DIARY OF AN ART DEALER

René Gimpel was born in 1881, the son of a picture dealer from whom he inherited two prosperous galleries in Paris and New York. Although he always maintained a great love for the French masters of the eighteenth century, he nevertheless had the sensibility and perception to recognise the genius of modern painters. His love of art went far beyond commercial considerations. In his diary, he observes with acute and loving detail the world he knew between 1918 and 1939. Some of the most fascinating pages are devoted to the artists he knew or whose work he admired: Renoir, physically broken, but still youthful in spirit, painting with the brush tied to his arthritic fingers; Monet reminiscing in his studio at Giverny; Mary Cassatt, tragically almost blind; Marie Laurencin and Picasso to mention only a few. Gimpel writes too of his colleagues, his brother-in-law, Joe Duveen, Nathan Wildenstein and Ambrose Vollard; of great collectors such as Henry Clay Frick and of critics—Apollinaire, Berenson, Venturi.

This is an extremely rich book, beautifully written in a lively and elegant style. It reveals a man of great intelligence, wit and above all generosity of spirit. In 1940 René Gimpel joined the Resistance and he was eventually arrested by the Germans. After stoically enduring great hardship, he died in 1944 in Neuengamme concentration camp. In the words of Herbert Read: 'this man, who had led a life which might be considered sophisticated and even decadent, proved that when it came to the test an aesthetic sensibility could embrace the noblest values of courage and self-sacrifice.'

HAMISH HAMILTON PAPERBACKS

In preparation

Harold Acton
MORE MEMOIRS OF AN AESTHETE

P. J. Campbell
IN THE CANNON'S MOUTH

Kenneth Clark
THE OTHER HALF:
A SELF PORTRAIT

J. Christopher Herold
MISTRESS TO AN AGE:
THE LIFE OF MADAME DE STAËL

Diana Holman-Hunt
MY GRANDMOTHERS AND I

Hesketh Pearson
A LIFE OF SHAKESPEARE

Hesketh Pearson
WALTER SCOTT

Robert Rhodes James
LORD RANDOLPH CHURCHILL

Cecil Woodham-Smith
THE GREAT HUNGER:
IRELAND 1845–9

RENÉ GIMPEL

Diary of an Art Dealer

Translated from the French by J O H N R O S E N B E R G

I N T R O D U C T I O N B Y *Sir Herbert Read*

A HAMISH HAMILTON PAPERBACK
London

R. G.

First published in France under the title
Journal d'un Collectionneur by Calmann-Lévy
First published in this edition 1986
By Hamish Hamilton Ltd
Garden House 57–59 Long Acre London WC2E 9JZ

Copyright © 1963 by Calmann-Lévy
Copyright © 1966 by Farrar, Straus and Giroux, Inc.
Design: Marshall Lee

ISBN 0-241-11761-5

Printed and bound in Finland
by Werner Söderström Oy

Contents

Illustrations

Introduction

by SIR HERBERT READ

The author of this journal was born in 1881. He was a picture dealer and the son of a picture dealer, and was therefore a witness of the revolutionary changes that began with the first appearance of Cézanne's genius and did not cease until a completely new conception of art had been established throughout the world. He himself had inherited a traditional approach to art, and to the end of his life maintained a preference for the French masters of the eighteenth century, above all for Chardin. This did not prevent him from recognizing genius even when it wore the mask of a new style—he could even admit that a contemporary painter such as Braque had attained to the perfection of this best-loved master.

What is immediately evident, as we read the pages of René Gimpel's journal, is that he possessed an acute sensibility which had not been blunted by a long commerce in works of art. The business which he inherited had been established in Paris in 1889 by his father, an Alsatian who had come to the French capital because as a French citizen he could not tolerate the terms of the Treaty of 1871. René Gimpel was imbued with the same spirit of revolt, and during the Second World War he and his sons were to participate actively in the Resistance. René was eventually interned by the Vichy authorities for his underground activities, released in 1942 but then re-arrested by the Germans. In prison he taught English to his fellow prisoners, to prepare them, as he said, for the liberation. He was sent with a convoy to Germany and suffered great hardships under which his health finally broke down.

Louis Martin-Chauffier, fellow-prisoner in Neuengamme concentration camp toward the end of 1944, described his end in a letter written some years later to Jean Guehenno (quoted in M. Guehenno's Preface to the original French edition of the journal): "Physically he was no more than a shadow of his former self, as was usually the case with all of them, but morally he had not changed, and that is infinitely rarer. Knowing that he was soon to die, he continued, as if nothing was happening, to speak of life and to give to his companions, overwhelmed by exhaustion, despair, and disgust, the example of the serenity of a man who, having nothing more to lose and having done what he can, is left with only one duty, which is not to flinch and to help others." Thus this man, who had led a life which might be considered sophisticated and even decadent, proved that when it came to the test an aesthetic sensibility could embrace the noblest values of courage and self-sacrifice.

I myself would not call the life that is revealed in the pages of this journal decadent, because I believe that aesthetic values are moral values, and the portrait of the author which emerges is that of a man devoted to his family and friends, generous and charitable, and above all intelligent. It is an extremely rich and varied book, in which we meet scores of famous people, and whether we meet them casually, for a few moments, or whether they appear frequently and become known intimately, they are always presented with decisive strokes, as if the writer had long meditated on the art of portraiture. It is not only artists and collectors who are thus made to live for us. Take, for example, the portrait of Clemenceau (January 11, 1919), the "Tiger" so stereotyped by cartoonists and journalists, half animal, half man: "Few wrinkles . . . his cheeks round, very round, like tennis balls. In caricatures, his forehead is brought forward, his eyes sunk, exaggeratedly; but that is all wrong. His mustache is thick but well trimmed, despite its vigorous thrust. They give him nutcracker jaws which he doesn't have. His chin is very round and his head really like a ball, very solid." Clemenceau, incidentally, is shown to have a real understanding of art, and was a close friend of Claude Monet, as Gimpel notes on another page.

The most fascinating pages are those devoted to the artists for whom René Gimpel had the most instinctive sympathy—Braque, Mary Cassatt, Forain, Marie Laurencin, Manet, Matisse, Monet, Picasso, Renoir, Soutine, Utrillo. The many entries devoted to Marie Laurencin constitute a full and intimate portrait of this delightful and inconsequent woman. Forain, too, appears frequently and is lovingly recorded. Then come colleagues in the trade—René's brother-in-law, Joe Duveen, Dur-and-Ruel, Paul Rosenberg, Nathan Wildenstein, Ambrose Vollard, and others—and inevitably associated with these the great collectors, Henry Clay Frick, the Rockefellers, the Rothschilds, Stillman (René himself was a collector, a passionate bibliophile). There are famous critics, too, Apollinaire, Berenson, Venturi—Berenson appears early and stays late, and always the impression given is repellent, *un Polonais felin*. The entries devoted to Proust are of the greatest interest. Gimpel first met Proust as early as 1907 at Cabourg, where they stayed in the same hotel. They were attracted to each other by a common enthusiasm for Vermeer. But the friendship did not ripen fully until fifteen years later, when Proust began to call on Gimpel in Paris. Proust died in November of the same year and Gimpel attended his funeral, but the diarist continues to recall incidents from their past association and publishes two interesting letters from Proust. He reports Alphonse Kahn's reminiscences of Proust's childhood, and the subtle observations of Fernand Crummelynck on Proust's work.

If René Gimpel was fascinated by Proust it is perhaps because in some degree he felt that he also was making a chronicle of his own time which would possess some of the same kind of interest. But Gimpel's model was Casanova. He tells us (October 8, 1920) that he made his first attempt to keep a journal during the first four or five days of the First World War, after having read Casanova's "admirable memoirs." People who have read Casanova only in prurient selections may not appreciate the validity of such a comparison. Certainly this is no casual journal: it has a purpose, part literary, part historical, and by virtue of its acute observation and lively style, will survive as a record of the social life of its period no less precious in this respect than Proust's novel. It is also, and this is not the least of its virtues, a lesson in art appreciation. René Gimpel had become, in the course of his career, an art "expert," to whom we owe many important discoveries and identifications. That was the practical side of his activity. But I find also in these pages something more than expertise—in short, a sensitive evaluation of beauty which is possible only to a poetic nature. In describing his feelings before Turner's "Interior at Petworth" (December 20, 1922) he suggests that it is easier to enter into the most unreal world of the poet than into that of the painter. "It is strange that we can move with such ease in the atmosphere of words and with such difficulty among the almost tangible images of painting." Everyone who has tried to write about the closed world of painting has experienced the same difficulty, but René Gimpel as a critic of art comes near to a spiritual penetration of this mystery.

NOTEBOOK 1

February 12–May 25, 1918

February 12 / Bombers and masterpieces

Since the last raid, Rude's *Marseillaise* has been shut away for protection in a huge box filled with sandbags. Dovecotes have been built for *The Horses of Marly*. Carpeaux's *The Dance* will be continuing its steps within the darkness of a double wall. Alas! even the Vendôme column has had a shelter built for it. What an insult to the brass of its cannons. Better to leave it exposed in its dignity and glory.

February 13 / At No. 57

57, rue la Boétie, that's where my offices are.

Five past four. Boni de Castellane, divorced husband of the rich American Anna Gould. His chest is too bulging, his shoulders too broad, his waist too nipped-in. He is dandified, very fair, hale and hearty, much too hearty, he is every inch the charmer, in fact: a great big doll full of grand airs.

Eight past four. Anna Gould, divorced wife of Count Boni de Castellane. She must be forty. Small and deformed, she is bent in a gourdlike curve. Her face projects a scarlet potato as an apology for a nose. She is accompanied by her new husband, the Duke de Talleyrand-Périgord, Boni's cousin. After his divorce, which plunged him back into financial straits but left his wife millions of francs' worth of debts, Boni's only moan was: "I was deceived. Anna Gould wasn't rich enough for me." With Talleyrand she is happy. Tall, stoop-shouldered, retiring, getting on to sixty, he has the grand air of ultrarespectability and benevolence of an old, reformed rake.

As it happens, they don't run into Boni.

With Berenson, the art critic

If small, lithe tigers could speak, they would have the voice and intelligence of this feline Pole. Behind that calculated sweetness a high old roaring goes on. He has velvet paws and killer talons of steel. He's let his beard grow to cover up the fact that he is only half a man. His eyes are blue—the better to deceive. Educated in America, he may or may not have been born there. Who knows? He lives in Italy, and some say he's English. His ambition, which is consuming, is to be recognized as the world's greatest expert on the Italian primitives; and he achieved his goal about three years ago. He is a dying man, but he'll go on for a long, long time. He doesn't do business or accept commissions, but he shares in the profits.

"Here are twenty-five thousand francs, M. Berenson."

"Thanks, Gimpel."

He came not long ago to settle in Paris: anxious, so he gave out, to work for the American Red Cross. The truth is, he was scared of the Germans breaking through the Italian lines and getting as far as Florence to bother him in his villa; and it is whispered that England refuses him entry. He knows the whole gamut of society and its milieux, but everywhere he has only enemies. The hatred he expends he gets back in full measure; but if he were in a cage with one of his detractors, he would not be the one to be devoured. His deadliest enemy is Bode, the director of the Berlin Museum, who has dared to study and understand Italian sculpture.

February 16 / Jacques Doucet

Jacques Doucet was walking on the avenue du Bois. He is past sixty but still as handsome as ever. His white beard, which I can remember being very blond, has always been clipped like a French garden. He wears his clothes as his mannequins do the dresses he designs. They are the errand girls' queens, he the prince of couture. He has an aristocratic air, so the nobility never found him wanting, and he had all it takes to please, from his blue almond eyes to his rapier wit. He has built up an eighteenth-century collection of impeccable taste, at a cost of a bit under three million francs. The public sale of it netted fourteen. And for that collection he created, with the help of Hoentschel the decorator, a superb setting, which he left the morning after the public auction. I live there today (19, rue Spontini). That sale! That departure! A tragic labor of love. He said as much, and I believe him. He loved Mme X, and she got a divorce for his sake. He was going to marry her, but she died. No one believed he could be so vulnerable, hated as he was for his pride, for which he suffered and because of which he has never received his just due for his works. He has not been admitted to the Institute, where he ought to sit in return for his magnificent gift to them of his collection of books on art and archaeology, a monument unique in the world and a treasure house for scholars, collectors, and researchers; it cost him millions. His too is the merit of encouraging artists, and of having recognized almost before anyone else the current renaissance of decorative art. How he was laughed at six years ago, at the time of his artistic about-face. Today he's beginning to have imitators. He continued his walk. We'll meet again.

February 17 / Our origins

I had lunch with Ernest May, the banker and collector. He's a Quentin Metsys, the Wise King with the curved nose and the clasped hands of the painting from the Rudolph Kann Collection now in the Metropolitan Museum. His is also the gold weigher's head of all the Renaissance artists, but with none of the avidity. It is rather the modern weigher of things and ideas. He's also very rich.

"I can see your father in you," he told me. "I was very fond of him. Didn't he die in America?"

"Yes, early in 1907. We were often taken for brothers he seemed so young. As indeed he was. But the quality, the sympathy he emanated was more than just sparkle. He charmed everyone with his perpetual smile and that ruddy face of his. Some of his friends used to call him the French Frans Hals."

"I also knew your colleague Nathan Wildenstein when he was just starting in antiques. He's come a long way!"

"That must have been at 56, rue Laffitte."

"No, before he had a shop. In the Cité du Retiro, in a second-floor apartment. He was then a middleman by profession."

"He began by selling ties in Strasbourg, then set himself up as an antique dealer in Vitry-le-François, and finished up in Paris. He's told me how at rue Laffitte, when he couldn't always pay his rent when it was due, he would have to wait till dusk to slip by the concierge's room. Twenty years later, at the Crosnier sale, he and my father bought Fragonard's *Billet Doux* for 500,000 francs; and in 1907, with the London house of Duveen,[1] and with me, he bought the Rudolph Kann Collection for 17 million francs."

"Your father helped him a lot, I know, at 9, rue La Fayette."

"Yes, but it was Nathan Wildenstein—this was in 1889—who advised him to take up the profession. My father was on the Exchange and right from the start had the great financiers as clients: the Rothschilds, Bardac, Albert Lehman, Strauss, Stern, and yourself, I believe. Then, knowing English, he took Wildenstein to England, where it was then possible to buy splendid French paintings at ridiculous prices. Old Martin Colnaghi's back room in Pall Mall was an inexhaustible mine. There, for 10,000 francs, they found Watteau's *The Poet's Dream*, which they tried vainly to sell for 20,000 francs. They kept it in a cupboard for ten years and when they brought it out again they asked 150,000 francs and David-Weill bought it. He had seen it on its arrival from London, but had been asked too little for it then."

"Myself, Monsieur Gimpel, I've never put down more than ten thousand francs for a picture. You remember Groult the great prototype of a nineteenth-century collector; he had the spirit. I'll tell you a remark he made which shows us all off, all true collectors. Groult was showing his friends a picture for which he'd paid a large sum, and they were congratulating him on it, but Groult interrupted them: 'I'd give fifty thousand francs more to have discovered it for a hundred francs.'"

[1] Joe Duveen, later Lord Duveen, was to become René Gimpel's brother-in-law.

March 2 / On Authenticating a Watteau

We were talking at No. 57 about disputed great paintings. Nathan Wildenstein said: "Michel Lévy claims that he has the real one and that the Kaiser's is a fake. But I've offered a million marks for the Kaiser's. That swine Wilhelm has my letter.[2] So the value of the canvas has doubled."

When he was asked who acted as middleman, he answered: "Two men, Ludwig Rosenthal, the merchant and court purveyor, who bought some manuscripts for Wilhelm, and one of the Kaiser's chamberlains who passed on my offer and insisted on having it in writing; I've got a copy. It was right in the middle of the controversy stirred up by the French collector, an item all the papers got hold of. Wilhelm had no intention of selling, but wanted an authentication. So! He didn't need mine; France was falling over herself to help him—above all, the French government, which was so afraid of upsetting him and had brought all the big guns to bear. Our ministers triggered off the Society of French Art, which, through the mediation of Alfassa the art writer, was charged with refuting every one of Michel Lévy's arguments. The entire Louvre got orders to march against Lévy. Everyone was quaking, and if Wilhelm's had been the copy, the government would have given orders to transform it into the original!" [8]

March 6 / Joseph Bardac and Arthur Veil-Picard, collectors, at No. 57

Joseph is Sigismond's brother. He has come to see the Hubert Roberts. He's the strong, successful banker type. Figures to him are steering wheel and gun powder, there to make or to break you; nothing less. His words and gestures have the authority of a mathematical sum. He ends all his sentences with "That's that." There is nothing to add; he always gives you a sum total. He buys on inclination, and at the same time profits from his knowledge of art to invest his money to advantage. I sold him Fragonard's *Billet Doux* for nearly 700,000 francs. Three years ago I bought from him the famous bust by Houdon, *Mme du Cayla as a Bacchante*, which I sold for exactly $200,000 to Henry C. Frick of New York. Last year I bought from him two little terra cottas

[2] The letter is dated June 11, 1910.

[8] Nathan Wildenstein acknowledged Michel Lévy's picture as genuine. I too am persuaded that it is by Watteau. (A note appended in 1939.)

by Houdon depicting the Brogniard children. I sold them for $32,000 to Joseph Widener of Philadelphia, who already owned the rather insipid marbles of them, which also came from Bardac, through the agency of Jacques Seligmann. Our banker had acquired them from Baron Pichon, who himself got them from the Houdon family. At one time these terra cottas had passed for plaster: there are two finer ones at the Louvre.

While Bardac, who owns the most beautiful Hubert Robert in Paris, was admiring the ones I have, Veil-Picard was announced. I had him brought up, and Bardac said to me: "I'm going to tell him I've just bought your Roberts." Veil-Picard entered and came slowly down the long gallery. His hat pushed down on his ears, his eyes slitted to kernels, his nose in his mustaches, his mustaches in his mouth, his mouth in his chin, his head down on his shoulders, his whole body sagging into his legs: that's Paris's leading collector. He has never sold any but a few insignificant pieces from his collection, except for two Boucher tapestries he didn't care for and a *cassone* now with Widener. This peasant from the Pontarlier region, whose rural origin is quite obvious both in his appearance and in a most frightful accent, built up his magnificent collection alone and without the benefit of advice. Bardac said to him, "You've come too late; I've just done you out of the Roberts." I watched Veil-Picard attentively. The shaft had gone home, and I distinctly read his thought: "I didn't want to buy these Roberts but I ought to have done so since this animal Bardac has taken them." He answered very simply: "You're right, they're beautiful." "Well," replied the banker, "you can have them. Just now I haven't the cash for such follies." Then Veil-Picard seemed to say to himself: "Aha, Bardac hasn't bought them, so why should I?" The conversation turned to past prices, and Veil-Picard informed us that the portrait of M. de Jars by La Tour, which netted some 500,000 francs in the Doucet sale, had been offered to him for 5,000 francs.

March 7 / Return of earthly chattels. At No. 57

This morning Nathan Wildenstein received the following letter: "Monsieur, I am the widow of Edouard Drumont, the rabid antiSemite. I hope you will nevertheless be impartial toward me. I have some pictures to sell. I wonder whether you would be kind enough to come to see them. . . ."

March 12 / A fake painting

A fake Gainsborough, a *Blue Boy*, has just been knocked down at the Hearn sale in New York for more than $32,000. It's harder to sell a genuine painting.

March 20 / At Mary Cassatt's

The poor horses which took me from Cannes to Grasse are war victims too; their stomachs don't even know what oats are any more. Phew, those hard climbs. At one point we marked time while the horses just pawed the ground. The driver didn't force them on; he knew it would be useless. My old friend up there was going to have to wait!

We arrived near the Villa Angeletto, at the end of the town, on the Gorge du Loup road. With my wife and two sons I got down and followed a narrow, steeply descending track to where the famous American artist lives. She and Whistler were the only representatives of their country in that constellation of painters who created impressionism.

Alas, the great devotee of light is now almost blind. She who so loved the sun and drew from it so much beauty is scarcely touched by its rays. But at least they warm that long, thin frame of hers—so typically Anglo-Saxon. She adored flowers, but her garden has grown desolate. She lives in this enchanting villa perched on the mountain like a nest among branches. The view extends far out over an undulating fragrant countryside, but the veil before her eyes thickens every day.

She takes my children's heads between her hands and, her face close to theirs, looks at them intently, saying: "How I should have loved to paint them!" My paternal heart is flattered, for Mary Cassatt was always independent enough to refuse to do a portrait of any child who wasn't pretty. Infant hygiene and Mary Cassatt are one and the same. Her children are always fresh from the bath; they've been raised in the English way, in the fresh air. Degas said of her: "She paints the infant Jesus with his English nurse." Perhaps she lacks the knowledge of her friends Manet, Monet, Degas, and Renoir—she herself admits it—but she expresses feeling to a very high degree.

She told me that a bomb had fallen on 15, rue Laffitte, just opposite the Durand-Ruel gallery, which had in it the whole Degas collection that's to be publicly auctioned next Tuesday. She was horrified at the idea that these beautiful works might have been destroyed. "Such a catastrophe," she said, "would have ruined Degas's niece, who with her wonderful care prolonged the great artist's life by three years at least."

I told her how Durand-Ruel, with his usual affability, spent an hour last month showing me the many Degas stacked in his gallery. Almost unbelievable—the number of vigorous sketches, hardly finished but very interesting, which can't really be ascribed. Are they by Degas or by some of his gifted friends? It's impossible to be sure. Durand-Ruel, who knows his masters better than anyone else, accepts advice freely from everyone competent to pronounce on this school of painting, to throw more light on the authenticity of these canvases while there is still time.

Seeing these paintings destroyed one of my illusions. A legend has grown up over the years that he kept his most beautiful pictures, that he showed them to no one, that his sale would reveal unsuspected aspects of his genius. This was an exaggeration. There are some pretty pastels, some very fine paintings, but very many elementary studies that tell us nothing, mere notes for the artist alone; numerous pastels which are quite incomplete or partially effaced—evidence of shocking carelessness and neglect. Some pastels are covered over in thirty years' accumulation of dust, so much so that Durand-Ruel, in an effort to prevent forgers if possible from finishing these pastels and even the paintings, has had very detailed photographs taken of all the Degas which are going up for sale and will distribute prints to all art institutions and libraries in France and abroad.

Mary Cassatt asked me if I had seen the etchings. I told her that I had, and told her, too, that the family destroyed the erotic works for fear of seeing a *Degas Erotica* published someday. Durand-Ruel showed me *The Fête of the Mistress*, an etching that he saved. They're very much in the raw, those women!

From Degas's collection of old paintings, Mary Cassatt has singled out the Ingres *Monsieur de Pastoret*. She has advised the Metropolitan Museum of New York to buy it.

In the course of our conversation, Mary Cassatt spoke a great deal about her friend the multimillionaire James Stillman, who died three days ago in New York. "His first purchases," she told me, "were two beautiful Boucher tapestries. Then I made him buy a Titian at Trotti's and two Moronis which came from the archbishop's palace at Trent. He paid $160,000 for them.[4] Then there was your Rembrandt *Titus*, which belonged to the Duke of Rutland,[5] your two Fragonards —*The Gardener* and *The Woman Grape Harvester*—and the Vigée Lebrun. That was almost his whole collection of old paintings, except for another Rembrandt.[6] He had a passion for wanting to buy my canvases. He had about twenty-four of them, and I hope he hasn't given them to museums: my pictures are for the home, they're pleasant and easy to take, and don't have anything for the public or for artists."

It was late and the day was declining when we left Miss Cassatt, whom one cannot, unfortunately, get to speak of the fascinating period of her life when she was the companion of Monet, Manet, Degas, and Renoir, whom she reveres. She doesn't, however, care for Gauguin, whom, she says, she never considered a painter. She calls Whistler a talented mountebank and Sargent a buffoon.

At Renoir's, at Cagnes

"Can M. Renoir receive us?"

"He didn't sleep last night," answered the servant. "I'll go and see. Shall I take your card?"

Renoir didn't know me; I was counting on the description the servant would give him of the carriage and pair, the hacks from Grasse. When she returned she said: "If you would be so kind as to bring madame into the dining room, we shall get monsieur down." Get monsieur down? Whatever did she mean?

The garden resembles a poverty-stricken farmyard, and the doors

---

[4] At his sale the Moronis together were to bring only about $40,000.

[5] Subsequently in the Barton Jacobs Collection of Baltimore, but nearly destroyed by cleaning at the hands of Duveen.

[6] Today owned by Ringling, the one-time clown. (Note appended 1929.)

and windows have the shoddy lozenges of those pseudo-Louis XVI villas thrown up in haste and by the dozen on beaches created overnight by speculators, the Dufayel type. The view of the sea and countryside is beautiful.

Renoir lost his wife three years ago; the house shows the effect of it: last night's crumbs hadn't been swept up.

On a table in a corner, near a window, there were some brushes, a box of water colors, and small ceramic squares decorated with flowers and with childlike designs of boats and pastoral trees; also some plates with his eternal nude woman, her knees crossed. I recognized the master's style and colors. Was Renoir doing ceramics?

Through the partly open door I caught sight of him: they were bringing him down, two women carrying him in a kind of litter. Georges Bernheim, the dealer in modern painting, said to me in Paris: "He's doddering." And that's how it seemed. I wondered what on earth I was doing there. Before me was a shell of a man. They lifted him out of the chair, holding him firmly by the shoulders to keep him from collapsing. But his bent-up knees didn't give. He was all unyielding angles, like the unhorsed knights in a set of tin soldiers. He rested on one foot, the other being huge, all swaddled. They sat him down again by tipping him backward.

Seated, he is a frightful spectacle, elbows clamped to his sides, forearms raised; he was shaking two sinister stumps dangling with threads and very narrow ribbons. His fingers are cut almost to the quick: the bones jut out, with barely some skin on them. Ah, no, he has his fingers—pressed in and spread against the palms of his hands, his pitiful fleshless hands like the claws of a chicken plucked and trussed ready for the spit.

But I still had not seen his head: it was sunk on a curved, humped back. He was wearing a large, tall English traveling cap. His face is pale and thin; his white beard, stiff as gorse, hangs sideways as if windblown. How has it managed that crazy angle? As to his eyes—well, it's hard to say.

Could I really expect this amorphous being to answer me? What intelligence could still exist there? I had to say something. I ventured on something like: "As admirers of your work, my wife and I have come to pay homage to the great painter. We salute the master."

He motioned to us to be seated and then to the servant to give him a cigarette.

She put it in his mouth and lit it for him.

Then Renoir raised his voice and said: "I have all the vices, even that of painting."

I stopped holding my breath. This jest, uttered clearly and in an animated tone, reassured me. I laughed. He smiled. His eyes, so dim just a moment ago, suddenly brightened. I told him: "On that table in the corner I noticed some ceramics in which I recognized your hand."

"Yes, ceramics were my first calling, and I'm teaching the art to my grandson who is sixteen and lives with me. Everyone needs an occupation, and this one seems to suit him. It's very difficult. The same color applied by two different hands gives two different tones."

"I've been told that you tried to mix your colors to keep them from changing later on."

"Yes, but will I succeed? I remember seeing, sixty years ago, the great Troyon in the Louvre, *The Return of the Herd,* with the steam from the bullocks' nostrils brilliant with the sun. But when I saw the picture again, several years ago, the sun on the animals' snouts had gone. That's why we have to search endlessly."

My wife asked him if he was fond of landscapes.

"Very much, but it's too difficult. I am classified as a painter of figures, and quite rightly. My landscapes are nothing but accessories. Just now I'm striving to blend them with the people I paint. The old masters didn't attempt that."

"What about Giorgione?"

Renoir didn't answer. He disapproved. Then I mentioned Corot, and he said: "There you have the great genius of the century, the greatest landscape artist who ever lived. He was called a poet. What a misnomer! He was a naturalist. I have studied ceaselessly without ever being able to approach his art. I have often gone to the places where he painted: Venice, La Rochelle. I've never come anywhere near him. The towers of La Rochelle, ah, what trouble they've given me! It was his fault, Corot's, that I wanted to emulate him. The towers of

La Rochelle—he got the color of the stones exactly, and I never could do it."

Throwing his cigarette into a bowl at his feet, he motioned again to his servant to give him another, and continued: "Landscapes are the painter's stumbling block. You think it's gray; but what colors there are in a gray landscape! If you only knew, monsieur, how hard it is to anatomize a tree with a brush."

"It's extraordinary," I said to him, "that at a time when nearly all the masters of 1830 were still alive, when that school was at its zenith of glory and admiration—its decline scarcely foreseeable—and when you admired their work so deeply—that you and your friends could create a rival school that is not only altogether different but is even a direct opposite."

"It was chance. There was a Swiss in Paris, Gleyre, who had a very cheap class in drawing, ten francs a month. I hadn't any money, which is what took me there. And there I met Monet, Sisley, Bazille. It was our mutual poverty that brought us together and thus made it possible for us, having formed a group, to bring into being the impressionist school. Each of us on his own wouldn't have had the strength or courage, or even the idea. The impressionist school had its origin too in our friendship and discussions. We had to struggle apace and stand by one another. In 1872 Berthe Morisot joined us, and to raise some money for ourselves, we all had a sale at the Hôtel Drouot which caused a riot. A man named Chocquet did us a lot of good. He was an old habitué of public sales, one of those people who like breathing in that dust, with its very special odors. He came into our gallery, spied a friend passing in the corridor, and called to him: 'Come and see the horrors being shown here.' The effect was altogether different from what Chocquet had expected. His friend admired our pictures. Chocquet was furious: 'They're obscenities.' He called in others. In no time, two rival factions sprang up, and came to blows. The police were called, passers-by rushed in from the street, the Hôtel Drouot was invaded, absolute mayhem. The doors had to be shut until peace could be restored. But after that, we had our supporters."

Recalling these memories of youth and strife kindled Renoir's eyes till they sparkled. Doddering? Far from it! Georges Bernheim was exaggerating. Had he never looked at Renoir's eyes? The chair-bound cripple with his quivering stumps: it all vanished when you saw those eyes. Those eyes, what animation and vivacity, what youth in them still!

I asked to see some paintings, and he instructed the servant to accompany us.

She took us along to a bedroom where two rows of canvases not on stretcher frames were fixed with drawing pins on the wall. Others were lying on the eiderdown on the bed. Sometimes, on the same canvas he had painted three or four subjects in all different directions; sometimes, pieces were missing, cut off at the corners. Pictures worth twenty, thirty, forty thousand francs left there like laundry hung out to dry. Many portraits. In the Midi sun, his last works lack that bricklike aspect, often so unpleasant, to which he has been partial for some years now; his heads also seem more distinguished. I was surprised. This was like a cluster of precious stones. Nonetheless these canvases aren't up to those of his youth. "But how can he paint?" we asked the woman.

"I place the brushes between his fingers and fasten them with the strings and ribbons you saw. Sometimes they fall and I put them back—but what's so astonishing about M. Renoir are those lynx eyes of his. Sometimes he calls me and tells me to remove a hair that's come off the brush and got stuck on the canvas. I look and see nothing till monsieur shows it to me: minuscule, hidden in a daub of paint."

"Does he paint much?"

"A great deal, ceaselessly. Many of his pictures he gives to charities, or to old friends or their children fallen on hard times."

The good woman has been in his service for sixteen years and she is disconsolate at not being able to talk about art, his sole pleasure, and so be anything more to him than a nurse. She took us into a little studio off in the garden and showed us the canvas on which the master was then working—a nude woman, with her back meticulously studied. The stretcher frame, instead of being held on the easel by a shelf, is hung and kept up by a counterweight, allowing Renoir to raise and lower his canvas easily by himself.

We rejoined the old man; I was rhapsodizing over the marvels I had seen, and I confessed my astonishment at the wealth of work in his studio. He informed me that he had sold more than three thousand paintings in his lifetime. I asked him if he would spare me one, and he replied: "No, not at the moment. I haven't enough to leave my children; in a year's time I'll see."

I didn't press the point but said: "It must be a great joy to you to realize how enormous the influence of your school has been in the world—your influence has been so strong that it's even overridden the faculty of different peoples to develop along national lines. Whether in America, Canada, Sweden, Norway, or even Germany, everywhere it's the French school they follow."

"Everywhere," he said, "and even in Germany, where everything has remained Gothic. They live as in the Middle Ages in their taverns; their architecture is still of that time. The Kaiser speaks like an old fossil: his sword and his God. By the way, have you seen the Degas exhibition?"

"Yes, at Durand-Ruel's." And I repeated to him what I had told Miss Cassatt.

"What a brute he was, that Degas! What a sharp tongue and what *esprit!* All his friends felt obliged to desert him in the end: I was one of the last to stand by him, but I couldn't hold out. What is incomprehensible is that Manet, who was so mild and gentle, was always controversial, while Degas, bitter, violent, and intractable as he was, was from the start recognized by the Institute, the public, and the revolutionaries."

"He was feared," I suggested.

"Yes, that's it. For my part, I kept his friendship for a long time by teasing him. One day he said to me: 'Renoir, I have a terrible, an invincible enemy.' 'Who is it?' I asked. 'You old fool,' he replied, tapping his chest, 'you ought to know that enemy of mine—it's myself.'"

March 25 / *Claude Debussy is dead*
Now he'll begin to be understood.

March 30 / *The Degas sale*
It took place last Tuesday and Wednesday, bringing in 1,966,200 francs. On those two days the Germans were still advancing on Paris and bombarding her with their long-range cannon, and the city had not

yet recovered from the shock of the previous week's explosion at La Courneuve, which had left fifteen hundred dead.

Durand-Ruel paid 258,500 francs for two Ingres, *Monsieur and Madame Leblanc*, the finest in the sale, with all due respect to Miss Cassatt. *Monsieur de Pastoret*, which she preferred, reached 99,000 francs, and *Monsieur de Norvins* was knocked down at 77,000 francs to Knoedler, the American dealer, who also bought Delacroix's full-length *Monsieur de Schwiter* for 88,000 francs. It is a vaguely sad painting, lacking the fire that made this master so great, a fire found rather in his compositions. The Louvre missed out on this painting; the place for it should have been our national museum; it's a pity.[7] Well, we'll do our best to get these paintings back. I wouldn't be surprised if *Monsieur and Madame Leblanc* had been bought by Mrs. H. O. Havemeyer of New York.

March 31 / On Oscar Wilde

Jeannotte is an American impresario, a one-time singer. I made his acquaintance around 1908 or 1909 in Montreal, where he had just founded an opera. In spite of being an impresario, he has good manners. He told me he was related on his mother's side to the family of Oscar Wilde. Jeannotte was very young when he met the poet at the house of an English duchess. It was in summer at a castle, teatime in a large company. The duchess took from a vase a magnificent rose in perfect bloom. She inhaled its scent, had it passed round, and everyone went into raptures, for its scent matched its beauty. It came to Oscar Wilde; the sun was bursting in through the open window; the poet sniffed the flower ardently, but in a flash tore off the petals and threw them out of the window. A tremor of indignation rose against this sacrilege. Turning on the opposition, Oscar Wilde said to them: "It would have been too sad to see such a rose wither." Their feelings were soothed.

April 1 / On a Corot

I was introduced to Mme Desfossé, and I said to her: "When Georges Bernheim offered you 800,000 in 1908 for your Corot, *La Toilette*, it was for himself. It is the painter's most beautiful picture."

[7] Since bought by the National Gallery (London).

She assured me that Georges Petit recently offered her a million for it.

April 2 / On a Fragonard and a leaden angel

Nathan Wildenstein has written me that he has bought Fragonard's famous *Young Girl Playing with a Cat* for 165,000 francs, and that it is the best canvas by this painter that we have owned. He added that he has sold our leaden angel to Hennessy.

A word is in order here on this latter object, which is something quite exceptional in Gothic art. We bought it about 1910 from a small antique dealer in Versailles. The angel is almost life-size and dates from the fourteenth century. Its unfurled wings rise straight toward the sky and give it the look of an ethereal being alighted on earth. It is blowing a long trumpet. Together with the *Angel of Lude*, in the Pierpont Morgan collection, it is the most beautiful piece of sculpture in this genre. Its trumpet was missing, and we replaced it. We were entirely ignorant of its origins until we showed it to Count de Bryas, who was amazed to find it in our possession, as he had known it for more than forty years. He had seen it in the garden of an old man at Boulogne-sur-Seine who never let anyone near the place because he was the son or grandson of the chief architect of the cathedral of Rouen or Chartres, more likely Chartres, and didn't want anybody to see what had been pilfered by his grandfather under cover of a fire.

We were never able to trace the mystery further, but this angel could well have been removed at the time of the fire on the roof at Chartres.

April 13 / At Renoir's

At Nice, in his apartment on the rue Palermo. His foot isn't doing too well, and there is some fear of gangrene. He has been brought here and is feeling better. His son, an unknown actor[8] who was wounded in the right arm in the war, had come down hastily from Paris, bringing some rolled canvases because of the bombing, to keep them out of harm's way. Among them, *Nude Woman* (1910), whose tones have already darkened slightly; she is painted lengthwise and nearly life-size.

[8] Since become a good actor. (Note appended 1929.)

A seated *Pierrot* with a red collar (canvas 50); a woman, his current model, with her left elbow raised and a yellow rose in her hand (canvas 90); the portrait of Dussane, of the Comédie Française, at home. She is seated and has the bearing of a sultana. This canvas too has already darkened slightly (1916). Renoir informed me that he has given it to the Luxembourg Museum. He explained that he paints that brick-red color so that later it may become a milky rose. When he wasn't so preoccupied with the decomposition of colors, his pictures didn't alter. We'll have to wait a good many years to learn if, at the end of his life, Renoir was right. It would be disastrous for the future of painting if it proved necessary to paint one tone to achieve another.

April 19 / The Americans' war

From London I've heard by letter: "One of the first American divisions sent into the firing line is 'The Rainbow,' so called because all the states of the Union are represented in it, in order that every home may feel from the first battle that war and death have entered the country."

At Renoir's

"Your wife has a charming face," he told me. "I should very much like to paint her. I would place her in a garden."

April 23 / At Renoir's, in Nice

In this small apartment he paints sometimes in the dining room and at other times in his drawing room, as at Cagnes, where every room in his house is a studio. Today his devoted servant and nurse, Mme Petit, ushered me into his drawing room. He has a model, a beautiful plump girl of twenty, rather short, with golden hair, large blue eyes, and a fine skin, with a purity of blood suffusing her face; a daughter of the fields, to judge by her fine health, but already of the town as well, with a dusting of rice powder and a tailor-made suit. I looked at the small painting which I'd seen last time and in which Renoir has seated this woman in a landscape. The other day he'd captured, as a soap bubble does, the sun's thousand colors in a falling sleeve of transparent tulle. Today it was a botch, a mess, and he knew it and said to me: "Twenty-seven times I've had this woman pose[9] and I can't get it to work; my picture was much better the other week; I ought to have left it. What do you think of these flowers I did yesterday but haven't finished?"

"I think they're magnificent and I wouldn't do another thing to them. Looking at them, I'm reminded of a phrase I read once in an astronomy book: 'The sun throws out flames thousands of miles long.' These flowers too cast immense flames; they blaze. Would you sell them to me?"

"Yes."

"How much?"

"Three thousand."

"That's a lot."

"I know, but these are my flowers, which cost more. I can't sell cheaply because of the dealers; I don't want to hamper their business. I have, for example, an old debt of gratitude to Durand-Ruel, who alone helped me to eat when I was hungry."

"I'll take your flowers. Why don't you sell me as well this portrait of the woman with the hat, your model? Ten thousand, you say? Done. And this woman in a glade? Let's add five thousand for that one. And if ever you'd agree to sell these washerwomen,[1] let me know; I adore the olive trees at the edge of that stream. When I leave you and return to Cannes, I look at nature and think of your paintings. You've shown me how differently each tree contains the sun. I marvel at the rightness of your olive tree coming up out of the ground, the trunk contained in the funny little hillock that rises with such dignity."

Renoir answered: "The olive tree, what a fiend! If you knew the trouble it gave me. A tree full of colors, not gray at all. Its little leaves, how they made me sweat! A gust of wind, and my tree changes in tonality. The color isn't on its leaves but in the empty spaces. I can't paint nature, I know, but the hand-to-hand struggle with her stimulates me. A painter can't be great if he doesn't understand landscape. At one time the term 'landscapist' was one of scorn, especially in the eighteenth

[9] Renoir's son, the actor, married her after his father's death. (Note appended 1922.)

[1] Renoir would have sold me this picture for around 10,000 francs. I came across it again this year for 800,000 francs paper money at Barbazange's, or 160,000 gold francs. (Note appended in 1927.)

century. And yet, that century which I adore produced great landscape
artists. I am of the eighteenth century. I humbly consider not only that
my art descends from Watteau, Fragonard, Hubert Robert, but even
that I am one of them. Watteau, what a genius! To have possessed all
knowledge so young! Watteau, Raphael, giants departed in the prime
of life. I swear to you, they knew they would die. So their talent advanced with giant's steps."

April 24 / Renoir ill

He has passed a horrible night writhing in bed. His articular
rheumatism has left him in a ghastly state. His big toe is crumbling and
is to be amputated.[2] My wife was going to pose, but the portrait will
have to be abandoned. His painting days are numbered.

The academician Barthou

It was his dream to enter the Academy; for four years he worked
toward his election, and to get it he pretended to lose interest in politics,
to which he will speedily return. He has a fine library, loves Hugo and
Lamartine, loathes Verlaine. I bought from him two of Samain's manuscripts: *Yalis ou le petit Faune aux yeux bleus* and *Au Jardin de l'Infante*,
the latter for 10,000 francs. Likewise some letters which the poet wrote
to a friend of his, a German. They reveal the dreamer powerless before
life. Barthou—such an obliging salesman—also let me have some of
Victor Hugo's notebooks.

May 6 / Degas sale

That of the artist's own works. It opened at Georges Petit's. At
no sale has the crowd been so numerous.

A witticism of Renoir's

Georges Bernheim had it from the artist's mouth and repeated it
to me. Renoir had painted the portrait of Bernstein the dramatist, who
had not paid him; whereupon the painter remarked: "He might at
least have put me off with a bouquet of violets."

[2] I believe they didn't have to operate.

May 7 / Degas sale

The first session brought in 2 million francs. All anticipations are surpassed. The Louvre bought the picture of the family (No. 4) privately for 400,000 francs. It is one of the most beautiful paintings in the world. If only he had painted more portraits!

May 8 / Bargains

Georges Petit, who has the face of a rutting, obese, hydrocephalic tom, tells me: "Fifteen or twenty years ago I went around to all the shopkeepers in Fontainebleau in search of pictures which Corot might have given them as payment. The two most beautiful, I found with a fruiterer whose account he hadn't settled for three years and to whom he owed four hundred francs. I bought them for twelve thousand and sold them for fifty thousand. Today they would be worth two hundred thousand francs apiece."

Degas sale

It's drawing huge crowds. Yesterday there were six thousand people at the viewing. The sale has now realized 6 million francs.

May 10 / War art

Apropos of the bombing, the newspapers urged Parisians to stick strips of paper on the shop windows to keep them from breaking.

My old city was never so beautiful. Spontaneously an art has sprung up, the art of paper strips. It looks as though there won't be any geometric designs left to invent: some are wonderful. Sometimes the ordinary shopkeeper shows more taste than the great goldsmith. An hour sufficed to create an art form. Alas! in one minute it can all be erased.[3]

May 11 / "The Invocation to Love"

Sepia by Fragonard. She is too blond and lacking in detail, but what passion! Bought for 15,000 francs from the widowed Mme Debussy, former wife of Sigismond Bardac.

---

[3] *L'Illustration* reproduced several windows. (Note appended 1930.)

May 14 / At Gallimard's, the bibliophile

Or rather at the actress Diéterle's house, 68, boulevard Malesherbes. Gallimard: looking like one of Napoleon III's generals with a goatee. A long carrot instead of a nose. His most beautiful book is *The Flowers of Evil*, illustrated with twenty-seven drawings by Rodin. The sculptor's miracle is that he took his male and female from Baudelaire's verses and gave them material form.

Gallimard told me that he owns fifteen hundred of the two thousand woodcuts illustrating the principal books of the nineteenth century. "The day after the death of a great engraver, I'd rush round to his widow or see his family and buy the complete works. I've made good use of my opportunities." His eyes were sparkling. What a book could be written on the cruelty of the collector!

While he was chatting with me I kept an eye on a man who was talking to Diéterle: Vollard, the wealthiest dealer in modern pictures. He is a millionaire ten times over. The beginning of his fortune goes back to the day in Cézanne's studio when he found the artist depressed and bought about 250 canvases from him at an average of fifty francs apiece. He parted with some but kept the majority until the time he could sell them for ten to fifteen thousand francs each.

"Do you know, Vollard," Gallimard asked him, "how the experts, in the next Degas sale, are going to present the sketches he did to illustrate Halévy's *La Famille Cardinal?*"

"They'll put them together in a single lot. Halévy never did understand Degas's talent, but Mme Halévy, who admired him, asked him to make sketches, assuring him that she would convince her husband. But she failed. Halévy chose the deplorable Morin."

Gallimard added: "I went to Degas myself to ask him the price of the *Cardinal* lot. He told me fifteen thousand. I accepted at once, but that evening he sent me word: he'd have to have 80,000 francs for them."

Vollard cried: "You can only trust the talentless artists to keep their word."

May 15 / On the death of Gordon Bennett

The owner of the *New York Herald* died yesterday at Beaulieu.

His ardent love for France sprang from his distaste for the American ruggedness which he himself personified. "The French journalist," he remarked to me one day, "is a foxhound, the American a bulldog."

I happened quite by chance today to visit the hunting lodge situated on Trianon land and adjoining its park, which Gordon Bennett rented from the estate. It's a miniature Louis XVI château and is called "The Lantern." He built a large aviary there for his owls, birds he loved above all others because they were the most victimized. The garden is abandoned; it is enclosed by a high wall. In a corner, under giant trees, I noticed a number of tombs—tiny tombs set close to the ground, with small marble plaques. I stooped to read the inscriptions: Dear little Toppy who died on . . . Beautiful little Ketty . . . Poor old Zata . . . Poor old Bill . . . Poor old Baby . . .

There sleep Gordon Bennett's dogs.

May 18 / Of art and love

Georges Bernheim told me: "In a little while, at six, I'm going to the brothel on rue Favart to see sixteen Toulouse-Lautrecs for which they're asking 100,000 francs. They'd have turned down 120,000 before the war."

"Quite possibly," countered Alforsen, a Swedish artist, "as business is bad in the houses. The women are finding too much work outside and the madams can't recruit enough female labor."

May 21 / A Rembrandt

I have offered $140,000 for the portrait of an aged woman, dated 1643, from the Montgermont Collection. She is holding a *lorgnon* in her right hand. Illustrated in Bode, Volume IV.[4]

May 22 / The Marquis de Chaponay Collection, 30, rue de Berri

The marquis lives in two eccentric old houses which he has had joined together. It is a charming place, with something of a château about it, and surrounded by an immense garden. About an acre of ground in all. He hadn't a single picture twenty-five years ago and built up a collection in less than a year, helped by the marquise. They hadn't

[4] The Duveens subsequently bought it for more. (Note appended 1925.)

told a living soul about it, and one day they invited twenty-five friends, all of them collectors. General stupefaction! The Chaponays with a collection, impossible! Great excitement in the Faubourg Saint-Germain. Then some prices came out which were sensational at the time: 200,000 francs to Durand-Ruel for a Nattier—a record. Nathan Wildenstein had offered 175,000 francs. Three hundred and fifty thousand francs for a Romney, a woman in white, which isn't even genuine. More than 100,000 francs for a Largillière, *Madame de Parabère*, which belonged to Count Boni de Castellane, to whom my father had sold it. More than 250,000 francs for a splendid Watteau of five figures painted on a gold background, with his old flute player on the left, and in the middle a dancer who might well be the brother of *l'Indifférent*. The panel on which the painting is done must have been part of an old harpsichord. The gold on the female dancer's skirt is quite radiant. A glorious and exquisite painting.[5]

What else does the marquis own? A slightly overporcelained Lawrence.[6] One or two Vigée-Lebruns. A Schall. A Mlle Gérard. A little Boucher cupid. A Gainsborough, the portrait of Peel.

May 23 / Groult

His widow is dead. What will happen to the collection? It's the question of the day. Camille, the son, had told us that she would set up a museum after her death and her sister's.

Groult was the great nineteenth-century connoisseur, the counterpart of M. de Julienne in the eighteenth century. Everyone has come across him, but nobody—I have asked around in vain—knows anything about him any more. He was full of wit. His sayings were much bruited about, and also his jests. I was very young when I knew him. He was a tall sturdy person, somewhat like Joseph Prudhomme. He often came to see my father in his gallery at 9, rue La Fayette; he knew me very well and would watch me work. One day an American asked my father about seeing Groult's collection. My father went along to see him, taking me with him to give me the opportunity of visiting the Groult house and its marvels. Groult looked at me and cried: "So

[5] Afterward owned by Baron Edmond de Rothschild.
[6] Subsequently owned by Arthur Veil-Picard.

there's the American!" My father protested: "It's my son." "No," shouted Groult, "it's the American. So this, M. Gimpel, is how you come, bringing a stranger into my house without my knowledge." And Groult, red with rage, continued in this vein. "But you know my son quite well," my father assured him. "Yes, and it's because I know him that I swear that this man [I was perhaps fifteen] is an American. I don't want to receive anyone, and I won't show my collection." Then, addressing me: "You like art, my boy?"

"I'm deeply interested in it, monsieur."

"Well, look at this Watteau, the portrait of M. de Julienne. You'll never see a canvas like it." He was right, it is perhaps the only known portrait done by Watteau,[7] oft discussed and indubitably his.

Then, as if my father didn't exist, he took me by the arm and led me into his huge galleries, where his collection seemed swamped in a vast disorder. But with what care and art was this disorder arranged! An object or a picture could be viewed from only one point, but from there nothing else could distract the eye. My father followed us. Groult, stopping me in front of two plain glass cases covered with velvet, told me they contained the most beautiful artistic creations in the world. With a conjurer's gesture he pulled off the cloth, revealing in one case wonderful butterflies, and in the other, mother-of-pearl shells; and he said to me: "You see the coloring of these butterflies, man has never been able to create any colors as beautiful, and the rarest pearl hasn't the brilliance of these shells, for which I paid between twenty and thirty sous apiece at Cancale. If they were rare like pearls, people would pay millions for them, and women would wear them. My butterflies too would be worth hundreds of thousands of francs. Humanity doesn't appreciate what it can have cheap. But even so, you know what I love more than my collection? A beautiful sunset. I keep five or six attic rooms in Paris, servants' rooms, and when toward six in the afternoon I scent a fine sunset, I climb the nearest six flights and contemplate nature in its sublime enchantment. Look, come and see the painter who has best understood color and light."

He took me into a room with Turners on a dozen easels, continuing: "The most beautiful, for me, is *The Bridge of Saint-Cloud*. The

[7] The Valenciennes Museum one is by Watteau.

first Sunday after buying that painting, I went off to Saint-Cloud to look for the exact spot from which it had been painted. I found it quite quickly. There was a house there; I bought it straight off and since then have spent all my summers there. It is in a different way as beautiful as my Turner." Groult's Turners were the joke of Paris, since three out of four were fakes. Did he know it? Perfectly well. He paid 200,000 francs for the genuine Turners; and for the fakes, grudgingly 300 francs. But it amused him to see bona fide connoisseurs admiring these daubs for fear of displeasing him. He carried the joke to the point of presenting a fake Turner to the Louvre for the fun of seeing it hung there by the curators, who hoped he would bequeath them his collection. And he let them go on thinking it. He didn't leave them as much as one drawing; so a few days after his funeral they had the fake Turner taken down, but then they began having hopes of Mme Groult and rehung it.

Shortly before his death Groult had transformed his garden on the avenue de Malakoff into a Hubert Robert landscape, with a water fountain, columns, and ruins. A walk led into the rue Pergolèse; I don't believe it was his. It was let to flower sellers, but he had arranged with them to be allowed to walk there after 6 P.M., when they had gone, and enjoy the flowers they left.

The only jest of his which is still mentioned often is this: A big manufacturer who had made his fortune in noodles used to entertain very smart people. A king, perhaps the Greek king, whom he had met taking the waters, came to Paris and Groult invited him to dinner. The king did not even reply. Groult then wrote to him: "You really ought to have come. We very much missed you, it was just a small dinner with people of our own kind: there was only the miller and his son."

May 25 / At the house of Mlle Brisson, the bookbinder, 68, rue du Cardinal-Lemoine

She has her studio in an old coach house in a courtyard. I was leafing through a book by Laurent Tailhade. "It belongs," she told me, "to one of my friends, a poet. He brought the author here to see me. Subsequently Tailhade sent me a very cordial note inviting me to his house, but his friend told me: 'Stay away; he'll receive you stark naked.'"

Mlle Brisson, a horticulturist's daughter, is a Paris gamine with wonderfully gifted fingers. How does she live? She has been reduced to making munitions during the war. She isn't a businesswoman; she loves books too much. She considers it her duty to read them so that she can decide just how best to bind them, and thus spends two days on each book, plus another three days in finding the leather and silk or the flyleaf paper. Then, when she has finished the binding, she asks eight francs. Her clients give her seven francs fifty. She'll end up in the poorhouse, this Paris gamine with the marvelous fingers.[8]

[8] She married an Australian lawyer and lives happily and in comfort in Melbourne, but always misses Paris, in spite of the many hours of misery she spent there. (Note appended 1939.)

NOTEBOOK 2

May 30–July 26, 1918

May 30 / En route for New York

7 A.M. Arrival at Bordeaux. With a heavy heart I embraced and said goodbye to my wife, who was weeping.

We passed by the docks, where we saw the *Lorraine*, completely camouflaged. It was like a stage setting seen at a distance of two feet; or, rather, like an enormous cubist painting with great sheets of ultramarine blue, black, and green, sometimes parallel but more often with the sharp corners cleaving one into another, and although you don't quite make it out, you can divine a reason, a plan, a guiding principle, a scheme.

Ship's log

Around noon, and after several optical signals the convoy ship leaves us, while French, English, and American soldiers walk the deck before lunch. At ten past two we sighted two transports coming from the west, laden with American troops and preceded by an English warship. I inquired why the insides of our lifeboats were fitted with nets. I was told they were there to hang on to in case of torpedoing. We proceeded until evening on a zigzag course to throw off the aim of hypothetical submarines. At night portholes and windows are closed with iron plates. In the corridor there are blue lights; in front of the doors leading to the deck, sailcloth curtains. I spent my evening aft, on the floor of the deck, with my back against one of those enormous steel mushrooms called capstans, pierced with loopholes for rolling up cables. Mine protected me against the wind. Delannay tells me that on old ships they were five times bigger, and that men worked them by passing iron bars across what I call the loopholes. Often the anchor chain would break, and with insane speed the capstan would spring in the opposite direction, crushing twenty men with the bars.

June 5 / About President Wilson

"When Wilson became a professor in 1890, he was appointed to the chair established by my mother, my brother, and myself at Princeton," Harold McCormick, a Chicago millionaire told me. "My brother was at Princeton when Wilson was studying there also, and subsequently I was his pupil at the same university. He taught Roman law, jurisprudence, political economy, international law. His courses were so popular that only the chapel was large enough to hold those attending.

"To make the American people understand why they had to fight, Wilson told them: 'It is for democracy.' Our enemies replied: 'Democracy is an empty word, invented as a pretext.' But I can tell you, M. Gimpel, that since adolescence, at his schoolboy's desk, Wilson studied the question of democracy. As professor he taught us the spirit of it. As president of the university he fought to impose it on Princeton, but was defeated by the conservative faction. Elected president of the university in 1902, he wished, for the country's good, to raise the level of education and to make the competition tougher. There was strong opposition. Then he declared that sports are necessary for all, that bodily health is essential to mental health. At Princeton he found only athletes who made a big display. He declared: 'It's not athletic meets I want, but health.' His opponents cried: 'What's to become of Princeton in intercollegiate competitions?' He assured them he didn't care a rap. As if that were not enough, he laid siege to a third ivory tower—the fraternities. They had grown powerful and ultra-exclusive, keeping out at the very least one student in every two. Those excluded were looked down on, not only at college but outside as well, not only in their student days but ever afterward. 'Let's stop this!' cried Wilson. 'This ostracism goes against the spirit of democracy.' But as aware as Wilson was that the students in the fraternities weren't the most intelligent, he didn't comprehend the power of their wealth, and he also underestimated the hatred he aroused. The directors and the professors joined with the students for the final attack on him. What precipitated it was the issue of building a college near Princeton for graduate students to do advanced or specialized studies. 'Very well,' said Wilson, 'but if we can find the money, it ought to be built at Princeton itself, for the students should be together now and in the future. Having the buildings at a distance would create a distinction between the students, and that's contrary to the spirit of democracy, which consists in giving the same chances to all.'

"Meanwhile, West, a professor of Latin and Wilson's adversary, had been canvassing those Princeton alumni who had made fortunes. In Chicago he suggested to a lavish donor named Proctor, who had grown rich in the soap business, that he should insist that the new college be placed at a distance. Wilson said: 'We must refuse this money given in a spirit contrary to the democratic principle.' Everyone said he was crazy, even my brother, who was on the board of directors. Refuse a million dollars! Say that it's harmful rather than useful! This president's an impractical visionary! Wilson assured them that if the donation was accepted, he would resign. The money was taken, and he went. Shortly afterwards the position of governor of the state of New Jersey fell vacant; it was put up to him, and he was elected. That's how he entered politics. The past can't always be reconstructed, but it is highly probable that but for his struggles to make his burning love for democracy prevail at Princeton, he'd still be there today."

June 5 / Stockyards

McCormick is not a self-made man; he was born rich, graduated from a university, toured Europe, and lived there. He does not lack distinction, and when he says he is from Chicago you're well aware that this is no butcher grown rich, no meat packer. McCormick described to me a visit made by some friends and himself to the stockyards of one of the meat barons who was obeyed like a general and feared like a sultan in all his establishments. The butcher took his visitors into the deep freeze, where the animals were hung in splendid array. Proud as an artist, he stroked the back of an ox, calling their attention to the color, the sheen, the form, the fat, the marblings. "You couldn't ever," McCormick assured me, "have sung with such rapture the beauty of your loveliest painting!"

Another packer whom he knew, whose fortune was more than $10 million, couldn't let a day go by without drinking a glass of warm blood. Worn out, finished, in the last days of his life he would drag himself to the stockyards, despite his doctor's interdiction and his family's pleas, to drink, gushing hot from the animal, his bowl of blood.

June 8 / On Renan

Our ship's steward is the brother of the famous philosopher Félix Le Dantec, the atheist of biology, or the biologist of atheism: the apostle of materialism, the adversary of Bergson. He died a year and two days ago.

The elder Le Dantec, the father, was Renan's doctor in Brittany. "When you think I haven't long to live, let me know," Renan had asked him. "I want to die in the Collège de France."

One day the doctor came home and told his family: "In two months Renan will be dead, and I don't dare tell him."

"You've got to find the courage, Father. Let's go to M. Renan's right now," said Félix Le Dantec.

"My father and brother returned home two hours later. I was there. In spite of their looking quite untroubled, my mother anxiously questioned them. 'How did dear M. Renan take the news?'

" 'Oh, very well. He took out his watch, reflected for a second, and said: "It's Monday today, Le Dantec; bring your family to lunch here on Thursday. Then I'll take my train to Paris." And we talked of something else.' " [1]

June 9 / Arrival

At eleven o'clock we saw land—far off, to the right, like foam on the line of the horizon. At noon we were saluted by seaplanes. A

---

[1] Renan left Brittany on September 17. He died October 2, 1892.

mother was scolding her little girl of seven, who retorted: "I'm awfully glad we've come to America. At least it's the country of freedom." A resounding slap! At two o'clock we made our way through the fleet of mosquito craft, the general term given by the Americans to their small, fast ships: warships of light tonnage, submarine chasers, armed yachts, transports. We even sighted a submarine with only the upper part above water; it arose from the sea as Amphitrite's retinue must have done. Four o'clock: the pilot came on board. Five o'clock: men from the Department of Health. No contagious illness was discovered. Five-thirty: all passengers in the smoking room, where Immigration puts you through a cross-questioning that comes close to impertinence. New York appeared, the lower part of the city, buildings of twenty to forty stories. They rise as one, looking more as if hewn from gigantic, awe-some cubes of stone than as if built by human hands. We docked and disembarked. Baggage examination. The customs officials, who used to be so prickly, harsh, and unpleasant, behave exquisitely to the French. At 8:30 I reached the Ritz-Carlton. I went along Fifth Avenue and into the park to have a walk round. The weather was heavy. The American women, those one-time icebergs, were clinging like cats to the arms of their sailors and soldiers. Love is in the air as in Montmartre or the Bois de Boulogne or Saint-Cloud on a fine night of the four-teenth of July.

June 10 / Some prices

I have sold to E. J. Berwind, the coal king, for $18,000, the portrait of Mme Labille-Guiard by herself, with her two pupils, Mlles Capet and Rosemont, illustrated in *Portalis*; Fragonard's *Les Deux Soeurs*, an engraving, for $194,000; David's *Jeanne de Richemont* for $228,000; Mme Vigée-Lebrun's *Marie-Antoinette* in red, for $120,000.

At 647

These are my offices in New York, a private mansion, one of the handsomest buildings on Fifth Avenue. A five-story marble façade next to Cartier's. Three windows facing the street: here that's a lot, since multimillionaires usually have only two—a tough country. Two of the display windows are beneath arches like the shops on the Place Vendôme. The rent of these premises costs me at the moment $36,000. Vanderbilt is my landlord. It's cheap. My settling-in last year cost me more than $140,000.

Flags

A flag hangs on our balcony, bearing six blue stars on a white rectangle surrounded by red. It is the Service Flag, showing that six people in this place of business, employers and employees, have gone into the armed forces. Naturally the flags of clubs, of the big stores, of banks, are covered with hundreds of stars. Deaths are indicated by gold stars. A Red Cross Flag and a Liberty Loan Flag have also been designed to show the public to what extent each establishment has subscribed to the Red Cross and to the Loan.

June 12 / At 647. Joseph Widener

He and Frick possess the finest collections in the United States. I called his attention to a Gothic tapestry, a Saint Veronica, of the quality of Spanish ones. I shall describe it later on. He came to see it and asked me the price—$85,000. He thinks it is splendid and would buy it if he didn't have to pay his enormous war taxes.

He has taste, but it is his late father who began the collection. Until the death of the elder Widener, Henry Duveen sold them almost all their tapestries, china, furniture, and art objects.

At the beginning, absolute crooks had gotten around P. A. B. Widener and had sold him fake paintings for as much as a hundred thousand dollars apiece, including a so-called Velázquez, by convincing him that the one in the Doria Gallery was only a copy.

P. B. Widener was a former butcher who had dabbled in politics and so had obtained concessions like the Philadelphia tramways. The following story is told of him. He was sitting in a Pullman compartment beside a traveler who began talking about him, saying: "Widener's just an ex-butcher!" Widener turned around and said: "Quite right, sir, but I'm not one any longer, whereas if you had been a butcher you'd still be one." (The elder Widener died several years ago. He was a very simple and affable old man.)

June 13 / The American Red Cross

In June 1917 the Red Cross asked the public for $100 million. It obtained $110 million. The campaign lasted one week. Before ten months had elapsed, it launched another appeal and obtained $170 million. This generosity is one of the finest aspects of the American effort.

That year there was a most remarkable performance at the Metropolitan Opera House.

A yachtsman who at Kiel had won a gold cup given by the Kaiser, put it up for auction. Knocked down, it was immediately put up for sale again by its owner, and this happened a great number of times. Thanks to Wilhelm, it netted possibly more than $60,000. In the end, when no further buyer was found, it was announced that the last bidder would have the privilege of breaking it up, and the gold would be given to the Red Cross. Inside they found lead. The cup given by the Hohenzollern Wilhelm II, king of Prussia and emperor of Germany, was plate.

June 14 / Roland Knoedler

He's the head of the long-established American house of Knoedler and Co., founded by his father, a German married before 1870 to a Frenchwoman. On the American entry into the war, Roland would never show a picture that commemorated the Allied cause.

His building is at 546 Fifth Avenue, near Forty-sixth Street. An English façade like a child's building blocks. An immense stone hall with ten employees to take charge of you and direct you to your area of interest, unless you only wanted to see one of the permanent exhibitions in one of the lower galleries. This place is a bazaar. You're looking for an engraving for five dollars that you'd find on the quays for five sous? You'll get it here. It's a Rembrandt etching you fancy, or a very rare eighteenth-century engraving? Five thousand dollars—it's yours! You need to have a glass cleaned, or a painting framed or repaired? At your service. But perhaps you want to buy a picture? Modern, you say. But what school? English, American, Canadian, French, Spanish, Hungarian, Russian? Name it; they'll show you it. An old master? They're less well provided there; they know less, they are a bit lacking in taste, but don't worry, they'll get you what you think you want. Will you spend one hundred dollars or one hundred thousand? Just say so. Speak, and you'll be taken to the right department.

How is this establishment doing? Not very well. Why? An old name, a long reputation for honesty, but no real intelligence. We'll come to the partners later on.

I was taken up to Roland in a room hung with red velvet. A Gallic type, sixty-five years old, he has a high forehead—and people with foreheads as high as that aren't intelligent; a flattened gray mustache, restless eyes. A likable appearance. Roland is described as a good sort. He's the man who played the gallant fool and married his old mistress. His wife now hobnobs only with priests. The New York clergy court her. She is their patron saint.

June 15 / At the home of E. T. Gary, the steel magnate

At 856 Fifth Avenue, by the park. He has a corner house. The staircase is marble, pseudo-Italian Renaissance. On the right, the reception room, which I enter. There are my Fragonards, the four from the Kraemer sale, plus *The Cage,* and on an easel Fragonard's self-portrait in miniature. The Louis XV wainscoting, bluish-gray, I like very much. Carlhian, the decorator, has followed my instructions well. On the floor, the old parquet that Gary wanted removed because he didn't consider it even enough; he didn't like the holes and cracks of time. He ordered them to be carefully filled.

His personal valet came down for me and showed me up to his bedroom. On the mezzanine and first floor he has nearly two million dollars' worth of pictures and art objects. But his bedroom reminds one of a poor transient hotel in a small American city. On the wall, a paper that was once white has become a greasy ivory. In this miserable place, under a baldachin made entirely of oak with padding at the headboard, the steel king sleeps. He is seventy-three, white-haired, with the body of an old and poor clown on whom life has not smiled.

Anti-Semitism

I've been shown a hotel advertisement: "No Jews, no dogs."

June 17 / The Bellini from the Crespi Collection

I bought it with Trotti and Duveen. Joe Duveen didn't care for it. Last year we had it sent to Ehrich, a small dealer over here, for him to sell. A fire broke out on the *Chicago,* the ship which was bringing it. The panel wasn't lost but Ehrich considered it ruined, as the paint had cracked. After an examination, the insurance company allowed us nearly the cost price. On calling at Ehrich's to examine the remains, I was amazed to see it hadn't suffered too much. The faces of the Virgin and the baby Jesus are completely intact. It had been packed in a zinc case and the fire dried the picture, which had peeled in places and even come away, and still shows a tendency to swell. The panel has to be kept flat, but it should be possible to transpose the painting onto canvas by a game of patience, juxtaposing the bits of scaling. Not much is missing, and it ought to be feasible.

June 18 / E. J. Berwind, coal king

He is a handsome old American with white hair and a stiff mustache who, despite his elegance, can't abide dandyism. He was the first American collector to appreciate our eighteenth-century paintings. His ancestors came from Germany, for which he has always maintained sympathies, despite his love of French art. I have sold him a dozen pictures which rank among the finest in the world. The interior of his mansion is just bric-a-brac. Almost everything is fake. Because he believes he has taste, he has never asked anyone's advice, and he is too violent and authoritarian to stand the truth. He would possess nothing, if he had not met me, except two large and superb Bouchers, which are truly remarkable. The last painting he bought from me is the finest David in the world, Jeanne de Richemont [2] and her son Eugène. This Empire woman in a white dress, with her great blue eyes and hair scattered in kiss curls, has all the aristocracy of maternal beauty. She is seated side-

---

[2] Jeanne Catherine Eglé Fulcray de Mourgue married Philippe Panon Desbassayns de Richemont, Count de Richemont, in 1798. He was born on February 3, 1774, at Saint-Denis (Île Bourbon). In 1816 he was appointed General Pay Commissioner of the Île Bourbon, then Councillor of State, Member of the Admiralty Council, and finally Deputy of La Meuse, on February 25, 1824, a post he held until the fall of Charles X.

ways. Her son, of whom only the head and upper body are visible, is an enchanting blond cherub with round eyes.

June 19 / With Bertron at the University Club

I had dinner with him in this great circle of intellectuals. Bertron is one of my clients. I have sold him some splendid pictures of the French school, including Fragonard's *La Bonne Mère*. I shall speak later of his collection. He has a handsome head with regular features, and is over fifty. He's the American type, with a young face and white hair.

Bertron is in politics and his secret-dream-come-true would be the Paris embassy.

June 20 / 120 Broadway. Forty-two stories

The lobby crosses the building from end to end. Three dead-end courtyards on the right, and three on the left. Eight elevators in each. A total of forty-eight. The first courtyard, nonstop to the eighteenth floor. Second courtyard, nonstop to the twenty-eighth. Various such combinations to avoid waste of time. From 9 A.M. to 5 P.M. the forty-eight elevators function continuously.

Anti-Semitism

Joe Duveen had hung a Van Dyck at the Frick home: two young men full-length, with strongly curved noses. Mrs. Frick urged her husband not to buy it, declaring that she couldn't bear to have those Jewish noses constantly before her eyes. The Jewish noses belonged to the brothers Stewart, nephews of Charles I, king of England.

On Joffre and Viviani

Today I passed Frick's private mansion. It was here last year that Marshal Joffre and Viviani were put up, while Frick went to stay at the Ritz. I was on the reception committee. On their arrival in New York our delegates were taken to City Hall and were received in a comparatively small room packed with at least five hundred people. The mayor welcomed them, and Viviani replied in his marvelous voice, so marvelous that beside me I noticed a sort of amiable giant moved to tears. Embarrassed at being caught out by my gaze, he said to me: "I don't know why I'm crying. I just don't understand."

Mrs. Benjamin Thaw—whose son enlisted in the La Fayette Squadron in August 1914, was decorated with the Croix de Guerre by Joffre, and subsequently killed—asked me to present her to the marshal. I invited her to the Frick house and took her up to Joffre, to whom I explained who she was. He could say absolutely nothing but "Ah, yes, yes!" He made fruitless efforts to find other words. At that moment an artist presented him with an art object donated by some society. He said, "Fine, fine, thank you," with renewed vain attempts to find some word. Then a little girl was brought up for him to kiss; he kissed her and said, "Little girl, little girl." Next there was something to sign. He asked for explanations, seeming to recover a glimmer of character. He refused, then gave in. But how could he have any character, this big fat officer with the great awkward belly? He has fine blue eyes, red cheeks like once-beautiful apples forgotten at a fruiterer's, white astonished eyebrows, and a stiff silvery mustache. When he opens his mouth, you hear the well-known voice, so often caricatured in the theater and at café concerts, of old Captain Ramollot. He has a good head, the head of a kindly grandfather. That's all. He is shown around here like Father Christmas to children. But his other identity, that of the Marne, must have stayed in France. There he goes now in the stone hall; taken by an arm, he enters a drawing room; pushed from behind, he finds himself suddenly in the library; drawn along by someone else, he follows into a gallery; then he's returned to the hall a hundred yards farther along. He knows neither why nor how he is brought a cape; he's propelled out into a car. En route to the inauguration. They were parading a dummy! The word went round that Viviani, jealous of the marshal's success, was no longer speaking to him. Joffre's movements created an absolute furor, but Viviani's share remained considerable. It was amazing that, beside the idol, the minister could arouse such enthusiasm. It was his speech that performed the miracle.

A reception was given at the New York Public Library for the French colony. There were four times as many Americans as French there. The public waited in two immense halls, then in single file passed through an endless succession of corridors and small rooms, the next to last of which was brilliantly lit, and so to the final hall, still one at a time. Joffre and Viviani were here. At the door stood two men giving helpful instructions: "Lift your feet, there's a rug, open your right hand to give a handshake." Ten feet farther on, an awning had been put up; approaching it, one was told: "The gentlemen are tired, so don't shake hands with them." And there, under the hangings, in the shadow, were seated Joffre and Viviani, almost invisible; one was quickly propelled through.

The detective I'd met at the Frick house, whom I saw this evening, gave me an explanation of this strange procedure. An assassination attempt was feared: that's why the public was filtered through corridors, the next-to-last room being violently lit to dazzle one, and the other, by contrast, plunged into shadow to bewilder one. We were made to open our right hands to facilitate arrest if we were armed, and told to lift our feet to give them a pretext, not for helping us, but for feeling our pockets and pinning us down if we were carrying firearms.

Encounter with an American woman

I've met an American woman whom Sargent painted twenty years ago. "He's an ironical, vulgar, and rude man," she told me. "He doesn't like women and insists that they are all liars. At the first sitting he started talking to me admiringly of the music of Fauré. 'I too care for it deeply,' I told him. 'But,' he replied, 'you've never heard it.' I protested. 'Then, if it's true, tomorrow bring me any pieces of his that you have.' "

June 23 / Ignorance

A dealer told me that at Kansas City, where he had shown a Van Dyck, two Rubens, a Teniers, a Lawrence, a Largillière, a Goya, and several other canvases, a visitor asked him if all those pictures had been painted by the same artist.

American senators

I had lunch with Hoentschel, Knoedler's nephew. We talked of the 25 per cent duty threatened on the sale of old paintings. "Yesterday," he told me, "I was called before a committee in Washington. A senator, looking very puzzled, asked me this question: 'Two weeks ago, sir, I read that a picture of Murphy's had been sold for fifteen thousand dollars, and a few days ago another Murphy brought in only two thousand dollars. Would you explain to me why Murphy's pictures don't all sell for the same price?' "

June 25 / With William Salomon, the collector

Up until just a few years ago the rich American bought only pictures. Surrounded by masterpieces of painting, his home was decorated in the worst taste. A hodgepodge of styles: Victorian, Napoleonic, 1889 Exposition, bronze work by Linke, decor by Jansen. The decorators didn't sell him furniture but pounds of bronze with a bit of wood underneath. Marble was valued only by cubic content. And since neither bronze nor marble could be put on the ceiling, it was covered with tapestries worked in gold.

When in 1901 I arrived in America for the first time, William Salomon was perhaps the only American whose home was arranged tastefully, with fine French wainscoting, handsome furniture, and pretty art objects, but no pictures. Those he bought subsequently, almost all from Duveen and me. The exterior of the house is of vulgar red brick— it is situated opposite the Metropolitan Museum at the corner of Eighty-third Street. Adjoining the building, there is a little wooden house in which a woman of ninety has lived since her childhood. There, where all her life has unfolded, she wants to die, and like the miller of Sans-Souci she has refused sizable offers by multimillionaire Salomon, who would very much have liked to build a gallery there.

I like William Salomon very much. The English who hedge round the title of "gentleman" with so many reservations would allow him full marks. It's a quality rare in Americans, who haven't had time to acquire polish. He is elegant, slim, gets his clothes from London. His voice is soft and he is rather a handsome old man, though of medium height. His black mustache and hair are agreeably sprinkled with white. He has not only taste but knowledge. He is the only American who can buy without a dealer. I am to see him again in a few days.

Frick, the collector

After leaving Salomon I ran into Frick in front of Cartier's. Frick is Swiss by origin, but resembles an old Scotsman, with a white beard cut just so, to the fraction of an inch, and washed with white soap. His suits always look new. He has rather a hard gaze. His features are so regular, his face so pleasant, that he seems benevolent, but just at certain moments you see and comprehend that you were mistaken, that his head is there, placed on that body, for his triumph and your defeat.

I greeted him and gave him news of Viviani. He asked me what the situation was in France. I answered that it was good. "You've just acquired a lot of fine things," I said.

"Oh, very little."

And he walked on. Four weeks ago he bought more than three million dollars' worth of pictures and art objects from Joe.

June 28 / At the home of the Du Pont de Nemours
On their immense estate the sun is radiant, the trees are green, the flowers sparkling. Six miles off, gunpowder is produced, and death.

Insignia worship
Many people have taken advantage of the presence of Allied soldiers to wear fake uniforms. To catch them, the military authorities one day ordered the officers to wear mufti. The haul has been copious.

On a Nattier
Some ten years ago Henry Huntington of Los Angeles bought a Nattier from Knoedler for about $90,000. It's the portrait of a woman reproduced in the little Nolhac edition. Very fine quality. Superb red drapery.

Now Joe reckons to get it back in an exchange. He asked me at what sum he ought to enter it on his books. "Fifty thousand dollars," I told him. "I'd still buy it for that price." This painting was at Reims, and for years I sought to acquire it. Its owner didn't want to sell it. He died. A middleman named Lacombe, a skillful bargainer, who worked for me, jumped on the first train to Reims, but on arrival there caught sight of Boussod, the art dealer, accompanied by another middleman, on the platform. The two men were going back to Paris looking so jubilant that Lacombe told himself they'd carried off the prize. He was reassured to learn that the funeral hadn't taken place yet, but he found it impossible to get into the house; he'd have to attend the ceremony at the cemetery. Meanwhile he began to be anxious about Boussod's return. He kept watch on the incoming trains. No one. So he went on. Back from the funeral, he was received by the widow. Learning that he was the first, he gave a sigh of relief. "Too late," she told him, "the Nattier is sold. A strange thing, monsieur. The day of my husband's death, one of the undertaker's men noticed my picture and brought to me a rich collector who had lately buried his wife. The collector made me a big offer and I accepted it at once."

And from the description of the two men, Lacombe recognized his rival in the undertaker's man and Boussod in the poor widower.

The L. Blair Collection

His splendid Boucher tapestries, his furniture, and his art objects are under wraps for the summer. We tried out the Pajou *Madame de Wailly* for his drawing room. I asked him $75,000 for it. Last year I sold him the wonderful white marble Louis XVI chimney piece from the Crillon mansion for $7,000, my cost price. "When it was installed for me," Blair told me, "I remarked on its beauty to the contractor, who specializes in fitting chimneys. 'Yes, it's nice,' he answered, 'but you've never seen the mantlepieces that Smith and Company make.'"

July 3 / With Joe. On the Fragonards of Grasse

"For how much," I asked him, "have you sold them to Frick?"

"One million two hundred and fifty thousand dollars. I haven't taken a penny commission. Morgan had exhibited them at the Metropolitan Museum, which I visited one Sunday. In front of the Fragonards I saw Knoedler, surrounded by his colleagues and employees. 'Aha,' I said to myself, 'they want to sell them to Frick.' Next morning I hurried around to Morgan's. 'How much are your Fragonards?'

" 'One million two hundred and fifty thousand dollars.'

" 'I'll give you a million.'

" 'Take it or leave it.'

" 'All right, I'll have them, but would you kindly telephone Mr. Frick that I'm letting him have them at cost?'

"Morgan telephoned, and Frick answered: 'Let Joe come over

to see me tomorrow morning.' I sold them to him and I've had that man since," said Joe. "Without taking any commission, I buy him everything he wants in European collections."

July 4 / Independence Day

One hundred thousand men were marching along Fifth Avenue from 9 A.M. to 8:00 in the evening. From my balcony at 647, several members of the French mission were watching the parade. Among others, Stéphane Lausanne, former editor-in-chief of *Matin*. Several years before the war his articles against Germany got his paper banned in Alsace-Lorraine. Now he's on top.

There was another propagandist, Kneicht, a Lorrainer of considerable wit.

Forty-two nationalities out of the forty-five recognized by the United States were represented. This parade made me comprehend for the first time the immense mixture of races from which this nation has emerged. Soldiers and sailors formed the head of the parade. This fledgling people has to have simple and clear demonstrations. The war was borne past them on somewhat puerile floats, the better for them to understand the effort required of them. The whole thing was a three-dimensional advertisement. An airplane drawn on an automobile, a mechanic at the wheel, and the propeller turning with a frightful, incessant din. Machine guns in a trench, with men on sentry duty, flat on their bellies. Next came a float, an advertisement for naval recruiting: men asleep, rocked in hammocks. Farther along, a boat demonstrating how mines are lifted. A naval electrical station, a veritable factory, flashed out its long beams. The cutting of hefty blocks of steel was shown, followed by a ship in the process of being built, and the motto: "A ship every twelve days." Next an antiaircraft gun trained unremittingly on the sky.

A procession of nurses bearing placards reading "We ask for 25,000" was followed by ambulances, tanks, and even torpedoes. The float of the YMCA, that admirable Protestant organization purveying comforts and amusements to soldiers at war, was very picturesque. Their concern is the moment of leisure in the trenches or dugouts; the piano, writing paper. The Salvation Army was baking cakes on their float.

Then came the procession of races. The Armenians carried a banner: "Suffering Armenia trusts in America." The Assyrians, whom I had thought extinct these three thousand years, likewise proclaimed: "Our trust is in America." China was wheeling along a pagoda. Bolivia, Montenegro, the Slovaks and Czechs, were represented in their national costumes; Panama, Central America, Honduras, Cuba, the Carpathians, Syria, Lebanon; Finland with the inscription "25,000 Finnish workers build boats for America"; Norway with "We have lost 830 ships."

The French were marching with two floats, that of Alsace-Lorraine, and another in which Rouget de Lisle was singing "The Marseillaise" at Strasbourg. They scored the hit of the day, for France.

July 7 / Henry Goldman, collector

He has the head of a German high official. His spectacles are like the prismatic lenses of a searchlight. A flabby countenance full of self-conceit. The fist banging on the table is the expression of his self-confidence. A wrangler, he rolls his *r*'s on a harsh note.

Again we discussed two paintings which I have sold him, a Clouet and a Gentile da Fabriano.

The Clouet is a portrait of Francis I. It is about seven inches high, and was called the Clouet of Toulouse, having been discovered in a château near that city.

German Bapst did me a thirteen-page analysis drawn from fifteen reproductions at Frazier-Soye's. He described it as three-quarter length, facing slightly left, and wearing a kind of beret adorned with a jeweled pin and a white feather. The pleated jerkin is scarlet and lets the shirt show through a sort of sleeve opening. Over one shoulder is thrown a cloak edged in sable and trimmed with pearls. The head stands out from a deep olive-green background.

Subsequently Bapst claimed to have discovered how this painting came to Toulouse. The famous cameo, *The Apotheosis of Augustus,* had been given by the church of Saint-Séverin in Toulouse to Francis I, and some time later, in 1553, the king, by way of thanks, made a gift of his portrait to the chapter. The cameo is today in Vienna. During the League troubles, it was bought by Emperor Rudolf of Germany.

The painting was done around 1530.

The Gentile da Fabriano is a marvelous picture. It had belonged to an English Canadian, Mr. Sartis, who, having come to settle in Paris, had lent it to the Museum of Decorative Arts, where it was on display for a long time, along with two other primitives, one a Lorenzo Monaco which I sold during the war to the Boston Museum on the recommendation of Walter Gay, the painter who was then its adviser, and who drew his commission.

Goldman's first purchase was a Rembrandt, the portrait of a butcher—a painting called *St. Matthew* so that it might be sold more easily. It is mentioned in Bode. He paid slightly over $120,000 for it. It was the subject to attract a lousy German: A Rembrandt painting of a man holding a knife! He found that powerful. It's no saint's head but very much a butcher's, with no spark beyond that of bestiality. Rembrandt took his characters from the people, the common people; he put his whole philosophy into their eyes. The quality of this painting is excellent, but it is a vulgar canvas.

Goldman has told me that he's bought the first Rembrandt mentioned in Bode and in the *Klassiker der Kunst*, for $2,000 in the Hermann sale. Hermann had paid the Austrian dealer Kleinberger $25,000 for it. Goldman has just disposed of it in an exchange with the Ehrich brothers, from whom he took a Van Dyck of the Rubens period, a Virgin and Child of Lord Hartington's collection. "I'd bought that Rembrandt," he told me, "just to study it for a few months."

American women

I knew Mrs. Gimbel as a young girl, pretty, intelligent, intellectual, interested in the arts and in literature. She loves her husband, who has no intellectuality. This evening I dined with them. When I made my goodbyes to her, I thanked her, but she overruled my thanks with her own overflowing ones. This evening was like a last glimmer of light for her. In a few years the eclipse will be total.

July 14

For the first time and across the whole of the United States the American government is officially celebrating our national holiday. This evening twelve thousand people thronged Madison Square Garden; all the seats were sold long ago.

The great success of the evening was the orator Paderewski, yesterday a pianist and today Poland's official representative. He no longer plays, for that's all finished; he fights, and how handsome he is! There he was on the stage, gaunt in evening dress, his hair disheveled and splendid, the divine tormented defender of his country. He spoke with ardor and beauty in a perpetual, stirring agitation. In celebrating our anniversary of freedom, he knows he was calling for the hour of deliverance for his country.

The Morgan chinas

Joe bought the collection for nearly $3 million.

Return to France

I am on board the *Lorraine*. Same cabin.

A vision of time past

The sea isn't too good. At the end of the deck some nuns were dozing. With their heads lolling back, they could not have been aware, modest as they are, that their faces were uncovered, exposed to every passing gaze. The thought came to my mind that traces of the past showed on their features. The sea made their faces look drawn, as if overcome with suffering, and I recognized—ah, but so strikingly!—the expression of those virgins of the seventeenth century who suffered attacks against their faith. I felt as if in a dream, startled by this vision and realizing how a like vocation, the same way of thought makes all these faces the same.

Transatlantic war

Two hundred Polish soldiers, eighty Slovaks, sixty Italians, twenty-five French, sixty YMCA members, some twenty members of the Catholic society, the Knights of Columbus, and lots of Red Cross. Members of all kinds of charitable societies, some businessmen, some police. In second class, rich Americans, people who in peacetime wouldn't travel without deluxe cabins, dashing off to France, crowded four to a stinking inner cabin, to dedicate themselves unto death. So many men of lofty purpose, gathered together like this, must be something fairly unique. The atmosphere is elevated, giving one a glimpse of what a better world could be like; and this is a better world. I, who normally keep to myself and my books on my crossings, feel the need to mix with this crowd—and I do.

July 20 / Offensive

The retreat continues.

Charity fête

My name was called and they offered me the vice-chairmanship. The chairman will be the Reverend Ernest M. Stires of that fine St. Thomas Church in New York. I accepted, only to learn a bit late that I was expected to deliver a speech. I am a man who speaks slowly, with hesitation, searching for my words and repeating them. I was extremely embarrassed, but they refused to accept my resignation.

Religious war

Le Dantec, the steward, has been describing to me how in his cabin this morning he had assembled the seven or eight clergymen representing the principal denominations, so as to fix for tomorrow, Sunday, the different hours of service and also designate the lounges where they would take place. "I really thought I must be sitting in on one of the old religious wars," Le Dantec told me. "I was right in the Middle Ages, with all of them wanting the grand salon and at the same time! There were frightful arguments, and shocking words passed between these clergymen. The Protestants maintained the most dignity, while the most rabid were the French priest and the Canadian one. There was a moment when they were practically at each other's throats. We had the hardest time in the world pacifying them. It was a ludicrous, deplorable spectacle."

July 21 / St. Thomas Church

I had a conversation with the Reverend E. M. Stires, and getting round his modesty, found out that it was he who built that beautiful Gothic church on the corner of Fifty-third Street and Fifth Avenue. He was not the architect but the guiding spirit. He had some of the plans redone four and five times, and designs *ad infinitum*; and even to this day he doesn't hesitate to ask a sculptor for three or four stone models for a single niche.

On Paderewski and the Poles

The secretary of our charity concert is Lieutenant O'Brien of the Foreign Legion, son of an Irish general, Croix de Guerre, military medal. His right arm is virtually paralyzed. Sent on a mission to America, he is now returning to France to escort a contingent of Polish soldiers. "These men are over thirty-one," he tells me, "so they wouldn't have to be soldiers in America, the age limit being thirty, but they are going to fight on French soil for their country's independence, a country which they don't even know, as they were born in America. Some don't speak English, the majority haltingly. They are nearly all married, and some earn as much as eight dollars a day. Six hundred Poles, on the average, depart each week for France, setting off to die on soil which isn't even their own. You don't often, in any race, come across such patriotism. I helped recruit them, with Paderewski, who's a genius. I don't mean as a musician, but as a man."

July 22 / Kornovaloff

He is a former president or vice-president of the Duma. Bertron gave me a note of introduction to him. He has the round sturdy head of a church warden, a fish mouth, and puckered eyes. He speaks little and in a low voice, like a deaf person. He criticizes Kerensky for his lack of drive. He affirms that the Allies' intervention in Siberia depends entirely on President Wilson's decision.

July 23 / The charity concert

We've collected more than $2,400. My little speech was a success, and if I ever speak in public again, it will be because this first effort has given me confidence. On my next trip to the United States I'll have to give some lectures on art.

July 25 / Lunar cemetery

It is 2 A.M. An oppressive night. On deck, to the front, passengers are sleeping. The scene looks like a graveyard of eternity, the cemetery of another world, a burial ground where bodies do not decompose but remain as at the moment of death. They have all been dead for centuries and will continue so forever.

All manner of dead are represented there; under dark blankets are those burnt in fires (whatever do they want, all these dead, with those lifebelts fastened on their backs or lying on the deck?); the suicides are stretched out on chairs, with slack arms and heads drooping pitifully, bloodless and mindless, on their invertebrate necks; a woman wearing mourning weeds is propped up on white pillows and black cushions; another, a diminutive blonde very animated in life, is now a doll that can no longer make its tiny sound. Those lost at sea, their faces white enough to frighten the moon, rest cushioned on mattresses and swaddled in wraps. The covers themselves are tragically beautiful, their folds have an absolute rightness about them, not as if arranged by some artist, not made false by any human hand. The bodies also are wonderfully true, each different in position, expression, personality.

Why is it that the old look less absolutely sealed in death?

A sailor on his back, lying flat on the lathes there, his hands in his pockets, is the only one with a look of slight decay. A simple, jolly creature who couldn't ever have been bothered by nightmares of death.

Most horrible, more horrible than those faces, are the hands, even those held as if in prayer, even those with fingers spread out, clinging flat against the body, expressionlessly dead. And there, look, the tragic futility of hands clenched in fists, and of others resting on the heart as if trying to grip it back to life or clutching at the vitals to keep them from slipping away.

A convoy

Twenty-one ships on the horizon. Soon we had passed them, they making for Brest, we for Bordeaux. A fine spectacle, twenty-one ships going to war!

The offensive

It continues victorious.

July 26 / Assassination of the Czar

We have not yet disembarked, but the newspapers are on board.

Kornovaloff said to me: "The czar was a perifidious man, and falsehood his mode of government, but the Bolsheviks have committed a great crime in assassinating him. They are thugs."

My wife

My dear wife was standing there on the dock waiting for me. "René," she said, "we're not to be apart any more, I don't want it."

NOTEBOOK 3

July 28–November 11, 1918

July 28 / Memento

On a bench: five soldiers with seven wooden legs.

July 31 / On Meissonier

When I arrived at his home, I found that huge, sybaritic tom, Georges Petit, seated in front of his little glass of chartreuse, like a cat watching a mouse. The conversation touched on Meissonier, and he told me: "He was a great painter. He was an intimate friend of my father, whom he appointed to look after his interests and manage his affairs. I personally sold *La Revue* for 400,000 francs, *Les Amateurs de Tableaux* for 500,000, *La Confidence* for 300,000. You've no idea of his tremendous conscientiousness. He owned an estate near Poissy, where he supported an absolute army of laborers. For his painting *L'Apropos* he had an inn door built specially, because he couldn't find one in the surrounding countryside. I sold that painting for 200,000 francs, and when I brought him the money he wanted to take only 120,000. He threw money about like a lunatic and couldn't have left more than a million or two when he died. He received Napoleon III with a luxury on the scale of Louis XIV."

"M. Petit, you ought to write down your recollections of Meis-sonier."

"I could, particularly since I possess at least two hundred of his letters. I have mentioned his great conscientiousness: listen to this. On that same estate he built a small railway and a track on which horses would gallop while he followed, making sketches, in a tiny locomotive. So you can understand that he hadn't time to paint many pictures. They're almost all in America. Vanderbilt owns quite a number. On his very first trip to Paris he hurried along to see Meissonier, who told him: 'You go to Petit's and fix it up with him.' And that's how we met somebody who subsequently became one of our biggest clients."

"The Meissoniers have gone down a lot."

"Gone down a lot, and come up again. A fine one can still command 200,000 francs."

On the "Angelus"

"M. Petit, did you know Millet?"

"Yes, and in fact I was involved in the sale of his *Angelus*, which first appeared at the Wilson sale where the fine Perronneau from the Doucet sale also came up. A dispute arose at that sale between Secrétan and Defoler, each claiming the *Angelus* had been knocked down to him. It had reached 180,000 francs. A bigger gambler than Defoler never existed. He proposed to Secrétan that they should draw lots for the Millet, and it was agreed. Their names were put in a hat; I was there; a page drew, and Defoler won the *Angelus*. Shortly afterwards he came to call on me; friends had been telling him he was crazy, that Secrétan had never intended to win that painting, and that he, Defoler, had been tricked, since both of the slips had borne his name. I dashed around to Secrétan, who replied that he would give 200,000 francs for it. He did a good piece of business that day, for at his sale that painting went for 800,000 francs to the minister of fine arts. This sparked off another situation, as the ministerial council didn't approve the purchase. So the minister came running to tell me the spot he was in. I paid a call on Alphonse de Rothschild, explained the situation, and he said to me: 'I don't care for the picture, but I'll take it to spare you and the minister of fine arts any embarrassment.' Waiting back in my gallery, I found an American named Sutton who had crossed the Atlantic to buy the *Angelus,* intending to show it across the whole of the United States. He'd missed out on it at the sale, and had just learned that the government didn't want it. I told him: 'You've come too late. I've just sold it to Alphonse de Rothschild.' Sutton answered calmly: 'Go offer him 850,000 francs.' I went back to Alphonse, who authorized me to dispose of the picture. So there it was—sold to Sutton, who commissioned Brandus for the tour. Admissions brought in $200,000, sales of prints $10,000, and when Sutton had extracted all he could from it, he asked me to resell it. Chauchard gave me a million francs for it."

Matisse and Mother Humbert

I mentioned Matisse to Petit, and he said: "His parents kept the door at Mother Humbert's, the queen of swindlers, where I used to be a frequent visitor. The concierge would even from time to time tell me about her son who painted, but I didn't pay any attention. I sold paintings to Mother Humbert, and, like every other sucker, I believed in that inheritance, in those imaginary millions, those nonexistent Americans, those Crawfords—yes, in that inheritance to which she had even given a legal existence by paying estate duties on it.

"She'd often shown me the huge triple-locked strongbox where she kept the securities, which she claimed she couldn't touch. When it was opened, you recall, there was only the proverbial trouser button.

"She gave superb parties at which I've met the president of the Republic. She had owed me 200,000 francs for some little time, and one day I went to get them out of her. In her anteroom I found a jeweler of my acquaintance waiting for her, but I hadn't time to speak to him, as she had me shown in at once. I asked for my money very firmly. She hedged. I insisted. Then she said: 'Since you need your money so badly, Petit, I'm going to pawn my jewels, a sacrifice I'd make for no other person in the world.' She thought I'd protest and demur, but I did nothing of the kind. She took me into her bedroom, where she flashed before my eyes at least two millions' worth of jewels, and asked me to come back the next day, assuring me that she would pay me, and I went.

"A fortnight later I called again at her house and again found the jeweler in the anteroom. He complained to me that he had left several millions' worth of jewels there for a fortnight and had not been able to get them back. A ray of doubt crossed my mind!"

August 3 / A mot of Forain's to Georges Petit

On the day when a Big Bertha shell dropped on the workshops of Barbedienne's foundry: "That's what's going to make the Rodins!"

August 6 / On the Americans

O'Brien said to me: "Two days ago I lunched at the front with General Mangin, who told me that the Americans made him wild with admiration, that in the last attack he saw them strip off their clothes and, bare-torsoed, start out fifteen hundred yards behind the tanks, overtake them, pass them, and even get in the way of their fire."

August 7 / Manet's portrait of his mother

Georges Bernheim tells me that he has just sold it for 150,000 francs.

August 10 / On a Monet and an Ingres

Georges Bernheim told me: "Rosenberg has bought a life-size Monet, a Japanese woman, for 150,000 francs, and he says it's a marvel. As for me, I've sold my Ingres black-lead sketch, *The Family of Lucien Bonaparte*, for 120,000 francs. It was drawn during the Hundred Days, and has ten figures. Lapanze, who was crazy about it, published it in *La Renaissance*. I bought it from Count Primoli. Now the sketch goes off to Copenhagen. Beistegui, who gave his collection to the Louvre, would have none of it because he thought the left hand of the child lying on the ground was not well drawn."

I didn't tell Bernheim my chief criticism, that the drawing is too pale and lacks firmness.

August 15 / On Renoir

When I returned to Paris, I was so glad to have made Renoir's acquaintance and so grateful for it to Georges Bernheim that I gave him at cost the canvases I had bought from the artist. Seeing them again in his gallery, without benefit of the Midi light, I was astonished to find them as beautiful as on the Riviera, and especially the portrait of the woman in the straw hat with three red roses in the middle and two yellow roses at the side. The canvases done this year are perhaps more beautiful than those of the last three years: they haven't that rather disagreeable brick-red color, but have grown pearly again. Georges Bernheim told me that he went to see Renoir earlier this summer, and he congratulated me on doing the same: "Like Vollard! There's someone who knows how to manage him. One day he brought him a parcel of fish from the market, threw them on a table, and told him, 'Paint me that.' Amused, Renoir did it, and Vollard carried off the canvas. Another time Vollard appeared before the painter in toreador dress, and Renoir, ravished by the color, did his portrait.

"On the other hand, Vollard holds his spittoon, brings him his chamber pot, and helps him to pee."

August 19 / At Claude Monet's

In the train taking us to Vernon, Georges Bernheim told me that I was responsible for the trip to Giverny, and that Monet might not receive us. Like Renoir, he doesn't like to be disturbed when he is working. I asked him if he knew Monet well, and he replied: "Yes, and on a certain occasion I treated him better than he's treated me recently."

"When was that?"

"You see, Monet had married for the second time—a widow, or perhaps it was a divorcée. She had a son who, on his mother's death, sold me eight of his stepfather's canvases for 8,000 francs."

"Why so cheap, when he couldn't be ignorant of their value?"

"They weren't signed, and the boy was not on good terms with Monet and could not get the painter to put his signature on them. They were nonetheless worth 40,000 francs with my testimonial. Monet heard of the transaction and sent me my cousins, the Bernheim brothers, to tell me he would like to buy back the eight pictures and to ask me the price. I wrote to him: 'M. Monet, you have only to send me a check for 8,000 francs and take the canvases.' He sent the check, promising me a present. I waited for it. Two years, three years passed. I decided to go and see him, and I said to him: 'M. Monet, I'm not asking you for any presents, but sell me some paintings.' He let me have twelve for

120,000 francs, and threw in a thirteenth. I had sold him eight for 8,000 francs. It was a rather expensive present, but then he's a very hard man. So a year ago I went to his house with my colleague Hessel, with whom I had gone half and half on a very bad Monet, and we took it along to him. He remembered the canvas and exclaimed: 'What a monstrosity!' 'Since it doesn't do you credit,' we told him, 'give us another in its place.' 'Not on your life,' he cried. 'There isn't in all my studio a single painting worth as little as yours.' Then we suggested effecting an exchange at a price, and pointed out a landscape and asked him the price. He replied that he wanted 10,000 francs for it, and we accepted. Monet took our painting and split it with one huge kick."

It was 1:30 when we arrived in Vernon. We got out of the train and climbed on the bicycles we had hired in Paris: transportation isn't easy in wartime. For some miles we followed the Seine valley, which is lovely just there, and so reached the celebrated valley where a number of artists are gathered around the master. I noticed large studio windows opening out of several peasant houses. We finally reached Claude Monet's wall, which is pierced by a large green door and a bit farther on by another very small door, also green. This we opened to enter Monet's oft-described garden. I regret my complete ignorance of the names of flowers, as I should like to name here the varieties I saw. A Maeterlinck would be needed for a garden like this. It resembles no other, first because it consists of only the simplest flowers and then because they grow to unheard-of heights. I believe that none is under three feet high. Certain flowers, some of which are white and others yellow, resembling huge daisies, shoot up to six feet. It's not a meadow, but a virgin forest of flowers whose colors are very pure, neither pink nor bluish, but red or blue.

A servant took our cards and told us that she'd go and see. Bernheim was nervous and whispered: "Don't be surprised if we aren't received." I asked him if that was not Monet coming toward us.

"Where? What's he look like?"

"There, under a big pointed straw peasant's hat. With a large white beard."

"Why, yes, it is he: he's coming."

We advanced. Bernheim shook his hand, introduced me, and

Monet said: "Ah, gentlemen, I don't receive when I'm working, no, I don't receive. When I'm working, if I'm interrupted, it just finishes me, I'm lost. You'll understand, I'm sure, that I'm chasing the merest sliver of color. It's my own fault, I want to grasp the intangible. It's terrible how the light runs out, taking color with it. Color, any color, lasts a second, sometimes three or four minutes at most. What to do, what to paint in three or four minutes? They're gone, you have to stop. Ah, how I suffer, how painting makes me suffer! It tortures me. The pain it causes me!"

Monet had come to the end of his monologue. I thought he would shake me by the hand and return to his work. I wanted him to stay a few minutes longer, and I said to him: "Excuse me, M. Monet, I'm the guilty one, it's I who wished to come. Georges Bernheim warned me, but I've been looking forward to this for so long! I sell old paintings, but adore the moderns. I adore your work. I get furious with my collectors when they tell me, 'It's finished, no one knows how to paint any more, the ancients will never be equaled.' What idiots!" Then, looking at his flowers: "How pretty your garden is. Mary Cassatt has so often spoken to me of it." "How is she?" he asked. I told him that she is nearly blind, and I sensed in the painter an old man's indifference. At this point Georges Bernheim said to notice how young M. Monet looked. I asked him his age, and he answered that he was seventy-eight. I complimented him, and indeed it's astonishing; I've never seen a man of that age look so young. He can't be taller than about five foot five, but he is absolutely erect. He looks like a young father on Christmas Day wearing a false white beard to make his children believe in old Father Christmas. His face is softly colored and unblotched. His small round chestnut eyes, full of vivacity, add emphasis to whatever he says. "Come into the studio," he said. It's a large rectangular room. About a hundred paintings are hung on the wall in three or four graduated rows. For the most part they are paintings of little interest, rather flat, without color: just foundations. But here and there a picture stands out from the others. I see one which seems to me to represent a thick forest with rifts of startling light, a forest of flowers which could be his garden.

My remark about modern painting had pleased him, for he brought it up again, saying: "I prefer a still life by Delacroix to a Chardin painting." As the conversation touched on landscape, I said: "You and your colleagues of the nineteenth century, you're the masters who brought the art of landscape to heights never before attained." Monet cried: "Don't call me a master; I don't like it." Protesting that I hadn't called him a master, I added: "You remind me of Renoir, who won't hear the word 'master' uttered." "I suppose," he observed, "that those Dutch didn't see nature as all yellow. Their colors must have changed. When we were young, we went around the Louvre comparing our cuffs with the linen of Rembrandt's people, and decided that his canvases were far from the original colors. Rubens, now, did beautiful landscapes."

Georges Bernheim mentioned Corot, and Monet said: "He didn't put enough paint on his canvases. I don't know what will become of them with time, varnish, and cleaning. I wonder what will be left of them. Very little, I'm afraid!"

Like Renoir, Monet is very much concerned with the chemical evolution of colors, and he admits that he thinks about it constantly while he's painting.

"Have you heard," Bernheim asked him, "that Rosenberg has bought your *Woman with Japanese Fans?*"

"He wrote me about it. Well, he's got himself a piece of junk."

"Junk?" repeated Bernheim, in astonishment.

"Yes, junk; it was only a fantasy. I had exhibited *The Woman in Green,* which had had a very big success, at the Salon, and it was suggested that I try to repeat it. I was tempted when they showed me a marvelous robe with gold embroidery more than an inch thick."

I asked the painter if he was serious, and he replied: "Absolutely." He showed us a photograph of the painting; I admired the head and found it beautiful. He told us with a certain artistic pride: "Look at those materials!" He informed us that it was a portrait of his first wife, who was a brunette and who put on a blond wig that day.

Bernheim had told me about an immense and mysterious decoration on which the painter was working and which he probably wouldn't show us. I made a frontal attack and won the day: he took us down the paths of his garden to a newly built studio constructed like a humble village church. Inside there is only one huge room with a glass roof, and there we were confronted by a strange artistic spectacle: a dozen canvases placed one after another in a circle on the ground, all about six feet wide by four feet high: a panorama of water and water lilies, of light and sky. In this infinity, the water and the sky had neither beginning nor end. It was as though we were present at one of the first hours of the birth of the world. It was mysterious, poetic, deliciously unreal. The effect was strange: it was at once pleasurable and disturbing to be surrounded by water on all sides and yet untouched by it. "I work all day on these canvases," Monet told us. "One after another, I have them brought to me. A color will appear again which I'd seen and daubed on one of these canvases the day before. Quickly the picture is brought over to me, and I do my utmost to fix the vision definitively, but it generally disappears as fast as it arose, giving way to a different color already tried several days before on another study, which at once is set before me—and so it goes the whole day!"

"I understand, M. Monet, why you don't like being interrupted; so with thanks we're going to leave you."

"Just come and see my dining room." The room he showed us is rustically simple but of an oriental subtlety, with just one basic color: yellow, tone upon tone, a Monet yellow, the color of his genius the day he mixed it—which is why it can never be repeated.

As we left him, the door almost shut, he called: "Come back to see me at the beginning of October when the days are drawing in and I take a fortnight's holiday; we'll have a chat then."

As I was pedaling along the road with Georges Bernheim, he said: "That was a fine reception."

"Splendid, so we'll go back in October."

"I'd gladly buy those panels of his: there must be about thirty."

"How much, Bernheim—300,000 francs?"

"Much more; at that reckoning they'd be only 10,000 francs apiece. Let's buy them together, exhibit them in New York, and we'll get our money back on the price of admission."

I told Georges Bernheim that I didn't think we'd be able to sell the panels in the United States because houses there are so small, and I added that also from the decorative point of view the canvases would be difficult to place, as they lack height; they would be ideal on the ground. They'd be perfect, I said jokingly, for a swimming pool.

"I'll tell him that," said Bernheim, "and you see how you're received in October. Anyway, he isn't a man to run after dealers. When I went to see him with Hessel, he told us that in his youth he sold a canvas for a hundred francs which today would be considered very important, and even then he received only fifty francs cash plus a painting by Cézanne, which he will show us and for which Hessel offered him 25,000 francs, but he refused."

August 21 / The Lorenzo Monaco of the Boston Museum

I bought it for 105,000 francs at the same time as the Gentile da Fabriano, which I sold to Henry Goldman of New York, and the Pietro Alamanno that I still own. I came upon this information by chance on opening an accounts book. I shall take pleasure, when I have time, in looking at my old books again and turning up information on prices in our time.

Evacuation of art objects

Edouard Kann,[1] who has quite a big collection, was telling me about it. He is the nephew of Rudolph Kann, who owned the famous collection that we bought, together with the Duveen brothers, for 17 million. He is the son of Maurice, who also had a very fine collection, the most beautiful paintings of which we acquired. He told me: "The Germans launched an attack on that fortified position, the Chemin des Dames. They wiped it out in a trice. The thing is, it was being guarded by only three territorial divisions and two English divisions decimated two months before during their retreat to the outskirts of Amiens. They had been stationed there partly to recoup themselves, their morale being very low. The Germans expected to meet resistance, but encountering none they advanced forty-five miles in three days, their guns idle. Ten thousand of our men, for the most part cavalry, swept down from the north, barred their way, and the Germans were halted by our first try at resistance.

"Then it was that the Beaux-Arts began having art objects re-

[1] He kept a journal during the war, he told me. It should be interesting. Kann, who died two years ago, was very well informed. He was an auxiliary and was attached to the Journalists' Center, where the latest news was always available and through which a great many interesting people passed.

moved. I didn't want to shift anything, but they insisted and offered me a huge wagon, into which they piled 1,600,000 francs' worth of possessions. Ten pictures, including my two Fragonard panels from the Crosnier sale, my Tocqué woman, my Largillières, my little Boilly, the woman with a bird, which cost me 23,000 francs, my Strasbourg bookcase and some other furniture.

"The Louvre, the Decorative Arts, the Petit Palais—all were moved out with incredible speed. It was quite a tour de force!"

September 4 / The "Angelus"

I have seen Brandus, of whom Georges Petit was speaking the other month. It was he who toured that famous painting right across America. I remarked that he must have heard some odd comments, and he replied: "Oh, masses of them! Almost everyone wanted to know how much it cost per square inch, and also why a copy wouldn't be as good. A tailor said to me: 'Your peasant's trousers don't fit him, they're much too short; so how can this picture be worth so much?' A visitor asked me: 'Why is this painting called the *Angelus*?' and added, 'It's probably the gentleman's name.' I overheard a girl asking her mother why the man and woman were so sad; the mother replied that they'd just buried their child. A conversation between two laborers went: 'Why are they looking at the ground in such an unhappy way?' 'Because the insects have eaten the seeds and they won't have any harvest.' "

September 6 / On Renoir

Not less than thirty years ago at a watering place, the painter met the beautiful Mme Stora, whose sons are antique dealers, and he asked to paint her. Benjamin Constant had also done her portrait. Several years ago Helleu saw the Renoir at the Storas', who considered the painting horrible, and he asked to buy it. They gave it to him for 300 francs, whereas they wouldn't have sold the Constant at any price. Since then Monet has bought the portrait of Mme Stora, which is, apparently, one of the finest Renoirs.

Vollard and Renoir

When Vollard was preparing his book on Renoir, he always used to go to the impressionist master's house with a painter named Bernard. Vollard would sit down at a table with writing paper and ink and appear to be catching up on his correspondence. It was Bernard's assignment to make Renoir talk while Vollard took notes of everything he said.

September 7 / On Nattier's "Baglione"

Helleu told me: "Your Nattier is one of the finest in the world. It's got that wonderfully graceful turn to the tulip. Twenty years ago Countess Armand commissioned Durand-Ruel to sell it. Degas and I showed it to the Countess de Béarn, who could have had it for 160,000 francs. Degas said to her: 'Buy it, and I'll be able to copy it.' She answered: 'I haven't any money.' 'You haven't any money?' I cried to myself. 'Borrow some then!' " [2]

Count Boni de Castellane

Boni, who had an income of three or four million, told me that he'd like to come into my New York establishment as a salesman at 5,000 francs a month, and added: "Or else I could get myself made a deputy or a senator."

September 9 / On Teddy Roosevelt, Jr.

Captain Snowden Fahnestock of the American Army, son-in-law of Mr. Bertron, whom we met in New York, dined last evening with his friend Teddy Roosevelt, who told him how some days ago he was searching the grand boulevards for a shop where he could buy a baseball glove. He approached an old gentleman with his wife on his arm and asked them, in terrible French: "Baseball, baseball, sporting house, where sporting house?" Taken aback, the couple looked at each other, then put their heads together, and finally the old gentleman took a notebook out of his pocket, hesitated between two or three addresses, and eventually gave him one. Teddy Roosevelt went along to it. He found himself in a licensed brothel.

[2] This picture is now in America. Bought initially by Ambatielos, a Greek living in Paris who lost his money, it was acquired by N. Wildenstein, who sold it to Erickson.

September 11 / On Rodin

Edouard Kann doesn't value Rodin's art very highly, and says of him: "He was an incomplete artist." He told me an anecdote related to him by Groult. Groult bred magnificent white swans in a pool in the middle of the garden of his property in the avenue de Malakoff. "Give me some of your swans," the sculptor asked him one day. "No," replied Groult. "I adore your swans," said Rodin. "Give me some, and I'll build them a marvelous pool on my estate. I'd like to have the enjoyment of seeing them always from my drawing room." "All right," answered Groult, "but first build your pool." Some months later Rodin informed him that the pool was finished. Groult replied: "My swans are expecting young, which I'll bring you myself in a month." He was as good as his word. Before putting them in the water, Rodin showed off his handiwork to the collector. The swans joyously entered the pool. Whereupon Rodin carried Groult off to his drawing room to let him spend an hour enjoying the sight which he'd promised himself. Alas! the edge of the pool was too high! The swans couldn't be seen.

September 16 / The art of Corot

His art lies in knowing how to let branches ramble. That's what I thought at Georges Bernheim's as I looked at a forest landscape with a glade that is a flow of silver. A woman in yellow kneels on the left, in profile; she is gathering wood, helped by a little girl in garnet red. (This canvas is about 24 inches high by 20 wide.)

Monday, October 10 / My third son

It's a boy, and my wife hoped to have a girl. She'll be very disappointed; I had tears in my eyes when I first saw him. He was ugly, his nose was flattened and elongated, his mouth enormous, but his hands were exquisite; the nails seemed edged with snow. He changes from minute to minute, and at 12:25 P.M. he was already pretty and had a human face. His eyes are blue, his nose small, his mouth likewise. What shall we call him? We've been thinking only of girls' names. Ernest too was disconsolate, as his mamma had promised him a little sister. But now he looks at the little creature with a huge smile and great joy. Pierre, wondering, remains grave.

October 13 / Victory

Germany has replied to President Wilson that she accepts his peace terms and declares herself, together with Austria, ready to evacuate the invaded territories, with a view to armistice.

I am going to call my son Jean Victor!

On Groult

Joe Duveen told me the following story: "Many years ago, when I was very young, we bought four marvelous Boucher tapestries in England. I took them to Paris, mentioned them to Groult, and made no bones about the fact that I was in a hurry to get back to London. He asked me to dinner, and there was company. At eleven o'clock we were alone. 'And my tapestries?' I said to him. 'We have time, take this glass of punch.' 'I don't drink.' 'You're wrong not to; try it.' 'No, thanks.' 'All right, then, come back tomorrow after dinner.' I returned the next day, he offered me liqueurs, which I refused, and for a week he continued this merry-go-round, but each evening he succeeded in making me lower my price. Because he knew I was anxious to leave, he forced me to stay on in Paris. Afterwards he admitted cynically to one of his friends that he'd intended to get me drunk. On the last evening I sold him the tapestries for 600,000 francs. He called his wife and asked her to bring in the sum. Then he counted out the six hundred notes, and he had me count them after him. It was eleven at night, and I'd had enough. Finally I got back to the Continental and deposited the money in the safe. At 1 A.M. I was awakened and called to the telephone. It was Groult: 'Hello, Duveen? You forgot to give me a receipt. Bring it to me immediately.' I hung up pretty quick. He had to wait till morning for his paper."

High prices

I was telling Joe: "I've offered Henderson £40,000 for his two Rembrandts—£30,000 for the portrait of the man alone. Try to get them when you go back to London. Five years ago I offered £100,000 for Lord Radnor's Velázquez, Holbein, and Quentin Metsys. Now you can give him £140,000 for them."

In his turn Joe has instructed me to offer 36,000 francs for the

Prince de Broglie's Rembrandt. I asked him to show me the Nattier he's had from Huntington in an exchange, but he told me that he had just sold it for £11,000 to Tombacco, an Egyptian.[8]

October 15 / Wilson replies

"Germans, you are vanquished. Address yourselves to Foch."

Wilson had been afraid France mightn't hang on. France had been afraid lest Wilson lack firmness. Everyone can breathe once again.

The Gustave Dreyfus Collection

I said to Joe: "I've asked Mme Jonas to sound out the son-in-law, Aboucaya. There are four heirs, and they can't keep the collection." Aboucaya answered: "If you've got a client, you can start by offering £600,000."

"I'll never pay that," cried Joe.

"You'll pay it."

October 17 / A Titian and an Andrea del Sarto

At Joe's I saw the Titian. It is not large, a portrait of a man in front of a balustrade like that of the Schiavona. He has a beard and forceful, cruel black eyes. The resolute right fist rests on a book. Twenty years ago Berenson wrote that this painting was a copy of a Giorgione. Now he attributes it to Titian. Giorgione must have had a hand in it, as with La Schiavona, today in the collection of Herbert Cook in London. Joe paid £25,000 for it.

The Sarto is of larger dimensions, a half-Italian, half-Flemish woman. An exquisite smile. She is in black, in décolleté, with a necklace, and she is looking to the left. A somewhat stiff white drapery, red sleeves a shade hard. The face is much superior to the rest of the painting. "I'll sell it for £50,000," Joe tells me.

The Duchess d'Uzès's armor

Has recently been sold for $70,000 to the Museum of the City of New York.

---

[8] Now in the E. Berwind Collection, New York. (Note appended 1929.)

October 21 / The Fragonards of Grasse

Chanas told me: "I sold them for Charles Wertheimer and got 850,000 francs for them. He gave me 25,000 francs commission."

October 23 / On Toulouse-Lautrec

"He was very much frowned upon by his family," Georges Bernheim told me, "until the day when he became famous. Then, Séré de Rivières, a relation of his and a very august president of the Seine tribunal, asked him to paint his daughter. Wickedly Toulouse-Lautrec gave him two nudes, women from a brothel, and made him put them on either side of the portrait. I've bought one of the canvases." "The portrait?" I asked. "Lord, no," shouted Bernheim, "I bought one of the brothel women."

October 29 / A Monet

I've just seen the *Woman with Japanese Fans* at Rosenberg's. Monet had told me it was a mediocre work. This canvas bears the same relation to a fine painting as a modern Japanese porcelain vessel does to an antique black china vase. Rosenberg is asking 300,000 francs for it.

October 30 / At Georges Lepape's, 44, rue Notre-Dame-de-Lorette

He is one of the leaders of the modern decorative art movement. No. 44 is quite simply five stories of windows in a wall. A bourgeois staircase with a chocolate-colored double door at each landing. He lives on the fifth, and he let me in himself. He has a nice jolly face, fat friendly jowls, and the glowing cheeks of a prize baby, with no chin. His gaze is sincere and his handshake unreserved.

The entrance hall is painted a cool yellow, a garden yellow, a bit like Claude Monet's dining room. Opposite is the dining room. On the right a grand staircase with openings at the top and side, plinths and cornices painted a pearl gray, and the wall hung with a modern violet-colored paper in long stripes of unequal width. A plain and very low divan covered in a silver material. Some chairs. A kind of large Tronchin whitewood table which he moves about and at which he works standing. In the corner, on the right, another table for working sitting down; above it, on the wall, two rows of books on shelves likewise painted gray.

During tea the conversation touched on cubism and Picasso. "I've been told," said Lepape, "that Picasso replied to a lady who wanted her portrait done and asked him for an appointment for a sitting: 'You need only send me a lock of hair and your necklace.'"

October 31 / La Toussaint

As I do nearly every Sunday, I went to the little Montparnasse cemetery and the tomb of my parents, whom I so dearly loved. The place next to them is for me. I carry with me a terror of not going down into that tomb at the precise hour.

November 7 / Revenge

We have entered Sedan. The German truce bearers are en route to the front.

November 8 / The plenipotentiaries

At eleven this morning Foch made known to them the armistice conditions. They must, by heaven, have found them hard. They were supposed to be empowered to negotiate, but now they want to refer the terms higher up. Foch has given them seventy-two hours. That's a lot for players who have lost the game.

November 10 / Abdication and flight of the Kaiser

The heading suffices.

November 11 / Victory

At five o'clock this morning the armistice was signed. The news got round Paris in no time, and everybody was telling you about it. No one was completely sure, however; but at eleven o'clock, at the moment hostilities ceased, the bells began to ring, the cannon to fire. I was on the Place de la Concorde; the Admiralty put out a multitude of flags. The atmosphere generally was restrained, with just a few student parades. People were going off happily to their lunch; that's all there was.

But at three o'clock, what a change! I made my way down the Champs-Elysées, where the crowd was solid. There was great animation, and suddenly I saw hanging from the end of a long pole a dummy—

Wilhelm II. He was dragged along and shoved onto a cannon which some workmen had set up on the edge of the pavement. The Kaiser was wearing black trousers, a cap, and a pimp's red sash. His conquering mustache was made of straw, and a white placard had been hung around his neck with the word *Assassin* in red. He was hauled before the statue of Strasbourg and there he was burnt, but the placard was not consumed and the word *Assassin* was not obliterated. The crowd was a sea of humanity. Cries, songs, hilarious processions down the rue Royale and all along the main boulevards. The whole of Paris had turned out. Droll sayings abounded. There was an English soldier who'd had a drop too much, and someone said: "That one's not had to put up with any restrictions." On the main boulevards traffic was at a standstill, except for enormous American motor tractors holding up to 150 people; and a Paris urchin joked: "Look, there's a tank!" Much mocking of Wilhelm. On all sides one could hear this song, or rather these two lines, given a working-class rendition:

> *He didn't have to go* [*to war*]
> *And so he shouldn't have.*

The Place de l'Opéra was like a whirlpool, as people kept pouring in from all sides. "It's a tango!" I heard a youth say, and the description was apt. I stayed on there till seven, and came back after dinner with my dear wife, who normally has such a horror of crowds but who loved it all this evening, because they were magnificent in their joy, at once hysterical and sane. A great warring people enjoying themselves to their hearts' content. And the people in mourning and in tears— they're happy all the same, for it is the day of glory. *FRANCE— VICTORY.*

NOTEBOOK 4

November 12, 1918–April 10, 1919

November 12, 1918 / The day after the armistice

    I spent my afternoon and evening on the boulevards. The crowd had doubled; incredibly, the joy had multiplied a hundredfold. Women were going wild but keeping their heads. I did not see a single drunk. Kissing, much kissing, but only a birds-of-passage kind of thing. The American soldiers are the most feted and they are also the most exuberant. They are the center of a mad whirl. On a traffic island in front of the Madeleine, a Yank was singing "La Madelon" practically without an accent, and was hugely applauded.

    My wife and I went in to Larue's for dinner, and two shopgirls called out to us: "Hey! There they are, the *nouveaux riches!*" Yesterday evening, on the balcony of the Opera House (the theater was closed), beneath the arch all lit up from the center, Chenal sang "The Marseillaise," but today the theater was open and the crowd shouted all but hopelessly for Chenal to come out again. Happily the people were to have their wish. At about ten o'clock it was announced that their favorite was going to appear, but time passed and she didn't come. A stagehand announced her every five minutes. Eventually he was booed, at which he cried: "Wait, she's on the pot!" The crowd burst out laughing and calmed down. Finally Chenal came out. She sang "The Marseillaise." The crowd fell silent and then there was pandemonium. It was nearly midnight, the last Métro had gone. Who cared? Tonight people go home on foot to the most outlying districts!

November 14 / Blériot

He's the first aviator to have crossed the Channel. The friend who gave me a line to him told me he buys works of art. I went to call on him at his residence on the avenue Kléber, and I was astonished to find someone with none of the look of a sportsman. He's precise, deliberate, and far more like a well-established director of a big insurance company. He said: "Ah, it isn't the time, it isn't the time; our orders have stopped. In six months we'll be making airplanes again, but meanwhile we're going to be turning out furniture for the devastated areas." He informed me that he prefers art objects to paintings.

A witticism of Picasso's

He was burglarized this summer. A friend ran into him at Léonce Rosenberg's, where some of his imitators were being exhibited. The dealer said to him: "You've been robbed." "Ransacked," replied Picasso, pointing to the pictures all around him.

November 17 / At the cemetery

With joy in my heart I've told my father that Alsace has been given back to him.

This evening my sons have gone to sleep with flags on their beds, even on the little one's cradle.

November 28 / My second visit to Claude Monet

Last Sunday Georges Bernheim and I were to lunch at the painter's at Giverny, but on Saturday evening Georges received the following telegram: "Am sick. Don't come." And on Sunday morning another telegram arrived, too late: "False alarm. Come."

We set off today to surprise the old painter. Bernheim took three pictures along in his car which he wanted to show Monet. We arrived around 1 P.M. Monet was in the doorway of that first studio he had invited us into for a few moments on the nineteenth of August last. He greeted us and invited us in. Those hundred unframed canvases in four rows all around the room I found no better than last time. Only five or six are good. Monet was genuinely sorry that we had already lunched. His beard is very white, his eyes quite round, and they are of a brown so dark and so brilliant that despite their tiredness they've kept a great vivacity. He seems to be run down physically, and isn't at all well. After lunch last Saturday he was taken ill in the large new studio where he is painting, and he lost consciousness for a time. A doctor had to be called. He said: "I've sent you both an invitation to lunch next Sunday." I replied that I had received mine this very morning when I was leaving for Giverny, but not Georges Bernheim.

We were all three of us standing, Bernheim with his pictures under his arm. He put quite a small one, eight inches high, into Monet's hands and asked him if he recognized this portrait, this young man with a large black beard. "But it is I," exclaimed the painter, "and it's by Renoir. I have a very similar canvas which X gave me, but it's a fake." "Aha, X!" said Bernheim. "What a line he's had in fake moderns. Now, M. Monet, look at this other canvas, your own of *The Church of the Calvary at Honfleur*. The master looked at it, remembered it, and commented with a big smile, "A work of my youth." He was delighted to come upon it again. "The church is well painted," he said. "Corot did it too. I don't like the trees there on the left; I'd cut them, cut them, cut them." "Impossible," replied Bernheim, "this canvas belongs to Jacques Charles, the manager of the Casino de Paris, and he wonders if you'd sign it." "I would indeed," said Monet, "but it will be right of center, to show him where to cut it. But it's split there on the left, so it's a Ville-d'Avray canvas." I asked him what he meant by a Ville-d'Avray canvas, and this is what he told me: "I was living in Ville-d'Avray and owed three hundred francs to a butcher who sent the bailiff around to me. When they were about to impound my things, I took a knife and slashed the two hundred canvases I had there. I left for Honfleur and some time after, when I'd had some success, my father sent me the money to settle my debt. I wired Sisley at Meudon, announcing my arrival, and we hurried over to Ville-d'Avray, but they'd all been sold. I went to the bailiff's to try to pick up the trail of my paintings, and he said to me: 'How can you expect to follow up anything so trifling? It's impossible! Your canvases were sold in lots of fifty, and each lot brought in an average of thirty francs.' "

I asked Monet if his father had been opposed to his painting, and he replied: "He had no confidence in my success. I was the worst pupil in my class, since all I did was sketch." Bernheim interrupted to show us his third painting, a view of the banks of the Seine. He had brought it to ask Monet to touch it up, as the two little figures at the water's edge have grown so dark that they look like silhouettes on a target range. But the master refused to do them over, as the work would suffer by it. He had painted it at Petit Gennevilliers.

I now urged Monet to sit down, and he said: "When I paint I can always stay on my feet; otherwise I tire quickly." We settled into very comfortable wicker armchairs. A woman brought us liqueurs; she had white hair and a youngish face with a high color; she must have been about fifty. She was Monet's daughter-in-law. We got onto the subject of the Curel sale, and Monet learned with pleasure that the family has kept one of his paintings which he greatly values: *The Bridge at Argentan.*

I tried to find out from the great impressionist which of the old painters inspired him, but he didn't give me any precise answers. He only said what we know already: that the French school of 1830 was stamped with the English influence of Constable and Turner. When we asked his opinion of these two painters, he said: "At one time I greatly admired Turner; today I care less for him." "Why?" "He didn't shape the colors sufficiently, and he put on too much: I've studied it quite carefully." "In London," I asked, "where you've done so much painting?" "Yes," replied Monet, "for I love London, much more than the English countryside; I adore London, it's a mass, a whole, and it's so simple. But what I love more than anything in London is the fog. How could the nineteenth-century English painters render houses brick by brick? They had to paint bricks which they couldn't and didn't see!" I told Monet that I attributed this tendency to the English passion for water color; and he answered: "Perhaps, and the great water-colorists were those who didn't make a specialty of it, like Delacroix."

This mention of England led us to talk of King George V's arrival today in Paris, and of the departure of the troops and their scheduled parade under the Arc de Triomphe. "You'll come and see them?" Bernheim said to Monet. "No, I think not," he replied. "I'm too susceptible; I'd die of emotion." He added candidly: "Not that I'm afraid of death. And I'm not frightened of it because I am very unhappy, very unhappy." He was clearly speaking the truth, and I felt for the old man. Bernheim was astonished, as I was myself. He asked him the cause of his sadness, and Monet replied: "Painting makes me suffer: all my old work with which I'm not satisfied, and the impossibility of doing well every time. Yes, each time I begin a canvas I hope to produce a masterpiece, I have every intention of it, and nothing comes out that way. Never to be satisfied—it's frightful. I suffer greatly. I was much happier when I sold my canvases for 300 francs. How I miss those days! And they were genuine, sincere—those people who paid 300 for my canvases. It was hard for them to spare those three notes. It's much easier for today's snobs to give me 20,000 francs." He turned brusquely to Bernheim: "Look, tell me, do you know where the study of the woman in green is? I'd love to find it again, it's one of my 300-franc canvases." Georges didn't know. He asked the painter to sell him a picture of flowers in a vase. The painter refused. Georges persisted for more than a quarter of an hour. The old man remained adamant, and when I queried him about his refusal he said: "So many canvases are memories, and some I consider too good and others not good enough to part with." At that moment Bernheim gave me the signal for leaving; we had to return to Paris. Night was drawing in swiftly, and he asked Monet to sign *The Church at Honfleur*. "Gentlemen," said Monet, "I don't have my tools here. Come with me into the big studio, and let's all put on our coats and hats to cross the garden." The painter's daughter-in-law followed us as far as that stable crammed with the immense canvases he painted during the war. Bernheim wanted to buy one. "Won't you sell me one?" he said. "Impossible," replied Monet. "Each one evokes the others for me." I looked at them and took pleasure in seeing them again. They are the more beautiful for being viewed one after another. The effect each time is a triple symphony of water, sky, and light.

So that Monet could sign, Bernheim removed the varnish with

his index finger. The old painter claims that the ancients didn't use varnish (he is mistaken), and that varnish yellows a painting. There he is right. "Yes," he said, "varnish has yellowed all the Rembrandts. As young painters, we used to go to the Louvre and put our cuffs up close to the Rembrandt collars; originally white like our cuffs, they had gone terribly yellow." Bernheim had finished his scraping, and Monet laid the canvas flat on an enormous rectangular trestle raised only about a foot from the ground; then he got down on his knees and signed it. On the white wood of that board some forty cardboard boxes, each containing a dozen large tubes of paint of the same color, were laid out very precisely. There were more than fifty very clean brushes in a glazed earthen pot, and perhaps twenty-five others in a second pot. Still more were lying about, all three quarters of an inch to an inch wide. There were two palettes, remarkably clean; they looked like new. One was covered with colors in little spaced-out daubs: cobalt, ultramarine blue, violet, vermilion, ocher, orange, dark green, another very clear green, and lastly a lapis-lazuli yellow. In the center, mountains of white like snowy peaks. "I don't see any black," I commented to Monet, who replied: "I gave it up when I was quite young. One day the American painter Sargent came here to paint with me. I gave him my colors and he wanted black, and I told him: 'But I haven't any.' 'Then I can't paint,' he cried and added, 'How do you do it!' " Bernheim returned to the attack: "M. Monet, won't you sell me a painting." His daughter-in-law murmured to him: "You are hard!" I came into it, saying: "Sell Bernheim something; ask him a big price for the flowers." Then Monet relented: "Oh well, 20,-000."

We returned to the studio and Monet went on: "I don't like to sell, I prefer buying back. I've bought back a lot in my life. Why, M. Bernheim, should I sell to you? There's only one person to whom I owe something, and that's Durand-Ruel, who was looked upon as mad and nearly attacked by the bailiffs on our account. It was in 1870 that I made his acquaintance. Daubigny introduced me to him, saying I had something in me. Another friend of that time was Clemenceau. He came to see me the other day. He wired me that he'd arrive for lunch. It was his first day off since the war; he traveled with two cars and four chauffeurs to avoid a breakdown. I expected to see him aged; but I think I can say that he has taken off ten years. We spoke of the Academy, and he said: 'They want to offer my name, but I've intimated that I consider the Academy should be only a salon and that I wish neither to make speeches nor to wear fancy dress.' At which point I told him: 'You've saved France.' 'No,' he replied, 'it was the infantry.' "

Monet has poor relations in America, the T. E. Butlers, 75 Washington Square, New York, and he asked us to send them $350 on his behalf. Just as we were going, on the doorstep, Bernheim succeeded in getting three more canvases out of him for 48,000 francs: two vases of flowers and some apple trees. He handed over the money in notes, which Monet counted very carefully; and that put me in mind of a number of people I know who like selling but long to keep both the money and the pictures.

December 3 / On Groult

A woman dealer who knew him was telling me that when Groult didn't like an object, be it the most beautiful in the world, he would say: "It's fit for target practice." Mme Arthur Meyer assured me that two days before his death, feeling his end near, Groult wished to burn his collection. Though it sounds incredible, one can believe it if one has known that capricious and irascible man who loved his collection like a mistress.

December 4 / The La Tour pastel

The one portraying President de Rieux has arrived at No. 57. It's the largest known La Tour. The magistrate, life size, is dressed in red and black. He is ensconced in his chair of office. He was the eldest son of Samuel Bernard. The frame was probably designed by Caffieri.

December 6 / Matisse

Except for his eyes, which are blue, everything about him is yellow: his overcoat as well as his complexion, his boots and his lovingly trimmed beard. As he wears spectacles, they are, naturally, golden. I met him in a little shop run by Guillaume, a young dealer who buys only extremists. I entered at the very moment when Matisse was leaving. Guillaume just had time to catch him by the arm. Indicating one of his canvases, he asked him the significance of a vertical blue band behind a green pot containing about ten flowers; the pot is on a little square juggler's table. The little table is as rickety as the painting. "It's simply a molding," the artist replied. "I don't paint natural wood." Guillaume said timidly: "It's just that I don't understand and I've got to explain to my clients." Matisse, curtly imperious, retorted: "My school doesn't explain."

December 8 / "The Poem of the World's Games"

A cubist play in four suites by Paul Meral, music by A. Honegger, dances by G. P. Fauconnet, at the Théâtre du Vieux-Colombier. The piece is by no means without merit, but it was hissed and there were even fights in the audience—apparently that's what happened last night.[1]

December 9 / Degas exhibition

I heard that shrewd connoisseur Camondo remark today: "There have never been so many backsides." Durand-Ruel told me: "Degas sketched all his life; some people own drawings done by him at the age of fifteen. In Italy he copied every picture he saw. He was a dreadful creature. When he parted with a picture, his dearest wish was that it shouldn't be sold and, given the chance, he wouldn't fail to speak disparagingly of it. For thirty years he wanted nothing to go out of his studio; occasionally we'd be allowed a study. When he came to see us, we had to watch that he didn't take anything off with him. He'd have been quite capable of taking back one of his canvases on the pretext of improving it, and we'd never have seen it again."

December 11 / On a Vigée-Lebrun and some furniture

Nathan Wildenstein reminded us that he had offered 44,000 francs for the Vigée-Lebrun *Polignac*, and he told Veil-Picard that he would willingly buy the Laroche-Guyons' pink furniture,[2] consisting of twelve armchairs and two sofas, for 1,200,000 francs.

---

[1] Honegger is today considered a musician of considerable importance. As for Fauconnet, a painter of tremendous promise, he died of starvation. (Note appended 1931.)

[2] The duke had two sons. He divided the furniture. One of the sons kept his half. The other sold his to Duveen. (Note appended 1931.)

December 14 / President Wilson in Paris

    Friends invited me to come and see him pass from their balcony, avenue du Bois, but I preferred to be with the crowd; and on the avenue du Bois itself, near the rue Spontini, I found an excellent place to stand: one foot on the border around a lamppost and the other on one of those railings that enclose grass plots. The cannon thunders, Wilson arrives on the scene. Frenetic cheering. There he is. Here he is. His grin resembles gigantic parentheses which he draws by turn nearer together and farther apart; it widens and shortens, and it is with this marvelous instrument that he wins the crowd, as by his familiar trick of waving his hat, turning it one way and the other at top speed—like a mirror for birds—holding it high in the air on the tips of his fingers.

December 16 / After the second Degas sale

    It reached nearly two million. Going in to Durand-Ruel's this morning, I counted more than 120 drawings and pastels on the walls. The syndicate has bought back extensively. In his office Durand-Ruel showed me two pastels, one of which portrays a woman actually decapitated by the frame (No. 29: *After the Bath*), and he explained: "I valued it at three or four thousand francs, and it made sixteen thousand. As for the other pastel (No. 189: *Interior*), a study for a larger painting, it started at fifteen hundred francs and was knocked down for more than fifteen thousand. These are two quite insignificant works."

    We were joined by Vollard. The shadow of his eyebrows puts his eyes in darkness. He talks a lot about what he is writing. He has a strong Auvergnat accent, this man of the Islands! The conversation reverted to Degas, and Durand-Ruel said: "The only way to give that man pleasure was to allow him to take offense. One always had to agree with him and give in to him." "I agree," replied Vollard. "Here's a typical instance: he had to move and was livid about it. I went around out of kindness, to help him. As I arrived, he was laying his pastels out in a pile on the parquet. 'Careful,' I told him, 'you're going to damage them. You ought to put glazed paper over each canvas and fix it to the back with drawing pins.' By way of answer, Degas started pitching into the stretchers with tremendous kicks, pushing them back and back till he smashed them against the wall in a frightful cloud of pastel and dust."

"He was tough," said Durand-Ruel, "and when he made a sale, he liked to put the squeeze on you." Vollard went on: "The day after I'd made a large purchase from him, he said to me, picking out a pastel: 'I'm feeling remorseful about having stung you for too much. I'm going to give you this pastel.' In a flash I knew there were two ways of accepting and that only one would be right. Either an indifferent 'As you wish,' or the noisy delighted exclamation that I did in fact opt for: 'Ah, how good of you, M. Degas.' It was the wrong choice. 'No,' said Degas, shyly drawing back his canvas, 'definitely not; I'm not satisfied with it.'"

In the presence of Vollard, Durand-Ruel repeated what he had told me the other day: "When he came into my galleries, I kept an eye out to see that he didn't take back one of his canvases." Vollard, who is never short of anecdotes, told us this one: "Degas saw a large Forain at my place and asked me its price. I told him 2,500 francs, and he offered to exchange it for one of his drawings touched up in pastel. So I called on him next day and he let me take with me a nude about a foot high; but in the afternoon he turned up at my place, saying: 'No, this drawing definitely doesn't satisfy me; I'm going to improve it.' I let him take it back, pleased at the idea of having a more finished drawing. Some time after, I asked him for it back. He was in the habit of retracing drawings that he was studying, without actually following their contours, and in fact enlarging them. He showed me my nude woman: she had put on four inches. 'But I'm not satisfied with it,' he commented. At the ninth study—it went on for years—my nude woman had grown considerably, attaining nearly three feet. When I protested, Degas replied: 'Vollard, you'll have to wait, because my model is pregnant.' A year later he informed me that his model had lost her figure and he'd never be able to finish the study. "Luckily," added Vollard, "I'd never handed over my Forain to him."

Finally, a story of a sum of money which Vollard owed Degas: he made an appointment with the artist to go with him and deposit the sum in the bank where he had his account, but Vollard couldn't make it and put through a credit transfer. He sent the painter a registered letter, informing him that the money was already in the bank. A distraught Degas came rushing over to Vollard's, shouting: "How am I supposed to get money out of a bank which I haven't deposited?" "And he the son of a banker!" Vollard added.

December 26 / On King George

After an airplane accident at the front, my brother-in-law Ernest Duveen was transferred to a hospital in London, where one morning shortly before noon the king's imminent arrival was announced. Only two or three of the fifty men there were seriously wounded, and that day nearly all of them were going to the theater. The order came to lie in bed, and they were furious. They put their pajamas on over their khaki and threw themselves fully dressed into bed. The king arrived; he questioned them, commiserated with them, expressed his distress at seeing all these men bedridden. One of them couldn't keep a straight face and burst out laughing right under the very nose of the king, who attributed the hilarity to the man's nervous state. Scarcely had His Majesty left when all the men were on their feet; then a wag shouted: "The king!" Everyone leaped into whatever bed was nearest—often two men in the same bed, in the general panic. One soldier landed in a cupboard, where he was left for an hour. Heroic warriors! Schoolboy antics!

December 29 / Beware

Going through the South Kensington Museum I happened to see two or three terra cotta busts by Bastianini, born 1830, imitations of works of the Italian Renaissance. I thought with some concern of the numerous busts by this man which can pass for antique! The lips are the only really weak point: too thin and too virginal, they lack expression.

December 30 / Advice to mothers-in-law

My wife's mother, Lady Duveen, has twelve children, ten of whom are married. She preserves the harmony among these households (and is adored by all) by always siding with her sons-in-law and daughters-in-law against her own children.

January 3 / On a Whistler

Croal Thompson, a dealer in modern paintings, took me to see one of his clients, Edmund Davis, the Englishman who in 1915 made a gift of British paintings to the Luxembourg Museum. He owns many Rodins, a number of which are marbles, and his pictures include Rossettis, Burne-Jones, and several Whistlers.

Thompson said to me: "Look at this one, *At the Piano*. I brought Whistler himself face to face with his canvas here, and this is what he told us: 'I was quite young, and had shown it at the London Salon, when I received a letter from a painter named Philipp asking me its price. I told him to give me what he liked. He sent me £30.'" Thompson added: "I sold it for £3,000 to Edmund Davis, who's been offered £20,000 on several occasions; and it's now worth 25,000."

January 8 / At Bourdelle's

The regiment of Captain Snowden Fahnestock, of the 77th New York Division, has organized a subscription and raised $10,000 to erect a monument to their dead, to be placed in Argonne near the Four-de-Paris, whence they launched their main offensive in June. The captain is looking for a sculptor, and Bonfils took us to the Impasse du Maine, to Bourdelle's. Studios to left and right. The artist occupies about twenty. He's quite a small man, in his fifties, and with a Midi accent. A graying goatee and mustache sprout from his skin, which might be described as North African. He has chestnut-colored eyes with extremely small pupils; they are very sharp and lively. He talks a lot, but when he's silent, darts hangdog glances at you. There we were, in the place where he lives—or rather where he sleeps. It's a kind of low-pitched semibasement room, very dirty, messy, and disorderly, full of odd objects, including many sculptures. Among them I noticed a small rough model: Rodin in his smock.

"I was his disciple," he told us. "People called me his disciple. Yes, perhaps I was. Now I've become an antidisciple of Rodin's. I owe a lot to him, a great deal of technique, but that's all. He killed his pupils—all of them, all his disciples. I branched away from him in my art and he saw it five or six years before his death. 'Why are you looking for something else, Bourdelle?' he asked me. And he was angry. He believed that he had attained perfection, that he had brought the art of sculpture to its final stage. How mistaken he was! He talked a lot and he talked well, but he was ignorant; he didn't possess inner force. Inner force is something very rare—and essential. So I split from Rodin. Of course he'd given me a foundation, but I didn't want to do Rodins. It never does to imitate a mannerism. Napoleon put his hand in his waistcoat. Another great man has to have a different mannerism or he'll be ridiculous. Let me show you mine, gentlemen, when it resembles that of Rodin. Look at this bust of the writer Charles-Henry Hirsch, it's in my first style, imitation Rodin, with all the exaggerated wrinkles, muscles, hollows, and even locks of hair. But here you see a more recent work."

And Bourdelle had us look at the head of a man modeled boldly by planes, and he continued: "It's not the same technique; it's architecture applied to the bust. You have to have architecture in all sculptures, and planes, planes, planes. In a large monument, this doesn't preclude giving sensitivity to a part of the composition, as, for example, to a female form. Rodin's *Marseillaise*, masterpiece that it is, lacks planes: in parts it is really far off. Now let's go into my studio."

We followed him as one does a guide, and like a guide he alone spoke. We entered a large room filled with bronzes, plasters, clays, small rough models, sketches, and finished works too. The outstanding piece was a life-sized *Heracles* with a gilded patina of an admirable burnt gold.

"A friend of mine," Bourdelle resumed, "a captain, posed for it. He was a superb athlete; he was killed at Verdun by a bullet in his forehead. See my Beethoven, he gave me a great deal of trouble. Have a look at this clay sketch too: *The Origin of the Organ*. The cello is silent and weeping with emotion, just look how it weeps. Now look at Isadora Duncan at the foot of a column. That was perfect. That would make a fine *Victory of Samothrace!* Now let's move on to another studio where you're going to see my monument to the independence of Poland. I began the project ten years ago. In high relief on a column I'd depicted the three Polands holding hands. The entire reception committee wept at the sight. When the Russians retreated I got down to work on it, and continued during their revolution and on through the Boche offensive against Paris. I was sure of myself. But then Michelet adored Poland, and you might say that Mme Michelet brought me up. I have also just been commissioned to do the Czech medal of Independence. I'm reviving the art of the medal."

"They're too blond," Bonfils managed to slip in rapidly.

"Yes, too blond," continued the artist, "and there isn't enough relief. It's time some relief was introduced. As long as the emphasis is on archaeology, Boche art will be the thing; medals are treated primarily by space, and it's by planes that they need to be handled: by the synthesis of planes."

At this point the sculptor broke off to glance at Captain Fahnestock's cross, a Christmas present to the gallant soldier. He handled it, gauging its thickness between index finger and thumb, and said: "It's not bad, but it too lacks coherence: once again no one seems to realize that a medal, if it's to have balance, has to establish a harmony between its volume and the width of the bust."

We moved on into the studio containing the Polish monument. "Look at the face of Adam Mickiewicz," he said, "the legendary poet of Poland: he who never despaired, who never ceased to foretell her resurrection. See how he moves in great striding folds, with his staff, his preacher's staff."

Bourdelle invited us to come into still another studio. It was very cold—all these rooms are horribly damp—but the sculptor led us on like slaves. There we saw classical figures designed for a monument to be erected in Argentina to General Alvear.

"You see, gentlemen, however large the work, I finish everything myself. Look at this gigantic horse: it all passes through my hands; I leave it to no one to finish my works. I worked such a lot with Rodin; everyone knows it's I who finished his hard marbles."

I noticed an allegorical figure. "That," he said, "was a project for a South American republic, for the governor of a province who was killed by a bomb. The committee didn't want it; their idea was to depict the governor in pieces, torn to shreds by the explosion. I sent them packing, that committee. For the common herd you've got to have cannon and rifles."

Bourdelle had been talking so much that it was only then that I was able to explain what we wanted. Bonfils had, of course, told him we were coming, and the sculptor had replied: "I won't have any competitions: and no approaching any other artist." I explained to Bourdelle that we had to ask him for a sketch or rough model, and he replied:

"That's not what counts, it's the execution, everything's in the execution. You remind me of a visit I had one day from Elie Faure, who brought along to meet me a young painter with a canvas of unripe apples and grapes. Everything on it was wrong. I asked the boy whether he had taken lessons. 'No, nowhere,' he said. How many young people like that do we have in France, with all the world's learning in their tiny brain; everything they've learned on their own. For my part, I'm at the beginning, I'm always just beginning. I have studied not only with Rodin, but with Dalou, another great master, and also with Falguière; and I owe something to each of them. But it's always a question of thought too, of long, careful thought.

"Look now, gentlemen," Bourdelle urged us, "at this little plaster, this nude woman on an arch; it's Selene, goddess of night. A woman of the world posed for it, a woman painter, a very rich woman who is quite independent. A figure like that is modeled rapidly, cast in bronze, and is sold quickly and in large quantities: that brings in money. But tell me, how much money do you have for your monument?"

"Ten thousand dollars."

"Ten thousand dollars, you say? But that's nothing, that's not enough. I have my wife and children to consider and I have no right to do what you want of me. What can one do with ten thousand dollars? Nothing. Scarcely a single figure. I see an American soldier between two crags, latter-day Thermopylaes. And on the rocks, the names of your dead. That will be beautiful, beautiful, beautiful!"

January 11 / Clemenceau comes to No. 57

I caught a glimpse of him with President Wilson, but I haven't seen him since the Abel Ferry funeral. Our military affairs weren't then going very well, and he looked preoccupied. Claude Monet was right the other day when he told me that he seemed grown young again.

In fact he looks so young that he wasn't recognized when he entered No. 57. The concierge announced him to me by a single ring instead of two. Wildenstein's son-in-law saw him through the office window and said jokingly: "There's Clemenceau." The man at the door even asked him his name.

He is too well known to paint. Painters and sculptors of the future will be wide of the mark if they portray him as a man more than sixty or sixty-three years old. In fact, he's been caricatured too much, and the tendency will be to distort his features. Since he's called "the Tiger," he's made into a creature half beast, half human. He has very few wrin-

kles and his cheeks are round, very round, like tennis balls. In caricatures, his forehead is brought forward, his eyes sunk, exaggeratedly; but
that is all wrong. His mustache is thick but well trimmed, despite its
vigorous thrust. They give him nut-cracker jaws which he doesn't have.
His chin is very round and his head really like a ball, very solid.

He was rhapsodizing over the La Tour. "It's the most beautiful
pastel I've seen," he said. "It ought to stay in France." He gives me to
understand that he'd love to find a Maecenas to present it to the nation.

Helleu said of Clemenceau that he talked about art like a shopkeeper. Certainly our Premier hasn't got the taste and learning of Helleu, but he has a fairly general knowledge of art. He is familiar with the
principal works of the masters and knows where they are. He was astonished when I showed him a Chardin not in the master's usual manner:
the portrait of the painter's wife, seated, dressed in middle-class attire,
with a basket of eggs by her side.

We spoke of the impressionists and he told me that the Americans have a portrait of him by Manet in which one of his eyes is missing
and his nose is awry.

I told Clemenceau: "I'm going to show you the most beautiful of
Nattiers, *The Marquise de Baglione.*" He replied that he didn't admire
that painter, but when he found himself face to face with the portrait,
he went into raptures and apologized.

He has read Giacometti's recent book on Houdon, and he said:
"Interesting from a documentary point of view, but it's vilely written." I
wanted to take him into another room to show him Fragonard's *The
Kiss,* but he demurred, saying: "I've got to go to No. 59 to see the doctor . . . very unwell." And when I persisted, he cried: "You must let
me get on with my arrangements."

January 18 / Historic date

Today the Peace Conference, out of which the next war will
come, opened at the Ministry of Foreign Affairs.

January 19 / In Sert's studio, 19, rue Barbet-de-Jouy

Rather than in a studio, I felt I was on the set of some theater.

His canvases are large like stage scenery. Sert isn't daunted by having to paint an entire church, which he is soon off to do in his country, Spain. He speaks of it as of a lark, for he works very quickly.

Three assistants in smocks brought in the canvases he was going to show me. These people prepare his foundations; I noticed huge canvases coated with a wonderful white enamel. He certainly works with fine materials. "I have studied the primitives and Renaissance art with much care," he told me. "Tintoretto was the greatest of decorators." "Perhaps," I replied, "but to compete with his rivals and do them out of commissions, he too often used cheap paint, and it has darkened terribly." Sert claimed mistakenly that the fault lay in the light, and cites as proof the fact that the master's ceilings have remained clearer.

The first work of Sert's I saw was in Paris, at the Keppels' home on the avenue du Bois, though it was destined for their English house. It had points of resemblance to Patinir, to the seventeenth-century Dutch, to Boucher. Sert pilfers wherever he passes. I'd met Boni de Castellane, a friend of his, there; this painter is quite a man of the world. He has a plump and polished exterior, a blond, handsome mien, but is too fleshy. Beneath his short pointed blond beard, lovingly trimmed, he's trying to hide the swelling of his cheeks. Doubtless an old ladies' darling.

The men in smocks placed a series of panels around me: they form a carousel of wooden horses, splendid horses under a circular dais, a kind of latter-day Field of the Cloth of Gold. An acrobat dressed as a kingbird is juggling with his trinkets. There are red fish in a tank. A bird seller straight out of a Persian fairy tale. I asked Sert the subject of this fantasy, and he answered: *Le Merveilleux Souvenir*. I painted it during the war, when we saw only awful things; and to escape the horror one had to go back to memories of childhood: the wooden horse, the acrobat, the white elephant, the birds, the red fish, as you have them here. Yes, that's it: "*Le Merveilleux Souvenir.*"

Sert's father was a big manufacturer who died young. He made rugs, and the child, already an artist, would furnish him with designs. He ponders his subject for a long time and then puts it swiftly onto his canvas. He showed me the rough sketch of a monochrome decoration ordered by an American by the name of Deering for an estate in Spain. It's the *Allied Victory*, which he did as early as 1915. A door, and to the left a magician of the year 2114 looking at an old map of Europe, in the center of which he comes upon a fortress: Germany. And the drama unfolds all around the room. Clocks in the sky sound the alarm, and the brave go off to war. Below: the Marne. The victorious troops of Gallieni. The first victory. Barbarism checked; the wisdom of old soars. Victory hovers like a heroic guard. The conflict erupts. Apollo on the side of the Allies—the never conquered sun. Peace. The triumphal arch. In the distance, the troops returning. An aureola. And in the air, the Ninth Symphony. Order, progress, civilization.

On Sert

I described to Berenson my visit to his studio. He was surprised to hear that I didn't know Forain's crack about the Spanish painter. Once Forain accompanied a wealthy bourgeois to an exhibition in which Sert was showing one of his large representational pictures. The bourgeois went crazy over it and wanted to buy it, but it was too big and he was furious. Forain tapped him on the shoulder, saying: "Don't worry; it'll deflate."

January 22 / "The Billet Doux"

We bought it in 1905 for nearly 500,000 francs at the Crosnier sale, and sold it two years later to Joseph Bardac. I've bought it back from him for 750,000 francs, but he's holding on to a one-third interest in the profit.

January 23 / Jacques Doucet, Maecenas

"How are the books going?" he asked me. He didn't give me a chance to answer, and went on: "I have all of Suarès's manuscripts. I go after the young ones: they're always short of a hundred francs a month. I've said to those whose talent I believe in: 'You shall have your hundred francs; bring me whatever you want to.' Invariably they have exhausted their year's allowance at the end of four months, and when they have money they no longer work. Then, as they have a debt of gratitude toward me, they bear me a grudge. At the Circle one day my father lent money to someone who was broke. Learning two years later that this person had money, my father asked to be paid. The person retorted: 'So that's all you can think about!' I've made an arrangement with a talented writer who told me: 'It's impossible to work for the public.' 'Work for me,' I answered. It was agreed that for a stately English lady and myself he would do a work, only three copies of which would be printed; indeed, an artist can't work for the general public."

"And Molière, M. Doucet?"

January 28 / En route to New York. The Durand-Ruels

We sailed on the twenty-fourth. The sea was rough, but Durand-Ruel stood firm on the deck. I joined him. His name is so bound up with nineteenth-century art that I find it interesting to question him on the origins of his family. He said: "My father's father was a notary before the French Revolution, which ruined him, and he had to flee. He returned to France around 1802 and set up as a stationer, then sold brushes and tubes of color, associated with the artists who came to his shop, and that's how we became picture dealers. The firm looked as though it were going under when it had only just become established, because my father hated commerce. He had prepared for Saint-Cyr and passed the entrance examination, but was turned down by the doctors because of his weak chest. He's never had a cold in his life, and he's now eighty-eight. So he carried on his father's business. But in trying to help the school of 1830 at its beginning, and also the impressionists, he did a very poor business. In 1886 he was on the brink of bankruptcy; he owed five million, and he left for America, where success was very long in coming. We aren't rich, we've never gone after money; the collection we own is worth only a certain amount."

January 30 / On Monet, Renoir, and Millet

I asked Durand-Ruel about that white-haired lady at Claude Monet's. "She's both his daughter-in-law and his stepdaughter. When Monet was quite young, he was entertained by a very rich man, M. Hoschedé, who brought two hundred guests down by special train to his estate in the country. He had started the restaurant The Abbey of Thélème, but ruined himself, and his wife was separated from him. Monet, who was now rich, installed Mme Hoschedé and her daughter at Giverny, in all due comfort and respect. He was a widower and had a son, who married the little Hoschedé girl. The son died. The little Hoschedé girl did some painting, and not badly, imitations of Monet. Wherever Monet painted, she would station herself behind him, copying both Monet and nature; but her canvases are smaller than those of her father-in-law, who has never allowed her to paint the same size." I asked Durand-Ruel if she signs them. He replied that she did, but that we had better be on our guard; although her canvases aren't yet passing for Monets, they certainly will.

"Is Monet well off?" I asked.

"Much less so than Renoir," replied Durand-Ruel, "who alone is really wealthy, and who in addition to his fortune has an important collection of his own works. Monet always was a sybarite. You get the best cuisine in France at his house. He's had a chef for twenty-five years. He eats like four. I promise you, that's not just a manner of speaking. He'll take four pieces of meat, four servings of vegetables, four glasses of liqueur. Millet didn't care about money, either. If he had only a thousand francs, he'd give five hundred to a friend in need. When he had almost nothing, he owed his grocer at Fontainebleau three or four thousand francs, three or four thousands' worth of early vegetables."

February 1 / On Degas

He became fiercely anti-Semitic at the time of the Dreyfus affair, and Durand-Ruel told me that very likely this was because he had many Jewish friends and he wanted to provoke them; but his Jewish friends persisted in not taking his anti-Semitism seriously. Many teased him. Camondo sent around his mistress to invite him to dinner; when he refused to come, she declared: "But I'm not Jewish." "That's true," answered Degas, in the hearing of twenty persons, "but you're a whore!"

"At the time of the trial," Durand-Ruel continued, "Degas turned up at our house one day, saying: 'I'm off to the law courts.' 'To attend the trial?' 'No, to kill a Jew.'

"Mme Halévy, a Protestant, invited him to dinner. 'But promise me,' she urged him, 'not to discuss either politics or religion, as there will be only Jews and Protestants.' Degas promised. It was a pleasant dinner; Degas, even more brilliant than usual, talked only about art and, over dessert, told how that same day he had had in a model, a woman who said to him that maybe Dreyfus wasn't guilty. 'You're Jewish yourself?' he asked her. 'No, monsieur, I'm a Protestant.' 'Ah, you're a Protestant. Well, then, get the hell out of here.' "

"He was a fantastic creature," said Durand-Ruel. "He didn't want his friends to buy his canvases, and he sent us a letter with a list of those who were not to be sold to." I asked Durand-Ruel if he possessed many autograph letters of painters. "Yes, many," he answered, "but few of interest, apart from Degas's which were always witty except when he was asking you to pay his rent. One thing: when a friend owned a painting by him, he had to hold on to it. Doucet had sold two Degas. One day he went to call on the painter, whose sight and hearing had greatly declined and who exaggerated his infirmities when it suited him. Doucet shouted at him: 'You recognize me? I'm Doucet, I'm Doucet!' 'Doucet, Doucet,' said Degas, as if searching his memory. 'Yes, I had a friend by that name, but he is dead.' "

February 6 / The Atlantic crossing

It is over, long and wearisome as it has been. The puppet show alone diverted us, attracting each day six children and 150 grownups.

February 7 / Disembarking

This morning I was as amazed as our forefathers were by the sight of the first train, when in the hall of the Ritz Hotel I espied a letter box specially reserved for airmail. There are flights every day for Philadelphia and Washington.

February 10 / Modernity in the Church

I was as bowled over as someone seeing an airmail letter box for the first time, on finding an elevator in St. Thomas Church, where I went to see my friend, the Reverend Stires. And a Gothic-style elevator, too.

February 12 / Pittsburgh

The great fortunes of the United States have come from here. Carnegie, with his $15 million income. Frick, who is slightly less wealthy; Schwab and Gary. The city is an agglomeration of twenty- to thirty-story buildings among brick huts. The factories are right in the center, and indeed in the neighboring streets one can see rails flowing like macaroni out of the furnaces. A hundred chimneys belch torrents of black smoke, so effectively that the sun is a rare sight and the night is often lighter than the day. How dirty one gets here! One's nostrils spew out as much smut as does the subsoil.

Amazed and horrified, I caught sight of a first-floor butcher's shop of human meat. Nothing but men's legs. Have I imagined it? What dream of blood is this? I drew nearer. They were wax. It was a display of artificial limbs.

This is also the country of the pickle. Over half a mile of enormous tall brick hulks of masonry where thousands of workers toil. All the neighboring streets stink of gherkins. The gherkin king, Heinz, is cruising on his yacht in Florida.

February 13 / Carnegie Institute

Donated by Andrew Carnegie to the inhabitants of Pittsburgh for the development of literature, science, and art. He was really the first great American philanthropist. He wanted to die poor. He didn't achieve that aim but nonetheless gave hugely. He has since been surpassed only by Rockefeller. The Institute has a museum of modern paintings.[8]

February 14 / A stamp collection

My uncle Henry Duveen died a month ago. He had built up a stamp collection which had cost him about £60,000. A European syndicate has just offered his son £200,000 for it, but the son will probably get £240,000.

February 17 / At Mrs. Otto Kahn's

Writing here is a great trial, and much application is needed. Thus, I emerge from a magnificent private mansion newly built, Italian

---

[8] A Sisley: *On the Marne.* Two Claude Monets, including a view of the Seine, and a Pissarro in very strong relief, very much enameled: *The Great Bridge of Rouen.* The best picture is a Puvis de Chavannes: a glimpse of antiquity, a celestial epic, with gods and goddesses, herdsmen and goats, Eros, the lute, quasi-winged horses, affectionate dalliance, obliteration of the sky, the earth, and human beings before the dazzle and blue violence of a sea which is no more than a vast lake. A large, somewhat muddy canvas by Raffaelli: *Boulevard des Italiens.* A rather pretty Boudin: *Trouville.*

Renaissance, whose architect is a highly talented Scotsman named Stein-house. There are superb pictures and art objects; and yet nothing inspires me. Though it is the most beautiful house in New York today, a mortal weariness falls from these stones, which cannot animate Mrs. Otto Kahn, for all that she is still pretty, is intelligent, and has excellent taste. Yes, she has beautiful objects, but though she owns them, they do not belong to her because she knows nothing of their history, she isn't immersed in their past. She loves them as one loves other people's children, without the pangs at one's heart. The art objects give as good as they get. They remain fixed there like street lamps that will never be lit.

Her husband has begun by buying French paintings of the eighteenth century, starting with a fake Nattier, or rather a fine old copy, the original of which is in Stockholm. He thought it was genuine because it was reproduced—and in color too—in Nolhac's book. They still have it and will keep it always.[4] They subsequently acquired two Paters and a Boucher tapestry, *La Halte de Chasse*; but the wife pushed her husband toward the Dutch and then toward the primitives. At that time she had influence over him: they had been married only briefly, and she had an enormous fortune. Otto Kahn had arrived from Frankfurt almost an immigrant and had gone into a large bank as quite a lowly employee. He was singled out for his very real ability, and married the daughter of one of the partners, who on his death left a fortune of $16 million to his two daughters. Mrs. Otto Kahn inherited the whole fortune shortly, on the death of her sister.

With so much money at his disposal, Otto Kahn resolved to storm the gates of the Four Hundred, a tremendous undertaking in this fiercely anti-Semitic society; so he invaded their sanctum, the opera. To gain control of it he bought up its shares—at a high price and even then with difficulty.

February 25 / At the Cleveland Museum
  Opening here: a small exhibition of French art into which some

---

[4] Later he let it go for a very modest sum to a small dealer, who sold it to Mr. Bayer of New York, who gave it to Wildenstein in an exchange. (Note appended 1931.)

English and Italian furniture has strayed. I pointed out these wolves among our *bergères* to the rather ignorant curators, and also got them to withdraw some fake drawings, in the eighteenth-century style, lent by the French designer X. I'm certain he did them himself. It's a way of seeing his work on exhibit in a museum. He has a modest talent as an illustrator, but is deplorable in his eighteenth-century imitations, and yet thinks he can take people in when he imitates Watteau or Fragonard.[5] The museum is a pretty little marble building, opened less than three years ago and already quite rich in endowments: a fine Puvis de Chavannes, *Summer,* a rather poor collection of primitives. I noticed a small painting, a Christ, in the manner of Simone Martini.

There is considerable interest in art here, as the city is rich, being surrounded by coal mines and oil wells. Automobiles are manufactured here and are so numerous that they can be parked only at right angles to the sidewalks. Williams told me quite seriously the other day: "In Cleveland or Detroit you have to be a beggar not to have an automobile."

Apart from a recollection of one or two public buildings such as the post office and the customs house, I take with me from Cleveland only my surprise at having found under my bedroom door in the morning the city newspaper provided free of charge by the hotel, and also the memory of my astonishment at discovering when I left my room in the evening that my key automatically turned off all the lights and switched them on again when I re-entered.

February 27 / A visit to the emperor of photography

Eastman, inventor of Kodak, that is to say the first film apparatus,[6] was born here in Rochester, which he adores. He still owns more than two-thirds of the shares of his company. It earned more than $45 million last year. I wouldn't be surprised if he produced 80 per cent of the cinematographic film in the world. His mother, I'm told, ran a

[5] I lent a superb Louis XIV wrought-iron console and two pictures by Drouais, bought for 20,000 francs from Guiraud, who had discovered them in Nice; a David taken back from Berwind in an exchange; a mahogany chest signed by Reisener; two superb Regency armchairs with Paris tapestry.

[6] A sensational lawsuit later disclosed that he wasn't the inventor of Kodak at all and that he had succeeded in depriving the true inventor of his rights. He was ordered to pay the latter an enormous sum.

boardinghouse. As a small boy, he didn't like going to school because he loved nature; hence his desire to photograph it. Eastman is about sixty-eight, small, with a severe, remote face; he is both chilly and choleric, with a bladelike nose and blue eyes.

His house, set in a large lawn, resembles a convent, and the interior is arranged in a harsh, indifferent way, for he is a bachelor. He goes out or has guests five or six times a week, but he is already at work at eight in the morning. Today, an exception in my honor, he started at eight-thirty: I had an appointment with him at a quarter past eight. I found him seated in his winter garden, going through the news and the stock-exchange quotations in the newspaper, while his magnificent organ played church music.[7]

When I went to Eastman's for the first time, I asked him where he kept *The Blue Rockets*, one of the most magnificent Turners in existence. It came via the Yerkes sale, and then the Knoedler. "No one," he answered, "can judge the beauty of a picture as well as I; I've a method of my own, and neither you nor anyone else can equal me because no one has as much knowledge of photography. When I look at a picture, I ask myself: 'If this view, scene, or portrait had been a photograph from real life, would it appear as it does here?' If the answer is negative, it means the painting is not right. Now then, after I bought that Turner, I saw that certain waves of the sea could not have appeared in a photographic print as he had painted them!"

O shade of Turner, did you shudder when the emperor of photography spoke thus?

[7] Yesterday I had a beautiful Romney hung in his house, the portrait of a woman of thirty with powdered hair, a white dress, and blue ribbons. He asked me its price. $160,000. He wasn't surprised, but he doesn't care for the arms, considers them badly drawn, and declares himself immovable on the drawing question. Nonetheless he owns a Rembrandt in which the hands seem dried up, mummified. He also owns a Raeburn, the portrait of a woman of forty, seated, in a white dress relieved by a violet-purple scarf. A pretty composition, but she has what looks like a broken arm buried in her lap. He has a charming Reynolds, a woman holding a bluish book with her left hand: she is an intellectual to the tops of her fingers. A velvety fur edges her cloak of cream-colored silk. His Hoppner depicts a pretty girl, with her scarf a virginal blue, but her blouse provocative. I greatly admired his Hals, a man in a hat who has the air of someone calling "Here I am!" He owns a fine Van Dyck, a man in armor, and a beautiful lengthwise Corot with two women and two cows walking in a meadow. A line of twelve tall trees bars the horizon.

March 1 / Visit to Jean-Julien Lemordant

He was a painter. The war left him blind. He arrived last evening on the transatlantic liner *Spain*. But who has put him in this cramped hotel room[8] that no daylight penetrates? Precisely because he doesn't see, I wish his room were immense, with the light flooding in. It was 3:30 when I arrived. His back was to the window, and behind him a small lamp was lit. He was stretched out in an armchair beside his bed, with his leg, which was also gravely wounded, resting on another chair. Two canes had been tossed onto the bedspread. His head and half his face are swathed in bandages. I reckoned, from the strong cast of his nose and his well-shaped mouth, that all his features must be fine and regular. His mustache is black and trimmed short. He had taken off his coat and was wearing a brown woolen waistcoat. His lieutenant's cap had been flung on the bed.

His career as a soldier was heroic. Le Goffic has sung his praises; Geffroy has written of him. His speech is open, his approach thoughtful. I spoke to him of Caro-Delvaille, who worked with him at Bonnat's and who is anxious to come and see him as soon as possible.

Lemordant has arrived here under the auspices of the French High Commission, to receive the Henry Howland Prize, which Yale University has conferred on him, and which is given every two years in recognition of a work of lofty idealism in the sciences or the arts. The award amounts to $1,500. For Europeans it just covers the cost of the journey, as they are required to come over to address the university.

The publicity office also asked Lemordant to bring his pictures; he has three hundred canvases and drawings with him, more than two-thirds of which belong to him. I am going to organize his exhibition in my galleries. I could tell at once that he has a generous spirit. Thus he refused to accept any profit from the sale of the catalogues; the money is to go to charity.

March 3 / At Henry Frick's

Ravens opened the door for me: Frick's servants, dressed from head to foot in black. Frick received me in his grand gallery where he keeps his most solemn paintings. It is an immense room hung with

---

[8] Room 224 in the Vanderbilt Hotel.

green. On the floor a carpet all in one piece and soft as moss. I have already described the man on my last trip, but since then he has grown stouter and entered a more advanced stage of elderliness: his face is crumpling, his pink complexion becoming patchy; his fair beard, which used to be a thick mass, is growing finer. But his cold eyes, grasping and hard under their genial look, remain a clear, beautiful blue. I told him about my Watteau, *The Betrothed Village Girl*, for which I asked him $130,-ooo. I had the impression that Frick has never seen a Watteau, although he declares the contrary. While I was speaking to him I kept glancing all around the room, and I acknowledged that this collection, which he will bequeath, with this museum, to the city of New York, is going to make a royal gift.

The finest picture is the Rembrandt self-portrait (1658. Bode 428. Collection: The Earl of Ilchester). He is wearing a sort of smock or robe of the richest yellow. Huge hands grip the arms of his chair. A wise and human potentate whose eyes fix on the beholder and overwhelm him. Another magnificent Rembrandt is *The Polish Cavalier* (1653). If his face were not that of a young man, I would swear that it is the Wandering Jew who goes there, in that landscape in which all uncertainties are summed up, in which home and hearth move farther away at each step, where the air is one immense doubt. His horse is at once pitiful and heroic, running for all eternity, with its limbs disjointed in that jerky movement, adapting to all terrains. There are two Vermeers; neither is entirely beautiful, but that may be because they have been retouched. The better of the two is the *Soldier and Laughing Girl*. A most handsome musketeer, although he is seen from behind. And how wonderful this tavern conqueror, with his immense brimmed hat, appears to the sweet young girl, who laughs as she gazes up at him, utterly without resistance. The other Vermeer is *The Music Lesson*, also with overtones of love. Several Van Dycks and several fine Hals, including his 1635 portrait, *The Burgomaster*, from the Kann Collection; also the *Woman Seated in an Armchair*, from the Yorkes Collection, and *Admiral de Ruyter*; but this painter never knew how to give his models the stamp of their social status, except perhaps in their hands.

March 6 / The Chaponay Nattier

Nathan Wildenstein has written me that he has sold it to Ambatielos with four small Fragonards for the sum total of £44,000, the Nattier being included for £34,000.

March 16 / In Caro-Delvaille's studio

It is situated at 15 Washington Square North, where rises a modest triumphal arch. One could almost believe oneself in London in this square, with its two-story brick houses so regular and alike. The square, placed halfway between the lower part of the city, that gigantic hive of business, and the residential district with its thousands of cars, seems as if by magic to belong to another town, another town really situated hundreds of leagues off, where the railway and even cars do not pass, and where the inhabitants, lacking all modern means of transport, exhibit the gravity of our ancestors, without any of the labored austerity of our provincial cities.

Washington Square and its environs were, until around the end of the last century, the very tight-knit enclosure in which were sequestered the families jealous of their ancient lineage, those who created that American aristocracy more exclusive than the court of the smallest and proudest of kinglets. But the luxury of the *nouveaux riches* who built their homes farther uptown, and the need for comfort, drove them from their base. Now it's the artists, the only really sensible people in this city, who have come to take refuge far from the noise and the multitude in these abandoned, dilapidated houses.

I informed the painter that the periodical *Art in America*, which wants to reproduce my David *Jeanne de Richemont*,[9] has asked me who could do an accompanying article, and that I have answered: "Only Caro-Delvaille." He has agreed to do so.

March 17 / At Frick's

On the wall there are seven pictures for which he has paid on the average of $200,000 apiece. Five full-length pictures: two Gainsboroughs, *Mrs. Baker* and *Lady Duncombe*; two Romneys, *Mrs. Milnem* and *Lady Warwick and Her Children*; and a Van Dyck *Portrait of a Woman*. Also there is Gainsborough's famous landscape *The Mall*. And, fitted in above the door, a Lawrence with two figures.

[9] Later in the New York museum.

April 8 / The Tapestry of St. Veronica

I have sold it for $80,000 to Mrs. George Blumenthal.

April 10 / Renoirs at Durand-Ruel's

Exhibition of thirty-five canvases, most of them small. Durand-Ruel bought them from the painter during these last two years. The catalogue apprizes us that the oldest date from 1878. Durand-Ruel told me: "I couldn't specify the dates, since Renoir retouches all his canvases before delivering them to us."

I admired two canvases of apples. Durand-Ruel told me there were five such groups of apples on the same canvas, which his brother and he found in the room of an old maidservant who had just died in the painter's house. They cut them up.

NOTEBOOK 5

May 5–November 3, 1919

May 5 / I sell a Houdon

    To Ledyard Blair for $120,000. It's the portrait in marble of Hue de Miromesnil.

May 7 / I sell the Drouais Roussels

    To E. J. Berwind for $200,000. They're *The Scholar* and *Little Girl with a Cat*.

May 13 / I sell "The Billet Doux"

    By Fragonard, to Jules Bache, for $250,000.

May 14 / Unfortunate publicity

    When I informed Brandus that I was leaving for Pittsburgh, he told me: "No city has such ugly women." Nonetheless, when Charles Knoedler went to sell pictures there thirty years ago, he spent every night at a brothel. When Chartran went there for the first time, the dealer accompanied him to get him portrait commissions, and as a great joke— it really tickled him—he swamped all the rooms of the house with

Chartran's visiting cards. The Pittsburgh husbands picked them up there, and for fear of being compromised shut their doors in the face of the artist, who everywhere else was received like a king. For the rest of his days he never stopped fulminating against this city. "It's inhospitable," he would say.

May 22 / I sell a Rembrandt and a Raeburn

Eighty thousand dollars for the two: to Bache, who is beginning to be quite a good client—$40,000 each. The Rembrandt is small, but of magnificent quality: the portrait of Titus. I've had it for years, and have missed out on selling it a score of times. My first failure was with the famous J. P. Morgan, the reason being rather amusing: it is painted on a panel and the wood shows some irregularities in its texture, and that's why he didn't want it!

May 27 / Florence Blumenthal

I lately sold her my gold-woven tapestry of St. Veronica for $80,-000. I went to her house the next day, to see how it had been hung. I waited first in her boudoir, into which a servant had shown me by mistake, and where there was a strong whiff of the scent women use today. Some moments later Mrs. Blumenthal entered.

Her house is the only one in New York whose atmosphere is genuinely antique. The inner courtyard consists of an authentic patio brought over from Spain.

"I'm rich, pampered, elegant, and people think I'm happy, Mr. Gimpel," Mrs. Blumenthal told me. "What it does to me when they say: 'How happy she must be!' " Her round, profoundly dark, nervous, and black-ringed eyes grew veiled. Small, thin, and long-lined, of ancient race, eloquent of Europe and the south, and of emotions exalted to the point of exhaustion, she has the complexion characteristic of a race of women nurtured for centuries by the sun.

"How can I be happy!" she said. "I've lost my son, a child of nine, the child I created! Woman is made to create, to create a being of flesh and blood. The child whom I created is dead; so I had to create something else, and I made this house, a personality of stone. We'll bequeath it, with the collection, to the city of New York, but its spirit will be gone, for these rugs caress the stones below; these small objects, the familiars of all this furniture they adorn, will have to be put away, protected behind thick glass."

"Flowers would be essential."

"Yes, you're right, it'll need flowers. It's so difficult to find flowers whose hues harmonize with old stone. Ah, Mr. Gimpel, I want you to hear my organ. One of your great organists who looks like Christ and has a positively ecstatic air about him when he plays, told me: 'Here's the only cathedral in America.' "

June 17 / Dr. Carrel

Dr. Lopez, a Spanish friend of mine who works at the Rockefeller Institute, arranged for me to visit the three famous buildings. I went through six floors of little rooms full of stills and retorts, laboratories very similar to the dens of the alchemists, whose theories are coming back into fashion. My incomprehension was total. Lunch was served at 12:30. In the dining room four tables, each laid for ten. Almost all the doctors kept their gowns on. Several brought friends. At our table there was Dr. Loevy, a surgeon, son of the former director of the Paris Observatory, and his brother, arrived yesterday from France, an officer who's been awarded the Croix de Guerre with three citations. Next to him a Polish Jew with a hard blond face. Dr. Carrel had reserved a place at our table, but he was late. When he came he turned out to be quite small. His head was extremely round, and I believe quite hairless, like a balloon! Although from Lyons, he had the neat, clean-shaven American look, but with a *lorgnon!* About forty-five, he has the physique of a myopic research worker. His eyes are an even, brilliant brown like those of La Tour's cheery-faced people. His lips are too thin, his mouth authoritarian. He asked Loevy about the price of food in France.

A frugal repast: A dishful of potatoes with three thin slices of bacon, and, to drink, water or iced tea. Seeing that I was French, Carrel invited me, after lunch, to join him in his office along with the two Loevys and Suarès. The American newspapers are full of an imminent revolution in France and it's naturally the subject of conversation everywhere. Americans returning from Paris paint the situation very black. Carrel wanted to know all about it and questioned Loevy with great anxiety. For me it was a pleasure to meet this man whom America claims for herself, whom we ourselves consider much more American than French, and whom we would hardly dare look on any longer as our own—to see this man, this Frenchman, get together Frenchmen, two of them strangers to him, behind closed doors in the hope of gleaning some idea of the situation inside his own country. He was anxious, his whole countenance showed it, but Loevy gave him full reassurances and his face relaxed again. Carrel showed me a dozen small paintings hanging in his office, which he considered very beautiful. "They were done," he told me, "by an old peasant named Tibault who paints after work as a hobby." These paintings resemble the pastels drawn by street artists on the Parisian sidewalks.

June 30 / Embarkation for Europe

On the *Aquitania,* with my wife and my son Ernest.

July 7 / Arrival in England

July 8 / France and the English

London is decked with French flags. In America there isn't a single one. Here friendship for France has solid ties. How erratic are the things of this world! Queen Victoria, idol of England, and considered the greatest sovereign that country had ever possessed, would shudder in her grave if she heard the epithets rained on her for having let the Germans overrun us in 1870. People held her responsible for the last war.

July 9 / At Christie's

It has its character, this famous London salesroom where nothing has changed for more than a hundred years. The same straight staircase, which would be monumental if it weren't overshadowed by a rectangular hall of such high, narrow proportions. On the first floor you arrive in a sort of anteroom, always full of objects and people. Opposite, the main room, which is very dirty, not very big, with the walls a wine-red, in the middle of which rises up a sort of jack-in-the-box in poor condition but of good wood with a fine patina on it. It's the auctioneer's seat, and in front of it a long table stretches out at right angles to it, surrounded by hard wooden benches, with an odd one caned, but both sorts battered.

It's wonderful! Here there's no need to pander to the clients paying out twenty, forty, fifty thousand pounds for pictures! In Paris Georges Petit begins by attracting customers with comfort in his immense gallery, providing hundreds of velvet armchairs. He shows them his pictures the way a goldsmith shows a jewel. He furbishes and gilds the frames, and of course cleans and varnishes the canvases, which are then spaced out harmoniously on the walls. A sale is more consummately got up than a first night, with good carpets too on the floor. Even at the Hôtel Drouot, that squalid hole, sales are got up a bit better. Christie's in England, in the country of comfort and cleanliness, has the audacity to offer sheer discomfort and a parquet floor thick with dust. Pictures worth a few pounds alternate with hundred-thousand-pound works, and are sold along with them, everything "just as it comes" on the walls. Three, four rows, the pictures one above the other, the finest sometimes perched just below the roof. With us, catalogues are superb. Before the war they cost an average of 50,000 francs to produce; here, not even fifty. No explanation or reference, no expert opinion or guarantee. What does it matter, since people still come! Let's look at these people. But first let's go and have a look at the picture permanently on view in the outer office to the right of the staircase, depicting a sale at Christie's around 1800. Now, to return to the main room: nothing has changed, neither the people nor the objects; all the period characters are here this morning in flesh and blood. They were here yesterday, and will be tomorrow! I can see an old Englishman with side whiskers and the eternal topper. A character out of Thackeray or Dickens, full of dignity and full of passion. All the men wear their clothes with an air. I notice two ladies looking at a male nude as if it were a stallion. An old woman wants to take their place: she is long and thin with a very small behind. The dealers have carnations in their buttonholes. Their shops may often be revolting, but they remain gentlemen. Mysterious colloquies, one very secret-looking between two individuals, one of whom is wearing a form-fitting frock coat, while the other, red-faced and rustic, with his stomach protruding, looks like one of those figures who sit in taverns in sporting prints. The latter is a lord, the former an antique dealer.

English engravings, French engravings

I called in at Graves's, where I saw the son of the collector who owned Fragonard's *Billet Doux*. He's the director of this firm, England's leading publisher of prints. "We ask French engravers," he told me, "to do plates of the finest eighteenth-century English pictures, because the English draw very badly." He showed me some examples by French engravers. I don't find them satisfactory; by drawing too well, our artists lose the ample, relaxed character of the English painters. Our engravers draw the bones under the flesh of the hands and show the veins right on the skin, and that's not English.

Orpen and Lavery

"Some days ago in Paris," said Crosnier, "I saw England's most popular painter, Orpen, who was there to do a picture of the Peace Conference, some thirty heads, but the best are sketches. He has his studio in the Astoria and is staying at the Chatham.

"In Boulogne on the way back I met Lavery, the English painter of society women, who told me bitterly that his government had commissioned him to paint the English army's daredevil drivers. 'They're very dirty,' he added sadly.

"His painting doesn't seem clean to him any more."

July 10 / Rembrandt's "Flora"

Sulley has just bought this picture, for which Lord Spencer always asked 40,000 pounds. He is asking me 25,000.

A Gainsborough

Lady Sampson or *Samson*: Sulley wants £20,000 for it; it is one of the master's finest. It was unknown, but is almost as pretty as Groult's.

July 11 / Return to France

Via Boulogne this time, and nine hours of travel instead of thirty-two. It's thanks to the peace, the peace no one is yet used to. It would be more precise to say that we haven't yet lost our habit of war. That's why I go from surprise to surprise today. How funny to see a train made up of French, Belgian, and German coaches. I was bowled over not to be asked for any bread-ration tickets in the dining car, and astonished to see hung there an advertisement for the Orient Express. The frontiers have been sealed so hermetically for five years that it seems incredible that they could have been opened in a few months. Looking out of the window, I saw tanks in a dump, and empty ambulance trains!

The La Tour is sold

Ambatielos[1] has come in on the deal, and Nathan Wildenstein has concluded the transaction for £48,000.

July 13 / Around the Arc de Triomphe

I arrived at 8:30 in the evening by way of the avenue de la Grande-Armée. The sun was setting, flooding everything with gold and concentrating its rays on the cenotaph, which it turned into a gigantic torch, while mounted troopers in sky-blue uniforms circled round the space, controlling the crowds which came pouring up the Champs-Elysées without a break. I went slowly round the Étoile. The gold dust was sinking away gradually, the vaults of the monuments were hung with shadow, and I looked upon the night of the dead. Smoke of incense was rising up; the cenotaph turned white. People's hearts contracted as the communion with the dead began.

Armand Lowengard, whom I expected to meet there, told an American earlier this afternoon, after having explained to him our cult for the dead: "Tomorrow twenty thousand men will file under the Arc de Triomphe in two hours. If our dead, our 1,600,000 dead, were to pass there, it would take them eight days, eight days; I've worked it out."

July 14 / The day of glory has arrived

The procession, the victory procession, was to set out at 8:30 from the Porte Maillot. I had seen the crowds lie down to sleep all along the triumphal way last night, and as this morning I had to cross the avenue de la Grande-Armée, being invited to No. 66, less than a thousand yards from our house, we got up early and at 5:40 were already attempting to

---

[1] Ambatielos was ruined shortly afterward. He hadn't paid for the pastel, which Nathan Wildenstein took back and resold fifteen years later to Maurice de Rothschild. (Note appended 1939.)

cross the avenue. It was too late. We had to drive our car around the Bois, where the troops were massed, and go by way of Saint-Cloud, Suresnes, and Puteaux. We did not reach our destination until seven o'clock.

At 8:32 Joffre and Foch appeared side by side on horseback. The people's gratitude went out to them. The two marshals were followed by delegations of the Allied armies. The Americans had a disciplined step, their flags were unmarked but fine, the Belgians looked fat jolly fellows, the English looked as though they were at Buckingham Palace. Then came the Italians. They were roundly applauded. And then the Portuguese, Poles, Rumanians, Serbs, Czechoslovaks, etc.

I pretty soon tired of seeing our infantrymen only from this balcony, through the leaf-covered trees; their crowning moment was when they passed beneath the Arc de Triomphe. That's where I wanted to see them and watch them pass, so I went down into the street. The Place de l'Étoile was a vast circus, an amphitheater unbelievably lofty, rising up in trestles, cars, ladders. How to get through? It took a great deal of perseverance to go around the Place, reach the avenue de Friedland, then the avenue des Champs-Elysées. Someone there lent me a periscope, a gadget brought into common use by the war. How can the infantrymen pass beneath the colossal arch without being crushed by its gigantic vaultings!

I looked at 146, avenue des Champs-Elysées, where I lived for so long; the fourth-floor balcony, the window of the room where in 1915 my beloved mother died; my mother who cherished the idea of being able to watch the triumphal return from up there. My eyes grew damp. Oh, Mother, you died too young!

The troops continued to file past, but it was impossible for me to see them because of the official grandstands. I ducked under them like a Paris urchin and, to my stupefaction, came out right in the road with three hundred generals behind me, and before me Clemenceau and Poincaré. Poincaré was exuberant, standing in full dress. Clemenceau kept slightly behind him, in frock coat and black gloves. He stood completely motionless, holding his topper in his hand. He looked grave. The expression on his face seemed to say to us: "It's not our celebration at all, it's that of the dead; they alone have the right to rejoice, not you."

Clemenceau had an almost grim look about him. His head seemed rounder, his eyebrows more fiery, his mustache fiercer.

July 15 / In the den of cubism

At Léonce Rosenberg's, rue de la Baume. A quiet little house harbors the revelation. An unobtrusive plate on the door: L'EFFORT MODERNE. I rang the bell and was let into a low-pitched entrance way, tiled very simply in black and white. I was shown upstairs to a large, long room forming a gallery. Here he has displayed cubes of canvases, canvases in cubes, marble cubes, cubic marbles, cubes of color, cubic colorings, incomprehensible cubes and the incomprehensible divided cubically. What is there on these canvases? Puzzles composed of patches of flat colors, interwoven and yet sharply differentiated. Léonce Rosenberg —tall, blond, and elegant like a pink shrimp—does splendidly: he keeps his gravity. I can take a lesson from him, a lesson in salesmanship, for Rosenberg manages to earn his living with all this; he must be an admirable salesman. I would like to see him at work. The sculptures are the most curious. I stopped in front of a marble ball cut like a Dutch cheese. I asked Léonce what it represented, and he replied: "It's a woman's head." I gazed, astonished, and then he added: "Only the form counts: it makes any representation of accessories—the mouth, eyes, and nose— quite superfluous."

I went up to an object made entirely of zinc cones, something like funnels.

"Whatever is that?"

"A clown."

It was droll enough, certainly. The arms consisted of two elongated cones, the legs also, but widening out to the base. The body: also two cones, fitting one into the other and forming a crinoline. I contemplated it and Rosenberg said solemnly: "These artists, these descendants of the stonecutters, of those who built the cathedrals—at least they have the merit of not trying to bowl you over."

I paused before each of these marbles and struggled, without any preconceived idea, to understand what the artist meant to depict. I didn't get there. I asked Rosenberg to explain, but he said defensively: "Our works keep their secret."

A second later, in front of a stone, a sort of volcanic eruption, he said: "It's all so clear."

Before something purporting to be a bust, but without a nose, eyes, mouth, or ears, he murmured: "We're eliminating parasitic wealth."

Which led him to fulminate against the impressionists, those crackpots, those characters who linger over detail, yes, over detail in which you lose yourself, detail that overwhelms you. "Ah," he groaned, "what we lack is the power to turn back the years; ah! if we had it! It's the vantage point of those who built the cathedrals. The simplicity of artisans striving to create an ideal Holy Virgin. We came on the scene when art was lost, but we've regained it. Where the impressionists deformed, we reform. Here, look at this." He showed me a kind of arch, a miniature aqueduct with two pillars, one straight and the other zigzag. "Isn't it utterly simple and magnificent?"

"What is it?"

"A seated man. Here we have the visual sense of the figure, not the constructive sense."

He pointed to a sort of big lentil and said: "It's a woman's stomach." I ought to have guessed it by the navel in the middle like a beer spout. "It's a *jeu d'esprit*, not of the senses," he added. "We are the descendants of Watteau, Delacroix, Ingres."

Finally I came to a statue that was all angles; it was marble but gave the impression of being coated in steel, armor-plated from head to foot. I was relieved: I now felt that I'd made progress, that maybe I no longer needed explanations, and I declared with the authority of something seen and clearly understood: "Now that, that's a knight."

"No," replied Rosenberg, "it's a female nude."

July 16 / At 57

Nathan Wildenstein told Arnold Seligmann: "I'm ready to buy the Prince de Beau's little Louis XVI table for 500,000 francs, and I'll sell it in Paris at a profit." [2]

---

[2] Some years later, when the franc had lost four fifths of its value, the prince sold his table to Joe Duveen for 500,000 francs (paper). Stubborn like many aristocrats, he didn't want to acknowledge the depreciation of our money—to his own detriment.

He then told us this anecdote about Doistau, that munificent collector. Wildenstein bought a miniature from him one morning, and in the afternoon the collector, miserable at having parted with it, came to buy it back.

Before the cenotaph

For three days the crowd has been filing past the cenotaph, on which each person can lay only a single flower. The procession is endless, the tears flow ceaselessly.

July 23

I have severed the old association with Wildenstein begun in 1889.

A Guardi

One of the most beautiful I have ever seen. Gulbenkian brought it to me. He bought it in England for four thousand pounds. It represents a fete in San Marco Square, which is decked out like a Venetian woman. Tents have been erected in front of the colonnade of the galleries, and one cannot see over their tops: beautiful tents like coquettes' canopies, blue, turquoise blue, trimmed with lace. Some hundred figures are milling about, self-absorbed pleasure-seekers.

July 26 / Berenson

He's in Paris and he sent me a line. I went to see him at the Ritz, at ten in the morning. He was lying down, a manicurist was with him; but she'll never round off those claws. He told me of the weariness that overwhelms him in the mornings. He is just back from Spain, and was enthusiastic over the cathedrals and churches which the French built there, and crazy about the works left by our sculptors. "It's the only place in the world," he said, "to study French art. Your thirteenth-century stonecutters had all the grace of Watteau; all your churches in France are restored, but down there they're pure. We don't want restored pictures or repaired statues and yet this fake architecture is approved and admired. It doesn't make sense. Then, your churches are

---

The table is today in New York at Jules Bache's, to whom my brother-in-law sold it at a very small profit. (Note appended 1930.)

empty but the Spanish ones are inhabited, it's their charm: they're in-habited by a great and magnificent lord, the Lord God!"

I talked to Berenson about the letter I've received from Soulié, and he told me: "I've seen a lot of Soulié this winter, especially in Chi-nese society. There was a Chinese woman around, a very disturbing Chi-nese woman." Berenson broke off, gazing dreamily at the ceiling, then resumed: "Yes, a very disturbing Chinese woman, who would have been the favorite of the Dowager Empress."

July 27 / Berenson at No. 57

I showed him the Ambrogio Lorenzetti on a gold background which he got us to buy in Italy for about 20,000 francs. Even he didn't realize it was as beautiful as this, having just barely seen it.[8] Looking at the relics which surround and frame it, forty of them at least, he said: "Relics—there's a source of lies for you; lies hardly outdone by those uttered during the last war about all that happened."

Talking of the Spiridon Collection, he set its value at only one million francs. With my eyes shut, I'd buy it for twice that much.

He finds the Duke of Alba's pink tapestries fabulous and also greatly admires his Fra Angelico.

July 31 / My former life

It ends today. I leave for London. What will it be tomorrow?

August 1 / My new life

I have bought a Gainsborough life-size portrait of a man from Sulley for £3,700. It's the first Lord Vernon. Despite its size, this pic-ture passed unnoticed in a recent Christie sale. It went for £1,000. I value it at £10,000.[4]

August 8 / St. Albans Cathedral

In the nineteenth century a certain Lord Grimthorpe, obviously a philistine, destroyed it by restoring it. To get himself a place in heaven, he made over enormous sums to this purpose. May he be damned and his soul engulfed in the most fiery depths of hell.

[8] This picture is today in the Boston Museum.
[4] It is today in the Philadelphia Museum.

August 29 / On Whistler

I have met an old man called Dr. Davis, who remembers clearly Whistler's first exhibition at the Dowdeswells'. He insisted on a sort of major-domo in yellow and white being posted at the entrance. London immediately nicknamed this character the poached egg.

September 3 / The price of a Pigalle

Looking through my accounts, I saw that I sold the bust of the Marquise de Pompadour, acquired from Countess Yolande du Hamel de Breuil (Château de Peschescal), to Jules Bache of New York for $160,000.

September 6 / Helleu on himself

At six o'clock this afternoon I was walking along the avenue du Bois-de-Boulogne when I ran into him, surprised to see this very snobbish Parisian mingling with the Sunday crowd returning from Vincennes. But as I watched him follow with his gaze all these women's fresh faces, I noticed that he was looking at them as he examines trinkets, for their beauty alone, without reference to their origin. I told him that in London at Dr. Davis's (from whom I bought some primitives) I saw engravings of his hung side by side with Whistler and Zorb etchings, and he replied: "You've the advantage of being young, so you'll see my engravings bring in big prices. The Marquis de Biron bought perhaps two hundred from a dealer on the rue Laffitte, commenting to him: 'If Helleu would only kick the bucket, I'd make money!'

"The other day Cartier bought my etching of Whistler for 1,800 francs. At the time I made twenty-five proofs of it and sold twenty for one thousand francs, a thousand francs the lot. When we're young we don't know how to recognize the masterpiece among our works."

September 11 / At Sulley's

There are three great art dealers in London: Agnew, Colnaghi, and Sulley, each of very good reputation, but Sulley comes first by dint of his incomparable fairness. He has an associate whom I've never seen, and whom Sulley himself no longer sees. Sulley is obviously incapable of lying; indeed he scarcely speaks at all.

He takes you up to a picture, stations himself behind an armchair, and opens his lips only to tell you its price, and even then only on request. When I asked about the Gainsborough, he answered: "I want £5,000 for it, it cost me a thousand, I'd let it go to you for £4,000." He let me have it for £3,700.

He keeps his enjoyment very much to himself, like his affections. I like him very much.

September 26 / Return to Paris

September 27 / A shot-up Toulouse-Lautrec

It's precisely that. It's a portrait of a fat brothel woman. Georges Bernheim, who showed it to me, told me that the last owner amused himself by shooting at it with a gun.

October 1 / Gainsborough's wife

I have seen her portrait. This painter, this man of refinement, who extracted the quintessence of female beauty, had a kettle for a wife.

October 8 / Tapestries by the gross

I have gone to London for a sale, and an old dealer whom I met told me how the father of the Lowengards had engaged a buyer for Spain; it was stipulated in the contract that Lowengard was obliged to take all the tapestries that he brought back, at a price of 150 francs each . . . even including the Gothic ones! (sic)

October 11 / Lord Foley's Collection

Sold on Monday *in situ*, at Ruxley Lodge, Claygate, in the county of Surrey. It's a horrible house, not a hundred years old. But what a marvelous collection! [5]

[5] Two entire services of Sèvres porcelain, extraordinary French furniture, two chests and some corner cupboards by Cressent, it's a model of the Schlichting Collection at the Louvre. There is a magnificent Greuze, a portrait of a little girl holding a basket of flowers and smelling a carnation. Her dress is white, the bodice relieved in pink. The canvas has varnish stains and the face is disfigured by it. It is much criticized, as no one here understands French art. They don't believe that it's by the master. I avoid the picture dealers; I couldn't refuse them my opinion. I go to the British Museum to see if it is mentioned, and there among the engravings I find the same personage in the same position as *The Gardener*, but with a simpler costume:

October 13 / "Sergeant" Sullivan

He's not a soldier at all but a lawyer. "Sergeant" is an old title given to the king's counselors. I dined with him this evening.

We talked of art, and he told me about a trial which took place about fifteen years ago in London: "A very pukka gentleman was invited for a few days to an Irish castle. After his departure, it was noticed that a Gainsborough portrait of a woman had disappeared. Following a complaint, a charge was laid and a search made. At the visitor's house a Gainsborough was found which the plaintiffs recognized as theirs, but they were mistaken. It was actually the same name and an almost identical face, but it wasn't the same personage; it was her sister. As for the stolen picture, nothing more was heard about it.

"Around that time, however, I received a visit from an antique dealer's sister. They worked together, but he had just bought a Gainsborough at a public auction for four pounds, and had thence severed his association with her. Here, I surmise, was the stolen Gainsborough, thrown into a minor sale because of the stir caused by the trial. I didn't see the antique dealer's sister again, but I heard that she had received 8,000 pounds for her share."

October 15 / Ballets Russes

I went back to see these ballets which stirred Paris in the years before the war, and knowing the influence this stage scenery and Russian costumes have had on our decorative art, I note with pleasure how our artists have simplified this oriental art which today seems very far removed from us.

Purchase of the Greuze

I've got it for £4,300.

October 17 / In front of a Rembrandt in the National Gallery

Rembrandt painted the way Hercules would have created man:

The Florist, engraved after the drawing by J. B. Greuze, painter to the king. Printed in the office of M. de Damery, chevalier de l'ordre royal et militaire de Saint-Louis. In Paris at Esnauts and Rapilly, rue Saint-Jacques. In the Town of Coutances A.P.D.R.

My picture, for I shall buy it, will not bring a high price. I'll go up to £7,000.

with his fist. Examining his boldly painted canvas, one becomes lost in the terrifying detail of a brush which the artist seems to have wielded five hundred times everywhere and in all directions. It is impossible to grasp his technique, which has the disorder of genius.

October 19 / Wagner in Paris

Today in the Salle Gaveau there were cries of "Wagner! Wagner!" This brought some whistles, but a soldier called out: "We've damn well won the right to hear Wagner!"

October 20 / A royal collection for auction

That of the Emperor of Austria. The people of Vienna have protested against the sale, but he's dying of hunger.

The Hubert Roberts of La Béraudière

800,000 francs. Not expensive.

The Pourtalès Vigée

600,000 francs, of which the heirs will see 500,000.

Final settlement with Nathan Wildenstein

We have exchanged final letters settling our separation.

October 23 / The collection of Charles I

The Duveens are studying the matter in great detail. William Salomon has promised them the money.

November 3 / An antique dealer's joke

At Stettiner's, the dealer in art objects, the daughters of antique dealers are called corner cupboards since, like those pieces of furniture, they're hard to place.

NOTEBOOK 6

November 5, 1919–May 25, 1920

November 5 / My library, my purchases

At Maynial's the first half of the manuscript of Anatole France's *Crainquebille* is available for 4,500 francs, and for the same price Barbey d'Aurevilly's *The Prophets of the Past*, with this astonishing dedication:

> *To Madame H. de Balzac*
> *in token of profound respect*
>
> This book was intended for the emperor of Russia. But I would rather have it in the hands of the wife of a man of genius—of him who was for all of us nineteenth-century writers a literary sovereign, our emperor!
>
> *Jules Barbey d'Aurevilly*

November 6 / The most beautiful Falconet

It's a marble statuette, the Galatea group, often reproduced in Sèvres biscuit. The statue comes alive and is a real woman. The artist has captured that unique, fleeting instant: the passing of inert matter into life. Wildenstein bought it from the director of the Rouen Museum for 500,000 francs (£20,000).

November 7 / A Bartolomeo Veneto

It is the portrait of Gabriel Sforza which Henry Goldman of New York has bought from me for 500,000 francs. With the rate of exchange dropping from day to day, this American isn't paying more than $60,000 for it. We had bought it for over 400,000 francs ($80,000) and kept it eight years. It came from the collection of Senator Crespi of Milan. It has the beauty of a brute. The jaw comes down like a trap, the nose denotes pride, the eyes attack. He is dressed in an ostentatious costume. Another beautiful feature of this picture lies in its shades of black.[1]

The Hamilton sale

Prices are rising in London. The Duveens, probably commissioned by Huntington or Frick, have bought a Romney for £54,600, about 2 million francs at the rate of exchange. It's no extraordinary picture. But then Romney is such a bad painter!

Beltran Masses on Matisse

Beltran Masses told me: "Matisse spent four months in Seville, and on his return to Madrid the principal Spanish artists welcomed him. I was among them. We asked him if Spain had inspired him and he replied: 'Enormously.' 'Have you any works to show us?' 'Yes indeed!' And he ushered us into a room where on a canvas we saw his usual white cloth, apple, and knife. I could have hit him."

November 12 / Spencer's Rembrandt

I told Wildenstein I had gone that afternoon to see Mme X, who has begun cleaning one of my primitives, and I added that she's very inept. "Why, yes," said Wildenstein, "it's she who cleaned Spencer's *Flora*.[2] She made the yellow flowers on the hat disappear. The Duveens, who had given it her to devarnish, said they were fake, but it isn't so; it's that woman who made the yellow go, since yellow can't stand up to a

---

[1] When this journal was begun, $100 were worth 500 francs; today they're worth 2,500 francs. Since July 1919, the franc had been falling every day, but one had so little notion of the depreciation of money that we were selling for $60,000 a picture that had cost us $80,000. (Note appended 1931.)

[2] This picture was subsequently bought by Mrs. Huntington of New York. (Note appended 1924.)

bad cleaning. Twenty-five years ago I had a picture of fruit including a cut melon. Before my eyes a woman restorer cleaned it and the melon began to dissolve as if under someone's teeth."

November 20 / My arrival in Strasbourg

I've come with my wife. We arrived at 9 P.M. I was worn out, but I was hardly in the hotel before I went out into the streets to see with my own eyes the incredible miracle: a French Strasbourg.

Not a single German inscription in the shop windows any longer. You read: La Brasserie de la Marne, La Civette, La Belle Jardinière, A la Parisienne, Paris-Parfums, France-Mode, Au Bambin, La Bijouterie des Alliés, A la Fauvette.

November 30 / Encounter with Vollard

I reminded him that I hadn't seen him since his visit to No. 57, when he came to see the La Tour, and he replied: "I prefer Renoir to La Tour." Vollard was full of praise for his own literary works: "I'm bringing out a Degas with fifty pages of illustrations and fifty pages of text. My Renoir is also going to come out. I claim no merit in writing it, for all my life I've only had to note down the painter's words. But it's going to demolish all the books written on impressionism, full as they are of theories that have no connection whatsoever to the masters of the school. Listen! I find my book on Renoir quite satisfactory. I read it to Renoir, who listened only absent-mindedly, but his eldest son, the actor, wrote me: 'In the whole book on my father I've only one word to pick on: it's "sentiment" in place of "sentimentality." And yet it's true that that's the word my father used. You have been too faithful!' "

December 2 / The Pourtalès Vigée

It portrays la Dugazon in the role of Nina, and has been bought for 440,000 francs by Nathan Wildenstein, who showed it to me, saying: "The picture made a very bad impression on me, I found it too yellow, but I remembered that it came from England, so I said to myself I could go ahead and buy it, that this was only the effect of a ghastly English varnish, and so it was. The woman's dress became white again and the apron improved a hundred per cent." Wildenstein was right.

December 3 / Death of the collector Frick

He has left his collection valued at $20 million to the city of New York. When I arrived in New York eighteen years ago, Frick was already a great collector, but he owned scarcely anything except moderns, eighteenth-century English pictures, and many painted around 1830, for forty years ago that had been the basis of all collections over there, and Knoedler was then selling them to him exclusively. He told me one day that he would never buy an antique piece of furniture or art object, and his home was arranged in the worst possible taste. But the king of collectors, Pierpont Morgan, died at the time Frick was building his town house, and all the objects from the deceased's collection which one would have thought were earmarked for the New York museum were thrown on the market for private sale. Frick got the most beautiful items. Unhappily for our country, he acquired the famous Fragonard panels of Grasse, which I always hoped to buy and bring back to France, but it was wartime and I was in the service! Frick didn't have Altman's taste, but he began buying intensively and the Duveen brothers obtained some very fine pieces for him. A long time ago my father had sold him the famous Romney, *Lady Hamilton with a Dog*, known as *Nature*. Also Lawrence's *Lady Peel* with a hat, the two I believe for $200,000—this was the price Frick normally paid. I shall always remember a visit I paid him after he had bought the bronzes from the Morgan Collection. I hadn't seen them and I was talking with him in his study when he got up as if on springs and asked me: "Have you seen my new bronzes?" Without waiting for my answer, he added: "Follow me." Nearly all his bronzes were in a room lined with low bookcases, and they were mounted on ball bearings, so that each bronze could be turned and seen from all angles.

Frick entered the room, started a bronze revolving, and said: "Look at that turning." Then he set a second bronze in motion, and a third and a fourth, and so on, going round the room and making all the bronzes revolve, and making me go around with him and with them and the room. I would have liked, if not to study them, at least to look at them. But Frick didn't care. The rich child was playing with his toys.

Renoir's death

He has gone from us at Cagnes, and I regret not having known him better. I intended to go and see him this winter—but Renoir has his historian and it is Vollard. The book he is bringing out will show us the Renoir I knew. I would say that during his last years people hung very much on the lips of the great painter. Crès has just published a slender volume in which some of his remarks are set down.

December 4 / The little salons

They multiply, and it's now impossible to keep up with them. Every post brings me one or two invitations. The artists will suffer by it. They thought it a way of not being lost in the turmoil of the big salons; the remedy tends to become worse than the malady. Devambez, who once was selective, is himself now inundated. In his ten little mezzanine rooms he shows four exhibitions. In his shop he sells prints. He's at 13, boulevard Malesherbes, next door to Potin the grocer. Strange neighbors. There are still good exhibitions at Mme Druet's in the rue Royale, and fine sculptures at Hébrard, rue Royale. As for Georges Petit, he's showing only society or fashionable bad painters.

December 8 / Mme Forain

She came to see my Gainsborough portrait of Lord Vernon, returning the call which I paid her this morning. I was taken around to her house to look at a fake English picture which one of her friends wanted to sell. The Forains live opposite me, on rue Spontini, in a town house with a studio that they built. I saw only the entrance hall and the vestibule, where a seemingly permanent disorder holds sway, like the evening after a move, when all the furniture has come and you go to bed asking yourself: "Can it possibly all fit in?"

She asked me whether I knew the engravings done by her husband, and I replied: "Very little." "They're wonderful," she said. "They're like Rembrandt's or Watteau's. Neither Rembrandt nor Watteau did any finer. I ought to show you his etchings, but there's no hope of getting into his studio, it's a sanctuary. When he goes away for a day or two, I'll let you know, as he doesn't like anyone to see what he's doing. He's even afraid of me because he's always tearing them up; he destroys a great many works, and I'm always trying to prevent it. When I succeed in stealing some pieces away from him, within a couple of days he's noticed and got them back again. In the morning I'll see him working on a canvas, painting a still life, and in the evening I'll find a female nude on it. No one knows what he's doing, no one. His work is going up fast in price. On a panel that's earned him 3,000 francs the dealers make 30,000. I worked it out the other day. My goodness, how he works! But he doesn't bother about finances. There's a dealer eager to organize an exhibition for him in London, and he's quite willing to send drawings but not paintings; he says he's afraid to have them transported, but it's really just that an exhibition would cause him too much trouble, care, and anxiety, that it would take away time from his work. Imagine, I'm now opening letters for him which date from 1914 that he's never touched!"

December 10 / The Forain family

It was 6 P.M. when I entered that first room on the right where someone was asleep the day before yesterday at eleven in the morning. All the Forains get up around noon. I looked for the bed, but at this time of day it's a sofa. Mme Forain was alone and busy copying a fake English painting which she takes for a Reynolds. Her canvases clutter the whole room. They're on the mantelpiece, on the armchairs, behind the furniture, on easels, on wardrobes. Disorder and dust.

A young man came in, holding a cup in one hand and a saucepan in the other. It was her son. "Ah, you've brought my chocolate," she said to him. "Put it on this bench. I want to introduce M. Gimpel to you, our neighbor from across the street. You see, M. Gimpel, the things we have to do, we make our own chocolate in spite of having had two extra servants for two months now." Mme Forain was telling the exact truth: in fact, for the whole house, including the kitchen, they have just these two servants, who have to do everything.

I asked Mme Forain the name of the English dealer who wanted to have an exhibition of her husband's works. She didn't remember, and of course the dealer's letter had been mislaid. "My husband," she told me, "sends drawings only to those who buy them, since drawings get damaged if they travel too much."

Thereupon Forain arrived. I hadn't seen him for twenty years; he no longer has a nutcracker head. He goes about at home in a wide brown hat; he is very bent; when he takes off the hat he reveals white hair and looks milder, a Napoleonic lock falls on his forehead, his brown eyes look like little copper coins. He joined in the conversation about the London dealer. His wife and son launched an attack to persuade him to agree. Both asserted that no English dealer would offer him a definite sale, not even a guarantee. They have a quarrelsome way about them, and the son repeated over and over, in a kind of leitmotiv: "The pound's now worth twice as much: instead of twenty-five francs you get fifty." In the end Forain replied: "I assure you I understand!"

Nothing will be settled this evening; they'll have to find the letter, which they know is lost forever.

December 13 / The Manzi sale

Two beautiful Gothic statues, kings with fake crowns, and a fine twelfth-century bust also much restored but with the face intact and dignified.

At Paul Rosenberg's

He's a dealer in modern paintings. We were at Rollin College together. His father and mother were Austrians; when war broke out, he was liable to deportation. Although born here, he had never become naturalized. But Rosenberg enlisted and was assigned to the Army Museum, where he did the honors of France's heroic souvenirs. He's no fool, with that face like a short-muzzled fox. His cheekbones are prominent and grained.

In the Deudon Collection, which he showed me, the most beautiful canvas is a Manet; a young woman in pink, lovely, pensive and sad, seated at a marble café table. The boredom of idleness weighs her down, the uselessness of her beauty depresses her, life stares her in the face like the marble of the table—cold, slippery, and hard. Rosenberg is asking 500,000 francs for it.[3] There is a fine Renoir, a garden with houses at the bottom of it. The garden is overflowing with the most beautiful spring flowers the human spirit could imagine. A superb Monet, *The Gare Saint-Lazare*, teeming, smoky, and metallic.

December 16 / The Manzi sale

The kings went for a song, as did the bust and two other statues. Demotte, Duveen, and I bought them.

[3] Since bought by Mrs. Arthur Sachs of New York. (Note appended 1928.)

December 17 / Mme Vigée-Lebrun by Pajou, in terra cotta

Nathan Wildenstein has just bought it for 225,000 francs. It's more beautiful than the Du Barry. A less haughty but more aristocratic bust, less authoritarian and more spiritual, less Versailles, more Paris.

December 18 / New Year's Day publicity

Taste is entering the home in the form of advertisements. Parisians are beginning to receive extremely pretty cards of all colors in their post. These ought to be kept: they'd make a picturesque collection. Ephemeral art objects thrown so soon into the wastebasket, images of our time, I regret their loss to future centuries which won't know us, or scarcely. Vuitton, the trunk dealer of 70, Champs-Elysées, has sent an original card signed "Grignon": blue branches, green leaves, pink, red, and white flowers rise from a rather small, faintly royal blue vase, a Gubbio shape but modern: flowering as if by a conjuror's trick.

I think I'd give first prize to Lalique—who started the trend. On an invitation to a glassware exhibition, he conveyed the impression of sculptured glass to perfection, simply by embossing on plain white cards a chaste nest of leaves in which a pair of white pigeons sit blissfully grave.

I'll certainly be going to Cartier's; he's invited me to an exhibition of his modern jewelry designed by Barbier. It has been left to Barbier to attract me in by sending me one of his charming reproductions, a chic Parisian girl in a short blue skirt patterned with large pink flowers. She has a hedgehog hairdo and a parasol the color of the woven flowers of her dress; she holds the parasol open, upturned on the ground. She is leaning against a veined marble base with a Louis XVI sphinx on it. The background is lilac, and a pine with a brick-colored trunk thrusts up heavy black foliage. Coming from Cartier's, she demurely shows off their delightful wares: on her arms, over long suède gloves, she has slipped two red and black bracelets. The fashion is for Negro art, and shop windows are displaying heavy bracelets made of bone; hers appear to be of tinted ivory. A long necklace of green beads loops down from her neck, rounded off by a green cameo of hard rectangular stone. Long earrings, also green, frame her face. So, this Parisienne will be getting me to Cartier's. Some interesting research could be done here; it's the beginning of a renaissance in the art of jewelry. Cartier has fixed a day.

December 26 / The Duke of Marlborough

He received me outside his Blenheim Palace, the residence of the famous general, built by an architect who had Versailles in mind, and for a great man who had been an honor to his country. The portico with its twin columns is tall and vast like that of a church. The duke has a noble air, standing against these overmassive stones, this triumph of cubism. Like the great lord that he is, Marlborough is very simple and very cordial. I haven't seen him for twenty years; since he was thirty. He has changed little, there are some deeper lines under the blue eyes. His slightly arched nose denotes forcefulness; his heavy eyelids, breeding.

He wanted to sell me some pictures, as the palace has become a big expense since his divorce from Mrs. Vanderbilt, although she provides him with an income. His apartments resemble those of the Great King at Versailles. His bedroom has an elevated, square-built bed with a canopy. There is a series of rooms with a sequence of Louis XIV's battles. The fine furnishings were bought by the present duke in the first years of his marriage. I saw his full-length portrait, with wife and children, by Sargent, who is only a second-rate painter: the painting is already getting dull. Marlborough has sold everything he is legally allowed to dispose of. I have taken a pretty Boucher oval and two Schalls, which my father once sold him.

December 29 / The Frick Collection

I've received the New York newspapers telling of Frick's death and of his collection. I noted the prices (in dollars) which I know to be correct.

Bellini, *St. Francis in the Desert*, $250,000. Titian, *Portrait of Aretino*, $100,000. Velázquez, *Philip IV*, $400,000. El Greco, *Portrait of a General*, $150,000. Rembrandt self-portrait, $250,000. Gainsborough, *The Mall*, $300,000. Van Dyck, *Portrait of Paolo Adorna*, $400,000. Gainsborough, *The Honorable Anna Duncan*, $400,000. Holbein, *Portrait of Cromwell*, entirely retouched: $200,000. Rubens, *Portrait of the Marquis of Spinola*, $90,000. Whistler, two pictures, $200,000. Millet, *Woman with a Candle*, $100,000. Rembrandt, *The Polish Cavalier*, $250,000. Gilbert Stuart, *Portrait of Washington*, $75,000. The enamels and bronzes of the Morgan Collection, $1,300,000.

January 1 / Commentaries

1919 has seen the peace signed and the soldiers passing under the Arc de Triomphe. But the war isn't over. Our mines are flooded, 500,000 buildings have been destroyed, from the North Sea to the peaks of Alsace, 1,500,000 combatants sleep under warring soil. Our railways have been used beyond their limits. We owe 40 billion francs. We can send nothing abroad. The value of the franc falls every day. The pound will soon be worth fifty francs. Under these frightful conditions, the cost of living is going up, salaries are doubled, trebled, and so they have to be. The Russian Revolution has all the bourgeoisie in a flutter. In every country there are enflamed elements which believe in the Soviet paradise. Both sides exaggerate. The Russian Revolution will carry out its ideals peacefully.[4] The wage earner is going to come out of bondage. Fierce convulsions shake the world and especially the Orient. We live in hard times.

January 4 / The Christmas tree

At home, with my dear children.

January 19 / In Forain's studio

I looked in first on Mme Forain. "Thanks for your letter," she said. "Forain's got the rosette of the *Légion d'honneur*. A minister told us, 'Forain won't get it because of his remark about how beautiful the Republic was under the Empire!' My husband grumbled to me: 'That rosette, what an infernal nuisance it's going to be.' "

I told her that as a result of my trip to London, Colnaghi is prepared to buy some etchings and drawings from him and organize an exhibition in its galleries, but they don't wish to buy any of his canvases, not knowing if the English will understand them.

Forain came into the room. How proud he is of his rosette, the gruff wag. He's full of good humor. Before he came in, his wife was telling me that she hasn't gone up to his studio since my last visit and that he's letting no one in. Forain replied to my congratulations with a "Follow me." We went up the big staircase leading to the first floor, then a spiral one to the second. It was 6:30 in the evening. By night, the

4 So I believed at the time. I've since changed my views (1926).

studio is barely lit, and it is in a state of phantasmagoric disorder. It's quite impossible to make an inventory of its contents, and one can't move in it without stepping on canvases, knocking against easels, upsetting boxes, covering oneself with paint, brushing the thick dust off chairs. In the middle of the room, on the ground, is a strip of linoleum, and on it the easel on which he paints and displays his pictures; it is surrounded by a number of little tables on which his brushes are strewn. He keeps his colors in a special piece of furniture, heavy and foursquare. This man, who puts so little color on his gray canvases, has a terrifying array of tubes. Like a pile-up of cartridge cases after a battle. Around the circle of tables, easels with no canvases but hung with dusters that can't ever have been washed, and stiff with paint. Beyond, the circle widens, and the eye can't distinguish much more. There are large canvases, a press, boxes of drawings in quantity, an immense mirror . . . a perilous maze!

"You don't know my paintings," he said to me. And he showed me, one after the other like a film, a procuress Bathsheba, several dancers, an operagoer eyeing a dancer, scenes from the law courts, a lawyer devouring his anxious client's possessions, war scenes, ruins, scenes of terror, a bloodthirsty German.

Any German who saw Forain's pictures would be sure to think their theme was "Justice Pursuing Crime."

Next, some little woman on a bed, a bed with the sheets gushing up like a beautiful expanse of water, the little woman showing her behind. Then several other nudes.

Then he showed me the drawings, red chalk on pink paper, lines fading out on the breast to show the very breathing; a catlike litheness, an almost tangible crush of roses, the portrayal of young flesh, awaiting and inspiring love.

January 28 / A saying of Ernest's

When his mother asked him if he had gotten to the letter Z, he replied: "Oh, Mama, I've gotten past it!"

January 29 / At Forain's

Mayer, one of the partners in the London firm of Colnaghi, accompanied me to Forain's, and the artist received us in exquisite fashion. He showed us his paintings on the war, and Mayer, formerly a German, and now a naturalized Englishman, found them admirable. The more ridiculous Forain's Germans, the more ecstatic Mayer became. Forain, who had no idea of Mayer's Germanic origin, was heaping the Germans with sarcasm, hooting with laughter, and Mayer laughed even louder. One by one he showed us: *Mother and Children Returning to the Ruins, German Snatching Eiderdown from Little Girl, Boches Guarding Prisoners before Calvary, Deportation of Young Girls of Lille*.

Mayer is prepared to give him an exhibition of forty canvases in London, and to guarantee him the sale of at least ten. Forain isn't keen to name any prices. He'd prefer Mayer to fix them. "I ought to give them a trimming," he said. Mayer wants only war or courtroom scenes.

Forain also showed us his drawings, and Mayer bought from him for 24,000 francs the originals of twenty-four colored drawings, published in an album of Devambez's. The artist also sold him some etchings, scenes of Monte Carlo, at 500 francs apiece, and some war drawings in color, all at 1,000 francs each, including a *General Pétain in the Trenches*. Forain had lunch with the general today and told us: "I call him Marshal Frigo. He's so cold, but it's because he's sensitive."

Mayer would have bought his complete series of etchings, but we'd been there two hours. Forain was worn out and said: "I'll settle it with M. Gimpel."

Forain showed us his etchings and his dry-point engravings. To me the most wonderful are those dealing with the story of Christ, and when we asked him how many proofs he'd made of them, he answered: "I run them off myself, in this press you can see in the corner. I print six, eight, twelve, and then retouch my plate; I take some more, touch it again, take another five or six, and then I start destroying my plate, ah! how I destroy it, if you knew!" "Oh, no," exclaimed Mayer, "surely you don't destroy it." "Why yes, I assure you I destroy it, I destroy it. It's finished, finished." And Forain ended his sentence in laughter.

February 1 / At Claude Monet's, with Georges Bernheim

He is eighty and hasn't changed since last year, apart from the fact that he complains of his eyes. "I see much less well," he said; "I'm half deaf and blind." However, he doesn't wear glasses. He is very hard of hearing. We talk of Renoir. "I haven't much longer to live," he said; "Remember, Renoir is gone." Then, he turned to Georges Bernheim: "All of you dealers should be pouncing on canvases in his studio." Bernheim explained that, by the terms of the will, the children can't sell the paintings until two years after his death.

The other day at Gallimard's Bernheim bought a beautiful Monet, *An Impression of Snow*, but Monet doesn't recall that canvas. Georges was sorry that he had not brought it and asked Monet if he wouldn't come to Paris. The aged painter replied: "Ah, no, I shan't come to Paris ever again, it's so unpleasant being in a hotel. The lights and the noise would bother me too much, my eyes are used to the soft light here." Monet can no longer bear strong daylight and always sits with his back to the light. We asked him news of his friend Clemenceau. "He comes here nearly every Sunday," he answered. "He was here last Sunday and even on the day of the Congress of Versailles, and he said: 'Yesterday everyone was congratulating me, and now they're all voting against me.' He had worked out his schedule in case he was elected. He planned to stay the night in his apartment on the rue Franklin. He didn't want to spend the night at the Elysée Palace and wouldn't have agreed to having guards. What a trick they've played on him! It's Briand who's dealt the blow. All these politicians strike me as clerks, clerks talking against the boss."

We returned to the big studio where the master's last large canvases are, and he said: "Dr. Gosset wants several for a place he's built in the country. I've told him I'd let him have them only if he'd place them in full light. I've begun getting offers, but I don't think I'll sell. I shall work until my death: it helps me to get through life, work has already enabled me to pass the hard times of the war. I get exercise, I can assure you, in this studio. Only a few years ago I was getting up at three in the morning, now at six, and I go to bed at nine. This life has preserved me. I've always enjoyed my food, which hasn't done me any harm. I eat less now, drink plenty, and smoke from morning till night. The work on these large pictures fascinates me. Last year I tried to paint on small canvases, not very small ones, mind you; impossible, I can't do it any more because I've got used to painting broadly and with big brushes."

We returned, all three of us, to the house, passing through the kitchen decorated with pretty blue tiles of a delectable cleanliness, into the dining room covered with Japanese prints hung on walls of a unique yellow, painted by Claude Monet. For the first time I went to the first floor, into the bedroom with its walls covered with canvases by the artist's gifted friends. There are admirable Renoirs, especially two small horizontal ones: a woman and child on the grass with a hen to their right; and another of the same size, of a woman on a sofa. It's like a Frago! At the head of his bed, a nude by Renoir: the face of a little girl, but the body of a beautiful woman. Very fine! There are Cézannes, Berthe Morisots, Renoir's *Casbah*. Monet bought the Cézannes, including an impression of snow in a forest, for 7,000 francs. "I offer you 70,-000," Bernheim said. The two Renoirs were painted at Giverny and given to Monet, but he bought all the others and has never sold a single one. "Oh, yes, once," said the painter, "a magnificent Renoir for 300 francs, but I badly needed the money and I wrote to Renoir: 'My dear friend, I'm extremely sorry, but in order to survive I've had to sell your picture.' Renoir understood."

Bernheim showed me a small Cézanne painted like an eighteenth-century piece, three people in a landscape, and told me: "You see this Cézanne, I've told you the story of how M. Monet one day sold one of his works for a hundred francs, fifty francs in cash and the Cézanne in place of the other fifty. And at the time this picture wasn't much of a gift."

"Yes," said Monet, "it was at Martin's, a dealer who never sold any but good pictures, who never put down more than a hundred francs for a canvas, and was satisfied with a profit of ten or twenty francs. Now, gentlemen, look at this Negro by Cézanne, I paid four hundred francs for it, and it was Vollard, too, from whom I bought it; he was only a novice. He's caught up since!"

We complimented Monet on his collection and he said to us: "I can assure you it's a pleasure for me, when I lie in bed, to see these lovely paintings by all my good friends!"

We returned to the drawing-room–studio where Monet generally stays and where Bernheim has always bought his pictures from him. We started talking about the collection that Rosenberg has carried off at

Nice, and Monet questioned Bernheim anxiously on his work *The Gare Saint-Lazare*. He wanted to know how its quality and tonality had stood up to time. Georges told him it was very beautiful.

"I'd be afraid to see it again."

"You're wrong."

Bernheim is right: *The Gare Saint-Lazare* is a beautiful work.

On an easel, just in front of us, we admired a small picture, a view of Vétheuil, and this is what Monet told us: "I offered it for fifty francs to the singer Faure. At that time, Renoir, Sisley, and all of us used to go with our canvases under our arms to offer our work to our few collectors, like Rouart. 'I need money,' I said to Faure, 'I need fifty francs; will you buy this picture from me?' 'It's all white,' he answered. 'I don't want it.' So that was that. Very put out, I carried away my canvas under my arm. Two years later Faure saw it in my house. 'But you've never shown me that,' he said. 'What! I offered it to you for fifty francs.'

" 'I'll give you six hundred for it.'

" 'You wouldn't get it for six thousand!'

"Clemenceau recently said to me: 'Loucheur wants a beautiful picture by you. How much for the view of Vétheuil?' 'Fifty thousand,' I replied, 'and if he takes it I'll regret it.' "

Georges Bernheim was very keen to buy one or two canvases, and he started the attack, always a difficult operation. It was hard work, but Monet sold him three canvases today for 18,000 francs each, including some hayricks and a view of Vintimille, very pretty but very sketchy, hardly grazing the canvas.

Monet assured me that he would like to have kept one canvas from each series he'd begun, that he hadn't had enough money, that he was young at the time.

"Have you kept any views of London?"

"Yes, for I did quite a few of them, and I was older. I spent three winters in London, where my son had gone to learn English. I so love London! but I love it only in the winter. It's nice in summer with its parks, but nothing like it is in winter with the fog, for without the fog London wouldn't be a beautiful city. It's the fog that gives it it's magnificent breadth. Those massive, regular blocks become grandiose within that mysterious cloak."

We then went on to discuss collectors, and I remarked to Monet that our French collectors are absurd with their absolute prejudice against mixing old and modern, but that I do it.

"I'll tell you," Monet replied, "that when we were starting out, Durand-Ruel said to us: 'The collectors find your canvases too chalky. To sell them, I'm obliged to varnish them with bitumen.' You'll understand, M. Gimpel, that we weren't exactly delighted with that, but one had to live!"

February 2 / A Pater

I picked it up at Wildenstein's. It's a little worn, it's *The Crowning of a Shepherd*, a rather large painting, which I sold to Agnew of London for 130,000 francs.

February 26 / Peary's discovery of the North Pole

He's dead. It was an amusing story. When he came back from the Pole and announced his discovery, he was treated like an impostor because a month before him Cook, another explorer, had returned from those parts and been universally feted, honored by kings, applauded by learned societies. But Cook had not discovered the Pole. In the polar regions he had learned of Peary's discovery, and had put on full speed to reach Europe first, where he boasted of his exploit. Peary was hard put to best his "rival," who was a man not without qualities.

March 5 / Death of Louis Duveen

My wife has eight brothers; this is the first to die. He was one of the most active members of the powerful house of Duveen, the world's leading firm dealing in pictures and art objects. Louis was a connoisseur of fine china, tapestry, and furniture.

March 21 / On Mary Cassatt

I was talking about her with Jaccaci; he too finds her on the decline. "She's become a viper," he said. "She was always very sharptongued. What she needed was a husband, or a lover. She sacrificed her chance of having children, sacrificed it to her art. When she was young and showed her adorable paintings of motherhood, no compliment irritated her more than 'One can feel that you're a woman!' She wished to be an artist exclusively. The other day I asked her: 'If you could start your life over again, would you marry?' She replied: 'There's only one thing in life for a woman: it's to be a mother.' "

March 29 / At Joseph Bardac's, the collector

Joseph lives at 1, avenue Marceau. His apartment is rather small but he leads a bachelor existence. He'll never marry. His collection, almost all in the drawing room, is noted for its gouaches in particular. I bought from him the two most beautiful pieces that he ever possessed: the bust of the Du Cayla by Houdon, which I sold to Frick, and Fragonard's *The Billet Doux*, which I sold to Jules Bache. Inborn taste plus a taste for speculation have made him a collector. Between the windows hangs a tapestry by Cozette. A Boucher, *The Painting*, has now replaced *The Billet Doux*. The shutters are always closed to keep the light from altering the gouaches. The two finest pictures are probably two pendants by Boucher, pastorals which were in Germany and which my father had bought in 1901 on the strength of photographs. Bardac would be only too glad to sell a portrait by Mme Labille-Guiard depicting Mme Elisabeth with a rather wooden regality. There is a fine Casanova suite of furniture. His favorite master is Hubert Robert, and he owns many of his works. They are hung in the dining room, apart from two small ones from the Doucet sale, which sold for around 80,000 francs,[5] and also *Porte Saint-Denis* and *Porte Saint-Martin*, exquisite pendants.

I asked Bardac how he started collecting. "About forty-five years ago," he replied, "my brother Sigismond gave us the taste for it. Noël followed suit, and then I. It was easy after the war of 1870; people didn't want anything old, it was all gold and red plush. I remember a lawsuit between a property owner and his architect. The former had instituted the action because the latter hadn't applied enough gold, and he was found guilty.

"At that time I bought at a sale in the Hôtel Drouot two boxes containing the most beautiful color engravings, one for eighty francs, the other for seventy. They'd be worth a million today, a million!

[5] *Corner of a Park: The Fountain*, 10 by 8 inches; *Corner of a Park: The Water Jet*, 10 by 8 inches.

"But I've better than that to tell you. A story I had from Hazard, the bronze caster of the Temple. He hadn't made money at his trade, but acquired some wealth late in life thanks to his collection of antique bronzes. He had a reputation for great honesty among his clientele; you could be sure he wouldn't sell you antique for modern; his clients obliged him to put on his invoice: 'Guaranteed modern.' "

April 23 / A meeting with Forain on my doorstep

I told him that I've got a magnificent thirteenth-century statue, and he asked to see it. He entered and I told him it was a St. Paul.

"No, it must be a St. Peter."

"But my apostle has a saber, M. Forain!"

"St. Peter is normally represented with keys, but he did carry a saber for you have him in the Gospels slitting Mark's ear, which he subsequently mends; and St. Paul always carries a naked sword. Read what Hello has to say about St. Peter and St. Paul, and the chapter in which the two apostles' spirituality is described in masterly fashion. Well, basically it's true, your statue gives more the impression of a St. Paul." [6]

I looked for Hello on my library shelves. Forain read the first page about the two apostles with great feeling, and from this reading I could sense how deeply Catholic he is. However, he didn't understand my statue, one of the masterpieces of Gothic art, but he did admire a little terra cotta by Houdon.

Since Forain's most active political period was during the Dreyfus affair, when he made such a violent attack on the officer whose innocence has since been universally acknowledged, I asked him: "So for a long time you believed Dreyfus guilty?" To my stupefaction, Forain replied: "I still believe it; I was sincere." "I don't doubt it," said I, "but what astonishes me is that you haven't changed your views." He gave me that most deplorable reason, so unexpected from a man as intelligent as he: "The General Staff couldn't have been wrong."

April 28 / Beurdeley Collection

He used to buy very cheaply, for he knew how to discover young

[6] I sold this statue to Raymond Pitcairn of Bryn Athen (U.S.A.). It is a masterpiece of the thirteenth century. Statue entirely polychrome. (Note appended 1931.)

talent; he had a nose for it. He was a pleasant, kindly person. He had asked me to sell for him in America the collection which will be dispersed tomorrow. He lived in a rather old house on the rue de Clichy, covered with paintings from the front door to the attic. I have drawn up a plan of his collection with as much accuracy as possible. The most outstanding paintings are hung on the three walls of the great gallery, in a large drawing room, in the dining room, and in his bedroom. The family, who didn't know who I am, watched me in astonishment as I took notes. Using the catalogue and my numbers, it was easy to master and re-create the plan.

April 30 / Law on the export of art objects

The Chamber voted a ridiculous law the other day. They imposed a duty of 100 per cent on the export of paintings and art objects.

Let them classify some objects of which we haven't got duplicates in our museums or on the walls of our churches, but to prohibit the export of art is to strike a blow at the spread of French thought.

May 8 / Abel Faivre, draftsman

I've asked Abel Faivre for news of the house he built some years ago opposite Anatole France's Villa Saïd, and we started talking of the writer, who after having intended to leave Paris for Versailles returned to his old house, which he had rebuilt.

I told Abel Faivre of my surprise on meeting Anatole France for the first time and being told by him, as if he had always known me, about the loss of his friend Mme de Caillavet and the immense grief it was to him.

"I'm not surprised," replied Abel Faivre, "for one day Anatole France said to me: 'I can take in great sorrows only by finding the words to express them.'"

May 11 / Sigismond Bardac sale

Bardac is dead. He was sharp and contrary, but sincere, as such people are. He was a good and fierce friend; I liked him very much. His sale began yesterday and is having a big success, the estimates are exceeded; and nothing much that is famous remains except for his La Tour pastels, as I bought his last really fine pieces two years ago.

The name of Bardac will long remain in the memory of the art world: the three brothers—Joseph, Noël, and Sigismond—all collected. Only Joseph is still alive.

May 14 / Death of Georges Petit

The people who have passed through this journal already begin to disappear. Only by dint of his immense business acumen was Petit a great figure in the art world, as in fact he never discovered a painter, and his taste inclined toward secondary masters like Meissonier, Besnard, and then Le Sidaner. Petit told me he had many of Meissonier's letters.

May 25 / Forain and faith

He absolutely insisted on giving me an etching which he has dedicated to me: *Christ Suffering Insults.*

If this series of etchings is so superior to all else he has done, it's because it possesses the religious faith of the great medieval epochs, and that's what I tell him. He speaks to me of faith, of the need to maintain it, to practice moral culture as one practices physical culture, so that on the day of the great cataclysm, the day of the clash between the physical life and the spiritual, the soul may be strong enough to resist.

I have questioned Forain on the origins of his own faith, and on the faith his parents probably had, and he explained: "My father was a respectable vineyard laborer without much religion; my mother was pious, but with the simple piety typical of our province. I was born in Reims. We're all Champenois in our family. My mother would have laughed at exaggerated piety: she was quite simply Christian and performed her religious duties regularly. On her last day she watched with serenity death's approach and prepared nobly and simply for her departure, saying, 'Put a taper here, another one there,' without any fear, in the very face of it.

"My piety sprang from having lived at the foot of the cathedral. I was five or six and didn't know why I looked at it like that. It illuminated my whole heart. I grew up. Around the age of eighteen life beckons, and you want to shock the bourgeois. What idiocy, to want to shock the bourgeois! This folly lasted until about thirty-five; then faith entered into me at one bound, and since then has only increased.

"Huysmans, my good friend Huysmans, developed as I did, and with the same rapidity. He speaks somewhere of the struggle between faith and passion. Passions are like military music. You hear it from afar, it grows, passes under your windows, stirring and magnificent, then begins fading, still beautiful, but weaker and weaker, and it vanishes. You have conquered."

NOTEBOOK 7

June 5, 1920–June 29, 1921

June 5 / Cézanne

Several dealers have just acquired the Hoogendijck Collection for a very high price. He was a Dutchman, only moderately well-off, who bought only Cézannes. His family then claimed that this was squandering his fortune and went to court to have him certified insane. They obtained a court order. Thus the unfortunate man died in an asylum.

The collection could not, in theory, leave Holland without a very large customs duty being paid. A certain person undertook to get the pictures past the frontier. He told the excise man that they were all his own work, which he was going to try to sell in Paris, and the man answered pityingly that he wouldn't have any success!

June 8 / Visit to Dunand

He lives at 72, rue Hallé, at the rear of a courtyard. The hall is very narrow. A board on which about ten helmets are hanging is fixed to the wall above the coatstand, on the right; they are trial models made by him for the Great War. Everyone knows now that he invented the one-piece helmet, that he made the designs in a war factory one afternoon and a thief stole them from him that night. This thief got to the Minister of War before he did, and when Dunand appeared there, it is said that they smiled at him as at an idiot.

All that is very remote to him. "I've better things to create than death helmets," he declares, "and anyway, what's the use of making them elegant?"

The actress Ida Rubinstein has ordered a helmet from him, which he is making out of aluminum. He turned it over, the better to show us the interior, which is superbly beaten and almost as beautiful as the outside. She is going to wear it in the role of Cleopatra. It is all white with a gold circling, and a green serpent rising out of it right in the middle. This is already in place, looking very dangerous.

Rubinstein is going to give a few performances at the Opéra, and if the hall is filled every time, she will lose only 500,000 francs, as each evening will cost her some 700,000.

Her friend, an Englishman, offered her a pearl necklace, and she replied: "I'd prefer a splendid performance." All the artists and craftsmen of Paris are working for her at this moment. Worth, the couturier, is preparing costumes which will cost her between 15,000 and 20,000 francs apiece. Beside the actress's costume lies a helmet twined with gold wreaths surmounted by a Gallic cock with its neck and beak thrust violently forward. Sometimes such lifeless objects meet with circumstances far more hazardous than those we normally have to face; for it is the helmet of Foch, of the victor in the Great War.

Dunand shows his work without ostentation or superfluous explanations, as if quite unaware of his talent. He is of medium height but gigantically sturdy; quite distinguished, although his face is veiled by a slight growth of beard. His eyes are brown, the color of old wood, his features regular like those of a Christ, but a Christ who has not suffered.

"I started," he told me, "by doing sculpture with Dante, that strange artist who works with solid blocks of steel. It's no exaggeration to say that he takes twenty years to finish some works. Of course there are some art forms which are merely a matter of patience, like the lacquer which I love so much! Just look, and think how much work goes into preparing this stuff and making it. Here you have some trial attempts. On these tablets you can see the various stages of preparation. At the bottom, the first layer of lacquer, then comes the second, and at the top the twentieth. So you have to varnish or paint twenty times—or rather forty, as the job has to be repeated on the other side to keep the wood from warping; otherwise it would crack, for you wouldn't believe how easily the lacquer can twist even the hardest wood into a semicircle. Actually, not forty but as many as a hundred preparations are required, since after each varnishing you have to polish and before each varnishing there have to be twenty seasonings, each lasting four days. It'll surprise you to learn that the seasonings require damp conditions, and a dark room where water flows continuously, and that success is more certain at the full moon. So you'll understand that it's a positively Oriental labor!"

Dunand had me touch two or three pieces of black lacquer, about the size of calling cards and deep and clear as mirrors; they are devoid of pattern, but the substance is so beautiful that I should adore to possess one.

There are also beautiful examples of colored lacquers on metals. All this is contained in a little room furnished in the modern style with a comfortable divan and pretty cushions. In a large showcase there are beautiful plates of silver and steel alloy. In farmhouse dressers which he partly opens we saw vessels which he calls "snakeskin," some of them magnificent. Next he showed us into the studio, where a child of twelve, his son, who strangely resembles him, was at work. The boy was hammering away exuberantly at the metal. Dunand took the little hammer from his hand and started beating the metal plate, his motion at once powerful and controlled.

I have often visited sculptors and watched the clay kindle into life under their fingers; the miracle is splendid, but not as impressive as seeing this flat, very delicate disk turning and turning under the hard blows of the hammer and taking shape to finish as a work of art. Dunand doesn't love money and his highest price is 500 francs. He finds happiness in the act of creation alone. He sells a great deal but makes no fortune.

June 15 / At Bourdelle's, the sculptor

I hadn't seen him since my visit to him with Captain Snowden Fahnestock, and he asked me immediately if the idea of the monument is still being considered. I reassured him, as he had given up expecting anything. It isn't the money but the thought that someone else might have been chosen to execute the monument that chills his heart.

Bourdelle speaks scornfully of the monument to Miss Cavell unveiled yesterday, presented by the newspaper *Le Matin* to the city of Paris. "What a dreadful idea," he said, "to go and put a Prussian helmet between the legs of that heroic nurse who was shot by the Germans. Just think, what a defilement, that helmet imposed for all eternity on this martyr!" [1]

He told me that he is giving a course in drawing for the pupils at the Gobelin tapestry works. But I gathered that he doesn't get on well with the administration, since he wants to see and do everything. "It doesn't interest me," he said, "to teach them drawing if I can't afterward see my students applying color and above all interpreting that color! And that idiotic method of teaching them only the antique, of letting them copy only Venuses and Apollos, and then five minutes later putting them on to the making of tapestry! They should start by teaching me tapestry again. My grandfather was a weaver, I remember him and a little of his methods. Give me a moment with the workmen to learn their trade, what I call the trade, and then I'll be able to teach the students something new!"

September 18 / Painting goes up in price

This applies to modern painting. The artists want to be paid more. The newspapers tell us that automobile parts have gone up by 80 per cent. Matisse is up by 75 per cent, so I'm told by Georges Bernheim, who has just signed a new contract with the painter, in association with Bernheim Brothers.

Remark of Renoir's

I've met an American who has read an article I wrote on Renoir in the American revue *The Dial*. "One day," he told me, "I called on Renoir, accompanied by one of my fellow countrymen who worked in the petroleum industry. The painter asked him his profession. 'I work in oil,' answered my friend. To which Renoir replied: 'We're both in the same business.'"

[1] Bourdelle was right. It is a frightful monument.

September 23 / A Goya

The Princesse de Bourbon; this painting has just been sold for 450,000 francs.

September 26 / A short conversation with Forain

We were crossing the rue Spontini when he said to me: "I've met your famous Greek collector Ambatielos, who bought your celebrated La Tour, the full-length *Président de Rieux*. The first thing he said to me, and let's not forget his accent, was: 'I've paid 1,200,000 francs for it.' I replied: 'When people spend so much money on a single painting, it must be that they don't plan to buy many.' He's a real *nouveau riche*.

"On the way back to La Bourboule, where he was staying, he saw a shepherd with his flock and dog. Getting out of his car, he went up to the shepherd and asked him, 'How much is your dog?' 'He's not for sale, my dog.' 'I'll pay a high price for him, name a big price.' 'No, he's not for sale at any price.' Ambatielos just couldn't understand it. He simply can't get over it!"

Forain took me into his studio and started painting. He was working on a picture representing a Calvary: a German is guarding some women, his "prisoners of war." But suddenly, with one sweep of a cloth, Forain removed a head and then replaced it, painting it almost as quickly as he rubbed it out. I told him I consider Georges Bernheim the most honest of the art dealers, and that he wants to buy some Forains. Forain considers this "most honest" just a phrase.

"Talking of art dealers," he said, "I lunched the other day with Mayer of Colnaghi's, who asked me my age. Maybe he wants to see me become an old master to get a better price for my work. I replied: 'Sixty-eight, does that reassure you?'"

I told Forain about the repartee yesterday in the Chamber of Deputies, when a member of the opposition cried out to his adversaries: "You're bowing and scraping, prostrate in the dust!" "Let's see you do that!" they called back at him.

October 1 / A witticism of Forain's

A son who had quarreled with his father went to the father's funeral. "It's the first time they've been out together," said the painter.

October 8 / My first journal

Among old papers I've come across a notebook, a journal I had begun in 1910. It lasted a fortnight, I hadn't the resolution to continue it. In 1912 I made a fresh attempt, but a mere two pages were the result. Oh, well, some real strength of character was needed to bring off such a task.

I tried again during the first four or five days of the war and again I stopped. I began the present one after having read Casanova's admirable memoirs. It was reading these that encouraged me to write. I am going to transcribe here my first attempts. I haven't kept the third.

> [*At this point the author interpolates ten dated entries for the year 1910. The journal resumes in sequence with the entry for October 9, 1920.*]

September 27, 1910

Count André de Ganay has brought me a small terra-cotta bust of a young boy, in an antique green, and wants my opinion. "It's modern," I tell him, "but very pretty."

Nathan Wildenstein[2] happened to arrive. He examined the object and said it was a fake, but remarkable, and added that some modern sculptors produce works much superior to certain ancient busts for which we may pay 100,000 francs. He mentioned a certain Leguay who twenty years ago made with consummate skill fake terra cottas that he sold initially for 1,000 francs apiece; but he produced too many and then couldn't find buyers who would pay over 200 francs. M. de Yturbe, who wanted to fox his friends, has one of the pieces, which Wildenstein got him for a few hundred francs. Wildenstein added: "Yturbe has never even paid me, he pretends not to remember the order, and the bust still adorns his mantelpiece!"

The Count de Ganay ranks among the cream of the nobility, and is always on the lookout for anything the aristocracy might have for the antique market. He keeps us informed. He thinks that one of his nephews, the Count de Saint-Sauveur, at present a soldier, will be the Countess de Béarn's heir. She has no children. This boy displays a keen taste for art. On his advice the other day the Marquise de Ganay bought

[2] At that time my associate. (Note appended 1931.)

from us the full-length portrait of the Infanta by Del Mazo, for 90,000 francs.

This morning I went to see Joseph Duveen, the eldest son of J. Joseph Duveen, who was the founder of the firm; he was born in Holland and arrived in England maybe fifty years ago with Henry Duveen, his younger brother. There they opened a small antique shop. They were the first to think of having an outlet in the United States. Out of the collaboration of the two brothers this powerful firm was born, and today it is the world's leading one. Joseph Duveen does business as he would wage war, tyrannically. He is an audacious buyer and an irresistible salesman. But he is childish too, and indeed asks me like a child what people think of him and his firm. "That you are a great seller and that you have the most beautiful pieces." "They're right, don't you think?" He showed me a large sketch, the architect Sergent's plan for their new house in New York, a copy of the Gabriel buildings on the Place de la Concorde. "When it's built," Joe told me, "French objects will go up by thirty to forty per cent, do you see?" "Yes, I understand, to pay your building costs."

September 28

The banker David-Weill came today to see a superb picture by Goya, a bullfight originally in the Salamanca Collection, and bought by me from Veil-Picard. His great friend Alphonse Kann has been urging him to come.

Kann drops in each evening to ask if his friend David-Weill has called on us. Today I told him that he had done so, but added that his client remained silent before the Spanish work, so Kann will have to engineer things.

Changing the subject, Kann told me this anecdote: "Baroness Adolphe de Rothschild went into an antique shop in Germany, asked the owner the price of a clock, and wanted to know if it came from a great house. 'An excellent one,' answered the dealer: 'I bought it from a baron who authorized me to give his name only after it was sold.' The baroness bought it and the antique dealer informed her that it had belonged to Baron Adolphe, her husband."

James Stillman, president of the First National Bank of America, came with his two sisters to see a Chardin. I addressed him in his own language, and he replied [in French]: "I don't speak English." After a silence he asked me [in English]: "When are you going to New York?" His sisters were rather shy in the presence of their great brother who had made good, and he was not very communicative himself! He simply asked the names and prices of the masters. If a picture interested him, he looked at another. His black eyes, hemmed in by large brows of the same hue, seemed fixed behind his spectacles, giving him an air of forcefulness and gravity. He is Rockefeller's banker. I told him that the Chardin had been sold and offered to show him a photograph of it. He had come to buy it and didn't want to see the photo.[3]

Friedländer, the German, who for some years had a certain authority as an expert on Flemish primitives, has just paid me a visit. His influence stems from the support Dr. Bode, director of the Berlin Museum, has given him. Moreover, he is extremely knowledgeable. I went to see him last July in Berlin to ask him for an authentication of a picture that I had got back in an exchange with Baron Edmond de Rothschild, a portrait by Bruyn that is today owned by Benjamin Altman of New York.[4] At that time I also showed him two vertical pictures of saints, of the school of Simon Marmion.[5] I saw Dr. Bode as well and showed him a splendid picture, an unknown Ruysdael, for which he wrote me a letter. He asked my opinion of the waxen bust attributed to Leonardo da Vinci which he had bought in London. This purchase caused a great stir a year ago and was discussed in the international press; an Englishman wrote that he had seen this bust being executed by an English sculptor named Lucas who lived in Folkestone. Opinion was quite divided, but Dr. Bode's enemies loudly delighted in the matter, among others B. Berenson, the critic of Italian art, who hasn't forgiven Bode for daring on occasion to give his opinion on Italian pictures. He cut out articles from all the papers and went about with his pockets stuffed with clippings. I saw him at the time, as he was staying at the Ritz. He was convinced, and rightly so, that the bust was a fake. Feeling ran tremendously high in Germany; even chemists were consulted; they

[3] Wildenstein had just sold this picture, but soon afterward the buyer returned it.
[4] Altman and I exchanged it when I sold him a Holbein.
[5] I sold them to Michel Dreicer of New York. They were to go to the Metropolitan.

took minute samples of the wax and found that it contained chemical elements unknown in Leonardo's time; but the Emperor Wilhelm II betook himself with great pomp to the museum and declared by the power of his sword that the bust was genuine.

September 29

James Speyer of New York is looking for art objects and Louis XVI furniture for his new mansion in New York; I showed him a Louis XVI suite that belonged to Mme Elisabeth,[6] and he says it's Empire. I showed him a pair of wall candelabra which belonged to Marie Antoinette, and he declares them Empire too.

Paul Warburg of New York, who doesn't like the French school, was struck with wonder before my two marvelous Nattier pastels which I bought from Sigismond Bardac. I have offered to show him the Veil-Picard Collection.

September 30

Around eleven o'clock I was ushered into Veil-Picard's on the rue de Courcelles, a mansion built around 1850 between a court and a garden. In the passage there is a statue of Apollo by Vassé, which came from the Duke de Luynes (Château de Dampierre). Veil-Picard appeared informally dressed. I asked him if I could bring Warburg around, and he replied in his peasant, Besançon accent: "It's all the same to me if he criticizes my collection. I know it's magnificent, I don't need to be told. Isn't it magnificent?" "Unique." "Come and see it again." I followed him, as he continued: "Who has any gouaches, who has any drawings? Nobody knows the gouache. Who, now, in Paris has a collection—apart from Groult, who's dead? And even he! Excepting for one or two pieces, what did he have? Let's not talk about Doucet; he has nothing. No Boucher, no Fragonard, barely a few pastels, and even then all of it small stuff.[7] But name me some collections: the Countess de Béarn, let's say, what has she got? The Fragonard from the Kann Collection. Yes, that's fine. And another Fragonard which I turned down. She has the Boucher that was in Mme Tussaud's waxwork museum in London and

---

[6] Since sold to the Baron Maurice de Rothschild.
[7] In 1912 Doucet sold this "small stuff" for nearly 14 million francs.

which is by Taraval. It's a mishmash, that collection! Come and look at my Fragonards: *Le Retour à la maison*, bought for 15,000 francs; *La Gimblette*, 25,000 francs. Go get your Americans so they may learn!"

October 1

Viewed the Veil-Picard Collection with Warburg.

October 4

James Stillman came with Mary Cassatt to show her my Velázquez. She's a great artist. She interprets maternity in a very Anglo-Saxon fashion; her infants are always fresh from the bath, and their mother only cuddles them when they've been washed. But how blooming they are, and how pink!

Mary Cassatt greatly loves old art, and it's really thanks to her that I've sold Stillman my Rembrandt *The Portrait of Titus*, from the Duke of Rutland's Collection. He paid $140,000 for it. Mary Cassatt bullies Stillman, and that's how she's made a collector of him. In front of the Velázquez she told him: "Buy this canvas, it's shameful to be rich like you. Such a purchase will redeem you." Stillman smiled. She already knew my Velázquez. She told me that twenty years ago it was owned by the painter Madrazo, who sold it for 6,000 francs since it wasn't authenticated. As for me, I found it with a German painter living in Paris, who asked me 50,000 francs, thinking it was by Del Mazo. I was certain it was by Velázquez; it would have been too expensive for a Mazo. I took it to de Beruete in Madrid, who gave me an authentication. It's a portrait of the queen, and the Spanish expert told me he considered it one of the most beautiful. I believe Miss Cassatt is confusing it with another canvas, since this German painter assured me his picture came from a sale by the Berlin Museum forty years ago, when that institution was trying to get rid of its rubbish.

October 5

Sigismond Bardac wanted to see the Velázquez again and quoted Carolus Duran's quip: "Velázquez and me." Carolus Duran used to tell how before he was born his mother went to a fortuneteller who predicted that she would have a son as great as Titian. And Carolus added:

"She was mistaken; she ought to have said Velázquez." The anecdotes about Carolus Duran are numerous. An American woman was posing in his studio; palette in hand, he cried, before putting the first touch on the canvas: "Come to me, Velázquez!" A moment of silence, and then the American woman said to him: "You haven't called loud enough, your servant hasn't heard."

This morning the Marquis de Biron saw a man who does fake Hubert Roberts. Biron owns a magnificent collection of frames. Bardac dropped in and we talked of the art of woodwork; Bardac is astonished that in seven years we haven't sold this magnificent suite of Mme Elisabeth's, which he so loves. He insists, and rightly, that the French understand woodwork, that it will take the Americans four hundred years, and that the English will never show a taste for it.

October 6

At ten o'clock this morning I went up to the Ritz Hotel, to the room of my friend Berenson, the American born in Poland, or of Polish parentage, who is thought to be English, and is called the Italian critic. He was lying down. His small face, like that of an anemic lion cub, looked very tired. He seemed ill, and I asked how he felt. He replied very gravely: "I'm in love, it's stupid at my age, forty-five. I haven't slept!"

And I asked him yesterday for news of his wife!

6 P.M.

Opening *Le Temps*, I read that a revolution has broken out in Portugal. The fate of the king and queen isn't certain: the queen to whom I showed the Rudolph Kann Collection two years ago. Wildenstein and I had bought the collection with Duveen, and to enhance its value we got the heirs to agree to keep the house for six months, to enable us to show the works in their setting. We were then snowed under with inquiries, and the whole of Paris, along with distinguished visitors, deemed it a signal favor to be allowed to visit it. There were more than twelve Rembrandts, some Hals, Van Dycks, Rubens, Memlings, Cuyps, Hobbemas, Ghirlandajos, a marvelous one of the French school, some Boucher tapestries, Lemoyne statues, Pigalles, etc.

The queen of Portugal, on her way to Paris, expressed a desire to see the collection, and I showed it her. For two hours I took her around the mansion. Her graciousness and her eagerness for instruction were touching. She found in it a bust of one of her ancestors in which she was greatly interested. He is a Bourbon. She talked to me of the magnificent eighteenth-century French plate in the Royal Castle in Lisbon, inviting me to come and see it. She left, declaring herself in my debt, and said that she would be able to thank me properly only if I came to Lisbon. If a woman could save a monarchy by her charm, it would be Queen Amelia.

October 7

Hector Baltazzi has given me the latest news of the revolution in Portugal. The king and queen are in Gibraltar, safe and sound. We talked about the frailty of empires and indulged in speculations on the fate of Austro-Hungary after Franz Joseph. I posed the question frankly to Baltazzi: "What do you know about the Mayerling drama? It's said that you were involved in it." "It's even been said," he replied, "that it was I who assassinated the emperor's son, Archduke Rudolf. I know the truth, it's simple and idyllic, but it's been soiled and despoiled. It is a lovely story; people wouldn't believe it. The victim was my niece, the daughter of my sister, Marie Vetsera." Baltazzi pronounces Marie in the English way, Mary. "The archduke met her at Countess X's, niece of the empress and daughter of a dancer. He was captivated by her wondrous beauty, and the countess connived to have them meet. How was Marie's mother to suspect the countess, who was always asking her to send around her daughter! So Rudolf, who was mad about her, asked the emperor, his father, for permission to marry her. He had been married in 1881 to the Princess Stephanie, who had given him only a daughter, and all hope of direct succession was lost. The emperor wrote to Rome, and the Pope answered that he could not refuse the court of Austria; but Franz Joseph did not give his consent. In church one morning, before all the court and in Rudolf's presence, she sang the 'Ave Maria.' A day or two afterward Rudolf and two or three friends dined in a hunting lodge at Mayerling. The dinner was very simple, the company sober; Rudolf went up to his room, where he found Marie, who had entered through the kitchen. They had decided to die: he fired a bullet into her left temple, then killed himself. They had written eight letters to the emperor and his entourage, and four to various members of the Baltazzi family. The eight letters were written in full lucidity, I am positive. At the sound of the explosions, the two friends who had remained below, one of them a Cobourg, went up and found the corpses. Cobourg took the eight letters and rushed to Vienna, but didn't dare present himself before the emperor; it was to the Empress Elisabeth that he broke the news, and it was she who informed the emperor. He read the four letters addressed to him as well as to her, in which the young couple said they were going to die because they couldn't marry. The young girl added: 'I die for my beloved Rudolf, and by his hand.' Franz Joseph immediately called together the family, and summoned certain counselors and Alessandro Baltazzi. It was decided not to publish the true version because religion forbade suicide and his son couldn't then be buried by the Church. Hohenlohe advised telling the truth. Presently they changed their minds and decided that doctors would examine the body and declare that Rudolf had killed himself in a moment of madness. The emperor had had Alessandro Baltazzi summoned to open, in his family's name, the four other letters, which confirmed the first four. In the one the young girl addressed to her mother, she asked her forgiveness, saying that she was going to die for Rudolf and by his hand. The contradictions sprang from all the hesitations, evasions, and confusion round the emperor: telegrams sent to sovereign courts like Germany and England were contradictory. At the time I was confined to my room, having been injured some days before in a driving accident. My head was bandaged, and when the reporters came to interview me they found me thus; hence the story that I was the assassin of the Archduke Rudolf. The countess was taken to the border. She lives at present in Munich with an actor."

October 8

Sir Edgar Vincent,[8] who owns the Rembrandt shown last year at the Grafton Gallery in London, came to see the Cuyp *Flight into Egypt* from the Kann Collection, which has the most beautiful, most golden sunset created by art before Turner.[9]

Sir Edgar, whose wife must be the prettiest woman in England, is

[8] Subsequently Lord Aberdeen. He was sent after the war as ambassador to Germany, where he constituted himself the inveterate defender of the Germans against France. They adored him and called him "Our Lord."

[9] This picture was almost completely destroyed in a fire on a French transatlantic liner en route to the United States.

himself tall and well proportioned, with a broad, short, pointed beard, a mild gaze, and blue eyes. He is really a magnificent old man. He was sent by the British government to Egypt at the time of annexation to look after financial interests; subsequently, when the Turkish revolution broke out, he was president of the Ottoman Debt. He had been in the Transvaal, having been sent with Barnato against the gold and diamond-mine magnates Wernher and Beit, former petty employees who had left Hamburg for adventure. Barnato was some kind of clown who had gone to South Africa to tread the boards, just at the time when the mines were discovered. He emerged as the great businessman of the Transvaal. He had amassed perhaps £6 million when he embarked for England. While on board, in the grip of delirium tremens, he plunged into the sea.

October 9, 1920 / At Cluny

I love museums on Sundays, as the crowds are so entertaining. Today at Cluny a father was showing his son some arms; "Do you see this gun, Paul?" "Papa, I want to do pipi." "It's a flintlock." "I want to do pipi, papa!" "Look, it was worked with this trigger." "Pipi, papa!" and the child started howling: "Pipi, papa, pipi, papa!" The father was furious at having to interrupt his lecture, in which he'd been intending to show off all his knowledge.

Visit to Claude Monet

Georges Bernheim came to pick me up at 9:30 in his "16" Pan-hard. A turn of the crank, and we were off to Giverny. He drove the car himself and we stopped at Rueil for gas. We got out, a donkey was browsing nearby, I went over to speak to it and stroke it. It belonged to two old women who sell haberdashery from village to village. They complained about business: "The cost of living," they said, "is so high these days!" But they added: "We were lucky to get this little donkey, he's so nice, it's sad that he's growing old, he's been very happy with us, he's like a child. We're going to feed him: he has lunch with us and shares our dessert, a pear today, and he gets a piece of sugar at every meal; he insists on having it, but he's so good, so good. I tell you, monsieur, he's like a child!"

Because of the donkey I bought two pairs of socks from them, and we drove on. At two minutes to noon we entered the house of Claude Monet, who has passed his eightieth year. He is as hale as ever, but a bit deafer. I asked about his eyes, and he answered: "They're getting worse, they're getting worse. I have to wear glasses for reading, and most of all for eating fish." He introduced his son to us, a man of about thirty-five.

"Monsieur is served!" announced the butler, dressed all in white, and we entered the famous dining room, so pretty because of its yellow colors, tone upon tone, painted by Monet, and so charming too because of its forty Japanese prints. Other prints decorate a small room preceding the dining room, this one with blue walls, similarly tone over tone, but the color slightly less successful. I took my place on the right of Monet's daughter-in-law. I could see the garden and its banks of flowers; Georges was opposite me, on Monet's right, and the one son on his father's left. Georges was facing two sideboards and admired them as much as I the garden. I then turned around and joined my cries of admiration to those of my friend. These sideboards are simple, and charming with their openwork panels, but why so interesting? Because they're painted by Claude Monet in two divine yellows, matching the three side tables and the chairs. Monet informs us that these sideboards come from the Fécamp district.

Bernheim mentioned a fake Renoir which he saw shown in the shop window of a dealer right on the rue Miromesnil. Monet told us about the fake Monets he has seen, on which the signature is always very good, better than the painting. Georges is of the same opinion. He considers that Renoirs are imitated better because people work at it harder, whereas they think it's easy to do a Monet!

"Is it true," Georges asked the artist, "what I've heard at the Rodin Museum?" "Perfectly true, I'm going to give the Hôtel de Biron twelve of my last decorative canvases, each measuring some four and a half square yards, but they'll have to build the room as I want it, according to my plan, and the pictures will leave my house only when I am satisfied with the arrangements. I'm leaving these instructions to my heirs, for I've painted these pictures with a certain decorative aim, and I want it to be attained. They will build on the boulevard des Invalides side, where there is more daylight, and even there I'll be up against the light, which has always defeated me. I ask myself how a Ruysdael or even a Holbein saw nature, and I don't manage to understand. Hobbema sometimes divined the light, as in his pathway in the National Gallery, but the great landscapist is Corot." "The *good* Corot," interrupted Georges Bernheim. "The *good* Corot," said Claude Monet. "I don't know about that, but what I do know is that he was very bad for us. The swine! He barred the door of the Salon to us. Oh, how he slashed at us, pursued us like criminals. And how all of us without exception admired him! I didn't know him. I knew none of the 1830 masters; they didn't want to know us. One day at the Robinson ball a storm broke out and people took shelter under the awning. Millet was pointed out to me. I said to a friend: 'I admire him so much, I must speak to him.' My friend stopped me. 'Don't go. Millet is terribly antisocial, full of pride, he'll tear you to pieces.' Daumier was as frightful as Corot to us; only Diaz and Daubigny defended us, the latter energetically. He was on the jury, and he resigned because we were turned down."

Georges told us a story about Sacha Guitry, with whom he lunched in London three months ago. Sacha arrived with his wife and father at a cheap restaurant near Paris, the owner recognized them and propelled them into the dining room, saying: "I'm going to announce you." And he yelled: "Three lunches, three!"

Talking of lunches, Claude Monet's was marvelous. First some hors d'oeuvres with the best Normandy butter, a succulent veal risotto with spinach, two chickens for five people: the first one roasted, which nobody touched; the second extraordinary, done with black olives; then a tart, a real tidbit, and fruit as beautiful as flowers. Monet has always adored the table. I watched him sitting over his little glass, his enormous little glass, for we had moved into his drawing-room-studio. Georges was talking to him about the magnificent pictures which Rosenberg bought from Mme Deudon in the South of France for 1,100,000 francs, among them *The Gare Saint-Lazare*, which Monet told us he sold direct to Deudon. In this connection, Monet told me that he had notebooks in which, up to about twenty years ago, he listed all the prices of the canvases he sold. He has a superb memory; thus Bernheim was telling him about one of his pictures which Alphonse Kann bought some days ago, *Two Women on the Sand*, and he said: "I did it at Trouville in 1870." In fact, the canvas bears that date.

I questioned Monet on his past. At twelve, he lost his mother, but already she had urged him to draw and had praised his plaster models. "I was expelled," he said, "from all the schools in Le Havre. I covered all my books with sketches—worse, all my friends' books. Later my father was opposed to my vocation."

Monet showed us the photograph of one of his canvases portraying his father looking at the sea; the picture is said to be in America. He sold it for 400 francs to Pratt, whose widow sold it for 40,000 to Durand-Ruel, and Monet wanted to buy it back from the dealer. He pointed out the pole with a flag on either side of the composition, and mentioned that at the time this composition was considered very daring. "I'm very fond of flags," he added. "On the first national holiday on June 30th, I went out with my working equipment to the rue Montorgueil; the street was decked out with flags and the crowd was going wild. I noticed a balcony, I went up and asked permission to paint, which was granted me. Then I came down again incognito. Ah! it was a good time, a good time, although living wasn't always easy. Durand-Ruel was our guardian angel, but as his admiration for us brought him to the worst financial disasters, he was obliged to move to America. For some time there was no longer anyone to buy our canvases from us, and then I sought out Georges Petit. It wasn't easy to persuade him. His father had done us a lot of harm. People who hadn't wanted impressionists on the rue Laffitte bought them on the rue de Sèze. Competition arose between the two streets and was very profitable to us. I remember, one day, going to Arnold and Tripp with two canvases under my arm, but I wasn't admitted to the back of the shop, where the two partners and their employees examined what I had brought. They were having a big laugh. I heard: 'It's Monet, the impressionist, what a scream!' And the laughter got worse than ever. Lifting the curtain, they saw me, and they laughed in my face as they handed back my two canvases.

"Three of us, Degas, Renoir, and I have had our revenge. We can say we have had a happy life, the others died too young—Sisley misunderstood, and Jongkind too! The latter was not even known in his own country. I have often mentioned him to Dutch people who have told me: 'We don't know who that painter is; he's certainly not one of our countrymen.' The greatest of the misunderstood was Delacroix; oddly enough he was misunderstood by successive generations too. He's one of my idols." "But," said Bernheim, "I've sold a Delacroix, *The Battle of Poitiers*, to the Copenhagen Museum for 300,000 francs." Monet replied, "Three million is what it's worth!"

The conversation shifted to living painters. Monet admires Vuillard but finds Bonnard, whom Renoir so much admired, very uneven. I'm going to meet Vuillard soon, and I'll tell him Monet's opinion, and Vuillard will blush fiercely.

We went for a walk in the garden. It's a perfect garden, a panorama of flowers whose beauty is deeply moving; they are so tall on their stems that they seem to walk along with us. Today for the first time Monet took me across the road and the railway line beyond which his garden extends, but where the landscape changes its appearance completely. There is Monet's pond where his water lilies float, surrounded by his pale willows, a pond which he has created as God created the caprices of nature.

We went back near the house, and passed a studio on the left, which I had never entered. I told him so and he showed me in. I found very beautiful works in it. I admired an immense canvas of a country outing, with four life-size women.[1] I asked him if he would sell it to me and he answered: "Ah, that one is special for me, it's my first salon 'reject.' Now the state is buying it from me for 200,000 francs, and has asked for two years to pay; it's to compensate me for the canvases I'm giving to the Rodin Museum."

Monet is a true Norman!

Opposite this picture I noticed a very fine canvas, even larger, a luncheon party on the grass, six persons. It has scaled away a little, as Bernheim pointed out to him. "That," explained Monet, "is because the canvas stayed rolled up for years with a man who had taken it in pawn; in fact, it was considerably larger, and when it was returned to me, I had to cut it down."

Among the beautiful canvases I noted two pictures of women in boats. In one of them they are rowing, dressed in pink and looking like pelicans; in the other, also women in a boat, they are in blue, the whole canvas is a blue harmony. It is his most beautiful work.[2]

[1] Today in the Louvre. (Note appended 1931.)
[2] I have since bought it. (Note appended 1931.)

Then we were back in his first studio. Georges asked him the price of two canvases, of ice floes: 30,000 francs apiece. Astonished, Bernheim offered him 20,000, but the artist didn't give way. Bernheim remarked that before the war his price would have been 10,000 francs and even quite recently only 18,000. Monet's son and daughter-in-law were sorry to see that Georges wouldn't buy the paintings, and Monet said: "There was a time when to sell a canvas for one hundred francs would have made me very happy, and I would have felt extremely honored."

However, I felt that Bernheim's very definite refusal had touched the painter's pride as much as in the past the rebuffs of Arnold and Tripp.

October 12 / Forain on Monet

We had talked with Monet of Forain, who was one of his great friends, and he had said to us: "Forain must have something to say about me, I'd love to know it." "I'll tell you at our next meeting," I had replied to Monet.

When I saw Forain come out of his house, I spoke to him of Monet. "A good friend, a good friend," he said. "I know a remark of Degas's about him. Monet was showing his water lilies for the first time; it was at Durand-Ruel's. Degas went to see them, then he went next door to Vollard's. Monet found him there, about to leave, and Degas said to him: 'I only stayed a moment at your exhibition, your pictures intoxicated me.' Monet went off and Vollard said to Degas: 'I thought you'd been angry with Monet since the Dreyfus affair.' 'Yes,' replied Degas, 'but for such an occasion I'm reconciled.' "

October 14 / A businessman's remark

Joe Duveen replied today to one of his employees who said to him, "It's one o'clock, and I want to go to lunch": "Sir, when I was young, I ate only on Sundays!"

October 16 / The Durand-Ruel Collection

There will never again be such a collection of impressionists. Perhaps a hundred Renoirs, a hundred Monets, Degas, Manets, Pissarros,

Cézannes by the dozen, pictures hung quite simply in two adjoining apartments on the rue de Rome. In the first lives Durand-Ruel senior and his eldest son. The collection is valued at 15 million and is the result of the father's poor business affairs. As he couldn't sell his pictures, he kept them. The eldest son, who showed me the collection, pointed out a Monet worth a good 30,000 francs which his father bought in 1878 for fifty francs at a time when this sum was hard for him to spare.

The apartment is a maze, for all the rooms are alike and all are covered with canvases of the same masters. The furnishings are horrible and must date from the time of their great poverty. It's all redolent of the poor Republic. Nearly all the bedrooms have iron bedsteads.

In the first room the very doors are painted by Espagnat. On the walls are several Boudins. Durand-Ruel told me Boudin was Monet's master and that they met on the quays of Le Havre, each carrying his easel. Boudin sensed the talent in this young man of seventeen who painted really quite badly and who was indulging himself there in Normandy in landscapes of an insipid oriental flavor.

There are Forains from the artist's youth; the "Fauve" showed no mean talent for painting even then. I saw Renoir's *Young Girls at the Piano*. There are four or five of these in existence because Renoir, having been commissioned by the state, studied the subject seriously. In fact he went too far and worked over the one in the Luxembourg too much, as he himself admitted to Durand-Ruel, and he was less successful with it.

We came to one of the most beautiful pictures in the collection. Renoir's *Woman Dancer*, an almost life-size dancer. Before the war Baron de Rothschild offered 500,000 francs for it. She is charming, this very straight, very white little dancer, with her frivolous tutu and her grave air of a little girl who has to earn her living. Durand-Ruel said to me: "She belonged to the famous Deudon, who, for reasons of inheritance, gave her to one of his cousins, and he sold her to us for 10,000 francs about twenty-five years ago.[3]

In one of the drawing rooms there are six still lifes: one of pigeons by Monet, two by Renoir, and three by Cézanne; the style of the

---

[3] Today owned by Widener, in Philadelphia. (Note appended 1931.)

latter is admirable. "All our Cézannes are signed," continued Durand-Ruel. "Several come from his friend Chocquet, a poor working man who ruined himself buying impressionists and whose sale brought in 300,000 francs. Today it might reach 3 million. His heirs were provincial; you can take it from me that they had no idea what a fortune they had inherited. Cézanne could not be approached, except through Vollard. Cézanne, who had been a close friend of Monet's, had long been absent from Paris, and when he returned and met him they dined together, gay and exhilarated, and made an appointment for the following day. But next day Monet received these lines from Cézanne: 'I was very glad to see you again, but it is better that this meeting be the last of our life.' Vollard, being on too intimate terms with the Cézanne family, has not told, and could not tell, all about him; but it is known that the painter left his wife and children, for fear of their influence. Monet told me the following story. He was on the street with Cézanne when the latter, walking ahead of him, stumbled. Monet put his hand firmly on Cézanne's shoulder to steady him, and the terrified Cézanne nearly fainted."

We passed on to another room with doors painted by Monet, who has no sense of décor. These are pictures, as Monet himself has acknowledged. There are fine canvases in this room, including two vertical pictures by Renoir of couples dancing: the chronicles of Sundays in Paris, of picturesque, secretive little suburban taverns where one dances with whoever asks one and where the shopgirl on her Sunday outing is the presiding fairy; her lover wears a top hat and she takes him seriously, until they get back to the city limits. One of the women here is Mme Renoir. She was very pretty, and already quite plump. Durand-Ruel owns a charming nude of her, a very small picture. Above the mantelpiece there is a Rodin *Maternal Caresses*, bought for 3,000 francs. A Monet, a very considerable painting, *A Hunt in Winter*, with Hoschedé, whose wife Monet married, in the background.

Here I saw again a little plaster medallion by Renoir, a profile of a young girl. Monet has a similar one, and Durand-Ruel said: "There are only two or three of them. Renoir is the man who most influenced modern sculpture, much more than Rodin, who stood apart, on his own. And he exerted that influence through his brush, by his form, masses, amplitude, and the sculptural nature of his figures."

I noticed two large and beautiful still lifes by Monet. "I bought them," said Durand-Ruel, "for 3,000 francs from Knoedler, who found them with a Pourville innkeeper whom Monet had also painted together with his wife; the two portraits are in America."

I entered a room with its doors painted by Albert André. They were executed in the studio of Renoir, who retouched them considerably.

I was surprised to learn that Durand-Ruel is very keen on Lewis Brown. "Degas," he told me, "valued him highly and came to watch him paint his horses; he considered him inimitable on this subject. Lewis Brown's early manner was somber and in the genre of Géricault."

Then we came to a small room with three Renoir masterpieces: first, *Sunday at Bougival*, a large canvas with all Renoir's friends.[4] In this connection, Durand-Ruel told me that Renoir always had many friends, as he was very intelligent: many rich friends, who saw no talent in his work but bought it to please him.

The two other canvases are portraits. The first is erroneously called *The Loge*, and Durand-Ruel considers it more beautiful than the one that is in fact *The Loge*. These are the daughters of Turquet, the Minister of Fine Arts and a friend of Renoir's; but the painting didn't please him; he didn't keep it. The other canvas is the portrait of a deliciously pretty girl whose name Durand-Ruel doesn't recall. Renoir had discovered her living in poverty in Argenteuil, and he asked her to pose, promising her her keep. She subsequently went into the theater and became one of the stars of the bohemian world. She is still alive.

Durand-Ruel showed me the other *The Loge*, considered Renoir's masterpiece, and I agree. He pointed out how the man's head and the woman's are nearly touching the frame because Renoir didn't leave any space around portraits. An empty space, for him, was an aesthetic failure. How right he was![5]

November 9 / *The choosing of the Unknown Soldier*

A soldier has been exhumed from each of the nine sectors of the front; the nine coffins have been brought to the citadel of Verdun and

---

4 Today in Washington, owned by Duncan Phillips. (Note appended 1931.)
5 These three canvases are in America.

placed in line. A soldier was called from the ranks to designate one of them. The other eight warriors will sleep in the citadel.

January 3 / Zarraga

He wanted to have an exhibition in London, and I've made inquiries in the modern-art galleries. There are three: the Leicester, the Independent, and the Chenil, but the Chenil only takes English painters. Matisse has recently exhibited at the Leicester Gallery and sold everything. However, the owners of this firm, and likewise Mr. Turner of the Independent, told me that in England people are still at the Corot stage, that the impressionists have come into the world without England's having suspected their existence, to such an extent that today when an Englishman is shown a modern French picture he doesn't understand it. These two firms are obliged to sell old paintings to subsist.

Zarraga wants to have his living assured him so as to be able to work seriously without troubling about his daily bread. I have introduced him to Georges Bernheim.

January 29 / Destroyed Fragonards

Fifteen years ago the Marquis de Biron, a keen searcher after art objects, noted when reading the Baedeker guidebooks that at Saint-Brice north of Saint-Denis there still existed a country seat that had belonged to Mlle Colombe, who was Fragonard's mistress. He went off there and found two portraits of Mlle Colombe. I bought them with him. They are at present in Baron Edouard de Rothschild's collection.

There are still a mass of exquisite souvenirs of the dancer, such as a pretty, half life-size terra cotta, *Mademoiselle Colombe and Cupid*, subsequently in the Edouard Kann Collection; a charming painted suite since bought by Mrs. Burns, the sister of the famous collector J. Pierpont Morgan.

The Marquis de Biron took along on his motor tour a certain Lacombe, a first-rate middleman and negotiator. This man told me last year that the owner of the house said at the time that as a child she had seen in one of the small drawing rooms painted panels which her father had had covered over with a coat of paint decorated with flowers, because the subjects were too wanton. I then said to Lacombe: "The odds are that these are panels by Fragonard. Let's go ask some questions and, if need be, scrape the new painting, under which we might perhaps be able to find the old."

Lacombe knew that the house has changed hands several times. We were there today. It belongs to an American, Mrs. Walton, at present in Nice. The Alsatian caretaker told us that the small drawing room is now natural wood, as Mrs. Walton has had the painting taken off by blowtorch. How sad!

The dead courtesan

The little Lantelme woman was for some years the prettiest girl in Paris, with eyes like saucers, and brows which nature had etched in with great strokes of charcoal. She died mysteriously, fallen from a yacht into the Rhine. She collected; and one day at Oscar Stettiner's, the curiosity dealer's, she happened to sit on a Renaissance coffer to which she gave some hefty kicks with her heels. "My coffer is worth 10,000 francs," Oscar said to her. "And my behind a lot more," replied she.

February 18 / The cubist exhibition

I don't like buying cheaply at auction the works of artists whom I know. But common courtesy obliges me to go and see Zarraga's canvases. Ah, he was a real cubist then; there is a *Man with an Accordion* with endless accordions. And a woman putting on her gloves, all cubic or in cubes. I couldn't buy these canvases, although I am certain that the next school of painting will emerge out of cubism.

March 5 / I leave for America

With my wife, on the *France*.

March 15 / The most beautiful Rodin

His most beautiful bust is that of Mrs. J. W. Simpson. I went to her house today. She told me she posed sixty times, thirty of them for the clay model, after which she left for America. When she returned, the figure carvers had gotten the marble in focus and Rodin worked another thirty days with her.

He told her that no model had ever consented to pose for that length of time, and that it was essential to him. That's why the bust of her was the best he'd done. Mrs. Simpson always kept in close touch with Rodin, and it was in fact through her that I made the sculptor's acquaintance. I asked her how much of the finishing was done by the figure carvers, as I've heard Bourdelle say that he did a considerable number of Rodins.

Mrs. Simpson vouches for the fact that Rodin finished all his marbles, which he used to cover with pencil marks—though certainly Bourdelle took some works very far, like an Eve in pinkish stone bought by Scandinavia, which Rodin called *"Bourdelle's Eve."*

March 20 / Carl Hamilton

He can't be more than thirty. He washed dishes and shined shoes ten years ago in an American university. He describes it himself with pleasure. Now he owns the world's finest collection of Italian primitives; he's bought almost all of them from Duveen Brothers, but his most beautiful canvas is a Bellini acquired from Sulley of London.

Berenson introduced me to him. Of medium height, he gives an impression of swiftness, although he is rather solid, and also of geniality and authority, but American geniality is always only skin-deep. I shall speak again of him and his collection.[6]

A shop to let

In a new building at least thirty stories high built at the corner of Fifty-seventh Street and Fifth Avenue. They're asking me $250,000; in other words, with the dollar at nearly 50 francs, 3,750,000 francs.

March 21 / Another Degas sale

The last sale took place in New York. Originally the Degas Collection had been secretly bought from the Degas heirs before the sale by Bernheim Brothers, Jacques Seligmann, Durand-Ruel, and Vollard, who

---

[6] Odd case. This man had made only a moderate fortune and had set about buying pictures for enormous sums, sometimes paying advances, sometimes nothing, as to Sulley, who took back his Bellini and sold it to J. Widener. Hamilton sold a number of canvases; the Duveens took theirs back except for those paid for in the first installments, and these latter were sold by Hamilton at public auction two years ago. (Note appended 1931.)

bought up a great deal. Jacques Seligmann, who until then had not bought anything but old pictures, protested loudly at the exhibition that he adored Degas and wanted to collect his works. All this maneuvering so that people wouldn't be surprised to see him making such sizable purchases. He put his lot up for sale two months ago in New York, and it was a flop. This time it was the Bernheim Brothers, Durand-Ruel, and Vollard who bought up. Bad sales befall even great artists.

Drunkenness

A great change has come over the United States which will have grave consequences! The government has prohibited the sale of alcohol; the latter has become so rare that it fetches the price of a work of art. Drunkenness is going to look for new gullets, and they will be rich ones.

March 26 / Monet's "Woman with a Fan"

Which we had seen at Rosenberg's, was bought by Albert Lehman, who, no longer liking it, has given it to Duveen Brothers in an exchange.

April 4 / Rembrandt's "Lucretia"

A knee-height portrayal. She is stabbing herself in her terror, with a ridiculous gesture. Neither realism nor idealization. A terrible lack of taste. Rembrandt is a painter of portraits, especially men's portraits. In his marvelous biblical and engraved scenes he is a stage manager of genius. This picture comes from the Borden sale in New York, where it was bought by a group of London dealers who then sold it in Holland; but it was returned to them, and here it is in America with the Ehrich Brothers, who are asking $250,000 for it, or 3,750,000 francs.

April 5 / The Montgermont Rembrandt

At Duveen Brothers. Much more beautiful and simple. This old woman knows life. What wisdom. It costs 2,500,000 francs.

April 13 / The Six Vermeer: "The Alley"

Sold for more than 600,000 florins. I had thought of buying it; I could have had it before the sale for 500,000 francs. The Louvre didn't come up with the money.

April 14 / The J. P. Morgans

I don't remember if I've spoken of Miss Greene, with her tanned complexion. I believe she was born in Cuba, she is even said to be a mulatto; her hair is frizzy, her cheeks are thick, her lips big. She's a figure sculpted by a savage of genius. And she's a "savage" herself: she is savage in her furies, in her preconceived notions, even in her marvelous intelligence. She's J. P. Morgan's librarian and the architect of that collection of famous, precious books. On ancient books and publications and old manuscripts, she possesses universal knowledge.

The Morgans are known in France, for his ancestor helped us in 1870, after the Franco-Prussian War. The Morgan Loan was popular with our fathers, as it made possible the liberation of our country. The famous collector was his son, and it's thanks to him that America possesses her art treasures. He was the moving spirit who fostered an army of art lovers. A great financier, he was at times fearfully attacked. His opponents always seemed to want to send him to prison. The colossus continued on his way, working for his country, and without a hint of bitterness. He died several years before the war, and his son, the present J. P. Morgan, still has to put up with some of the ferocity with which his father was fought.

Miss Greene had just had a veritable battle with him. "He's a great man," she said to me, "and I want him to show it; that's why I'm angry. He's got to work like his father for his country, shutting his eyes and stopping his ears. I've told him that otherwise I'll quit, as my function is too limited in this library. My energies would be better employed somewhere else. As a financier he's already much greater than his father, who left enormous bundles of shares worth nothing.

"If you knew how remarkable he was in his struggle against President Wilson; he made truly gigantic gestures. Since from the outbreak of the war he'd lent money to France and England, Wilson had him summoned and said to him: 'Stop your loans to those two countries, as they're being spent on the manufacture of munitions and the United States must remain neutral.' 'But I'm not neutral,' replied Morgan. 'But I want you to be,' retorted Wilson. 'But since I am not neutral, no force in the world can make my spirit neutral!' That day's conversation ended there.

"The war continued and Morgan helped France with all his might. Wilson called for him and started again on the same lecture. The President had to use persuasion, for no article of the Constitution gave him such power over Morgan, and Morgan knew it. 'I shall stop helping France,' he replied, 'only when Congress passes a law forbidding Morgan and Company to support her.'"

And Miss Greene concluded: "You see the man in that reply. He would advance the spread of art if only he'd devote himself to it. He must become president of the museum, he really must; he's refusing, but it's absolutely essential!"

April 27 / On Degas and Mary Cassatt

Mrs. Havemeyer has sent me a booklet, a lecture she gave on April 6, 1915, at a dealer's on the occasion of an exhibition of impressionists: at Knoedler's, I believe. Mrs. Havemeyer was one of the first people to appreciate these masters, and her purchases very often helped them to subsist. I've told Mrs. Havemeyer that she ought to have sent this booklet, which is full of anecdotes, to the libraries. In it she tells how she bought for 500 francs the first Degas to enter the United States, and Degas thanked her, saying he was sadly in need of money. It was Mary Cassatt who had advised her to make the purchase—Mary Cassatt, Mrs. Havemeyer tells us, was her guide and inspiration, and the "godmother" of her collection. She informs us that the American artist was not a pupil of Degas and that she met him a year after she became acquainted with his works. Here is an extract from a letter written by Mary Cassatt to Mrs. Havemeyer:

> How I remember, nearly forty years ago, when I saw Degas's pastels for the first time in the window of an art dealer on the Boulevard Haussmann. I pressed my nose against the glass, absorbing all I could of his art. That changed my life. I saw art as I had dreamt of seeing it.

Then followed for the two artists long years of friendship with occasional short separations because of Degas's ill-natured words. He painted her several times, as in *At the Milliner's*. He admired her, saying: "I can't stand the thought of a woman painting like that." He said in front of her canvas *A Child before a Mirror:* "It's the most beautiful painting of the nineteenth century." Then he added sarcastically: "It's the baby Jesus with his English nurse."

Miss Cassatt called Degas a philosopher in his painting, and Mrs. Havemeyer shares this view. His philosophy developed greatly through his contact with the life of the streets, which he analyzed. He frequented the boulevards, the cafés, the Opéra, the races. Then he would go back to his studio and begin his canvas; when it was finished it wasn't an exact, formal representation of the music hall, the rehearsal, or the jockey and the horses; it was always a subject treated in depth.

Mrs. Havemeyer asked him one day why he always painted ballet scenes. He replied: "Because only there can I find again the movements of the Greeks."

May 9 / On Mary Cassatt

Mrs. Havemeyer tells me that after a trip to Egypt Mary Cassatt was so impressed by Egyptian art that she couldn't work for a year.

They're prudes in Boston

There is currently a very fine exhibition of modern art in the New York museum. Among other canvases, a Degas: an old oil lamp illuminates a table. The man leans with his back against the door, and he is looking at a woman who has begun to undress. She is sunk in a chair. Is she perhaps weeping? She has intelligent eyes. There is cheap paper on the wall. What is life for him, for them: what emptiness! Their life is like the wallpaper with its dirty flower pattern. At the back, a narrow iron bed.

The picture was shown to the purchase committee of the Boston Museum, which was going to buy it, but some women were against it, saying the picture was immoral: this couple weren't married, as the bed was a single bed.[7]

May 20 / Mrs. Gardner

Among the fantastic American collectors of this period, she is one

[7] I've since discovered that the real title of this picture is *The Rape*. It is in Philadelphia. (Note appended 1931.)

of the most influential figures. She was eighty-two the other day and is paralyzed. I'd seen her only once, over fourteen years ago, in Boston, in the Spanish house, with a patio, which she had built. I recalled a dried-up woman rushing through the various floors of her house, with me behind like a fatigue party that she had to train. Today, stretched out reading on her chaise longue, she seemed like a creature already entered into eternal beatitude.

She built her house outside Boston, not far from the city. The exterior is just four brick walls. Some years ago the Boston Museum moved quite near here. Incidentally, this museum has just bought some gigantic Catalan frescoes. There is a Christ pronouncing a blessing, a Christian Jupiter, whose lines exceed in their swiftness and expressiveness the known limits of pictorial art.

The day was very warm. Entering by a very small door, I came into the coolness of an interior in a tropical country; the arches low, the double columns supporting them decorated with capitals dating from the twelfth to the sixteenth centuries. The square courtyard is full of green plants; and the ground is a fresh-looking carpet of moss. Some sculptures stand here. I noticed four fine columns like young girls, and partly glimpsed a double curving staircase rising in a corner. The windows and stone doors are all antique. I discovered two beautiful Roman statues, some Chinese sculptures. Unhappily the house is shut up and all the objects put away, so we shall have to go around it another day.

May 21 / The value of the Frick Collection

The newspapers tell us that the estimate made by the U. S. Treasury is $13 million, instead of the $30 million of a year ago, owing to bad business. They give us the price of each object and even tell us that Frick left twelve pairs of shoes, eight dozen handkerchiefs, a soft hat, and the Fragonards of Grasse, which cost him a million dollars and are today estimated at $700,000. My father had sold him *Lady Peel* by Lawrence and *Nature* by Romney, each for $100,000. They are worth twice that sum.

June 7 / On Puvis de Chavannes

I have had a conversation with Burroughs, the American painter who is curator of paintings at the Metropolitan Museum, where an interesting exhibition of impressionists, post-impressionists, and living painters like Matisse, Picasso, and Derain is being held just now. I said to him: "People laughed at the opening of this exhibition; I'd allow no one to laugh at anything, however experimental. I don't laugh, I'm too afraid that the future will come to laugh at me."

"When I was a young student in Paris," Burroughs told me, "I had been given a letter to Puvis and some days later I met him at the Indépendants, looking at each canvas most attentively. There was just then a much-talked-about artist who had a theory: when a cloud fleeting across the sky had the air of a camel, he had to paint a camel; when a branch trailing to the ground gave the impression of a serpent, he felt obliged to paint a serpent!

"I, in my pride at knowing Puvis and being able to talk to him, went up to him and said how ridiculous I found it all, and Puvis replied: 'It's the first time I've seen him, and I don't yet feel I can take the liberty of criticizing him.'"

June 8 / The Five-and-Ten

What a stirring book could be written on the lives of the American pioneers of commerce and industry! They have nearly all vanished, like Widener, who was a butcher; Carnegie, a petty employee. I knew a number of them and learned a great deal from them. They were alike in their desire to get at the truth and they left no stone unturned.

My friend and old client Bertron introduced me to one of his friends, F. Kirby, who has an income of at least $2 million, and who in his first job made $2.50 a week. He was earning only $40 when he thought of getting married.

How did he start this enormous business? Here is what he told me: "Some young men were employed in a little novelty store in a small town called Watertown, in New York State. The most able of them was called Woolworth. He was paid $3.50 a week, and his father was a farmer. The boy's duties were sweeping and tending the boiler, later selling. One day his boss said to him that he wanted to improve the quality of the goods, but that first they would have to get rid of unsalable stock, at no matter what price, and asked him if he had any ideas. The young Woolworth had an idea. From all the stock, all the departments, he collected this merchandise and set up a counter by the door of the shop, where he piled it up, topping it with a placard with just two words: five cents. Nearly the whole lot was sold on the first day. He then thought of opening a shop where he would sell everything for five and ten cents. Several of his friends, including Kirby, followed suit, and today there are nearly fourteen hundred of these stores throughout the United States, and there are some in England as well. And for pride and publicity, Woolworth built in New York the tallest building in the world, which bears his name and cost him $15 million."

Kirby lives in Wilkes-Barre, Pennsylvania, where he opened his first store. We arrived there last night with Bertron, who would love to have his friend establish a museum, with me as adviser, but Kirby gives his money predominantly to schools. When he talked to me of his beginnings, he told me that for a long time he used as his office table the packing case in which his first merchandise was delivered to him.

Kirby adores trout fishing, and to my horror he offered to take us out on an expedition. I had never cast a line and had no wish to kill. As I had been told that fly casting is very difficult for a beginner, I said I wanted to try it, as I would thus be sure to return empty-handed; but we had a guide who never left us and who, seeing my clumsiness, was constantly taking the line from me, to such good effect that I have seventeen fish to my credit, Kirby twenty-five, and Bertron nine.

We talked of James Hill, one of the great railroad kings, who died five years ago and had put together a magnificent collection of nineteenth-century paintings. Bertron told us about his beginnings: "He was a dock worker somewhere in Canada, and used to have lunch and dinner in a restaurant with about twenty-five other dock workers, all thrifty and all sparing in their tips to the waitress; but on Christmas Eve Hill got up and asked them all if they were prepared to give the girl the same sum as he. They said yes, particularly as they knew Hill was even stingier than they. He put $20 on the table. They were horrified, but they were men of honor: they had given their word, and they kept it.

"Twelve days later Hill married the waitress."

June 29 / Mme Curie

I re-embarked on June 25 on the *Olympic* for England and France. Mme Curie is on board with a gram of the famous radium she has discovered. This gram, costing millions, was presented to her by the women of America.

She is traveling with her daughter, but is nearly always by herself. She walks a great deal on deck, very nervous, her hands always restless; she fidgets with her fingers incessantly, playing with them without being aware of it. Her face is white and rather thin. She has eyes like a blind person's, with very tight eyelids which blink open and shut perpetually. She has a rustic simplicity about her, in her thick cloth dress. She is a Pole and has that austere look which is common to the peasants of her country.

NOTEBOOK 8

October 6, 1921–October 3, 1922

October 6 / Van Zype on Vermeer

Van Zype will have done Belgium and France the service of being instrumental in the foundation of the Belgian Academy of the French Language. He has been rewarded with the title of Perpetual Secretary. He and his wife came to have dinner with us.

"Have you got your Vermeer *The Geographer* here?" Van Zype asked me. "No," I told him, "I'm not bringing it into France because of the import regulations and the frightful duty I'd have to pay. Beautiful foreign works won't be coming into France any more, it's infinitely sad."

Van Zype, who wrote that fine book on Vermeer, is far from knowing all his subject's works. Of the ten pictures in America, he has seen only *The Sleeping Servant* of the Rudolph Kann and Altman collections.

I asked him if he doesn't think Vermeer, like not a few painters, trafficked in the sale of pictures and even carpets. Except for a great painting which he did several times and on the best canvases, you never find the same carpet and never the same picture on the wall. If he was occupied by a trade, that would also explain his producing so little.

Van Zype remains skeptical. Looking at *The Painter's Studio* from the Czernin Collection, he said to me: "There is Vermeer at the back." "Well," I replied, "in *The Courtesan*, in Dresden, you find a man in the same clothes, and I'm quite certain we have a Vermeer self-portrait there. I've just been studying it, and everything confirms me in my view." Van Zype looked at it, only to say of this cavalier raising a glass: "No, I can't imagine Vermeer drinking." In the face of such sublime naïveté I don't insist.

He doesn't care for *Alleyway in Delft*, but adores the Budapest *Portrait of an Old Woman*. Before the Berlin *Woman with a Pearl Necklace* he murmured: "The moderns think they've discovered light!" and continued: "Where could it be truer, more alive, more pure and simple than there?" Van Zype believes in the authenticity of the Brussels picture *The Man on a Chair*. He is mistaken. He adores *Diana and Her Nymphs*, from the Hague museum; "so limpid," he adds. I informed him that *The Servant Girl and the Cavalier* in the Frick Collection is so much restored that the heads in it are almost modern. "That's the case," he says, "with *The Coquette* from the Brunswick Museum." He doesn't care for the Bredius *New Testament*, or for *The Letter* at the Amsterdam museum. He finds this work too heavy, too complicated. He likes the Coats one very much. He admires the portrait in the Arenberg Collection, with its admirable mass, its volume. He doesn't know *The Astronomer* in the Rothschild Collection.

October 13 / On Degas

Durand-Ruel has been showing me a canvas of a woman arranging flowers in a vase. "It's astonishing," he said, "how he could paint flowers, yet he couldn't look at them, he couldn't bear their scent."

Durand-Ruel showed me a large figure of a dancer, a woman. The artist spoiled the figure a bit by retouching with dark slashing strokes.

A fine Courbet, *Peasant Returning from Village*, which he bought for ten thousand dollars in New York before the war.

We talked of M. K. Matsukata, the Japanese who has just burst upon Europe and cleaned the dealers out of modern pictures to set up a museum in Tokyo.

He spent up to 800,000 francs with Georges Bernheim, and even more with Durand-Ruel. He took from them Millet's *Four Seasons*, large decorative panels. To Claude Monet he gave 200,000 francs for just one of his panels which the painter showed me at Giverny during the war.

October 27 / On Jean-François Millet

Brame, the modern-picture dealer, said to me: "I knew Millet when I was quite small, in 1875. My parents told me one Sunday: 'Today we're going to the country to lunch at M. Millet's.' They dressed me in my best clothes. Millet was already someone, and to go and eat at his house was an important event, even for a family like ours.

"I remember of that luncheon only a numerous family and a patriarchal atmosphere. Millet didn't actually say the *bénédicité* but there was the odor of it.

"I possess not a few letters which he addressed to my father, and many of them relate to his environment, which so absorbed him. The most amusing of these letters is very far removed from the spirit of the *bénédicité*. Here is the story: One Sunday at his house in the country a young girl fell headlong on the ground. 'Aha,' they said to her, 'we saw everything. Why don't you wear pants?' 'You're mistaken,' she replied, 'I've got pants on.' In fact she hadn't, and somebody who had a camera said to her: 'I'll prove the contrary to you, since I took a revealing snapshot of your fall.' It wasn't true, but Millet did a drawing of the indiscreet fall. He tried—so he himself wrote—to get as close as possible to nature. The drawing was to be photographed, to be presented to the young girl as conclusive proof!"

December 5 / Some remarks of Forain's

I hadn't seen Forain for a long time. His face is still young, only the hands have aged, their skin is translucent and white, with skeletal bones. At present he is devoting himself entirely to painting and is doing some dancers. Why dancers? An old gentleman offers a ballerina a gold piece, with his respects. "It's the first trophy," says Forain.

He showed me a courtroom scene with two women in blue and red on the right, and said to me: "This isn't working out because of the straight edges of the witness box, those parallels which Delacroix so rightly called the murderous lines. Hogarth fixed a mobile copper line to his palette and called it the line of beauty."

December 11 / A Vermeer and Edmond de Rothschild

Just a year ago, I bought the Vermeer *Geographer* for £20,000 from the du Bus de Gisignies Collection; it was formerly in the Pereira Collection. It passed into the Kums Collection and was sold at public auction twenty-five years ago for about eight thousand francs. When du Bus acquired it, he hid it; no one was allowed in his house. He died not long ago; his nephew, the Count de Reinesse, inherited it and sold it to me. The picture had terrible cracks, but I realized that this was only the varnish, which was mixed with a frightful green color that readily came off. I then discovered not only a date, 1657, but also the signature, which had not been seen before. I mentioned these facts in an article I wrote for *Le Connoisseur*, which carried a reproduction of the picture.

December 21 / C. L. Fraser, the English illustrator

He had talent but, alas, during the war he got a touch of gas in the lungs, and yesterday a brief illness was enough to carry him off. He was thirty-one, born in 1890. One senses in his art the Russian influence of a Bakst, and the French influence of Bonfils, Lepape, Barbier.

I have just arrived in London and am going to see his exhibition at the Leicester Gallery. His most outstanding work is the set of drawings he did for an old English opera, *The Beggar's Opera*. (I would translate it: *L'Opéra de la cour des Miracles*.) He was not a creator like Beardsley. He revealed too many outside influences, but might have taken on more personality with the years. He was not born with an original talent, but is superior to the French whom I have named because he is a philosopher and paints, more than the costumes, the face and its spirit. With only his brush Fraser plays all the roles and with consummate cleverness shows the actor all the attitudes to strike: those of the Scold and the Neighbor's Wife a well as those of the Coquette offered for sale or of the innocent but suspicious Young Girl!

England will gradually come to be proud of C. L. Fraser, who was a soldier and an artist. And so France also must get to know him.

January 1, 1922 / Importation of art objects

The law has been repealed. Some masterpieces not yet in our museums will be classified as historical objects.

January 22 / Marcel Proust

He telephoned me at 7 P.M. to ask if he could come to see me at midnight, and of course I replied that I had no objection.

It is strange that, with my mind so full of precise memories, I cannot recall how I met Marcel Proust, who was then thirty-six. I know that it was in the Normandy seaside resort of Cabourg, in August 1907, at the Grand Hôtel, where both of us were staying; but we were not the sort to speak to each other without having been introduced. In fact, I would say that he didn't usually chat with anyone. Cabourg has since become a fashionable place, but at the time it was *"très famille,"* as the bourgeois say. So the presence of a playwright with a familiar face, like Francis de Croisset, caused a sensation there, and the presence of a singer like Gaby Deslys caused a scandal. Proust, who had published only one book and two translations of Ruskin, passed unnoticed. As for the casino, it hardly existed except for certain young girls and young men; you went to bed early at the hotel, and Proust would come down regularly at 8:45 in the evening, when everyone was about to go to bed; he had just gotten up. Despite the sometimes overpowering heat, he never left the hotel and even in the hall wore a thick wool twill overcoat with numerous heavy linings, dating from years gone by; it was so faded it looked stained. I laughed a lot at it. Proust's pale, ivory-colored face was edged with a very black, slightly curly beard. He had the great eyes of men from the African deserts. The last time I saw him he told me in passing that the old Dutch painter Jan Vermeer of Delft had brought us together; this indication didn't bring anything back concerning our first meeting and I didn't dare ask him about it, but he certainly had not forgotten it. The doctors, whom he ridiculed—his father among them— had assured him that the sea would do his asthma a great deal of harm; it did him a lot of good. He returned there in 1908, still quite satisfied with the salt air. He claimed to be able to breathe only at night, and that is why, he said, he slept during the day. It is difficult to know with Proust what part sickness played in his imagination. To gather information useful to his work, he would endure any pain, risk any infection. And if he could stand the salt air, it was because he felt impelled to study seaside life. Had he returned to Cabourg when he had nothing more to learn there, his asthma would probably have worsened. I saw him there once more in 1908, and that was the end, he never left Paris again.

At Cabourg we would meet every evening, and we never spoke to anyone. He would sometimes see a tall, very large woman descending the grand staircase—her name was Orosdi—wearing a faille dress with a train; her head was somewhat Oriental and she was superbly self-assured, with red flowers on her shoulder, an Empire-style trinket in her hair, and diamonds falling from her ears to flash like shooting stars in the air; and he would exclaim, reminded of the floats of laundresses on the boulevards in Mardi Gras: "What about that, old fellow: here comes a carnival queen, more carnival than queen!" From time to time he'd have a visit from a writer, such as Bernstein the playwright, who amused him very much; but I never saw him talk with any resident of the hotel, and yet he knew the name and history of each one. When he went up to his room around midnight he would play checkers with some servant and question him on everything that went on under this vast roof. He gave enormous tips; if a dinner cost him ten francs he added twenty for the waiter. He based a large part of his work on the information he obtained from servants.

In 1907 Proust had already worked out a general outline of the entire series of novels, for he spoke to me of the controversy that would be raised by his ticklish subject, though the first book, *Swann's Way*, which he published only five years later, in 1913, did not contain anything daring. The second, *Within a Budding Grove*, on the first dangerous promiscuity of adolescence, appeared eleven years after his first stay at Cabourg, but the Great War was upon us, raising the hemline of women's skirts with each passing year, and the book caused no scandal; no more did the following ones, which had become very bold.

Marcel Proust adored Balzac and was always urging me to read and reread him. His second favorite author was the Duke de Saint-Simon. Like them, Proust had amassed an encyclopedia of information in his brain. That time by the sea, I used to spend the greater part of my days looking at churches in the tiniest Norman villages. I don't know if my friend had visited them all, but he knew everything they contained.

Here, it might be a mosaic paving three foot square; elsewhere, a capital in the cellars, down in the crypt.

Another thing I remember: some days after I had met Proust he said to me—and I've never discovered how he knew about it, living isolated as he did: "Why have you kept it from me that you've had a revue performed in a Parisian theater?" Yes, a revue that I'd written had been done in a little district theater; it had had a modest success, it was an adolescent fantasy, but hadn't come to the attention of the general public; however, Proust, the greatest literary detective the world has ever known, had learned about it, on the little beach of Cabourg.

January 23

Marcel Proust arrived at half past twelve midnight and stayed only two hours because I didn't press him; I began to be very tired. I hadn't seen him for fifteen years. He seemed to me almost as young as he was then, but he is now neatly turned out, his clothes are smarter and newer, and he has cut his straggly black beard. His face is no longer as pale as it was, but on the other hand it is swollen like his whole body with uremia, and he has somewhat the air of a stout fifth-form schoolboy tall for his age.

We had hardly shaken hands when he said: "I'm not going to look at your marvelous things; I've come only for you. You're surprised not to see me wearing that crushed-violet overcoat of mine that you used to make such fun of. It's still in existence, but I didn't dare put it on."

Proust always felt the cold; even in an overheated room he doesn't take off his thickly lined overcoat.

"A remark has been reported to me," he said, "which the English ambassador made about me at a grand dinner he gave. The first words flattered me no end: 'Proust is the most remarkable man I've met in Paris.' You'll understand that when an English ambassador says such a thing about you over a full dinner table at his embassy, you feel considerable pleasure—even pride; but the end of the sentence was: '—because he keeps his overcoat on at dinner.' That chilled me, it was a great letdown, utterly disappointing."

Settling Marcel Proust near the chimney, I lit a big wood fire, though the radiator was piping-hot.

We talked little of his great literary successes. Of the Prix Goncourt which he received, he said: "I scarcely knew what it was; it's just a publicity machine. Léon Daudet came to break the news, exclaiming: 'I must embrace you.' And he embraced me. I would have preferred to be kissed by other lips. I always annoy Daudet, as whenever I meet him, from whatever distance I catch sight of him, I call out to him: 'Dreyfus is innocent.'"

I told Proust how in his book *Within a Budding Grove* I rediscovered Cabourg of the years 1907 and 1908, when we were both staying there, and he replied: "Officers from I've forgotten what company have written to me that they recognized Coutances—where I've never been —in it; and I wrote as much to them, assuring them they were mistaken. They replied that my description of Coutances was too precise, that I might not want to admit it but I couldn't change their opinion. I wrote them that they were right. So they were happy."

We talked of people we knew, like Helleu, whom he likes very much, and Forain, whom he can't stand. But I remember Forain calling Helleu a milliner who paints like a hairdresser.

About his book *Pastiches et Mélanges*, Proust told me that Princess Murat was displeased with the way he had described her absurd receptions. He adds: "She reproaches me for those few pages, and complains: 'That's what I got for inviting him.' As though it were something special to be one among five hundred guests. I did meet her at the Opéra ball, or rather I happened to come across her, and she deigned to hold out her hand to me, absent-mindedly, of course, and when she realized, she blushed.

"At the same ball, Monsieur K., who'd also come in for some rough treatment from me because of his stupidity, his mania about precedences, was hanging around. He's worse than Saint-Simon. I watched him circle round me, saying to himself: 'Should I hit him? But he looks very ill. However, a slap . . . a good slap . . . it would do me good. Only, it's possible he might collapse. And where would that leave me?'

"Meanwhile, I was asking myself: 'Is he going to hit me or isn't he?' The possibility advanced and receded by turns. Finally I saw it evaporate. But, between ourselves, I am fairly safe writing what I see, since I'm so near death. It's true, for three weeks now I've been given up. For months at a time I'm confined to my bed or my room. Fifteen years ago I could still get up at five or six in the evening; now it's ten o'clock at the earliest. Often I go to dine at the Ritz at eleven, and in a small room, so as not to be bothered. I've come from there this evening. Ollivier, the headwaiter, wanted to stop me from coming here. He said: 'You don't go to people's houses at this hour.'

"My taxi is at the door, it's driven by the husband of my faithful servant, a woman to whom I'm devoted, as she knows how to stave off ill-timed visits from Slavic or American women who come, or want to come, and sit on my bed and who exclaim, thinking to please me: 'Oh, M. Proust, we have only two books by our bedside, one by you and one by M. Paul Bourget.' By M. Paul Bourget! That's hardly flattering!"

Proust reminds me that at Cabourg, where we met, it was Vermeer of Delft who brought us together. I speak to him of my *Geographer*, which I don't have here. He loves the Dutch painters. Of all the Rembrandts, his favorite canvases are those belonging to Baron Gustave de Rothschild, and this is what he told me: "I adored those pictures from the day I saw photographs of them, but I had also seen the faces of the Baron and Baroness Gustave de Rothschild, and this association of those beautiful Rembrandts with the faces of the baron and baroness I found horrible. Then I took my courage in both hands and wrote to the baroness that I would love to see her Rembrandts one day, when neither she nor her husband would be there. To my surprise I received an answer. She mentioned a Sunday when they were going to the country."

Then he told me the story—if one can call it that—of a dinner party given by the Queen of Rumania. "It was at the Ritz," he said. "I was invited for nine. I had given warning that I would be a little late, but I arrived at eleven, and they hadn't waited for me. Of the meal that had been ordered, nothing remained. The queen immediately took me in hand and said: 'I'm a writer myself.' I burst out laughing. What a charming thing to say, 'I'm a writer myself.' She didn't understand my laugh—luckily, as I would perhaps have missed the rest of the conversation, in which I laughed a lot more. She continued: 'I've written about the czar, and you do understand: I'm a queen myself. You do realize: he was a king, and since I am a queen, we're two of a kind. Don't you see?' And to make sure of getting the fact through into my thick head, the queen touched her nose with the index finger of her right hand and spread the hand out horizontally as though to touch—somewhere across an infinite distance—the nose of the czar, whom she couldn't fail to reach thanks to the magical powers of royalty. She continued: 'Same kind: he czar, I queen.' She spoke pidgin French. 'Those who have written or will write about the czar were never, and will never be, his equals. I, I am his equal; they saw or will see him from below, always from below. It isn't the same thing.' The queen, to make it clear to me that it wasn't the same thing—we were of course seated—this time placed her right hand flat on her knees and slowly moved it, raising it obliquely in front of her to the tip of the nose of this czar shot so long ago, eloquently showing by this gesture how poor hacks, poor puffing asthmatics, could never climb such a slope and attain the genius of a queen. I laughed, oh, how I laughed!

"I laughed again when she spoke of her people's love for her, her people whom she cherished, and even more, whom she healed. She had only to touch paralytics to see them walk; her miracles occurred daily.

"She spoke and I laughed; that's how we communicated."

February 2 / A visit to Forain

I asked him if his political drawings bring him many letters, and he answered: "Few from France, but at the time of the Dreyfus affair, many from abroad, especially from Scandinavians. They'd often write me that my talent could hardly express my goodness of heart. Letters of this kind are like politics: they irritate you. You start with moderation, then you're insulted, so you reply with increasing violence. By now it's all over, my career ending, a few paintings to do, no more battles and noise, all that past buried."

I spoke to him of Proust. He used to know him at the Strausses. "His books are deadly and amusing," he said. "He is amoral. He brings up certain subjects. That reminds me of Mme Strauss, Bizet's widow, who replied to a lady who asked her what she thought of incest: 'Madame, I can't answer you, as I'm only disposed to commit adultery.'

"She was celebrated for her wit, Mme Strauss," continued Forain. "The Strausses defended Captain Dreyfus furiously. But when she saw him mute and insignificant in his box at Rennes, brought back from

Devil's Island for the retrial, she cried: 'We've taken up a simpleton by mistake!' "

I told Forain the story of the slap Proust was waiting for, and he told me the one about the man from Marseilles who was arguing in a Paris café with a fellow sitting next to him. Finally he said: "Let's go settle this thing out in the street!" The men went outside, and with one punch the Parisian knocked down his antagonist, who got up again black and blue, saying ruefully: "So in Paris they don't break up a fight!"

Forain spoke to me of his youth in Reims. When he was quite small he used to put butter on paper to make tracing paper and copy pictures. "And then," he added, "there was the cathedral, oh! what a cathedral!" Later he went to work at the Louvre, where he watched Fantin-Latour copying Veronese. "It was magnificent!" he exclaimed.

I asked him whether he found etchings as difficult to do as paintings. "Absolutely. I used to go over my plates with the same intensity."

I mentioned a fine painting of his that I saw in the Durand-Ruel Collection, called *The Folies-Bergère*. "I sold it to them for 400 francs."

We went on to discuss modern painting, Matisse, Derain. He can't stand them. "These people only want to shock," he said. "They hit out blindly, and for them it's art. They don't know that painting is the most beautiful of professions—second only to selling paintings."

Forain gave me a malicious look.

February 27 / Ollivier on Proust

He's the famous headwaiter at the Ritz. It was he who wanted to stop Proust from coming to my house the other evening. I told him that the writer is very fond of him. "And I like him too," he replied. "He's so good, concerned about everyone. If an employee has a head cold, he sends over his doctor. Unfortunately, I don't see him often enough, every week or ten days, and sometimes even less—when he's spending a month in bed. He always orders the same dishes. Here he has an appetite, but at home he doesn't eat. He orders the best wines, but he never drinks more than a drop of them. He must be very rich. He sometimes invites friends, and they chat till five or six in the morning. I know these night birds: I don't mean people who go in for orgies, but intellectuals like Proust. You have them in all big cities, and many more of them than you might think. I can spot them in daylight. They always look like miserable corpses. Proust often brings books along, and I serve him in a little room where he can write. He writes near the fire, always with his coat on. The fire has to be enormous. Proust insists on a constant temperature of eighty-six degrees. When I've been in the room ten minutes, I'm roasted, but you can't tell him that. He often tells me to stay, questions me, asks a thousand details, which he stores up. He's put me into one of his books, exactly the way I am. The funniest thing is that his servants lead the same life and resemble him. They have to be up all night to wait on him. They sleep by day and acquire all his habits. He has a maidservant who has brought along her whole family and they practically live together. The whole house is lined with very thick cork, since the day is the night for him, and so he has to protect himself from both daylight and noise. That costs him a lot; workmen coming in are paid their weight in gold to hammer silently. The windows are never opened when he is there. The carpets are never beaten. Imagine!"

March 1 / A crack of Forain's

It was told to me by Feral: "Twenty-five years ago I was dining in a restaurant, Forain was at the table next to me, and opposite, a little farther on, Caran d'Ache, then a very well-known draftsman, and known to have a weakness for maidservants. That evening Caran d'Ache was coughing his heart out, and I heard Forain call out to him: 'You must have forgotten to shut the skylight!' "

March 29 / Sale of the Renoir studio

The first 103 pictures have just been bought for 1,500,000 francs by the newly founded firm of Barbazanges, which has an option on the remaining 600, divided into six sets. These options are graduated over several years, with a minimum price already fixed, but when the next option expires, the Renoir family, even if they get a bigger offer, will have to give preference to Barbazanges, who otherwise will buy at the minimum price, say 10,500,000 francs for the lot. Orosdi is financing this firm; it has already bought Courbet's *The Studio* and sold it to the Louvre.

When Barbazanges had signed, he got together the Durand-Ruels, Georges Bernheim, Rosenberg, Bernheim Brothers, Hessel, all of whom knew about the deal but estimated it at only 7 million. He offered them a share, which they refused because there were too many small pictures, which is true.

The lots are equal, each one including only six or seven very beautiful canvases, plus some twenty very fine fragments, and that's all.

Today Barbazanges has only one superb horizontal Renoir, of the painter's last model, a woman seated on some material of green stripes on a white background. On the left there is a straw hat with roses. He is asking 350,000 francs for it.

April 7 / *Excavations in Egypt*

A dealer has told me that before the war he employed 150 Arabs on excavations which he had undertaken on the edge of the desert in secret, as the Egyptian government would have taken his finest pieces away from him. These 150 men kept the secret because Europeans were held in awe by the Arabs. "I had only to threaten to kill one if he talked for him to believe it, but the war changed all that, and now it's the European who is afraid of the Arab, who will kill him for a trifle. The war put a spirit of independence into the Arab's heart which has made him dangerous."

The excavations have stopped. An unexpected consequence of the war.

April 20 / *I love spreading my vice*

Ernest Duveen, my brother-in-law, has just been appointed artistic adviser to the king of England.

I said to my brother-in-law that this would be the time to start keeping a journal. Such an association with a royal family is a rare source. He is going to begin one.[1]

I gave this advice last year to Kelly, an employee in my firm taken on by Wildenstein—a very artistic boy who knows all the artists. He is doing it.

The Renoir studio

The Barbazanges have telephoned me to say that the canvases

---

[1] He didn't. (Note appended 1929.)

have arrived. There are too many small ones and only two good portraits, including the one of Mme G., wife of the bibliophile. We've met the latter at his mistress's place. Mme G. is the typical petite bourgeoise who helps the maid with the housework. These domestic virtues made the husband turn to an actress. Renoir, a good friend of the wife, also did the portrait of the mistress.

The second interesting portrait is that of the thrice-married Mme Nathanson. Nathanson committed suicide. She is blond and smiling: perhaps she smiled too much! Now she is married to Sert, the Spanish painter whom I've already mentioned.

The most beautiful canvas is fairly small; I believe it's no more than twenty inches wide. They are asking 100,000 francs for it. It is a view of Guernesey, with rocks on the seashore and a group of children in the brilliant colors of early August.

Then there is *Castle of Mists, Montmartre*, where Renoir lived (50,000 francs), and a *View of Pornic* (85,000 francs) in pastel shades, depicting a summer haze, a white mist, a somewhat hopeless yearning for the eternal Orient.

The Le Breton Virgin

Alphonse Kann tells me that this Virgin bought the other day by Duveen Brothers is fake, that it was made forty years ago, at the time of Viollet-le-Duc. The Duveens have already dispatched it to America. Kann's opinion is not gospel but must be taken into consideration. I didn't look at it with the thought that it might be fake, but I didn't like it.

A thirteenth-century statue

I have just sold my Gothic statue, the *St. Paul*, to Raymond Pitcairn of Philadelphia, for $110,000. With the dollar at about eleven francs, that works out to some 1,200,000 francs.

May 23 / The Prud'hon exhibition

It is being held at the Petit Palais. Prud'hon has his place in a certain period of the history of our art. That applies to every great artist: for though he may be ignored, he cannot be excluded. But what in fact did Prud'hon do? He was the offspring of Clodion and the father of

Carpeaux. His only merit was being a poet in the age of Napoleon, and the age of steel, and of having paved the way for romanticism.

May 30 / At Forain's

"What's new?" he asked me. "What do you know about politics? I've got to do my *Figaro* drawing by tomorrow noon. Why ever did I take on this weekly drawing? It is such a bother, I think about it too much!"

I asked Forain how the projected work crystallizes in his mind into the final clear invention.

"I do have some help. It's the old fable of the guardian angel and the demon, good and evil. Use a modern term and say the subconscious. There isn't anything else, but there is that." "It helped you a lot during the war." "Because I believed in it." "How did you hit on your famous caption for the two French soldiers: 'Let's hope they hold out.' 'Who?' 'The civilians!'" "I don't know. But I do know that Carpeaux said to me one day: 'You work and turn out a masterpiece, you work and produce another, but it's forty years later.'"

During this conversation, Forain's drawing got quite far advanced. He would have it finished in two hours.

"I went faster," he told me, "when I didn't need spectacles. The glasses distort, they distort and slow up my work."

Forain asked me if I knew the banker J. P. Morgan, who had just arrived from New York. He then went on to tell me of his trip to America, and in particular of an afternoon spent at the Vanderbilts' place at Newport, in their "Sugar Castle."

"There were fine paintings," he said, "beautiful works of art, but not a tree outside. Everyone was going through that lovely collection without really taking anything in, when all of a sudden Mrs. Vanderbilt took a mechanical toy out of a box and made it go. It was a Negro smoking, you can imagine; all these uppercrust Americans were enthralled; they looked at it for an hour, two hours, they didn't weary of it, you should have seen them! What funny people they are, what funny people!"

July 12 / Picasso

We met at Paul Rosenberg's. He speaks good French but has

retained a strong Spanish accent. The head of the cubist school is a blood pudding, a bleached blood pudding. He's not yet forty, has brown eyes like very worn counters in a child's game. The face of this pudding is cut by six perpendicular lines—as though the strings of its muslin bag had been untied—falling from the eyes, the nostrils, and the corner of the lips.

September 7 / Price of art objects

Despite the world economic crisis, I've seen a Persian rug at the Bacri Brothers for which they are asking 800,000 francs. Larcade tells me he has taken an option for 9 million on the unicorn tapestries found at the Château de La Rochefoucauld.[2]

September 19 / The Pellerin Cézannes

In his villa at Neuilly he must have at least a hundred of them. It is hard to look at a hundred Cézannes; it's a hundred clashings of cymbals in your head: my head rang for hours. You feel the effort, the toil and travail in his painting, and yet it appears more and more complete.

It's been an interesting visit, but although I stayed for two hours, the details that I so love to pinpoint have eluded me. In the middle of the garden there is an *Eve* by Rodin; to Kelly, who accompanied me, together with Hoffner, a painter, Jan Juta, and his sister, I pointed out that its patina has become very ugly, because the sculptor gave his bronzes their patina artificially, and when they are exposed to the air, nature takes her revenge for his deceit.

Pellerin sends admission cards to whoever asks him for them.

His house is a square building traversed along its entire length by the central hall. On the left, two drawing rooms; on the right, the staircase; and farther on, the dining room. There and in two first-floor bedrooms are hung the Cézannes, plus four Renoirs, three of which are magnificent. The taste shown in this house is abominable. The portrait of President Poincaré in evening clothes, black silhouette with its great ribbon, is next to the portrait of Erasmus after Holbein, but on embossed, colored hide. The armchairs are in the "rocking style" or in the

[2] He sold them for 17 million to John D. Rockefeller. (Note appended 1929.)

Louis XIV "caned style." As in America, the pictures mount along the staircase. In the United States you would be given a catalogue; here at least you are allowed to browse; no servant follows you, the hospitality is agreeably relaxed, and decorum prevails.

But the Cézannes! You would have to describe them all! They need a bard to do them justice!

September 21 / Some advanced works

Léonce Rosenberg's: an exhibition by Severini, an Italian who paints clowns with paper flutes; they're not bad but the colors ring false. At Hayden's gallery there's a sub-Derain, a woman painter of the fluid style, called Irene Lagut. There's also a good sculptor called Csaky, probably some fierce Balkan, since in his busts he does away with nose, eyes, and mouth, and cuts the skulls in two. Foreigners, like this Csaky, have done damage to French lucidity; they have indubitably a muddling effect on the good sense which some of us possess.

September 25 / Four statues by Pajou

The Four Seasons, at least life-size, are marvelous. They are at Nathan Wildenstein's, who bought them for 75,000 francs from Ancel, a dealer on the quai Voltaire, who in turn had bought them from Leroy, the Versailles dealer. I went to see them with Stotesbury from Philadelphia; Wildenstein has asked him for 1,250,000 francs for them. I myself want one million francs from him for two plaster groups by Clodion, from the Doucet sale: life-size female figures holding basins. Two other groups are in the Museum of Decorative Arts, and in the Peyre Collection.

October 3 / On Renoir

The Durand-Ruels have shown me the portrait (painted in 1865) of a woman of about thirty-five, which they bought today and which was unknown to public and critics. Its background is green. Renoir was very young at the time, and although this painting has qualities, it shows inexperience, for instance in the horses, which lack suppleness. The model is still alive, and is in her nineties. It is she who sold them this canvas. Renoir loved a young girl of that family, the Lecoeurs—the

Durand-Ruels believe it was the sister of this woman—but the father rejected him as a dauber with no future.

I asked the Durand-Ruels if Renoir believed in his own talent. "Everywhere he went," they said, "in all the inns, he forgot his canvases." Do they believe that many unknown Renoirs exist? "Perhaps there are a few rolled up somewhere, but probably most of them have been destroyed. He left near Bougival, together with a number of small articles, eight large canvases today worth 200,000 francs apiece, and when he returned there eight years later, the innkeeper said to him: 'I'm glad to see you. Do take away this roll of paintings you left behind here.' His pictures were his way of paying his rent. Thus, when he left his Montmartre studio he didn't want to pay the landlord, but left him his canvases; it was Father who forced him to take them along."

NOTEBOOK 9

October 23, 1922–May 22, 1923

October 23 / In Italy

The Sistine Chapel is chaos, but an ordered chaos. Michelangelo, faced with a broad arched ceiling, created with his brush the illusion of beams or rather of vast stone masonry divided in a kind of colossal, highly architectonic trellis with a multitude of comparatively small rectangles, through which the sky may just be glimpsed, since these rectangles are filled with so many huge figures that the corners of blue are rare.

I tried to see the lyricism which painters and writers have found here. Michelangelo bowls us over like children, but I rebel and refuse to find this work gigantic just because I see giants, however strapping! The artist allows us no repose; it's a torment, and an eternal torment is not part of our souls and therefore does not exist in nature. Thirty years later he painted the great fresco at the back, *The Last Judgment*, in which his faults were aggravated; it's an explosion of flesh. Michelangelo's paintings are like a cannonade. I think, in contrast, of Puvis de Chavannes, of that silent creator whose every picture is a prayer. Yes, Michelangelo's painting is fine because Michelangelo is a powerful draftsman and a prodigious technician; but his work, being essentially profane, would have been more in place in an ancient temple, where the divinities were always an enlargement of man. Michelangelo was a romantic in the manner of Victor Hugo, but without his contrasts. He has raised himself above mankind, above his fellows; but he has not established contact with the mystical forces which should have been essential in a place like this. His contemporaries no longer understood such things, and Michelangelo lacked the genius to reforge the links of the divine chain. Perhaps, aware of his impotence, he sought to achieve his end by painting on a large scale; at all events, he has managed to dazzle us from that day to this, and for a long time to come.

I think today I've seen evidence which supports my statement: I have never heard noise in a Gothic church, but here the visitors passing through unleash a deafening hubbub. They're responding to Michelangelo.

By what enchantment do those who know only the name of a single painter know Raphael's? They do not know Giotto. Was it his quality of precocious youth and his premature end? There are other reasons and they are more profound.

His frescoes in the Vatican do not even possess the qualities one finds in the Sistine Chapel; Michelangelo at least has his sense of the colossal, which always amazes us, plus an astonishing vision of architecture. In his compositions, Michelangelo arouses our interest in the figure; all Raphael knows how to do is paint pictures, striking pictures. He has given us *The Fire in the Town*, *The Expulsion of Heliodorus from the Temple*, or *The Repulse of Attila from Rome by Leo I*, treated exactly as some present-day artists might treat *The Assassination of President Carnot at Lyon* or *The Crowning of a Village Queen*. But, being more childlike, Raphael is more naïve. Michelangelo has covered his surface so well, his giants match so effectively the scale of the architecture, that his compositions form a decorative whole. Raphael would forget about the wall; he simply painted pictures, and so the question arises: Was Raphael a great painter? He did marvelous portraits, and that would be enough for him to qualify as a great painter. In his portraits he reaches the heights of a Memling, a Roger Van der Weyden. His frescoes were perhaps a concession to contemporary taste and are typical of his time; but when he painted Francesco Maria della Rovere,

Bramante, the Duke of Mantua, or his own portrait, they are truly beautiful. But these portraits are so true to nature, in contrast to his rigid
compositions, that they stand out like someone walking into a costume
ball wearing dress suit and top hat: and the intruder in the hat represents life and feeling. How ugly and poor are the colors in Raphael's
never-ending ball: there's never a true red or blue. Italy still suffers from
Raphael's water-colorish tints. A Frenchman disguised as a Catalan
won't have the air of a Spaniard, and Raphael's saints, his evangelists, his
poets, his philosophers, are not at all like the moral figures he wished to
portray; they lack spirit. Nothing is more insipid than a Virgin by Raphael. Since he doesn't know how to paint feelings in these conventional
faces of his, he renders what he takes to be sentiment by postures of the
arms, and the legs move too, the legs of a man in flight are expected to
express terror. Thus, all the characters in his paintings are terribly posed
and rigid. The painter seems to have said to each model: "Don't move
now, I'm going to take the photograph." Besides, there is no cohesion
among the multitude of figures. Raphael was never able to make us forget the studio. We observe a lack of unity. Each individual plays out his
scene without concerning himself about his neighbors: that's why the
whole is so discordant.

How can one hesitate between Raphael and Michelangelo? The
first is only a young man full of grace, the second is an athlete. Their
painting is in their own image.

At the end of the Raphael rooms I paused in the tiny chapel of
St. Nicholas, and here I found repose. The tourists don't linger here:
these are only Fra Angelicos! It's practically a cell. How he must have
liked it here, the divine monk Brother Angelico, the painter of paradise.
Yes, give me paradise if it is as Fra Angelico has painted it, he who
painted with the hope of making us happy. That was his message. His
pictures are flooded with azure, his blue recalls the color of the skies on
days of love; of love and grace, when grace touches us. With his divine
intuition, Angelico had a vision of paradise here on earth. Take me
there, Angelico!

October 24 / The Corsini Palace

There are five or six magnificent pictures: a little triptych by Fra
Angelico, pure as an ancient lily; a *Portrait of a Man* by Bartolomeo

Veneto, a painter who in some of his works came close to the greatest masters; the sumptuous gowns conjure up barbarian luxury. A *Florentine Lady* by Piero di Cosimo; no doubt she was much caressed by gold, kisses, and silks. Holbein's portrait of Henry VIII covered in gold; his apparel is as if damascened, there is no armor so beautiful, and so effective, that the enormous Henry VIII doesn't appear as villainously fat as he was. This is a masterpiece, and it is truly the portrait of a king. It's to be noted that Van Dyck outdid himself in painting Charles I—the same goes for Clouet with Francis I and for Velázquez when he painted the queen, though he didn't care for her. Therefore one might say that a masterpiece is not so much a result of inspiration as of careful observation.

"Innocent X" by Velázquez, in the Doria Gallery

Morgan would have offered a million dollars for it.

Velázquez was faced with a ruddy Italian, and the artist, accustomed to the pale complexions of his country, unhesitatingly steeped his brush in red the color of wine and brought the bon vivant devastatingly to life.

Like Velázquez, I am less interested in the Pope than in the man. That face is a whirlpool of flesh, and blood, and life; the eyes are searching. "You've come to see me." "You, you're plainly no fool." "As for you, you're an imbecile, away with you."

Those eyes, painted so tellingly by Velázquez, must have frightened Innocent himself; unless they helped him to understand his own success.

Beholding himself here, he must have taken to heart the words "Know thyself."

October 25 / At the Vatican Museum of Antiquities

It's a necropolis of marble. Good and bad side by side, like men after death. It's the Pompeii of sculpture, a tremendous world, an empire. And it is only an infinitely small part of a vanished and mysterious world; yet by spending days here one must surely be able to enter into communication with its resident spirits. The temples are at the Forum, but their gods are here. The ashes of the Romans are scattered to the four winds; their busts, hard, rough, and stony like their faces, are lined up in a throng, arranged in tiers like the dead in the catacombs. They bring to mind the milk of the she-wolf and the skull of the wolf.

Here Laocoön is no longer the melodramatic priest of Apollo strangled, with his sons, by two serpents; here he is strangled by fate. The Belvedere Apollo is no longer a god but a man more beautiful than a woman, and more beautiful because beloved of a woman.

Here stands the powerful torso of Hercules. If he moved, he would raise the temple.

Here, the *Discobolus*, summing up the art of the Greeks, and their life. Even before hurling the discus, he is the crowned athlete; the statue symbolizes the eternal alliance of skill and strength, basis of all power. Greek sculptors, O citizens of the world!

October 29 / The Baths of Diocletian

In these baths a church was built called Santa Maria degli Angeli. And in the church there is a gigantic Houdon, *Saint Bruno*, done when the artist was twenty-five. The vulgarity of this work, which was inspired by the building it rests in, shows how dangerous for our Villa Medici artists is the bad taste that has so long reigned in Rome, side by side with genuine masterpieces, and even blended and confused with them.

Michelangelo designed a convent and a cloister to be housed in these baths, and planted somber cypresses. It was a site for meditation.

Now the National Museum is installed here, with a collection of antique sculpture. Nowhere better than here can the poverty of Roman sculpture be realized, although the Romans sculpted as if possessed! They were possessed by a rage to copy the Greeks and it lasted for centuries. What an admission of impotence!

The National Museum has some admirable Greek statues. The most beautiful are always of the period called Archaic, a word which never fails to upset me. This excellent word, which makes the layman think of someone groping, feeling his way, signifies an art at one and the same time at its inception and in all its splendor.

October 31 / Berenson on the Italians

I am in Florence. Mussolini has been appointed president of the Council. Much talk of Fascism. Berenson commented: "These Fascists are the same people who requisitioned my most precious wines three years ago in the name of the Florentine Soviet Committee; then they were Communists. They don't know what they are. The only lucky Italians are those who live abroad. I've lived here for thirty-two years and I've never seen a government, and that's their way of governing. Like their police, who lie low during strikes. When the government comes up against some difficulty, they disappear; when everything is settled by the nature of things, they reappear, triumphant. But nevertheless everything works in this country. That's because Italy isn't a nation; it is a civilization!"

After dinner Berenson, that model of integrity, tried to sell me pictures, and very bad they were!

November 1 / Florence and Botticelli

I am spending only forty-eight hours here, and I wish to say only a few words about Florence—why, then, do I feel impelled to speak of Botticelli rather than of those who came before him: Cimabue, Giotto, and the others I admire, and of whom he is only a lymphatic and pagan descendant?

With the Florentine insolence of his period, he raised the heavy veilings of his madonnas, throwing transparent ones over them instead; he brought them down from the sky and made them walk the earth among the sturdy blades of tapestry flowers; that is the essence of his *Spring*.

This pagan festival wasn't enough for him; the Virgin, who was formerly holding the divine infant, is undressed and shown to us nude; she rises from the water and he calls her Venus. She is the initiatress.

Botticelli met Savonarola late in life—Savonarola, the fiery monk who despite the Medicis and in opposition to them saved the honor of Florence after the defeat inflicted on it by Charles VIII. Savonarola clamored and fought against the Medicis and the dissolute popes, and finally he was publicly burnt.

However much he wept and repented in his old age, Botticelli's greatness is not dimmed by the fact that he played a part in the dissolution of public morality. The dissolution of the arts themselves is merely an inevitable consequence. Fragonard and the profusion of fondled behinds that he shows us is immediately followed by the Revolution. Botticelli, last scion of an epoch otherwise greater than the eighteenth century, still preserves not only the fine manners of his race but the grand manner! The frescoes of Giotto are a biblical manifestation; Botticelli's *Spring* is an embodiment of the lyricism later to be found in Wagner, who, great though he was, could not have written a religious song for the early Christians. Music has not yet found its Giotto. Gounod is church music for silken robes. Botticelli's *Spring* similar in kind to that of Siegfried. Both are equally pagan. Both are bedecked with flowers. And both dangerous to youth. Both speak more to the senses than to the spirit; that is why they are inaccessible, and hence even irritating. They depict impossible happiness because they are the image of happiness. Thanks to Botticelli, the Florentine Renaissance died at the height of its beauty. With his image of womanhood, he was the link that joined the world coming to an end and the world about to be born. In his image of womanhood he developed the secular spirit, which led to an exploration of its mystery. In bringing her toward humanity, he removed her from man. Soon afterward, in *La Gioconda,* da Vinci was to evoke the enigma which will never be solved but which will go on tormenting all painters in their works, all the tireless commentators on the inscrutability of woman. Ever since man and woman ceased to commune with God, they have failed to communicate with each other. Botticelli stands at the point of departure of these diverging lines rushing down from the heights and fleeing each other. Spring has the power to bring people closer together but it cannot unite them. Botticelli's is a striking portrayal of this limitation. Those women and those fauns, so close to being human, are living images of desire; but as soon as their pleasure is over, they will be gone and the gesture forgotten.

November 13 / Italian swindlers

An Italian dealer will show you two busts, pendants, and he'll admit that one of them is fake, a fact which is perfectly obvious. The one he'll sell you as a genuine antique is equally fake but less visibly so.

November 19 / Marcel Proust is dead

How quickly they vanish, those who have entered the pages of this journal. I am glad to have caught at least a glimpse of this elusive man. Since my marriage, and because of his nightwalker's life, I've seen no more of him. I am sure he has completed that prolonged and fascinating history of the Guermantes and Swann (several volumes still remain to be published), for he told me back in 1907: "I'm writing an erotic book." And if eroticism there is, it appeared only toward the fifth or sixth volume.

He was always saying, "I'm going to die," and you no longer believed it. He must have been fifty. Society people, of that grand world which he adored, were beginning to feel that he took too much interest in them. Probably they will not regret his death. In *Pastiches et Mélanges* he went so far as to give names, and his history of the Guermantes is a *roman à clef*.

What a commotion has gone on these five years around him who, in his horror of noise, had his whole apartment padded with cork, from ceiling to floor!

This writer will be emulated and, above all, imitated. He brought into literature what science would call microbic analysis. How fiendishly powerful were his lenses and his analysis of what he saw! As though he wished to explore the atom itself and its system. Having carried this to its limits, he has made it quite impossible for a school of writing to develop in the same direction. He will be compared with Saint-Simon, whom he told me he so loved; he is more introspective. He also adored Balzac. He will not be read by the masses, but nonetheless he will endure!

November 20 / The mask of Marcel Proust

I met Helleu, who said: "Do you know where I'm going this afternoon?" "No." "I'm going to sketch the head of Proust; his family, or rather his brother, has asked me to do it. It's no joke; what a grisly assignment!"

Although Helleu made a grimace, I could sense how pleased he was to have been commissioned for this grim task.

November 21 / Proust's funeral

We gathered at the church. I went to the funeral parlor on the rue Hamelin, and while I signed the book an old man was speaking very loudly to the undertaker's employees, saying: "I was his professor of Greek." I got into conversation with this man, who told me: "I gave him lessons at Houlgate, where he spent his vacations with his family, and it was all quite serious; his father used to attend the lesson. I had him at thirteen, he really loved Greek, did little Marcel, and already his dream was to become a writer. He didn't care for playing. He was always trying to draw my wife aside, far from the animation of the beach into the quietest spots, to speak, he said, of literature, and he would ask both of us: 'Do you think that one day my plays will be performed at the Comédie-Française?' "

The old professor never saw his pupil again, as he said himself, but he is very proud of him now that he is dead. He is glad to attend this funeral and wants to know if there will be many men of letters.

"What do you think of Proust's books?" I asked. The old professor of Greek, stooped and quavering, replied: "Ah, monsieur, Proust's books are a bit difficult for me!" Charming!

At the Church of Saint-Pierre de Chaillot, all draped in black, there was not much of a crowd, fewer than four hundred people. The men of letters weren't there; they do not know Proust.

The priest in the pulpit pronounced some words to the effect that Proust was not a believer.

November 22 / Helleu on Proust

"Oh! it was horrible, but how handsome he was! I have done him dead as dead. He hadn't eaten for five months, except for café au lait. You can't imagine how beautiful it can be, the corpse of a man who hasn't eaten for such a long time; everything superfluous is dissolved away. Ah, he was handsome, with a beautiful thick black beard. His forehead, normally receding, had become convex. But I've bungled the job. What can you expect, when I had to work with electric light? We were there together for two hours, and with the electric light on my copperplate, I could only see the plate; I didn't see what I was doing. Ah, but he was beautiful!

"His old housekeeper told me that he had said: 'When I am dead, have them call in Helleu to do my portrait.' It's a funny appointment to make. He wanted it because I had done Whistler, Sargent, and de Montesquiou. This morning I went to the printer's; I'll run off two or three proofs, none for the trade. He was handsome; a cast should have been made. If only the window could have been opened, but they were afraid of rapid decomposition; they were wrong, with its being cold like this. But how beautiful he was!"

November 24 / With Forain

I brought up the subject of Botticelli's *Spring*. "Do you know," he asked, "that the two women were English whores driven out of Rome? They're the English type, with long teeth."

I watched him at work, and he explained his manner of painting: "I've not invented this, but the preparatory sketch has to be complete; it is important to establish masses, and they must be well defined; masses exist only through light. How one longs later on to alter the light and with it the masses! It's all related. Those broad brush strokes are quite deliberate. That's how Hals and Rubens worked, perhaps not Titian; no, Titian didn't, and he was greater than the others. Ah! there is no method; there are only different ways of feeling. The greatest difficulty is to know when the work is finished, when it should be left alone."

Forain moves from one canvas to the other; here he paints a courtroom scene with a woman feeling unwell; there another courtroom with an expert scrutinizing a necklace—damning evidence seen through a magnifying glass. Forain modified it with his thumb, rubbed out the judges' heads, saying: "They don't give a hang."

The day was declining rapidly. Forain plunged into his boxes, full to the bursting point with drawings, and pulled out several of them, all widely different. The most interesting one was a Chardin water color, *Blowing Bubbles*. I asked him if he copied the picture directly, and he replied: "No, I did it from memory, having seen a reproduction." It is astonishing in its exactitude. Other drawings included Fragonard women, with a very eighteenth-century flavor. The artist wondered why it is that the Americans don't understand the eighteenth century. I replied that they find it frivolous, and he said: "But frivolity is the perfume of life." And Forain is so moral! Sometime earlier he was quoting a maxim he had read: "You must be a wife to be a mother," and added, "That's not modern." There is one particularly amusing drawing: the sharing of hypothetical dividends: fat shady bankers jostle the table with their bellies, to the typist's amusement. Then there was a drawing of war: it's from the time of the torpedoing of unarmed neutral vessels; on the beach, a Dutch youngster with his mother; the child puts his hand into the water and takes it out again, saying: "Mama, there's wheat in the sea." I told Forain that I went to Reims the other day. "Ah, it's my city," he said. "It's all because I spun my top on the cathedral pavement that I've become an artist."

November 25 / Quote from a jeweler

One of Cartier's employees has told me that their boss always says: "You have to make the client feel a passion for the stone."

A letter from Proust

I must have received it at the end of 1907. It isn't dated.

> 102, *boulevard Haussmann*
> *Yes, the first pledges which two mortal beings*
> *Exchange seated on the ground at the foot of a tree*
> *Stripped by the winds, on a rock made of dust.*
>
> These verses of Musset come back to my mind, dear sir, when I remember your pledges at Cabourg and your solemn promise to come to see me on your return. Instead of which, *complete silence.* I have only half a regret, for I have been seriously ill since my return, and have left my bed only three times. I receive absolutely no one and would not have seen you either. But a word, at least, from you would have touched me, while your silence has hurt me and has rather cruelly made me think of myself as "a seaside connection" of yours. I hope my condition will improve sufficiently to allow me to return there and that the sea air may accomplish its annual miracle for me to the extent of enabling me to resume the chats in the hall in the retreat of the damned, where I'll tell you what happened after your departure: some very curious things. You have missed some amazing spectacles. Au revoir, dear sir. I hope your mother is well. Please give her my regards and believe, I pray you, in my friendship for you.
>
> *Marcel Proust*

I have had several letters from Proust, but this evening I could find only this one. We had spent the month of August in 1907 and 1908 together at Cabourg, and in the evenings we used to sit from nine o'clock onward in the highly animated hall of the hotel, and it's that corner, with our two chairs or armchairs, which he referred to as the retreat of the damned.

The happenings and the amazing spectacles he refers to were of course nothing much—some quarrel, perhaps, or someone's intrusion into one of the cliques. But Proust so magnified details; his observations were so minute; he gave such importance to things which to others would seem trifling, but which, when he spoke of them, would really be transformed into exciting and fascinating events.

December 2 / With Lemordant

I had not seen him again since my visit to Penmarch.

Nervously I told the painter that I had a present for him, called a Radiola—a new invention, wireless telephony—and that every evening at about six he could hear the concerts sponsored by the Eiffel Tower, and at nine those sponsored by the company that sold the apparatus.

I didn't dare bring the contraption into the studio, but left it in my car, for it's no easy thing to persuade the great blind artist to accept presents. However, this really is a marvelous invention, and luckily his resistance was weak, and I rushed down to get the thing. It was nearly seven o'clock. For the first time the heroic blindman can be in touch with the joys of the outside world. He was so moved that he could not grasp the simple explanations I gave him about which knobs to turn, and he said: "Come back another day, tomorrow if you can, or the day after; I'm overwhelmed."

December 3 / Another letter from Proust

I've just found it. He wrote upon receiving the announcement of my marriage, which took place in 1912. It does not bear any date.

> Dear Friend,
>
> I congratulate you most sincerely. I was a little disappointed to receive this printed card. It seemed to me that we were just a shade more intimate and that you would have written to me. But doubtless I have confused my personal wishes with reality, and besides you must have so much to do and so much to think of. I have never been married, but I can imagine. I beg you to tell your mother that, among

the feelings which the news of your marriage have awakened in me, she has not been forgotten. Her joy and also the little cloud of melancholy at being separated a little from a son such as you, I understand all that so well. I hope that you will be able all the same to spend much time with her and that your wife and she will understand and love each other.

Your very devoted
Marcel Proust

How life moves in a circle! With the same post as this letter, I am sending one to my friend Lauris, asking him to arrange for me to visit the Rouart Collection. And that at once reminds me how that other time it was through him and thanks to you, whom I did not yet know, that I was granted permission to visit the Kann Collection, which, however, I never visited after all—like everything I've failed to do in my life, everything else my health has deprived me of.

December 6 / At Forain's

"I once knew," said Forain, "a Count de C. who twenty years ago used to walk every day in the Bois de Boulogne. His father, a country gentleman, had lain with all the farm girls and given them numerous children, for whom he always reserved subordinate positions in his household. After his death, scenes like the following would occur from time to time at the château: one day the shoot had been deplorable and the young count summoned one of the beaters, his brother, into the drawing room to say: 'If our father had been present at this shoot he'd have called both of us *cochons*.' At this moment sounds were heard in the corridor, someone was coming and entered the room; the beater immediately straightened up and put his hands to the seams of his trousers, saying: 'Next time I promise Monsieur le Comte he will be better served.' "

December 7 / The etching of Proust made by Helleu

He has told me that two copies only were run off for the family, and he added: "I've destroyed the plate, it's not nice to keep a dead man at home, not even one like Proust."

December 8 / Substituted statues

They are at the Château de Grancey-le-Grand near Dijon. Nathan Wildenstein had been told that there were two thirteenth-century marble statues there for which the Count de Mandat-Grancey could get 50,000 francs. They are in the chapel some sixteen feet underground. The watchman told me that in summertime people from the neighborhood come out to see them and they are mentioned in all the books.

They are fakes; they must have been done some thirty years ago; the originals must have been of stone, dating from the beginning of the fourteenth century.

On Baron Maurice de Rothschild

While looking for Proust's letters the other evening, I found one from the baron. When still very young he was already a rather bad sort, and Baron Edmond, his father, sent him to hunt in South Africa. It was a way of being rid of him.

Around 1910 he inherited a fortune from his godmother, Baroness Adolphe de Rothschild, and an enormous collection. As Maurice didn't want to work at the bank, his father, to keep him busy, sent him to Nathan Wildenstein, and entrusted him to Wildenstein.

What an amusing time that was at No. 57! Maurice was always being hidden, there were swift entrances and exits, as he was a client the others weren't supposed to see, but word got out and the Seligmanns and Duveens made for him, and Maurice let it happen, as there were many things in his collection which he didn't like, a lot of fakes he wanted to be rid of, and which he coolly sold or exchanged.

One day, when I hadn't yet met him, Wildenstein said to me: "I was at the baron's this morning; he wants to see you to speak to you about America, where he'd like you to sell some of his pieces. He'll expect you tomorrow at eleven at his home, 47, rue de Monceau." I went and was immediately shown up into his bedroom overlooking the Parc Monceau; he wasn't there, and the bed was unmade. Suddenly I heard someone calling from the next room: "Is that you, Gimpel?" "Yes, it is I." "Well, come in." The voice came from the bathroom; I entered, and what did I see? Rising from the bath, not Diana but His Excellency the Baron Maurice de Rothschild.

Shortly afterward I left for America. He entrusted several pieces to me and gave me a letter, the one I found the other evening.

December 11 / Marie Laurencin

She came to see my children and to paint them, and was accompanied by Mme Raoul Aaron, who introduced me to her; they went to school together, and they started talking about old times. They had lost track of each other, and it was through my asking Mme Raoul Aaron one day to come with Marie Laurencin that they met again.

"You were rather eccentric," said Mme Aaron.

"Yes, I was and still am; it's one way to make life livable."

"Yes. And your life has not been funny; not funny at all—do you remember? We sat down side by side and you told me the story of your life. And we both cried."

"That's it, we cried," said Marie, laughing.

Marie has a snout like the phantom figures she paints; her creatures resemble her. She has this pointed snout and blue eyes; in paintings she makes them black. "Did you begin to paint young?" I asked her. Mme Aaron interrupted, "You remember, you said, 'I've got to earn some money.' I advised you to do fashion plates. You considered it, and tried one or two, but your talent rapidly outgrew that art!"

"Yes, I painted, I did some drawing. One day my mother told me, I don't know where she'd heard it, that to be a great painter you had to know how to draw braids. So I always sat in the back row; that's where I belonged."

"Certainly not," protested her friend.

"Certainly yes. Do you remember, one day I found on the floor a list in two columns—made by some of the girls. The first column ranked us in order of beauty, the second in order of intelligence, and I was at the bottom of both. They were right, I was rather dim, I'm not very intelligent. The ability to paint is a gift, a sort of instinct. I was at the bottom, and yet I don't think the others have gone much further than I. Then there were those braids; being last in line, I could see them all, so I sketched them. I drew nothing but braids, and I showed them to my little friends, asking: 'Will I become a great painter? Look at these braids, try and recognize them.' There was one they always recognized simply because it was the longest. I took them to my mother, who burned them; she burned many of my sketches; she was right, they were so poor, and my mother had taste; you remember she used to go on her own to muse in front of the pictures in the Louvre, in front of Leonardo."

While we were talking, the children came in and my wife asked if she wished to paint them, for Marie Laurencin paints only children who appeal to her, she had warned Mme Raoul Aaron, she had even written. The children did appeal to her, very much so, in fact, and so did my wife, whom she would also like to paint, and to whom she said: "You are my type." They discussed horses: my wife would like to be painted on horseback. Marie adores horses and remarked: "But you know, I don't make them true to life, they are my horses. Ah! how I love horses. When I worked in the Forest of Senart, three beautiful horses, three thoroughbreds, would come every morning to greet me."

Then one of our dogs put in an appearance. Marie was wild with delight, saying she had to paint this dog, Asta, with the children, and adding: "They're so beautiful, dogs and children together!"

It was decided that at 10:30 tomorrow Marie Laurencin will begin the portrait of Pierre, who is due to leave with us for America. She said she preferred to paint him at home in his normal surroundings, but when she learned that on other days he is out at that hour she said: "No, no, let's change it, I don't want to upset his routine; then he won't like me, he'll think of the sun and he'll be right: we mustn't restrict him." We assured her that the restriction would be slight.

Marie Laurencin talks rather like a Paris urchin, a conversation strewn with surprises; her face is pleasant, that's all. She went on to talk of her friends: André Gide, Giraudoux, Paul Morand, whom she doesn't see very much. "I'm a woman," she said. "I like to stay at home, except that I love traveling, because there's nothing that relaxes me better than a journey by sleeping-car."

It's only a year since she started doing portraits, such as that of the son of James Hyde or Robert de Rothschild's little girl.

She talked of Mme Aaron, saying: "She thought I was rich; that's not quite true. I have two picture dealers, Rosenberg and Hessel; they are in partnership to purchase my canvases. I don't know what I'd do without them; as I've said to them: 'I'd have to walk the streets.' And it's not at all certain I'd make a success of it. And she thought I was rich. Ah! You don't know my story; a few days before the war I married a

German, which cost me six years of exile in Spain; I was divorced a year ago."

"Because he was German?" asked my wife.

"No, because he was an alcoholic, which is worse. I shan't marry again now. He's lost his money, his whole family is ruined; from time to time I go to see the family in Germany; the other day I gave my sister-in-law two hundred francs in French money for her little girl; she was so delighted! It's a noble family, I was a baroness; all that, title and money, is gone and means nothing. What does the title matter to me, except that just once in a while I dredge it up for people who use false ones. Society people like that are so malicious. For example, I was recently at the house of the Marquise de Polignac. Now, I don't know if you've read Giraudoux's last book, *My Friend from Limousin*, there's a woman in it; people have said it was me because she marries a German before the war, she paints or is an artist of some art; but she has scandalous adventures, the impression is given that she was Giraudoux's mistress—which was never the case with me—and her children are stillborn. So the Marquise de Polignac asked me: 'You've never had a stillborn child?' 'No,' I replied, 'I've never had a stillborn child; I've never had anything more than a puppy or a kitten.' "

December 12 / Marie Laurencin starts the portrait

She took out an album and started to draw with a Hardtmuth pencil and some colored pencils. Pierre had posed for barely thirty minutes, and the resemblance was already there. She asked him what his favorite animal was and he answered that he liked cats best, so she is going to do him with Petit Gris. Ernest was looking at her drawing and saying: "Oh, I'd love to know how to draw like you, I was fifth in drawing." "Myself, I was always last," she replied. Then she turned to me: "Ask Jeanne Aaron. But I was better at needlework, because I was shortsighted and did the petit point well. That list I found on the floor was perfectly fair. You cannot imagine how useful it has been to me in my life to know that they put me at the bottom of the list, and how often I've thought of it!"

"Why was it useful?"

"Why? Because it made me think, because it enabled me to take stock of myself, because it kept me from overestimating myself. It gave me a sense of proportion, seeing how other people's opinion differed from mine on this essential point. I owe a great deal to that list!"

December 13 / Her tubes of color

Apart from black and white, she has just four in her box: cobalt blue, deep madder red, ocher yellow, and emerald green. I hardly know what use the drawing she made yesterday has been to her. Today she turned up with her little canvas, on which she had traced only a green line very vaguely indicating the oval of the face, and two small lines for the eyebrows. She applied white, which she transformed at once into pink; she started with the nose, which she doesn't really do at all—no one has ever seen a trace of it in any of her pictures—and at the end of an hour she left her canvas with everything indicated on it, and already a certain resemblance in the eyes.

December 14 / A letter from Manet

It is framed, at Dr. Fournier's, who is selling out and retiring to Marseilles. It was addressed by the painter to his mistress and went approximately like this: "Your doctors are asses to stop you from eating fruit. Here are some strawberries and plums; they won't do you any harm."

And the fruits are rendered in water color.

Fournier, a doctor of venereal diseases, and the son of such a doctor, owns several highly erotic pictures, which seems strange for a man who searches out the depths of the miseries occasioned by the act of love!

Fournier has, from his mother, a Hubert Robert which he wishes to sell. When he inherited it, Groult looked him up and told him his picture was fake but that he was prepared to relieve him of it. "It shook me," said the doctor, "getting such an opinion from such a connoisseur. But I made inquiries. He often returned to the attack; in the end I made it clear that I wouldn't sell him my picture, and a day or two later, when I had a dinner party, and he knew it, around seven o'clock I received a wreath, with his card, on which he had written: 'With my eternal regrets.'"

At Marie Laurencin's, 12, rue José-Maria-de-Heredia

I called on her, together with my wife, who said to her: "Your apartment's like your paintings." "You're quite right," she replied. "It's always like that wherever I live."

She lives in three small rooms, with some imitation and some Louis XVI plasterwork, but all done up with paper, fabrics, and modern furniture; a great deal of blue, a delicate blue.

First of all she introduced her cat to us, and we talked about two angoras she'd seen at a shop on the rue La Boétie, for which she was asked 1,700 francs. She wanted some friends to buy them: "They made a mistake not buying them," she said. "They would have been like ostrich plumes stalking through the apartment!" Next she showed us a bird in a cage; it sang ravishingly but was a mechanical toy. We listened to it in silence, while the cat tried to catch it in his claws; happily the wirework of the cage was close and he couldn't have killed it. Then she held up under our noses a little toy lamb, which had cost four francs ninety-five. "I'd been sick and had received too many flowers; I was tired of them, and said so to Hessel: so he sent me this lamb, which arrived the day I was about to die. It's dusty, perhaps it'll have to go to the cleaner's."

Marie Laurencin has scarcely any paintings in her apartment; all her canvases were confiscated during the war, then put up for sale, and the lot brought in thirty francs. She has just started on a portrait of the Baroness Gourgaud.

On her bedroom mantelpiece she has a photograph of her ex-husband, a very handsome youth and very distinguished. My wife took him for an Englishman. "He appealed to me," she said, "because he had beautiful manners and danced well." Then she showed us an album with photographs of her pictures. Her maid Blanche's daughter, little Olga, was in many of them and she called her in so we could see her, telling us the mother was so stupid and her stupidity so irritating that, to have her around less often, she gives her two days off a week. Even so, her apartment is immaculately kept, because the artist adores tidiness to the point of mania. Little Olga is fat and chubby-cheeked.

Marie Laurencin gives her pictures titles such as *Diana, The Sirens, The Circus, The Three Graces, The Angels*—titles which often bear no relation to the canvases.

Finally she showed us a little boy's head, explaining: "Ah, that, that's a son of mine. From time to time I make myself some children; I need children. Often it's a little girl, and these children are very much my own."

December 15 / Marie Laurencin works seriously and steadily

She applies the paint, a great deal of paint, in an almost unnatural way: that's because she uses so much white. Her paint is just a tinted white. "Yes," she explained to me, "I can leave a picture unfinished, and I appreciate the charm of a sketch, but I don't do any; the impressionists' pictures are sketches, and that's why it's hardly likely that they will survive."

I was surprised to hear such a judgment from the lips of this artist who is a direct descendant of that school. It should be said that she has no artistic culture; thus she knows nothing whatever of the old masters; she asked me the styles of my drawing rooms and wanted to know if they were handsome: she couldn't decide for herself. Of the history of art, she said to me: "I learned it at school when I was a little girl."

She has always been terribly nearsighted and has difficulty in going down a staircase. She drags along a cane, but only as the aftermath of an operation she has had and talks about a lot. "Oh," she said, "it's not particularly unpleasant to be very ill, the solitude and emptiness is so relaxing; it's an impression which has its value, being alone with pain. I knew I was very ill, but at the time one feels such indifference that one is tempted to cry out: 'Let death come.' No, I'm not afraid of death. As I say, I knew I was very ill and yet I asked myself all the time: 'So when shall I be able to move about?' Dr. Martel, who three times has operated on me and saved me, gave me an authoritative answer: 'You'll walk when the leaves are falling.' He didn't believe it himself and he remarked to me once again only last night: 'Doctors know how to lie so well.' "

December 20 / "Interior at Petworth" by Turner (National Gallery)

I can't describe it, I don't know what it is, I don't see what it is. It's easier to enter into the most unreal world of the poet than into that of the painter. It is strange that we can move with such ease in the

René Gimpel's father

The Gimpel Gallery at Trouville in 1898

The Duveen children: the eldest, Joseph, is sitting on the right.
Florence, the youngest, was not yet born

René Gimpel and his wife Florence in the garden of l'hôtel de la rue Spontini, which was built by Jacques Doucet

Jacques Doucet

Renoir in his studio

Forain

Marcel Proust by Jacques Emile Blanche

Dedication by Marcel Proust to René Gimpel in a copy of *Sodome et Gomorrhe*. It reads: 'I have just spent several months near to death. My health has not been good enough to correct the mistakes in this volume, I have not had any proofs, but, such as it is, it comes with my affectionate gratitude. Marcel Proust

'And I would so much like to see you.'

Joseph Duveen

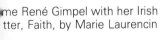
me René Gimpel with her Irish
tter, Faith, by Marie Laurencin

Ernest Gimpel (later known as Charles) with Asta, an Alsatian, by Marie Laurencin

Peter Gimpel with the cat Pompom, by Marie Laurencin

atmosphere of words and with such difficulty among the almost tangible images of painting. I don't want to know what this interior at Petworth represents. Why plunder the unreal? Besides, I couldn't enter the interior at Petworth, I wouldn't dare enter; it's enough that the door is wide open for our contemplation. I wouldn't dare go in, I'd be afraid of being burnt up; the air looks so hot, so boiling hot, and the mass of air is so thick, so voluminous! Only the soul of the painter can survive in it; perhaps other great painters as well are in fusion, in preparation there; it's no place for recognizable nature or even for a partially idealized one. In the interior at Petworth, moving strains are being brought to birth.

December 21 / The Pre-Raphaelite painters (Tate Gallery)

Burne-Jones was the greatest, Lady Waterford had some inspiration, Rossetti is a bit thin but a poet, Watts is hardly one of them, he was merely grandiloquent; the others were insignificant extras: Windus, Sir Patrick Spens, Miss Siddal (1834-62), Ford Madox Brown (1821-93).

It's not a school; it's a group. It left nothing behind and could not be expected to, for having sprung from opposing strains, its birth was a defiance of the laws of nature, like that of the mule. Instead of mining their strength from their own race and from their immediate predecessors, they turned to foreigners for inspiration, to foreigners who'd been dead too long. It's a child of old parents, and it bears the mark of ennui on its face—of deep and frightful ennui!

These painters, who sometimes did good work—but counter to any national trend, since they rejected tradition and even trampled on it—did their country harm: the modern English school is struggling in the chaos created by them. Had it followed them, it would have been Post-Pre-Raphaelite, which would have been absurd; it was ridiculous enough to be Pre-Raphaelite. They had broken the charm, and the young of today, not knowing where to turn for support, look to the last talented English artists: Lawrence, Constable, Turner. At a loss to fill a gap of a hundred years, they flounder. What a disaster!

December 30 / I buy a French primitive

I have paid £800 for it (about 51,000 francs). It vaguely resembles a Chinese picture. It's probably from the southwest of France.

January 3 / Considerations

When I told Aubry that I am having my children's portrait done by Marie Laurencin, he said: "You're right, she's a great artist, and her greatest merit is never having lost her feminine sensibility. All the women paint like men, look at Mme Vigée-Lebrun. Marie is perhaps anemic, and yet her colors are lovely, she has a way of expressing herself fully, she seems to want to put everything on a canvas, as if each canvas were to be the last and must express everything she knows. I knew her a little when she was with Guillaume Apollinaire; they loved each other very much. She was also married to a German with whom she had lived for quite a long time. There've been a lot of intrigues against her in the salons, what stupidity! But she is highly appreciated by Salmon and Max Jacob."

January 5 / Marie Laurencin finishes "Pierre and Ponpon the Cat"

She didn't want the child for this last sitting, and since yesterday the portrait has changed considerably. As to the likeness, it is more moral than physical. "People are very nice to me," she said. "They're always telling me: 'I didn't believe you could get such a resemblance.' I've also nearly finished the portrait of Baroness Gourgaud," she continued. "It was hard for me, she's not my type, she's an American, all teeth and a dried-up body. But when you get to know her, you see that she's good; she's so vigorous that she needs a round of pleasures and lots of people around her; curiously enough, she has a small religious spark in her. Your wife is more my type; since I first saw her, and I might say I only caught a glimpse of her, I've been talking only of her to everybody, asking if they know her. I met a lady who believed she knew her and asked me what she looked like. I replied: 'She has a charming voice, which goes so well with the way she lets her arm rest on her face.' The woman didn't understand at all; she had never noticed the grace of this gesture. It's a sensitive gesture. I can imagine your wife living in the forest with beautiful horses. I can tell that she is deeply moved by the silent miseries of animals and that her pleasure in owning them is tinged with anguish. She isn't one to care about going out and doesn't need society as part of her daily life; she can find enough elements of activity in her own elegance of thought and in its refinement. Haven't you got a photograph of her? That would be sufficient for me to paint her portrait and give her a surprise." "No," I say, "the few photographs ever made of her have always been monstrous."

Just then Marie Laurencin went up to a photograph, saying: "Pierre told me it's the portrait of a sister of your wife named Eva; she too must be a rare spirit." "You are right, madame." "She is sensitive," continued Marie Laurencin, "she has the sensibility of a flower. Yes, that's it. I can't put it any other way: a flower's sensibility. I'd like to know her. She too must feel the wounds inflicted every day by crass barbarians."

Marie Laurencin went through the photographs one by one, and it was unbelievable what she could read in them; she knows this, it has often been said to her. She was charmed by the photograph of a brother of my wife's, Ernest Duveen, an extremely sensitive person. Discovering a photograph of me in a drawer, she said: "You are headstrong and complicated, you love philosophy and you ought to write. You need to probe the heart of life; it's not given to you to love the theater." She is right, I don't love the theater, and I'd just admitted to her that I had written some plays. Marie Laurencin is astonishing; she sees all, and she's nearsighted to boot. She told me that she doesn't want to be distracted by any art other than her own; that when she was exiled in Spain she wrote a great deal to her friends, that they found her letters exceptionally well written, that in fact she can write letters like nobody else, and that some people wanted to publish them but she was against it, for quite apart from anything else, they contained a number of remarks about real people, so that it would be the height of bad taste. She has just written a story called "Translation," which has not yet appeared, for the American magazine *Vogue*, and has been paid $100. "None of it will be understood," she said. "That's the reason for the title. *La Nouvelle Revue Française* wanted me to give it to them. But I firmly refused; I want to be admired for my painting alone, and I don't want my painting to be admired because what I write is admired. I've worked enough at my art and for my art. I toil over a canvas, a canvas ought to be worked over, so much paint is necessary, and with my kind of talent the effort mustn't show. I wrote verses in Spain because I was barely working. I can tell you that I won't let myself get absorbed in serious books that force one to think, in philosophy. These books strike at my independence. Oh, yes, sometimes I read verse, which passes like a song. The verses of my friend Valéry give me pleasure. And then I do take a stand against certain groups, certain people who disturb me. There is a Bulgarian artist, a madly talented Jew, Pascin. What a book illustrator he could make! After an hour at his house I can't stand it any more, he smokes a pipe, he drinks liqueurs, so I leave him, saying: 'It's too dirty at your place, there's too much disorder. I am order itself, untidiness and dirt gravitate against the independence of my thought.' "

I told the artist that Aubry loves the feminine sensibility in her work, and I added: "Perhaps you won't consider that a compliment." "Oh yes, I want to remain a woman, and I'll admit to you"—Marie Laurencin suddenly blushed—"that each day I make myself do some sewing, as it's the most feminine exercise there is; it reminds me that I am a woman. And I don't go in for embroidery, but darning; honest darning, done in all seriousness, is a duty passed from woman to woman."

As Marie Laurencin was about to leave, I asked her if she wasn't going to varnish the picture. She replied that she never does. She said, "I wouldn't know how to do it, you do it; I love seeing how my pictures look varnished. But I would advise you to put it into an old frame, white and gold go well with my pictures, white because of the gray, but particularly the gold, as there isn't any yellow in my painting." I admitted that I would prefer a modern frame. She replied: "Then take it up with Doucet, who's given so much thought to the art of the frame; or else I could recommend a framer who studies modern styles. And then there's Mare, who also designs modern frames." "We'll see on my return," I said, "and a little before my return you might begin the portrait of my eldest, to give his mother a surprise."

"On your return," she said, "we'll be seeing each other, we must keep in touch now that we've started to know each other."

In the course of the afternoon I met Georges Bernheim and told him that I've had one of my children done by Marie Laurencin. "But she must paint your wife," he said. "She's absolutely her type." Marie Laurencin said the same thing this morning.

January 6 / I leave for New York on board the "Paris" with my wife and
    son Pierre

Watching the immigrants from the upper deck, Pierre asked me
why all those poor people weren't with us. What am I to answer him?
"Because they are poor." Hmm!

January 13 / I arrive in New York

I am staying at the Ambassador Hotel. I saw Demotte, who told
me he has sold a Roman statue to my friend Raymond Pitcairn and for
$20,000. That's about 300,000 francs.

January 15 / Joseph Barnard

An excellent American sculptor, very much engrossed in carving
himself a fortune out of the trade in works of art. In the South of France
fifteen years ago he bought a cloister and brought it over here, reassem-
bled it, and is now asking a million dollars for it.[1] I met him at Demotte's. The artist can see with only one eye, the right eye; the other
squints terribly to the left, a twisted disk. His face is chubby and close-
shaven; his black hair is sprinkled with gray, with odd tufts springing
from his skull like horsehair out of a mattress. He is of medium height.
His fingers are curious, they are so square and above all so small that they
seem to have only two phalanxes.

He talks of art as if it were a cabalistic science of which he is the
only astrologer; he speaks to impress. He's a sort of Rasputin of criticism.
The Rockefellers are his imperial family. And the dealers court him. At
the same time they are afraid of him. He has just helped to sell to John
D. Rockefeller, Jr., the Gothic tapestries of La Rochefoucauld for
$1,100,000, or about 18 million francs.

Barnard has filled his cloister with Gothic pieces that he got together in our country for a song twenty years ago. He told us that in a
small village near Perpignan the mayor one day took him into a sort of
cellar where he found the fine El Greco *Christ* now in the Louvre. The
worthy mayor offered it to him for one thousand francs. Barnard, author-

[1] He sold it for almost that price to John D. Rockefeller, Jr., who gave it to the
Metropolitan Museum, a museum of Gothic sculpture. (Note appended 1932.)

ized by the local administration, cabled the New York museum, offering it for five thousand francs, and the Metropolitan turned it down!

As far as antique sculpture goes, he has luckily never understood anything but ornament, or he would have carried off all our fine statues.

The beautiful Renoirs from Durand-Ruel are here: *The Loge, Dancer, Woman Bathing, The Fisherman's Children, At the Concert* (also called *The Loge*), *On the Terrace*. This last is the portrait of the demimondaine de Maray, then a little working-girl, who also had her young sister pose, to feed both of them. I went up close to the canvas and saw cracks under the black bodice; Durand-Ruel told me that these are the result of lacquers used as an undercoat which dried while still fresh. Beautiful blacks. The artist rarely used them: it was a color that didn't tempt him. He didn't like yellow either; he said it was always an enfeebled red.

The Durand-Ruels aren't selling these canvases, which are part of their private collection.[2]

Divers facts

An American dining with me told me that in 1872 the ground on which this Ambassador Hotel stands was sold for $10,000.

He was talking to me about American farms and told me they cover such vast areas that the machine plow will take a day to complete a single furrow.

We discussed Prohibition, that fatal ban on alcohol. He told me that people can get all they want to drink anyway, and that the bootleg liquor is such poison that every day there are people who drop dead after a few drinks. People who had never drunk alcohol before do it now because it is forbidden, and these people get to be the worst alcoholics.[3]

January 16 / Renoir, Degas, Rodin

I took my wife to Durand-Ruel's to see the Renoirs, which she found enchanting; she asked Durand-Ruel which one he preferred and

---

[2] They began selling them that winter; and they haven't kept even one. (Note appended 1932.)

[3] It was the beginning of Prohibition, which has since caused much deeper ravages. (Note appended 1932.)

he replied that he didn't know, that he wouldn't choose the most famous, *The Loge,* but would rather have *Dancer,* who in actual fact was never a dancer at all, but the daughter of one of his servants.

My wife told Durand-Ruel that Marie Laurencin has done Pierre's portrait. She added that she wasn't satisfied with it, that it wasn't like him, and Durand-Ruel said: "Renoir did a portrait of my wife that didn't resemble her. Look at this woman on the left in this canvas from Bougival; it's Mme Renoir. She had a turned-up nose and thick lips. She was or became his 'type,' his ideal woman, so he gave that nose and those lips to all women; but worst of all, when Mme Renoir had aged and grown inordinately stout, he swelled out and aged all his models, whom he deformed as nature had deformed his wife; that's why we find those monsters in works done toward the end of his life." Monsters! Durand-Ruel exaggerates!

I told him I liked *Woman with Cat* rather less. He told us she was a model who turned up drunk every day at Renoir's, and once, drowsy with wine, she fell asleep on a chair, and it was thus that the painter put her on canvas. And, in fact, she stinks of alcohol!

Durand-Ruel showed me the complete series of Degas's sculptures, seventy-two in all, female dancers and horses. The founder Hébrard purchased from the Degas heirs the right to reproduce them, and he will do twenty-two series, one of which will go to the Louvre, donated by the heirs; all the others will be sold for from 600,000 to 750,000 francs each. In doing horses, Degas sculptured the sinews. His dancers are all vigor, and it is their effort rather than their dancing that he captured in his sculpture. As a sculptor Degas is even greater than as a painter. Sculptors will have to study him. Durand-Ruel told me that Degas never sold a single one of his wax figures. They were found covered with dust, frequently broken; sometimes a horse had lost its neck, which was then fixed back on with wire.

All his life Degas was a bohemian; his meals consisted of an egg or two and some milk. Every morning he would give his maid five francs for meals for both of them. "He spent nothing," added Durand-Ruel. "Several times, however, he owed my father 200,000 or 300,000 francs, because he was building up a collection. He was often swindled." I can scarcely credit this statement of Durand-Ruel's, as his sale proved him to have been a great connoisseur. "In order to get our money back," continued Durand-Ruel, "we bought pastels from him; for one of them he made us pay 100,000 francs." Several of his sculptures were discovered in an old grand piano given to his parents on their marriage; he had removed the strings to make more room, but it wasn't a safe place, as some drawings that Forain had given him were found covered in mold.

I talked to Durand-Ruel of the book just published by Rodin's secretary, Marcelle Tirel, under the title *Rodin at Close Quarters, or the Inverse of Glory*, a rather picturesque narrative. "Oh," said Durand-Ruel, "toward the end of his life he became a blackguard, thoroughly dishonest. Even with the museums he'd set prices which he would then treble when they sent round for delivery. One day I bought some marbles from him, and when I dispatched them to America, I asked him, in conformity with American law, so as not to pay entrance duty, to give me a certificate attesting that these were, of course, original works. He replied: "I'll give you nothing of the kind; these are marbles done by my workers; I didn't touch them.""

Durand-Ruel took me into a room where there were only still lifes and flowers by Renoir on the walls. I made some comment about Renoir's remarkable versatility, and he said: "You know, he used to paint plates at Haviland's. He earned fifty francs a day, and the other workmen seven. 'Do you want Watteaus, Fragonards?' he would say. He had discovered all the secrets of the great masters. He told me that from time to time he would feel moved to paint dark like Díaz or like Rousseau or Fromentin. Without copying, he would do a Díaz, a Rousseau. He signed these canvases neither with his name nor with that of the master he was imitating, but they were sold over good signatures!"

Public auctions

The results at such a sale are unpredictable. This evening a Ziem was sold for $8,000, or 120,000 francs. According to Durand-Ruel it would have brought 15,000 francs in Paris. A Lhermitte went up to $6,000, or 90,000 francs. In Paris it would be worth 10,000 francs.

On the other hand, a marble *Eve*, life-size, a unique model by Rodin, was knocked down for $2,900. It is easily worth 200,000 francs. I bought it with Sidès.

February 5 / Vermeer signature

Today I found the signature of Vermeer, the word "Meer," on the picture called *Woman and Servant* in the Frick Collection. I've already found it on my picture *The Geographer*. I know of undiscovered signatures on other Vermeers. In the Frick picture it is high up and to the left of the jewel casket.

February 28 / John D. Rockefeller, Jr.

Yesterday's and today's newspapers announce that he has just bought the Gothic tapestries of La Rochefoucauld for $1,100,000, or, at the current rate of exchange, more than 18 million francs.

A Gauguin

"Why be angry," the artist wrote on the canvas, in the Tahitian language. The young Durand-Ruel (third generation) showed it to me. When I look at this picture I feel the charm of a return to nature; it is all contemplation and interior life. In order to attain this miraculous state, Gauguin, the former banker, must have had to throw off his civilized skin and take on that of a child of nature. A woman, standing in the foreground, seems molded by repose; she is tranquil because she doesn't have our nerves, our nerves which assimilate nothing. One day a mass exodus away from machinery will take place.

The Caruso sale

The superb tenor had married an American who was crazy about him. She had money, and he left her a great deal more.

This paragon of civilized womanhood is selling all the collections, and all the theater costumes. All his effects are up for auction, all kinds of souvenirs, his theatrical case, and the one he took on his honeymoon.

When a woman is callous, her lack of feeling attains extremes unkown in men. In England a year ago the following divorce took place: During the war a woman fell in love with a man and wrote to her husband at the front: "I don't love you any more. It's going to make you desperate; you'd be better off getting killed."

A young Englishman to whom I was talking about this today mentioned two similar cases in his regiment. A man was killed, the regiment had his sword and revolver sent to his wife, and she returned them, requesting that they be sold.

Another woman greeted her husband from behind a door opened just a crack, saying: "I thought all the really brave men in France were dead!"

Oh, Tahiti! Oh, Tahiti!

March 1 / A Vermeer sold

Knoedler has sold *Young Girl with a Flute*, known in Paris as *The Tonkinese*. It's truly one of the master's most beautiful works. It's going into the Widener Collection.

March 9 / A Whistler and a Corot

They are in the Baltimore Museum's temporary building. The Whistler is called *Waffing*. At the edge of the Thames on a café terrace he painted Legros the engraver, and the woman known as The White Model, who often posed for Whistler. Hers is a discolored whiteness; she is the image of death waiting deep within ourselves, which questions our spirit, argues, explicates. Beside her, the apoplectic Legros looks more fatally, more hopelessly dead, bon vivant though he was! The Thames is overburdened. How can it carry all those boats? They jostle one another, they're crushed together, it's absolute havoc. In the midst of this din and the immense commotion, the human figures are completely still, while the boats before them are the symbols of a merely material existence and its needs. From their very souls these beings seem to plead for some distant life, far from the boats and their remote passage.

In Corot's *The Shepherds of Arcadia* an enormous tree overshadows all the planes and dominates the horizon itself. Within this shadow the shepherds converse and dance; a goat takes part in their revels and gives a humane note to the festival.

March 13 / At Nathan Allen's, 368 West Park Place, in Kenosha, a small town near Chicago

Bache, who is his banker, informed me that in a single cotton transaction he had made $10 million. He lives in a tiny wooden house. He owns a Rembrandt dated 1655, the portrait of a rabbi, and paid

$100,000 for it. He isn't even aware that it is mentioned in books. The rabbi's expression reveals a tragic disposition and a hard past. He also owns a Titian, a doge, a rather flat picture, but nevertheless with a hint of Venice the fair. Nathan Allen has two pretty little Corots as well.

March 15 / At the Chicago museum

I've made this trip to see the museums and I have spent two days in this one alone. Mrs. Potter Palmer has bequeathed some magnificent impressionists; a Mrs. Kimball has given some English pictures and a fine Rembrandt, a portrait of the artist's father. Ryerson has lent his magnificent collection of primitives. There is a superb *Maître de Moulins*.

March 21 / At the Detroit museum

The president of the museum, my friend Ralph Booth, is unfortunately away. The museum, housed in an old brick church, is still in an embryonic state; but elsewhere construction work has begun on an enormous building; once it is completed, the gifts will pour in.

Detroit is the city of automobiles. Ford manufactures five thousand automobiles a day here and makes $100 million a year, taking a profit of only $55 per car.

As for the particular characteristic of Detroit, it is this: I've not seen a single horse here.

March 22 / At the Toledo museum

George Stevens and his wife, exquisite people, are its directors. The very pretty building was erected thanks to the generosity of a certain Mr. Libby, who has some very beautiful canvases and will bequeath them to the museum.

Mr. and Mrs. Stevens, who are only moderately well off, are devoting their lives to the museum. He gave up a fine situation for this post, which has obliged them to live, if not drably, at least quite unpretentiously. This devotion to the cause of art is found throughout the United States, and gives an idea of the fervor that convulsed the Middle Ages, when its churches were erected.

March 24 / At Eastman's

Eastman has built a conservatory of music which cost him $4 million; he's given it to the university. He showed it to me. Eastman's idea is original: he wants to force the public to learn to love music by way of the cinema. He puts on the finest films for fifty cents, which is nothing here; people flock to them, and hear a magnificent orchestra, for which they come back again. This cinema, open from 1 P.M. to 11 P.M., pays all the expenses of the conservatory.

I told Eastman how much I hate machines, and he replied: "They're to help man get through his work quickly, so that he may have more time for his pleasures."

I looked at his collection again. He has just bought a superb full-length Raeburn, *General Hay MacDorvell*—in a red riding coat and white breeches. What elegance was deployed for war in the eighteenth century!

March 25 / Miss Frick's twins

Some ten years ago Frick bought a small primitive painting found in France and sold to him as an Antonello da Messina. It represents a *Compassionate Virgin*, with Mary Magdalene and another Mary, Mary Jacobé or Mary Salomé, and on the two gibbets the thieves, with the donor to the right. But opinion was divided: some said it was Flemish; Berenson was the first, I believe, to declare it French, of the school of Avignon, which became the general view. This primitive was considered by many the pearl of the collection.

A week after my arrival here Miss Frick telephoned that she wanted my opinion on a picture, and to my stupefaction she showed me a panel almost identical to the first, a little smaller but without the donor; she asked me if it is by the same hand, and which one was likely to be the original. I replied: "Yes, it must be by the same hand, and at first sight the first seems to me to be the original. But then I love it so, that old friend!"

"Will you let me have your opinion in writing?"

"Ah, that's something else again; in that case I'll have to ask you for time to examine the panels."

Miss Frick went off, and I quickly realized that the work found last was the original, that the other, much studied and loved as it had been, was an old copy. I made some notes, quite an exhaustive fifteen-page study in fact, which I sent to Miss Frick.

I saw my brother-in-law Joe Duveen today, and in the course of our conversation he said: "Oh, by the way, you gave your opinion on Miss Frick's pictures; I take the opposite view; I've given her a certificate that the one they had first is the original. Look at the photographs." As he took them out of his drawer, I asked how they came to be in his possession, and he replied that he had them from Miss Frick's secretary. They were very poor. Joe had photographed the original photographs, which were themselves defective. He went on to expound his thesis. I replied that anything could be said about such deplorable reproductions. He asked me to go back and take another look at the two pictures, which I did. I came away even more convinced that I was right. When I went down to Miss Frick's library, her secretaries talked to me about the panels, and I told them what I thought, but at that moment Miss Frick's private secretary came in, and that same evening Joe, informed by her, phoned me to say that it was better not to discuss this question before third parties. I replied that I quite agreed. Joe wanted to avoid a controversy from which he'd emerge much diminished. He's brought a hornet's nest down about his ears. He has no knowledge of painting and sells with the support of experts' certificates, but his intelligence has enabled him to keep up a cracked façade in this country, which is still so little knowledgeable.

March 26 / A $10,000 bet

It's to do with Miss Frick's twins. I dined with Joe and some intimates to whom he confided our differences. Forgetting his discretion of the day before, he let himself be drawn in the heat of conversation into challenging me with a bet of $10,000, which he mistakenly believed I wouldn't accept. He asked me whom I proposed as experts. I named Berenson, Friedländer, and my nephew Armand Lowengard, and he accepted.

Joe doesn't realize the stir his bet is going to create. Already this evening one of the people present asked me, after having heard our explanations, and in front of Joe, if he could have a thousand-dollar share in my stake.

March 29 / Miss Frick's twins

I have explained the bet to Miss Frick, who knows I'm right; she taxes me with having chosen Joe's hangers-on as experts, but I assured her that Berenson and Friedländer wouldn't compromise their reputation to please Joe; as for Lowengard, his conscience would not let him do a thing like that.

April 9 / Miss Frick's twins

Joe has realized the stupidity of his bet and that he's put himself on the spot; he asked me to go to Miss Frick to tell her that he had been mistaken and that he will give her and her mother $25,000 for their charities.

Miss Frick replied to Joe's offer: "Tell your brother-in-law that I don't take money from a lost wager. Tell him too that you've saved him $25,000, and that pride goeth before a fall."

I didn't report this last remark to Joe, who is already red-faced enough.

April 16 / My exhibition of Gothic art and primitives at the Art Center, 65-67 East 56th Street

It has opened today and will run for two weeks. The main attractions are the following pieces: a superb twelfth-century fresco nine feet square; also five French primitives, a Jacobello del Fiore, a Giovanni di Benvenuto, an Andrea Vanni, and five thirteenth-century statues.

May 19 / Manet's "The Music Lesson"

The woman, life-size, is seated to the right on a horrible sofa, holding her music book on her knees; she wears a low-cut black dress and is about thirty. Beside her there is a bearded man whose gray-green trousers are cut in the fashion of the day. He is playing the mandolin. We are far from the music lessons of the eighteenth-century, which were only a pretext for love. Here it's a pretext for painting, and this is perhaps the sole flaw in this picture, this snapshot in which no one is thinking of music. The great pictures are silent and sad in the manner of this one. Manet's *Music Lesson* is as sad as Calvary. It is a Calvary. Who is this man with his flowing hair in the manner of the late romantics, and this rather intellectual woman? I don't know. But I do know that Manet has set down their essence, what they are though they're not aware of it. The psychologist has scrutinized them so closely; he has entered so profoundly into their spirit, that it is our own heart he pierces when he shows them like this in their narrow existence, in their oppressive, unbearable everyday life which strangles them like the tunic of Nessus.

"Claude Monet" by Edouard André

Hutchinson, president of the Chicago museum, told me this morning that this painting had been commissioned for the museum. André did two of them. Monet is there as I have described him, except that his face is truly the color of water lilies. He has precisely that beard which doesn't look real but makes him resemble Father Christmas. His eyes look out at an angle, with a malicious, mocking expression. It's the look with which these days he bitterly defends his prices. And why shouldn't he?

"Edouard Manet" by Fantin-Latour

It was bought by Hutchinson from Manet's widow. After having seen *The Music Lesson*, I was disconcerted to see in front of me a Manet looking every inch the fashionable man-about-town of the day, his beard well kept, brushed, curled, soft and caressing, almost uniquely suitable for love. He is wearing an impeccable flat-brimmed hat that widens out toward the top and looks as if it had come straight from the hatter's. One hand is gloved, he is holding a stick, his trousers are gray and his coat well cut; my title for it: *Manet Steps Out into Society*.

Turner's "The Dutch Fishing Boat"

One of my father's friends was Mimerel, the engineer who discovered aluminum. I always remember his saying one day that water should be considered a solid substance and that if science would plumb this idea, it would make fascinating discoveries. Working on this principle, he was then trying to evolve a boat that would skim over the surface of the water.

The great painters, who are great in a different way from the great engineers, have long since understood the solidity of water, whether they be Turner, Manet, or Whistler.

In this picture a huge wave lifts the heavy, peaceful fishing boat. How solid the water must be to raise it like that! It is its solidity that has led man to venture on it, and its solidity is what makes it dangerous, what breaks and engulfs. Turner is the master of this, of the tempest, of death striking at us through our fear. We know that these people, on these boats, are condemned. Nothing can save them and we are riveted, helpless ourselves as we stand on the shore, while they move on to perish in the vicious seas.

May 20 / Impressionists at Harold McCormick's

A Monet: *Algiers*. An undistinguished Manet: *Drinker with Jug*. A Puvis: *In the Heather*.

May 22 / With Harold McCormick

The pictures belong to one of his brothers. I had lunch with him and one of his daughters. A droll family: Harold married Rockefeller's daughter, but divorced her for a singer, a Polish woman. One of his daughters has married a riding master, a Swiss.

After the meal he insisted on taking me to see the Museum of Natural History, where he paused for a long time before the stuffed apes, and I could scarcely drag him away from them.

I had come on business and had brought along some pictures, which he asked in due course to see. I showed him an exquisite Virgin, which I attribute to the Master of Flémalle, and Harold, who a moment ago couldn't leave the apes, exclaimed: "How ugly she is!"

NOTEBOOK 10

May 23–September 27, 1923

May 23 / Vermeer's unknown signatures

Ever since I discovered the signature and the date 1665 on my Vermeer of Delft *The Geographer*, I have thought that other Vermeers must also be signed. Shortly afterward, I found his monogram, M.S., in an ornamental pattern right in the center of the lute in *The Woman with a Lute*, from the Johnson Collection of Philadelphia. This painting isn't genuine, but is an old copy of a Vermeer. The same ornamental pattern and the same monogram appear on the virginal in Vermeer's *Music Lesson* at Windsor Castle. I've also seen this decoration on a virginal in a picture, I believe by Mieris, in the National Gallery. It is perhaps the monogram of a maker of musical instruments, but beyond a doubt Vermeer adopted it. At the Frick house I've since found a rather clear signature on the jewel casket in *Woman and Servant*.

After long study of the work by Hofstede de Groot, with the splendid reproductions of thirty-seven known Vermeers, I reached the conclusion that the painter signed nearly all his canvases. There are only six signatures lacking, in six pictures which I haven't seen.

Allegory of the New Testament is monogrammed very plainly, and the artist uses the same decoration as on the virginal of the Windsor picture and the lute of the Johnson one.

In *Allegory* this very large monogram forms the pattern of the Cordovan leatherwork at the top right. I shouldn't be surprised if it was even dated on the *mappemonde*. In *Woman Reading* from Amsterdam, the same signature, the same sort of decoration, is on the geographical chart at the bottom, but placed inside the arms.

In *The Singing Lesson* in the Frick Collection there is something written on the paper which the man and woman are holding in their hand. At the bottom of the paper there would be a date.

In *The Taste of Wine* in Berlin, I noticed "Meer" on the roll of music paper falling from the table. It can only be seen in full daylight. Perhaps there is a date as well. In *Soldier and Laughing Girl* in the Frick Collection, it seems to me that "Vermeer" and a date are inscribed on the card. In *Young Girl with Flute* in the Widener Collection, I read "Meer" on the left above her right shoulder; the date must be at the tip of the collar. In *The Pearl Weigher* in the Widener Collection, I read "Meer" under the table, on the leg, in the hollow square formed by the molding. In *The Milkmaid* of Amsterdam, the monogram is in the form of a decoration at the base of the wall on the right. In *Girl with Guitar* in the Huntington Collection, the monogram is seen very clearly, at the bottom, in the triangle formed by the table and the hanging rug.

May 24 / Vermeer's unknown signatures

Today I have studied *Young Girl Writing* from the Morgan Collection, which must surely be signed on the coffer, like the one in the Frick Collection. I seem to make out a date on the coffer, something like 1666, to the right of the central ornament. I wouldn't be surprised if *Young Girl with Virginal* from the Beit Collection wasn't signed on the music book. I also think *Woman with Jug* at the New York museum must be signed, and the picture in the Gardner Collection as well.

May 26 / With Joe

His success stems from his taste, his boldness, and also his gift of organization, of which the following is an example. For twenty-five years the best art critic in England was Humphrey Ward; now Joe has had all his articles copied in triplicate, for his three branches, with an index, and when he wants to buy a picture or an object, he looks to see if Humphrey Ward mentioned it and what he said.

At the moment he is having bound all the letters he has received from Berenson over a period of fifteen years, similarly with an index. The expert speaks in them of all the fine Italian pictures from all the great European collections, and as this critic has written only two or three slender books, these letters, which constitute vast volumes, will be of great interest. I have advised Joe to bequeath them to the British Museum, together with his firm's business correspondence, and when he said, "It's too secret," I replied: "Specify that it's not to be opened for a hundred years!"

This week Joe bought a Holbein in Austria for £40,000; last week, Lord Spencer's Hals for an enormous price, also a Mantegna; and two weeks ago at Christie's, Van Dyck's *Portrait of Alexander Triest* for $146,000; also a Cuyp for more than $90,000. At the William Salomon sale in New York a month and a half ago he bought three vases by Orazio Fontana for $100,000, a Fragonard, *Mademoiselle Colombe*, for $40,000. In two sessions he ran up a bill for $400,000. A month ago he bought a Dürer. At the same time he showed me a Fra Angelico and a Rembrandt, *Portrait of a Man in a Red Toque*. A few days ago he sold Lord Carnarvon's Lawrence *Woman and Child* for an enormous price, and Turner's *The Queen of the Adriatic* for $300,000.

Joe has told me that Nathan Wildenstein and Arnold Seligmann have bought Joseph Bardac's thirteen gouaches for $80,000.

To make up for his lack of knowledge, he surrounds himself with all the great experts. Bode and Friedländer cost him only a few gifts to the Berlin Museum; but Berenson is expensive, as he exacts 25 per cent of the profits, whether he is assisting in the purchase of a picture or giving his opinion or introducing the client. I too pay this fee. Joe has made numerous gifts to France, to the Petit Palais, to the Louvre, to various propaganda societies, and has indeed just been awarded the rosette of the *Légion d'honneur*. He hopes one day to receive a peerage in England.

May 27 / The Ursuline convent

Once again I was on the train bound for Chicago. Reading *McClure's Magazine*, my wife was attracted by a photograph of a young girl on horseback, riding astraddle: an advertisement by the Ursuline Sisters of Middletown, New York, who recommend their school, claiming that in their convent the pupils are educated just like at home, with instruction in music, languages, riding, and sports.

May 31 / At the Cleveland Museum

Here I saw Renoir's *Pont-Neuf*; it belongs to a Mr. Coe. This is the picture that brought in the highest price at the disastrous sale of Renoir's paintings, and his friends', in 1874. It is signed on the left, "A. Renoir." It shows the blue Paris of the banks of the Seine, with a realism like Zola's and a poetry like Baudelaire's; with a multitude of amusing little figures: a mother out walking with her little girl, the Frago retinue, the eternal Crainquebille, the doughty and treacherously stubborn policeman. It would take a long time to describe this picture!

If this museum continues to be so well managed, it will become one of the two or three finest in the United States. The New York one is scandalously administered, but grows rich without moving a muscle, thanks to bequests, like our glorious and miserable Louvre. A day will come when the other museums here will give New York hard competition. Cleveland cultivates the civic spirit; it doesn't wait for the dead but approaches the living. That's the way to make a great museum. Someone named Wade has made fantastic donations. His example was followed by the Mather brothers, the Prentices, the Coes, the Severances. The director of the museum, Mr. Whiting, is a cold man with a warm heart. His assistant, Milliken, is full of youthful enthusiasm, and collectors can't resist his smile. America will never know what she owes to these pioneers of the ideal; she ought to erect statues to them or at least engrave the names of these outstanding servants of their country on the museum walls. People will want to know who they were, but they are anonymous. Some men, throughout the country, have realized that the frenetic manufacture of machines is going to lead America into the most intense materialism. On the other hand, America's deification of the machine is understandable, considering that it has put her so quickly on a rival footing with the whole world and has brought comforts into places which were desolate only a short time ago! For example, in Minneapolis and St. Paul, two cities with 400,000 inhabitants each, the first white woman was born around 1840 and died some ten years ago. How far they have come in eighty years! Before, there was nothing but Indians and the wilderness. It's not to be forgotten that this era of construction, such as the world will never see again, coincided with great mechanical discoveries, none of which had yet been perfected, such as the railway, electric power, the telephone, telegraph, etc. The squalid, illiterate immigrants from Europe were to accomplish cyclopean labors, and when they had made a little money, they would pass the pickax to the latest arrivals.

It is to these people, or to their still rough-hewn children, that the greatness of a Memling, a Rembrandt, a Renoir, a Cézanne, had to be taught. The marvel is that from this bizarre population great leaders have emerged. At the beginning they were preoccupied with the material needs of their weaker brothers, but thirty years later, when their labors were coming to an end and they were thinking of handing down the reins of authority to their juniors, they constructed schools, erected universities, and built museums.

The director, Mr. Whiting, wanted to show me the collections in the city; that's why I returned to Cleveland. Mr. Milliken and Mrs. Whiting accompanied me as well, for the city is so dirty, its factories so numerous, that rich people live in the country, where we went by automobile. There are some pictures by Dearth to be seen here as well.

Mrs. Prentice has a Luini, two Pinturicchios, a Rembrandt, a Watteau, *Betrothed Village Girl,* which once belonged to me, a Constable, a Terborch, a Reynolds. Mrs. Prentice is beautiful, with white hair, though she is not yet fifty; her eyes are blue tempered with gray reflections. She took us around her garden, which she prefers to her collection; she carries her refinement to the degree of appreciating the qualities of special kinds of leaves.

Mr. Severance, her brother, who lives across the road, has a Turner: *Fire in the Houses of Parliament, London,* a canvas as sad as it is magnificent. He has a Van Dyck, a Romney, a Reynolds, a Cuyp, and one or two Gothic statues.

These two collections will probably go to the Cleveland Museum, as neither Mrs. Prentice nor Mr. Severance has any children.

June 1 / At the museum

Today it was the turn of the Mather brothers' two collections, then that of modern pictures belonging to Mr. Coe; he has three Cézannes, including *The Deserted House;* seven Renoirs; a Gauguin *Woman Seated in the Shade of Palm Trees,* signed and dated 1891; some Monets, a Degas.

June 2 / *Eastman seen at 8:30 this morning in Rochester*

While he had his breakfast, the organ was being played. I showed him my Vermeer, which I let him have for $180,000. He finds it beautiful, so beautiful indeed that he wanted me to show it to his housekeeper, his organist, and his Negro servant.

The Eastman Kodak Company made $18 million this year from the manufacture of film.

June 5 / *A Vermeer signature*

At the Metropolitan Museum I had *Woman with Jug* taken down for me. I examined it for more than an hour, and saw something which looked like Vermeer's monogram, the letters M and J, on the window at the center top in the horizontal section to the left, and I think I could even make out the date, 1661 or 1664.

June 6 / *A Vigée-Lebrun*

Nathan Wildenstein has sold a Vigée-Lebrun, of the Russian period, to Barton Jacobs of Baltimore for $50,000. It is a portrait of Princess X.

June 7 / *The fakes in the Metropolitan Museum*

The twelfth-century seated man from the Dreicer Collection is made from ancient stone, but the figure has been so much retouched that it has no character. It's not worth a thousand dollars. The St. John said to be modern is, in fact, old. The seated king is modern, it's a horrible thing. There is one fake that nobody suspects; it's a little Roman statuette, a very elongated man which the museum bought four years ago from Alphonse Kann in Paris. It's easy to see that the figure has been slashed with some instrument to give the impression of natural breaks. The robe has idiotic folds which don't look right at all. The pattern of the lacework has been cut with a knife.

Kennedy on Whistler

He has made up a catalogue of the painter's work. He is a former dealer in engravings, and so old that he has no more face than a fish on a slab. I've been told that he is endowed with a prodigious memory and that he talks of Whistler in a most interesting fashion, but I could get nothing out of him, except that he owns some two hundred letters from the artist, many of which are unimportant, but others very curious. I advised him to bequeath them to the New York Library.

"I could write about Whistler," he said, "but I leave that to fools."

The Wilkes-Barre Museum

It will owe its existence to me. I was in Wilkes-Barre today with my friend Bertron to talk business with his very rich friend Kirby. On my arrival, Kirby rang the president of the museum, a lawyer, Mr. Gilbert S. MacClintock, of 44 South River Street, asking him to come and confer with me. He turned out to be a charming man with a few white hairs already, although he can hardly be older than forty. "I've always dreamed of a museum," he said, "and a year ago a magnificent piece of ground came up for sale. Hoping against hope, I rushed to see Mr. Kirby, without whose cooperation nothing can be done here, to explain to him the need for a museum; but he had already received your letters of a year before, where you brought up the subject, and which he told me to read. And so I found him perfectly well disposed toward the project; he signed a check for me and helped me to find the remainder speedily."

An American dinner party

We were twenty guests at Kirby's. The city's leading men were present, the best informed, and yet, outside their business sphere, none could keep up the most commonplace conversation. From seven till eleven they all sang without a break. Each one had before him, printed on four sheets, fifty popular songs; someone would call a number, the orchestra would play the tune, and they sang in chorus. Hardly had they come to the end of one song, when the next number would be called out and another song would begin.

After eleven, we moved into the drawing room and Bertron encouraged me to talk art, but the only subject they cared to discuss was the Ruhr.

June 9 / A new Vermeer

Joe has informed me that a new Vermeer has just been discovered in Paris, that £12,000 is being asked for it, and that he is going to buy it for £10,000; that Hofstede de Groot has certified it as genuine; that it is a large portrait of a young man like the one in Brussels, but with a hat.[1]

June 11 / With Joe

He told me that he has bought Edmond Veil-Picard's Hals, *Young Man with Mandolin*.

June 12 / Miss Frick's twins

She shows them to everyone qualified to give an opinion and has by now no less than twenty testimonials; she has told me that only one person shares Joe's opinion: the curator of the Cook Collection in Richmond, who Joe said was an idiot. Miss Frick has given me the photographs to show to the three experts I have chosen as arbitrators.

June 13 / I leave for France

With my wife and Pierre on the transatlantic liner *France*. I don't know anyone on board except Brandus, who has his offices at Nathan Wildenstein's. He is thirty years old and takes exhibitions of paintings from town to town; he has an excellent memory and he repeated to me some of the comments people make.

"What are the Sèvres vases used for?"

A woman who bought several pictures from him said, "Send me two of each."

At a rather large exhibition of old and modern pictures someone said: "You must have worked hard to paint all that!"

In front of a picture by Alma-Tadema called *The Reading from Homer* he was asked over twenty times where Homer was.

[1] Joe bought it and sold it to Bache; it is a frightful picture, probably by Bourdichon. It is worth 5,000 francs. (Note appended 1929.)

Before an antique table supported by columns in the shape of torsos, someone exclaimed: "What marvelous machines you must have in France to make those columns!"

Before a picture entitled *The Shepherds of Arcadia* someone remarked: "What funny clothes you wear in France!"

June 14 / A Boucher

Brandus tells me that he has sold Bache a Boucher for $60,000 which fetched some $15,000 at a public auction near London last year; Wildenstein subsequently bought it for around twenty-five or thirty thousand dollars.

June 15 / Wildenstein's affairs

"Your friend Nathan has made more than 5 million francs this year," Brandus told me. "His first transaction was the sale of Fragonard's *Pledge of Love* to Mortimer Schiff; he sold Asher Wertheimer's two great Paters to Berwind; then, for more than $60,000, a well-known picture by the Master of Flémalle, *Portrait of a Woman*; the Vigée-Lebrun to Barton Jacobs; a horrible Greuze of a drunken man, for $15,000 to a collector from Portland, Oregon; a primitive to Friedsam with Kleinberger as a go-between; some decorations in the Lancret genre to the New York museum; an Ingres drawing, two Nattiers, some pieces of furniture to the St. Louis Museum; a small tapestry to Whimpfeimer. On their behalf I sold Bache the oval painting by Drouais, *Child Holding a Flower*, for $60,000."

"That picture is worse than candy melting in your mouth," I said to Brandus. "It's candy that sticks in your throat. For my part," I continued, "I helped Wildenstein sell the life-size Clodions from the Doucet sale to Stotesbury of Philadelphia for $70,000; and for the same price, the four life-size Pajous, which came from Ancel and Leroy of Versailles." Brandus asked me how much I got from Barton Jacobs for the Chardin *Woman Playing Knucklebones*, and I replied: "Thirty-five thousand dollars."

June 16 / Multimillionaire's remark

Brandus is the cousin of Bernard Franck, army contractor and

European collector. He told me that when Morgan bought his 125 eighteenth-century dance cards for $200,000, the American asked him how long it had taken him to get them together. The Parisian collector replied with a sigh: "Thirty years." Said Morgan: "It's only taken me five minutes."

Franck was so overcome by the unhoped-for sale that he went personally to the bank to cash his check. Secretly he started another collection of dance cards, which this time cost him quite a lot; he did not bring it out until Morgan was dead.

Hoping to find other such Americans, he built up still other collections of needle cases, music boxes, etc., pouring no end of money into objects which today aren't worth a quarter of what he paid for them; that miraculous Morgan sale was the worst transaction of his life.

June 19 / Frick's first picture

Charles Knoedler, who is on the ship, has told me: "One day Frick entered our galleries and saw a Bouguereau portrait of a little girl; he bought it because it resembled a daughter he had lost; and that was perhaps the starting point of his famous collection!"

June 20 / We disembark

How enjoyable is the journey from Le Havre to Paris!

June 21 / The Fragonards of Grasse

The elder Guiraud, of 1, quai Voltaire, told me: "Thirty years ago I had in my pocket a year's option on those Fragonards and I went to see Baron Edmond de Rothschild, who didn't want them; I failed at every door. Wertheimer gave the owner £28,000. At that moment J. P. Morgan was on his yacht at Cannes, where the dealer, who had never before sold him anything, approached him, took him off to Grasse, and let him have them, making a profit of ten per cent."

On Lord Carnarvon and Carter

Ernest Duveen was telling me about them this evening. He is a close friend of Carter's, while another of my brothers-in-law, Victor Walker, was for twenty-five years the inseparable companion of Lord

Carnarvon. Ernest is therefore in a position to know a great deal about the famous discovery of the tomb of Tutankhamen at Luxor.

Carnarvon wouldn't have died of that insect bite if he hadn't given so much of himself. He had been working on that site for years, he had spent a great deal of money on the excavations; he no longer believed in Carter; he was going to look for another partner and buy a right of excavation elsewhere.

An hour before Carter's departure for Egypt, the voyage that was to lead to this marvelous discovery, Ernest had lunch with him, and wished him good luck as he left.

Carnarvon was not just a lordly silent partner; he was a genuine Egyptologist of considerable merit and a very fine connoisseur. In his contract with the government he had made sure that he would have full possession of whatever might be discovered, but the findings were so vast that this was impossible; besides, the king is not easy to deal with and won't readily let objects out of the country. Carter is of course prepared to negotiate and has said he would accept half. A syndicate of Parisian couturiers has offered him £20,000 for the privilege of copying the clothing and ornaments, but he hasn't yet accepted. Carter, by his arrangement with Carnarvon, had the right to only a certain percentage, but his partner's death gave him additional rights, and he is perfectly capable of not giving anything to Lady Carnarvon, who is terribly fond of money but who nevertheless told him that she renounced in his favor all the rights connected with articles in the press, lectures, and films. Carter is going to tour the American cities; he may not be an altogether disinterested scholar, but he's not a man of means.

June 23 / Bardac's gouaches

Edouard Jonas has told me that Arnold Seligmann has sold them for $150,000 to Mortimer Schiff of New York.

Prince Gagarine's Rembrandt: "Man Holding his Hat"

He has offered it to me for $60,000. I doubt if it's genuine.

June 25 / Marie Laurencin telephones me

She asked me when she could come to sign her latest canvas, for in my absence she did Ernest's portrait. When she says sign, she means, "When can I come for my money?" She will get 5,000 francs a week from Tuesday, as she is very busy until then. I told her that she is quite well known in America, and she replied that it is, in fact, the only country where she is known at all.

She wanted me to tell her what I thought of the portrait; I admitted that my wife doesn't care for it. The artist replied that that is not a bad sign, that she is afraid of being understood too quickly.

Caro-Delvaille lunches with us

He is aging a great deal these days and he speaks of our time with terrible bitterness, the bitterness of an old man. He is quite right to censure artists for drawing women's legs apart and showing us their sex; and I agree with his remark that if art is plebian, this might well be the fault of the naturalism of the generation which preceded his own. He talked to me about his friend Lecomte du Nouy, who is said to be the son of Maupassant, and not of his supposed father, who was a painter of stained glass and a protégé of the Queen of Rumania. His mother had a literary salon. Du Nouy has become a collaborator of Dr. Carrel's, and perhaps the most valuable one. "He leads a strange life, du Nouy," he said. "Athlete, author, cowboy; then war broke out and he was a military courier traveling by car; since he met Carrel, he has displayed unheard-of ingenuity in the construction of scientific instruments, without ever having been a great mathematician. Carrel explains his ideas to him, and the type of research he wants to do, and du Nouy produces the instruments he needs: instruments of such sensitivity and precision for infinitesimal measurements that no doctor in France can understand how to use them unless he's a mathematician.

"Du Nouy represented the Rockefeller Institute at the Pasteur Anniversary. He has been offered a chair at Nancy. There his works are known, but in Paris, where it is thought that nothing is invented outside the metropolis, no notice is taken of communications from anywhere else!"

I shall see Caro again next week, when he will begin a portrait of me.

June 26 / I leave for Oxford with my nephew Armand Lowengard
  He studied there in 1913 and 1914 and is going to receive his degree in a ceremony that was postponed because of the war.

Oxford
  In this town I am moved above all by the prevailing air of peacefulness. I am trying to come to grips with the psychological atmosphere of the place. For that, I have had an admirable guide in my nephew.
  It is certainly hard for a Frenchman to understand the students' way of life, and I must make an effort to discover the meaning of it all. Each college has its ancient garden with time-honored trees, and the upkeep of these gardens costs millions every year. A few young men in slippers are sitting about in broad wicker armchairs tilted well back; others spend almost the whole of their lives looking out of their windows. The students get up when they like, or rather when they can, since they go to bed when they please. Don't they work at all? They do, a little. At night one can see the lights on late in the room of some studious boy. But he'll have to shut the curtains if he wants to work seriously; he must hide or else be in constant dread of irruptions by students, who arrive like a whirlwind and before whom books must hastily be put aside. Armand often heard the phrase "Here we hate intelligence" ("We hate brain"). They are required to attend one or two lectures a day, which amount to about four hours' work in all. And yet it is from Oxford or Cambridge, her sister and rival, that the most outstanding intellects of England have emerged. The professors themselves are not very remarkable: just occasionally they have some brilliant scholar, perhaps a distinguished Hellenist. One might expect that there would be some competitive spirit between the colleges, a desire to outdo one another in exams. But no such thing exists except in sports, and then competition is as gentlemanly as it is keen. Are they meditating, these boys leaning on their elbows at the old windows? How they would laugh if you asked them such a question! And they would answer: "But we aren't thinking about anything." And it would be true. Would it then be correct to assume that these people are somehow inferior? One might well believe it, as the entrance examinations are very easy, though the final ones are less so. It is obvious that the professors scarcely count, that the colleges

belong to the students, but though they see little of their teachers, who seem to be there only for the sake of tradition, their relationship is comradely.

What, then, for heaven's sake, do these young people learn in the city of intelligence?

Things which are taught in no other place on earth. It is here that are formed and set those qualities which made England's greatness possible, and which are not to be found in books, any more than the Frenchman's good sense or his genius for improvisation. In these peaceful crenelated courts, England teaches that all agitation is vain; that one of the secrets of a happy life is to watch it pass from one's window; that running won't help you go farther and that jostling is hateful. Here Great Britain's irreducible traditionalism is kept alive. As if to stress the greatness of this principle, each college likes to see the son follow in the footsteps of his father; for the son the entrance examination is, as it were, a mere formality; and he will even be given the rooms formerly occupied by his father, with, if he's still around, the same servant.

With such a heritage, grown through the centuries, when the country is in danger, as in the last war, the Great War, they are the first to go, these young boys who think of nothing in particular as they lean on their windows. Not many from 1913 and 1914 are left; and in the group photographs one comes across in all these rooms, Armand has counted more dead than living: officers all, aged eighteen.

July 1 / Darnetal's journal

He took my advice, and began writing it, but has given it up. I did not think it was very good and gave him some advice without discouraging him. I read in it that Manet's *Le Bon Bock* has been bought for about a million by Rosenberg. By now everyone knows that the exact price he paid was 800,000 francs.

A remark of Forain's

A woman has just been telling me how once at a distinguished party she was wandering about the room with Forain when he noticed an elderly woman with her hair falling over her forehead and ears and some curls even on her nose. He whispered to his companion: "What do you bet she's bald under all that!"

July 5 / Princess Murat, née de Rohan-Chabot

She wanted my opinion on a Flemish primitive and Marie Laurencin took me to her house. Her primitive is very interesting; it isn't by a great master, but it is French. A red cloak, rather surprisingly, is draped round the shoulders of the Virgin who is bending over a Christ with reddish hair, a yellow body with frightful wounds and the eyes of a drowned man.

The princess is quite a character; I do believe she wears a wig. Her hair is as black as that of a Chinese; it is parted down the middle of her scalp and covers her head like a roof of well-twisted thatch. Some horizontal curls resembling miniature stovepipes fall to her cheeks. She is in her sixties. The tea she serves is really excellent. She is amiable, sprightly, enthusiastic, mad about art, can't stand the eighteenth century, loves the times she lives in, and is a patron of modern art.

Marie Laurencin told me later that she is the only woman in the world who knows how to liven up a formal party; that she is divorced, but not in the Court of Rome, because that's expensive.

Before going to see the princess, I went to pick Marie Laurencin up at her home. While she was changing, I looked around her drawing room with its "modern art" furniture, and her dining room, which she uses as a studio. One has to guess that it's meant to be a dining room; there is a chaise longue in it, a tiny harmonium, and a mandolin, for Marie Laurencin is fond of music. She had just stopped working on a canvas which was still on the easel: women with doves. There are small bookcases in both rooms, nothing very exciting in the way of books, except perhaps the twenty-volume Bibliothèque Rose. I was soon to learn that these aren't books from her girlhood, but her grown-up books, as she gracefully admitted that they are the only ones she can read, being so stupid! As for Giraudoux or Suarès, she insists that she doesn't understand them! I was talking to her about the impressionist painters and she replied that she scarcely knew them. She knows nearly all the moderns personally, but for the most part she has no idea what they're doing.

July 9 / On Robert de Montesquiou

I'm reading his memoirs, which have just come out and which are totally uninteresting. He calls Marcel Proust a poor writer. That's because Proust made him into the principal character of his novel. And what a character at that. Some people go so far as to say that Proust's description of his vice, and the savage way in which he wrote about it and exposed it, shortened his life. I remember Proust's remark about his friend and victim: "No one can say things more reasonable and act more unreasonably than he."

July 17 / Duveen's Vermeer

Nathan Wildenstein told me that it was found in Paris, and that it was left hanging for years at Feral's, the expert of public auctions, until the day when it was bought for 2,000 francs by Neumans, a Belgian who is rather knowledgeable about the Dutch painters. This man sold it for 10,000 francs to Perdoux, who speculates rather wildly in paintings; he, in turn, showed it to Hofstede de Groot, who certified its authenticity and was paid 50,000 francs for his certificate. Duveen paid £10,000, or 750,000 francs, for it. Nathan Wildenstein has assured me that the picture isn't genuine.

August 1 / Ralph Booth

He is the president of the museum of Detroit (Michigan). He owns eight newspapers. Last year he had a chance to run for the Senate, which he refused because of the museum, whose moving spirit he is; people were flabbergasted by his decision. He is a collector; last year he bought a Bellini for really nothing, for $25,000, from a German dealer living in Switzerland who had himself acquired it for £60 in a London salesroom, Robinson and Fisher.

August 25 / Fragonard's "The Jug of Milk"

Edouard Jonas arrived today at Le Touquet and told me he bought this painting at the end of July. The picture is on its old canvas, and he must have paid some 300,000 francs for it.

September 1 / The Case of "La Belle Ferronnière"

Back in Paris last night, I went along to the Ritz, where I met Louis Levy, a distinguished American lawyer, who told me: "I'm here for your brother-in-law's case; all the English and American papers are going to have us on their front page." I asked him how the case started in the first place. "One fine day in New York a journalist asked Joe on the telephone if the picture *La Belle Ferronnière* which the Kansas City Museum wanted to buy was authentic, and your brother-in-law replied that only the one in the Louvre was genuine, that the other one was just a copy.

"The interview was published; hence the lawsuit. And what can the owner of the picture claim from us? If the experts say her picture is a fake, she need only keep quiet about it; if they say it is genuine, it will be very valuable, thanks to whom? thanks to us."

The Autun Ingres

The newspapers are letting out polecat howls: "It's ruined, it's the state's fault!" I saw Brisson, the canvas restorer, who told me: "I've just come from there; it wasn't anything. I've revarnished it and it's magnificent."

September 2 / "La Belle Ferronnière"

I saw Louis Levy again, and he resumed yesterday's conversation.

"If this picture were genuine, it would acquire inestimable value, thanks to us. Meanwhile, for this old rag the woman is asking $500,000 in damages, which at the current rate of exchange comes to 8,500,000 francs; it's not surprising that the case is causing such a stir over here! The most amusing and incredible thing is that the sale to the Kansas City Museum was far from settled, and the sum of $50,000 had simply been mentioned—a donor was still to be found. Joe will be in Paris this evening. We have ten experts coming from all corners of Italy, Holland, England. Berenson is arriving from Florence. When your Minister of Fine Arts refused to let us take the disputed picture from the Louvre, we had authorization requested by the United States Ambassador, and it was granted. What publicity for Joe. And how important he's going to seem to his American clients! What do people here think about it?"

"They're amused."

"Why?"

"To think that your splendid multimillionaires will see a halo of glory sparkling round Joe's head simply because he declared that a horrible copy of a famous picture was only a copy and, to prove it, had to call in the most celebrated experts from the four corners of the world!"

September 4 / Six panels of savonnerie at Edouard Jonas's

I've never seen anything more beautiful than these panels of a folding screen. In the middle of each of them there are two birds sporting and kissing in flight; at the bottom there are splendid vases, and flowers rise from them which are open to bursting point. He must have bought them for around 200,000 francs. Unfortunately one of the panels, bearing a crown, has about ten inches cut out at the bottom.

"La Belle Ferronnière"

I have seen Joe, who told me that the inquiry has begun at the American consul's, and that Berenson was cross-questioned for three hours; apparently he was hard put to contain his fury; but how clever he is, the old boy!

The lawyer asked him: "You've given a good deal of study to the picture in the Louvre?"

"All my life; I've seen it a thousand times."

"And is it on wood or on canvas?"

Berenson reflected a moment and answered: "I don't know."

"What, you claim to have studied it so much, and you can't answer a simple question?"

Berenson retorted: "It's as if you asked me on what kind of paper Shakespeare wrote his immortal sonnets."

September 12 / Marvels

Joe showed us a Holbein, from the Meklenberg Collection, bought, he said, for £30,000. Then he showed us the Van Dyck, the Cuyp, and the Bellini from the X Collection, sold last spring at Christie's, and a magnificent Lancret series. I gave the Veil-Picard Hals a close look; it's a fake beyond any doubt.

Afterward I had dinner with Joe and spent the evening with him. He was as happy as a child, thinking that on the day of his death he'll be remembered as the man of *La Belle Ferronnière*. How can anyone be so naïve!

September 14 / With Caro

We were going down the Champs-Elysées; the setting sun was as beautiful as the day before, and Caro said: "You know, Claude Lorrain was greater even than Turner because he knew how to draw in space." He talked to me about his life in Paris twenty years ago when he knew the great artists. Of Degas he said: "He was a reprobate. He threw nude models out on the landing and tossed their clothes over the bannister. At Pissarro's funeral Mary Cassatt said to him: 'You're nasty to your brother, you're beastly to your sister; you're bad, you're bad.' He just uttered a raucous snarl, the snarl of his life." Caro met Oscar Wilde at the home of the painter Blanche and said of him: "He *was* naïve. He said to Blanche: 'Look, the coat I've got on is going to astonish all of Paris.' 'It won't astonish anybody,' Blanche replied. Oscar Wilde couldn't get over it."

September 16 / "La Belle Ferronnière"

Armand was telling me about the experts' report yesterday at the Louvre; the comparison of the two *Ferronnières*; the arrival at 8 A.M. of the experts, who must have had to get up at six—d'Estournelle de Constant much earlier, as he lives in the country; and the crowd of journalists yelling because they weren't let in. The Louvre administration didn't want them, but put the blame on the lawyers. They were screaming at Armand: "Berenson is a bloody German, you'll be hearing about it from us!" Then a rumor spread among them that some American journalists had slipped in among the experts, and the pack had to be appeased, tangible proof had to be given, they had to be convinced. Once everyone was inside after showing their credentials, Armand introduced the great experts of world renown to the wretched directors of our museum, who didn't know a single one because, sheltered in their ivory tower, they're out of contact with the world of foreign scholars. When Sir Charles Holmes saw the second picture, the younger sister, he burst out laughing and had a hard time stopping.

The only interesting aspect of this huge hoax is that the experts all agree that the Louvre picture is by Leonardo.

The lawyer of the opposition asked one of the experts why he wore spectacles; and how he dared, if he didn't see clearly, to assume the title of expert.

Bredius, the former director of the Hague museum, told me recently that when he was called in on a case in which the authenticity of a Van Goyen, the seventeenth-century seascape painter, was being challenged, the American lawyer presiding as judge was surprised to see that he knew so much about the artist, and asked: "But how old were you when Van Goyen died?"

September 18 / Drawings by Guardi

A specialist told me a way to recognize them: nearly all were done on paper bearing the watermark G.K.; he also told me that a great many fakes are produced in Venice, that the color of the sepia is different, the fakes having no light, so that placed in the shade they show dark, while the genuine ones become phosphorescent. All these are additional considerations to that of the drawing itself, which can ultimately be judged only by the expert.

September 19 / What a Reynolds!

Joe showed me *The Portrait of Lady Crosbie*. She is dressed in white, standing as though interrupted in a swift movement, her gown swept into a whirlwind of silk, and so substantial that one seems to hear it rustle. She is standing on a plain, tall as in a huge exclamation mark; the horizon lies low behind her, and she herself splashes the blue sky with her beauty. On her left, two windswept trees.

No other picture of the English school shows as clearly how much these masters influenced our French landscapists of the nineteenth century.

September 20 / The Bolshevik commissars call on me

Comrade Benois and Comrade Triensky. The latter is chief commissar of the Hermitage, the former is responsible for the paintings there. Triensky saved the museum, I'm told. His attitude toward life seems one of lofty, unaffected indifference. He is suffering from a painful attack of lumbago, and was trailing a plain walking stick well behind him. He is a man of great energy, but his sort are the worst of their kind: they're the pale ones. Benois is roly-poly and very much a man of the world.

I expected Princess Murat to arrive any moment with Marie Laurencin, and that she would be astonished to see Benois, whom she knew very well and believed to be dead, as so much false news comes out of Russia.

These two Russians spoke lovingly of their museum, which extends over an area surrounded by more than nine miles of wall. They assured us that life goes on normally and invited me to go there.

The wife of the man who, with Lenin, led the Revolution, Mme Trotsky, is inspector-general of the collections. When I asked them if she had good taste, they replied that she had the good taste to leave well enough alone.

September 26 / With Marie Laurencin

I went around to her house; she was working on scenery and costumes for the Russian ballet *Les Biches*. She asked me to take her along to Rosenberg, who has owed her 12,000 francs for ages. He buys pictures from her in half shares with Hessel for about 60,000 francs a year. "I spend 100,000 francs a year," she told me. "I'm a spendthrift but without ostentation; it doesn't show. Look, for instance, at the many pairs of shoes I keep in that cabinet in the passage, they cost me a fortune, there are thirty pairs at least."

She makes money painting portraits, but says that from now on she wants to paint only the gullible, that is, her special favorites, the people idiotic enough to discover a resemblance where there isn't any. She has just done Chanel, the couturière, who asked her to do her portrait but has turned it down. "Yet I pay her for my dresses," said Marie, and added: "She's a good sort, but a peasant from the Auvergne. She wants me to try again, but she'll have to do without; I'm going to pretty up the one I did of her to sell it. Rosenberg is keen on it; he's collecting my canvases for his children, to give to them when they're thirty."

I told Marie that my wife had had her portrait done by Beltran Masses, and her face turned crimson—she would have liked so to paint my wife herself, as she loves her gestures and her voice. She asked me if my wife was happy, and I replied that there was always some restlessness in her; and Marie said: "Calm, indifferent people haven't got souls of the same moral value as those who are restless; it's a proof of the quality of her spirit."

She gave me a poem to read, which she had published in the *Nouvelle Revue Française* of last July, No. 113, under the title "Little Bestiary." It is cubist in style, and she told me laughingly that she was paid forty-seven francs for the three pages, which represent ten years of work.

At one point she said of a certain woman: "She is like grass, fresh and tender."

We talked of Manet; she told me that Bernstein, the playwright, had his portrait done by Manet when he was quite small, and I replied that in that case something of the writer's will certainly survive. Bernstein has a picture of Marie's, and a fine Goya besides, a child in red.

We went out to have tea at the Golfers' Club on the avenue des Champs-Elysées; she wants to join the club and learn to play golf, as she's afraid of getting fat.

Finally we ended up at Rosenberg's, and she asked him for 200 francs to pay for her dinner this evening.

September 27 / On Claude Monet

Georges Bernheim reproached me with not having visited Monet for a long time; all the more so as he has had two operations on his eyes, which have improved his sight.

Georges has just bought two of the painter's seascapes, very old ones, which he sent to his first salon in 1867; he mentioned the fact to Monet, who expressed the desire to see them. "Nothing to stop that," replied Georges. "I'll bring them to you tomorrow, and since you have to spend a weekend on your back, I'll hang them on the wall opposite your bed during that time." Monet accepted, and when he saw them again, he said to Bernheim: "On the day of the private viewing, Manet came across the room to join me, saying: 'But where are those two pictures on which everyone's congratulating me and which I didn't paint?' When he saw them, he exclaimed: 'Oh, the swine! He's even imitated my signature.'"

The pictures are now hanging on Georges Bernheim's walls; they've darkened, and they no longer look like Manet's in the least; only influence remains.

October 4, 1923–May 27, 1924

October 4 / Princess Youssoupoff

I went once again to the Russian restaurant, with my wife and her sister Eva, and the princess was there. She is indeed beautiful. She is pale, dark, and severe.

How strange it is. The Princess Youssoupoff, niece of the Czar, has, if you gaze long at her, something of the implacable beauty of those anarchist women, more terrible than the men because they dominate them.

And one can't help thinking that that brain, behind those eyes which are so dangerously averted, has undoubtedly had its share of responsibility in the crime.

On Crommelynck and Verhaeren

I was to lunch with Crommelynck at the house of a Miss Bertin who has written a children's book called *The Golden Wooden Shoes*, which La Sirène is going to publish and for which Maeterlinck wrote a preface; but the playwright had flu and didn't come. Mlle Bertin swears he is the greatest man of the theater of modern times, and that moreover he is being compared to Shakespeare and Racine: according to her, his *The Magnificent Cuckold* is surely the most prodigious study of jealousy ever made. He was born into a family of artists; his uncle was the greatest Belgian actor of his time, and his father too was an actor. Mlle Bertin showed me a photograph of a painting, a portrait done by Crommelynck's young brother. He lives in Brussels, is only twenty-one, and his art seems astonishing. I read in the photograph the influence of the primitive Flemings, of Cézanne and the cubists, a strange combination. He works for months on a portrait.

The writer is a marvelous talker and a very simple man. He lives in Saint-Cloud, in the same house as the widow of Verhaeren, that bell-ringer of verse. She didn't want to let her husband leave for Rouen; she had a presentiment. Should he leave? There was a moment of hesitation; but it was wartime, the great Fleming went, from a sense of duty, to give his patriotic lecture there, and the train killed him. His widow is heartbroken; she was nearly thirty-five when she married him but their love was very deep. The poet had begun to write at a late age, and fame didn't come too quickly; to help him, his wife lived for a long time like a hireling.

Now his house is a salon. Mme Verhaeren has eyes like the waters of southern lakes, and when a word offends her they cloud like those pure waters under the impact of a soiled pebble.

With Berenson

He and his wife are staying at the Hôtel Beau-Site. I went there for tea. He was surrounded by an admiring group of sophisticated young women who were reminding him of all the witty remarks he'd ever made, such as: "O God, grant me this day my daily idea, and forgive me yesterday's."

Mme Berenson was talking about the case of *La Belle Ferronnière* and her husband's remarks at the trial. The lawyer for the opposition said to him: "In the past you have written that *La Belle Ferronnière* wasn't by Leonardo da Vinci; did you inform the experts at the Louvre that you've changed your mind?" "There aren't any experts at the Louvre," said Berenson.

Berenson denied that he had come to Paris specially to testify in court: Joe Duveen would have thought him a traitor. He remarked on the stupidity of judges who seem to think that one can answer simply "yes" or "no," and he gave us an example of a question where either "yes" or "no" is an admission of guilt: "Have you given up beating your wife?"

Mme Berenson mentioned a trial in England in which the defendant was a doctor. He was asked at least twenty times: "Did you attend Mr. So-and-so?" "Yes." "Did he die?" "Yes." The famous doctor was done for after that.

At this point my nephew Armand arrived. Berenson asked me about the latest authors. "What do you think of Cocteau's newest masterpiece?" "That it is very banal." He agreed: "It's an insipid novel, but it's the latest snob thing to go into raptures over it. The boy is just a brilliant talker I love listening to, but not half as much as he loves someone to talk to! And whenever he opens his mouth he takes you straight to paradise."

This evening I repeated that phrase to my wife, who doesn't care for Berenson, and she said: "What does Berenson know about paradise?" I kept quiet in the face of that trenchant reply.

"The paradise of Cocteau," continued Berenson, "is artificial, and that's why it is so beautiful; and the most beautiful thing about his conversation is that he says nothing."

Berenson went on to tell us that he is studying the Byzantine manuscripts at the Bibliothèque Nationale, and that he is living in a dream. He had a great deal of trouble in getting hold of them; no one knew where they were and he had had to write to Italy to obtain the reference numbers. When he protested because there was no catalogue, he received the answer: "It's very fortunate, as we'd be besieged by curiosity-seekers from all over the world!" They didn't dare use the word "scholars."

I said goodbye to Mme Berenson and so did my nephew. Berenson followed us out and in the corridor he asked Armand for some money, some money the latter had changed for him. The expert grimaced when he saw that the pound had gone down, and he complained about the Duveens not having any money in Paris. As we went out, Armand said to me: "It pains me to have to visit that hypocrite. I do it for business; otherwise I'd never set foot there. You saw his face fall when he discovered that he'd lost a few francs; luckily I brought him the bank slip. He'd like us to pay his expenses in Paris and give him an advance on his commissions; that's why we pretend never to have any money in the safe except what we need for our current expenses. You've seen how the snob plays at being disinterested in the eyes of the world; well, you ought to see his letters asking for money, the baldness of it. He pretends to work but does nothing; he knows a lot and produces nothing, because he wouldn't want to be equaled or even approached. He'll never give you any information which might be useful, he'll never offer to take me with him to the Louvre. When I had dinner with him in Florence, this man of learning took me aside and said: 'Do you know that that lady opposite you was Princess Tralala before she married?' Once, in the days when he wasn't so powerful, he said to Bauer the antique dealer: 'A man as scholarly as yourself shouldn't be a dealer, it's horrible to be a dealer.' To which Bauer replied: 'Between you and me there's no great difference; I'm an intellectual dealer and you're a dealing intellectual.' Berenson never forgave him that."

October 21 / The Hague

I haven't been to Holland for a very long time; I've come here with my wife to see a Boucher tapestry; it's ghastly. So much the worse. I'm glad I've come, and from my first sight of a Dutch interior, I've reveled wholeheartedly in the past. In this country where art is long since dead, beauty is preserved by an incessant repetition of the past; though it is immutable, it has no luster. On the other hand, Holland, with her low roofs, was taken unawares in recent years and when she had to put up large department stores and all the other big buildings, she turned unabashedly to modern German efforts; while we, out of false patriotism, persist in denying their genuine artistic and functional application. It's a simple perpendicular style, a bit flat but not cramped; its soaring lines are almost unbroken from top to bottom; the houses are four or five stories high and their large windows let in floods of light and air, in keeping with modern principles of hygiene. Holland could not turn to France, which had nothing to offer her except some poor attempts at metallic construction: a heresy, as metal is fit for nothing but armaments; cast and painted steel can hardly be expected to improve in appearance with age. It is when sculpture has a prominent place in architecture that France gains a position that no other nation can wrest from her, as none possesses sculptors of quality.

Here I am at the Dutch court of Terburg, with its separate building units assembled in a kind of quaint open-air salon, vividly colored, with its parterre of brick creased like the skin of a little old woman: a parterre lightly overgrown with a faint moss. The architecture has the picturesque quality of houses built piece by piece, with corridors at sharp angles, semi-concealed staircases, and everywhere white walls with an air of rude good health. It's the kingdom of the good housewife, of the procreatrix devoted to her function.

The museum

It has only six or seven remarkable pictures: two Vermeers of Delft, the Paul Potter, let's say three Rembrandts, three Holbeins, a Van Dyck, one or two Rubens.

Paul Potter's *The Bull* amazed our ancestors, as there was nothing to equal it until the nineteenth century. What about now? I hate comparisons, but in comparison with the scope of nineteenth-century French landscapes, even a Ruysdael is lessened. The greatest landscape artists of old were those who did landscapes as if incidentally; Baldovinetti, Botticelli—one only has to look at his garden of flowers and herbs in *Spring*—or Rembrandt, Watteau. One of the most beautiful landscapes in the world is *View of Delft* by Vermeer of Delft.

The artist's technique was to scoop out thousands of little hollows for enameling, into which he poured melted gold.

October 22 / In Amsterdam

I paid a visit to the director of the museum, the most Latin of Dutchmen, Schmidt Degener, who is quite young, perhaps forty. He's been here for a year. It was he who organized the Dutch exhibition in Paris, to whose success he owes his present position.

Unfortunately we had only a few hours to spend in the museum and we rushed about like tourists. Half the rooms are closed, and without his assistance we'd have seen nothing.

October 22 / In Rotterdam

We went to see the Vermeer of Bredius, *The New Testament* which is better than one would think from looking at reproductions.[1]

The Crommelyncks

His play *The Magnificent Cuckold* caused a scandal; the cuckold lifts his wife's breast out of her bodice; the members of the audience who enjoyed seeing it applauded; the rest booed. I hadn't gone to see it, as I get so tired of the eternal stories of adultery; but I saw it yesterday, and it's quite a good play.

This morning I had lunch with Crommelynck and his brother at Mlle Bertin's. In fact, Crommelynck wanted to meet me because I was a friend of Proust's; he was anxious to find someone to talk to him about the departed writer. I told him about my last meeting with Proust and he said that it was exactly as he would have imagined.

November 11 / Guillaume Apollinaire, blackmailer

His friends have been weeping pages over him, but just before the war he was paid by Jacques Seligmann to put out a signed pamphlet in which he attacked the original of *The Good Mother*, by Fragonard, a masterpiece he had never seen. I had sold this picture to an American, S. R. Bertron; this fellow Seligmann was trying to undermine my client's confidence in me, and he paid his creatures to get up a polemic. Everyone knew this and Apollinaire could not have been ignorant of Seligmann's motives. Several times Thiébault-Sisson devoted whole articles to the defense of this picture in *Le Temps*. I had one of the pamphlets, but have mislaid it. But where are the others? In America, where Seligmann had them distributed to his clients and to mine? They were printed in Paris by a German who disappeared when the war was declared; the affair dates from that time. Would he still have a packet of them? There must be a set in the archives of the Seligmann firm. No one in Paris has ever seen even one.

November 15 / The three Carnarvon Gainsboroughs

They have been sold to Joe Duveen for at least £120,000.

---

[1] Subsequently in the Friedsam Collection at the Metropolitan Museum of New York.

November 18 / Anniversary mass for Proust

More people came to it than to his funeral. Everyone wants to have been a friend of his.

November 22 / On Colette Willy

I have been offered the manuscripts of *Claudine*, which were published under the name of her husband Gauthier-Villars but which are in his wife's hand. I haven't actually seen them but am told that they are covered with marginal notes by her husband and taskmaster: "Good. Fair. Excellent. To be developed."

Colette has described how her husband would shut her up every day like a schoolgirl kept in class after hours. He would put the key in his pocket and say to her, "Six hours of work today."

December 3 / The Stoclet Collection in Brussels

I have never seen a collection of such fine taste. I went to view it last Saturday, but got through only half of it; I'm going back and will speak of it again. It's the cathedral of the North.

December 10 / Forain, the Crommelyncks, Caro, and Mlle Bertin lunch
with us

I invited Marie Laurencin too late, and she said: "I'm sorry about it, but come one day with Forain; or arrange a tea for him and the Princess Murat." I mentioned this to Forain, who finds Marie amusing; but as for the princess, he tells me that she likes to go counter to current fashion to make an impression, that she's always after a sheep with five legs, the sheep at the moment being Marie Laurencin. "The Princess Murat was my pupil," he added. "I taught her to ride a bicycle." Forain doesn't care for Marie's portraits and he said to me: "There are thousands of people around who can do that sort of thing, and each wants to stand out from the rest." Forain groaned at the sight of my Derain *The Two Sisters*. When we sat down at the table, the conversation continued on the moderns, and came around to Cézanne; and poor Cézanne, dead for some time, was trampled on by everybody; and though I was amused by the stupidities of these highly intelligent people, I was saddened by the thought that Forain, who is perhaps seventy, is consulted by the jury of the Prix de Rome on the merits of young people of twenty-five. They are separated by fifty years, and it is really a tragedy that the judges are old men completely insensitive to modern art. Only young Crommelynck said not a word, while all the others agreed that the Cézanne picture *The Card Players*, at present on exhibit at the Salon d'Automne, was simply frightful. "No!" shouted Forain, "don't talk to me about it; those men with thick bones like pipes, stuck together like that. I love hands that are elongated, flexible; these hands, they're hands that don't even know how to cheat!" A burst of laughter. "I knew him well," continued Forain, "and he always used to say: 'I can't finish a picture.' But the masters, the old masters—their pupils were bound by strict contracts, and by God those apprentices worked, for later on they had to do their master's pictures. Today there's no art any more; it's all artifice." Caro approved, and so did Crommelynck; and then there was a stupid digression full of contradictions. Forain said: "There's no such thing as sincerity in art, it's not necessary; don't speak to me of a sincere artist; if he's sincere he's a failure. People talk about nature, but we have to look at nature with our backs turned." Caro agreed, adding that at the same time one mustn't let it fade from one's eyes. The conversation reverted to Marie Laurencin and to the matter of likenesses, and Forain said disgustedly: "No, no, you don't have to ask an artist to produce a resemblance; don't start talking to me of doing men as they are." My wife put forward the idea that the lack of resemblance may stem from the fact that artists are often dreamers. "No, no, never," cried Forain, "artists are never dreamers; not real artists, only some amateurs!"

Crommelynck ventured to say that the same craze for deformity could be found in the literature of our time, but that he found it strange that painters should make the best writers.

They all agreed that they saw no talent in Ibsen. Forain loaded him with insults as he had just crushed Derain. He condemned his specimens of the human race. Henry Becque was subjected to five terrible minutes.

We talked of the Théâtre du Marais in Brussels, which is putting on plays by young authors; I told Crommelynck that I seem to remember Stoclet had taken an interest in this theater. "Yes, he did, but from afar; I believe he gave only 50,000 francs, and in two installments." "There are times," Forain replied, "when that's a considerable sum of money."

January 2, 1924 / On Corot

A London dealer, Rothschild, has told me that his father was a personal friend of the painter's, to whom he never paid more than £120 for a picture, and for the same amount Rothschild would often ask him to add a figure, a cow, a house. Corot would comply gracefully; whereas Jacques, the fourth-rate painter, would exact an extra twenty or forty pounds to pad his canvas.

January 4 / On the cathedral of Reims

An architect told me that during the war he was stationed at Reims, and that in building the defenses he got down to the subterranean quarries from which the cathedral stones had been taken. He saw tracks there of the wheels of the last wagons, and at intervals of a foot the hollows for holding the oil lamps that gave light for the work. He found eighteenth-century lamps and kept some. The quarries were buried once more by the bombing.

March 25 / Vandals

A specialist in Egyptian art has told me that he is waiting for a large Egyptian statue. To get it out of Egypt, it was cut into forty-six pieces, and the work of reconstitution is being done in Paris. This happens every day.

March 27 / The first Lady M

We had dinner with her at Giro's. She is the daughter of a clergyman, and was married at sixteen to a man of about sixty-six; he liked very young girls (a taste which he pursued in art). He went after portraits of little girls and built up a magnificent collection of antiques. My brother-in-law, Ernest, made sales to him totaling about £1½ million. His wife bought the equivalent in pearls. They had a secretary, J. C., with whom she was in love and whom she made into a man of means. The war gave her considerable pleasure, as she founded two hospitals for young officers.

At Dunand's

He has considerably enlarged his studio since obtaining such satisfying results with lacquer. He even employs four or five Chinese, but

Bonfils tells me that despite some big orders and the splendid quality of his work, he isn't doing too well. We went into the room where the Chinese were at work with that wonderful patience of theirs. He has gone back to their methods, using eggshells broken into thousands of tiny fragments and strewn on the lacquer. We saw some very beautiful and some very modern designs. The lacquer dries in a damp dark room with water flowing perpetually from the top of the walls. The lacquer takes twice as long to dry during the moon's first quarter. Between each preparation, the drying lasts three days.

Several artists are working at reproducing in lacquer a pale and dusty picture by the pale and dusty Dhurmer as a door for a lady by the name of Gompel. Dunand is asking 18,000 francs for a three-panel screen just under four feet high.

Remarks made by Degas and repeated to me by Guiraud

A young artist once asked the painter how he had achieved success, and the painter replied: "In my time, one never did achieve it."

The painter Michel Lévy had an income of 5,000 francs a year and had managed to put together a superb collection of Watteau drawings; he himself repeated to Guiraud this cutting remark of Degas's. They had shared a studio and each had done a portrait of the other. One day Bernheim offered Michel Lévy 45,000 francs for his Degas, and Lévy sold it. Degas heard of it, and when he met Michel Lévy, Lévy stammered some excuse, spoke of his poverty and of all the comforts the sum had meant to him, the house in the country, etc.

He met with no sympathy. "You've committed an act of meanness," Degas replied. "You knew very well that I couldn't sell the portrait I painted of you."

Guiraud added that Degas's life was exemplary and that those who called him a reprobate didn't understand his lofty concept of duty.

A Degas exhibition at the Georges Petit Gallery

The sale of the studio had done the painter's reputation some harm, despite the large prices brought in; there were so many studies, unfinished pictures, damaged pastels. But today the crowd is silent as before a great revelation. Certain pictures are reminiscent of Vermeer;

but the Frenchman is far more intelligent than the overly patient
Dutchman.

A Fragonard

Wildenstein is asking 1,500,000 francs for *Education Does Everything.*

April 2 / A Memling for Melbourne, sold by Agnew

Count Sala, the representative of this firm in Paris, has told me
that this painting was found in the heart of France, in the house of a
kind of peasant who had a series of primitives and who wasn't unaware
of the value of his picture, with which he wanted to provide dowries for
his daughters—he was successful.

It was through the concierge of his building, in the Place Vendôme, that Sala was put on the track of this picture, and he assured me it
was a masterpiece. He also told me that Melbourne had bought a Titian
from them which was at least as beautiful as the *Ariosto* in the National
Gallery.

On Forain

Allard, who has the exclusive rights to Forain's pictures, told me
that his latest pictures were the finest; for when Forain was younger, he
resembled in turn Degas, Renoir, and Daumier.

Degas made two famous remarks on this subject: "Forain stands
on my own feet," [2] and "Forain paints with his hands in my pockets."

Allard complains that he isn't producing enough, but that is because he doesn't care about money. The artist has often said to the
dealer: "If I wanted money, I'd take a copperplate, draw three lines on
it, and the whole world would be scrambling for it."

If he seems to keep his prices up these days, it is because he had
to see his work at low prices—almost unsaleable—for so long. Allard
himself says: "The value of his pictures still fluctuates greatly and I keep
the prices high in all the public auctions; that's why Forain needs me.
Apart from that, he's clever enough to manage his affairs on his own."

[2] Rouart assures me that this remark was made about Besnard.

April 9 / Picasso exhibition at Rosenberg's

It consists of twelve pictures, each at 100,000 francs, and some drawings, and it runs from March 28 to April 17. Rosenberg showed me a marvelous Claude Monet, *The Red Boat*, priced at 300,000 francs.

April 10 / A third lot of Renoirs

Georges Bernheim bought the Renoir studio today, with Barbazanges. They purchased the second lot four months ago and it was immediately carried off by the collectors. Today's collection is insignificant: fifty-five canvases, some of them the size of a large visiting card. When they are half the size of a small pocket handkerchief, they are worth 15,000 francs. These rapid sketches rarely cover the canvas.

May 15 / I leave for Milan

I am going to see Prince Gagarine's Rembrandt.

May 16 / The Duomo

Seeing it again after quite a number of years, I felt the same disillusionment as many a time I have experienced on rereading books which I had loved in my youth. How works vanish in the flatting-mill of the critical sense. Like so many travelers, I believed the cathedral to be sheer lace and had likened its hundred spires in my thoughts to a hundred fabulous tapers; today they reminded me of bone penholders sold at the seaside or at Mont-Saint-Michel, with little magnifying glasses inside them through which you see views of the district.

Its ornamental sculpture was cut with so little care that instead of forming a whole with the stone it seems to be stuck on all over. The interior of the cathedral is pure and has more dignity; but the church is overly vast. It is perhaps to cover this lack of intimacy that the clergy adopt the stratagem of burning quantities of incense. Incense of stone is more persuasive, more meaningful, more inviting.

La Brera

There are three Crivellis. The artist has placed his creatures among leaves and patterns of green and gold, and once he starts a curve he stops only when he can go no farther, and then in such a way that the beholder is unaware of it. Even in the human body, the artist senses the harmony of a supreme and indeed sublime scroll pattern, and I wonder that he can still maintain a line. His human figures are like the elongated and supple foliage of exotic trees; these paintings are not at all displeasing to the passing viewer, but how trying it must be to live one's whole life with a Crivelli!

I stopped before a Gentile da Fabriano, a master I adore because he was so respectful of the things he painted; he takes us into a paradise always simple but not without a radiance of glory. His Christ and his Virgin have the innocence of those who are so good that they fall victim to scoundrels, but at the same time they are armed with the grace that made lions recoil in past ages, when human beasts persecuted the new believers. He doesn't give us an exact image of paradise like Fra Angelico, he doesn't paint God the Father with a white silken beard of real hair, and pink cheeks; he doesn't give us groupings of angels touched by the miracle of adolescence and dressed in trains made of silk rent from the heavens in their flight; he doesn't bathe his world in a blue haze peculiar to himself and to the monk caught in his ecstatic reverie; Gentile da Fabriano's paradise is not really seen. He paints on a golden background, and it is in this gold, or behind this crackled metal veil, or before it perhaps, or before us—who can tell?—that his paradise is found; I would say that he pours it into us, the beholders, whereas we are ourselves drawn into that of Fra Angelico. To attain Fra Angelico's paradise, we would make any promise, but to enter Gentile da Fabriano's we must have been good all our lives.

Because of this subtle difference these two painters are at once strangers and brothers. There is a delicious Benozzo Gozzoli of the same spiritual family, more vividly imaged and a little more childlike. Benozzo Gozzoli succeeds in making us believe that infancy is paradise lost. Ah, how the art of that time knew how to create paradise! Art today shows us a woman washing her behind.

How I regret the twice lost paradise of Benozzo Gozzoli! He is a painter I should love to have known, especially when I was very young, for he alone could have initiated me with shattering force into the supernatural beauties of art. I dare say, though with regret, that I've somewhat outgrown him, but it's like an adult reading a fairy tale he did not know as a child. My spurious superiority comes from not having been brought up on him.

There are three Andrea Mantegnas, including *The Dead Christ*, who reclining, his body prodigiously foreshortened, with his head high and his feet toward us, seems to move to follow us, like the eyes of bad portraits. The painter has taken pleasure in doing his Christ in layers, as when he paints cities in an infinite superimposition of planes and lines, lines which recall the sectionings of trees, of those great logs, displayed in natural history museums, that reveal unsuspected centuries of age. But Mantegna achieves this effect in a space of eight or twelve square inches. His Christ is solid in death, as a God must be who has taken great suffering upon him.

The three Bellinis failed to move me. By showing us too well how thoroughly he knows the art of painting, he loses the respect of holy things.

May 17 / Poldi Pezzoli Museum

Luini bores me as his name bores me; he's a Prud'hon without the spark of chaste love. I noticed a fine Boltraffio in the manner of a Vermeer, and a beautiful *Samson and Delilah* that is supposed to have been painted by Carpaccio. There is a charming Allegretto Nuzi, a painter who joins simplicity of spirit to vividness of costume. By Mantegna—a Virgin who knows that her infant will slip from her and already clasps the *bambino* tightly to protect it from death; the grief of all mothers, the perpetual threat, the pain which in a different way is as intense as that of childbirth. Is it because of this suffering that the Virgin was spared the travail of giving birth? This is what Mantegna seems to imply. A Botticelli: *Virgin with Golden Hair*. Factitious Renaissance gold applied to lewd beauties. This beautiful Florentine had nothing to fear. Her gods had not suffered, so why would she have turned to asceticism? Is that why she has permitted gold, the unclean metal, to stream from her forehead and caress in its wicked flight the humanity surrounding her? Why should she have sought to appear of divine essence; the Virgin of Botticelli was not that. She was a pretext, an illustration for the Bible.

Finally, the picture of a woman in profile, a work attributed originally to Piero della Francesca and at present to Verrocchio. It is perhaps

Italy's most precious jewel. But why? This woman is not beautiful, she is only pretty, and not even that for certain. Is she a great lady? She is, undoubtedly, a very rich one. Has she depth, and does her soul contain a mystery? She is intelligent and highly resolute, no more. Her portrait is Italy's jewel because never was any subject better painted. Never has any goldsmith composed or executed a more beautiful pendant. It was the first time that a painter considered the human face, the countenance, as a colossal jewel holding the greatest of fires. It is an artist's creation of living flesh more beautiful than any molded by nature, and its luster makes his touch caress this shining jewel.

Leonardo's "Last Supper"

I don't believe I've been back to Milan since about 1901; but I recall that I didn't then understand the greatness of this work. Da Vinci's miracle is that he explains all, yet allows each of us to develop his own theme. He doesn't impose a formula. This god-painter has no commandments, so it is all the more difficult to follow him, and also all the more formidable. This god is the god of intelligence. I seek to measure mine, thinking of his. There is no other god of intelligence; the other gods are too powerful to need to be intelligent. Their "intelligence" lies in their "Let it be!" and it was! I do not find any religion that has created a supreme, intelligent god; there are clever gods, but that's all. Nearly all the gods are rancorous, proud, megalomaniac. Man cannot create a god, he can do no more than render him in his own image. It's impossible to evaluate the intelligence of a Napoleon, whereas it is so easy for us at a distance to take the measure of his faults; but a Leonardo appears to us adorned with all perfections. If he was capable of faults, they are inaccessible to us. All philosophy can be disputed; one cannot begin to contest Leonardo's work. Nature has its flaws, and how immense they are. Where are Leonardo's? Undoubtedly he embodies a supreme kind of intelligence and that is why we, his inferiors, cannot attain to a total understanding of *La Gioconda*. In *The Last Supper* Leonardo was bound by the text "One among you will betray me"—but in *La Gioconda*, how did he arrive at the finishing touch that has become the question mark? How did he know that the painting was finished; at what moment? This man is the god of intelligence. Wagner cannot rival him, for he represents the crossroads of passion. But what passions are alive in Leonardo? He affects ours, but his are noble and unseen. A Gentile da Fabriano, a Fra Angelico, would have transported the Last Supper to paradise; Leonardo didn't forget that Christ had fierce men of action around him. He was not afraid to show that divine acts actually took place on earth. Looking at the work, one feels that it is permeated by the words of Christ: "One among you will betray me." The shock is registered instantly and in a different way by each apostle, and each face has its own expression that only the versatile Leonardo could have rendered. And these expressions have as much of the future of the prophets as of their past.

The Gagarine Rembrandt

He is asking $130,000 for it. The paint has peeled in many places; the wooden panel on which it is painted is full of knots. And is it by Rembrandt? I strongly doubt it. In fact I don't believe it.[3]

The Ballets Russes

What decadence! They are finished; they no longer have a star; and worse still, they no longer are an ensemble. They still concentrate on the musical and painting aspects. Mme Laurencin has painted pretty sets for Les Biches, and the whole ballet comes to look like the figures she paints. In the corridor I heard a woman say to a man: "Look around the house, all the women look as though they were by Marie Laurencin; she has fashioned a type just as Boldini created the eel look fifteen years ago."

May 27 / I buy a Degas

I have bought it for 70,000 francs. It's a portrait of Mlle Rouart.

[3] It was bought in Detroit, authenticated by Valentiner. I've seen it again. I don't believe in it. (Note appended 1929.)

NOTEBOOK 12

May 28, 1924–January 14, 1925

May 28 / A Manet—"Workmen of the rue de Berne"—at Bernheim's

This picture comes from the Hoentschel Collection; Georges has just bought it in half-shares with Barbazanges and he is asking 850,000 francs for it; he even says that at that price he'll hardly make any money. He has been offered 700,000 for it by Knoedler, who sold *The Bar at the Folies-Bergère* to the National Gallery for a million, having paid £10,-000 for it before the war, or 700,000 francs by today's exchange. *Workmen of the rue de Berne* is a charming and graceful picture, but those aren't Manet's essential qualities. Manet's *Plum* was bought from Rosenberg the other day for about a million francs by Mrs. Arthur Sachs of New York, and it's a masterpiece.

With Marie Laurencin

She doesn't want to free herself from Paul Rosenberg's guardianship, since for years he has been giving her about 50,000 francs a year, but she'd like him to pay her more. These days 50,000 francs are the equivalent of 15,000 gold francs. She doesn't want to try a bluff and say she has other propositions, for these money questions weary her. She wants to think only of her art, from the time she gets up to about five in the evening, when she stops. Rosenberg leaves her free to do portraits, water colors, etchings, drawings, without asking her for any commission. She sells a copperplate for 3,000 francs, a water color for 1,000, and a water-color drawing for 600. She has painted only three portraits since January; when I expressed my puzzlement she replied that the portrait of a woman gives her a great deal of trouble, that she picks and chooses her clients, that she couldn't do two at once, that pictures of children are easier for her. Already it isn't easy for her to do two genre pictures a month. She has just been asked to paint Chenal of the Opéra-Comique, but she is hesitating.

On Anatole France

Mlle Brisson, who bound books for him, told me that he was deeply moved by the celebrations in honor of his eightieth year, but he has a horror of growing old, and for a month the whole world hasn't stopped reminding him of his age.

June 5

I showed Crommelynck the Degas I have bought and placed in my Louis XVI drawing room. He is astonished that the proximity of this painting overwhelms my lovely Greuze, *Barberie de Courteilles*, and a fine Vigée-Lebrun. Even my La Tour, from the Doucet Collection, seems a little conventional, although it is a finished work and my Degas is only a sketch.

Crommelynck talked to me of the piece *Romeo and Juliet* adapted by Cocteau after Shakespeare, at the Théâtre de la Cigale. "It's a marvelous spectacle," he told me, "but the house is half empty. Many people go for a lark, to joke and laugh aloud. The costumes are all velvet and painted, even the lace on the sleeves, even the folds of the crinolines. The effect is magnificent. The back of the theater is also done in black velvet. It's a sort of tragedy in slow motion. I do assure you Cocteau has genius."

June 15 / On a Velázquez and a Dürer

Armand tells me that the Velázquez recently discovered by the director of the Vienna Museum in the stacks of the Imperial Palace, where it had been for two centuries, is marvelous.

Recently a picture dealer sent in his card to this director, who happened to be very busy just then and made him wait an hour; when he received him, the visitor had a marvelous signed Dürer under his arm, for which he was asking only 100,000 gold francs instead of the million it was worth; but the museum didn't have a penny, the Society of Friends of the Museum wouldn't agree to a loan, and it was a dealer who advanced the sum, giving the museum time to sell some frames and some copies.

A sale at the Louvre Museum, which has made history

People flocked to the sale as to a celebration and I went as though to a funeral. Mme Thiers's pearl necklace was being sold. I know it was not right for a museum, but nevertheless it makes me sad to think that we've won the war and have to liquidate our riches. The cost of living has gone up and the Thiers and Dauze Foundations no longer have enough money. The sum realized will be shared between these two institutions and the Louvre: 13,000,000 francs or 4,000,000 gold francs, when the necklace cost 300,000 gold francs in 1881. That's some consolation.

June 20 / With Crommelynck

I talked to him of Vermeer of Delft, whom he adores, and I called his attention to some of my unpublished notes on the Dutchman. I told him that we may be sure the personage on the left in the picture *The Courtesan* is in fact the painter, that moreover he is wearing the same apparel as the man at the back in Count Czernin's picture called *The Painter's Studio*, who, by common consent, is considered to be Vermeer. Moreover, the stance of this man is exactly that of a painter who, to do his own portrait, would be looking at himself in the glass. Also he is somehow on the fringe of the scene. There is still another detail to be considered. His left hand held a palette, which has been replaced by a glass— frightfully drawn—whereas a jug there on the table is marvelously done.

At Nathan Wildenstein's

I called on him with a rich American to whom he showed the

most beautiful Greuze[1] that I know, the Countess de X playing the mandolin. He asked him 1,650,000 francs for it, 475,000 francs for Fragonard's *The Happiness of the First Kiss*, and 550,000 francs for two tiny Fragonards which come from a Russian collection in Berne.

June 25 / The Duke of Marlborough

I went to see him at the Hôtel du Rhin. He informed me that he has put up for sale at Christie's a very beautiful chimney piece for which he paid £3,000 at Mme Lelong's many years ago. The Duke made out the article to be first-class. He waxed enthusiastic and urged me to put one of my representatives on a train to rush to see it and cable me details. Then, with swift and graceful authority, he pushed a catalogue into my pocket. His own pockets were full of them.

June 26 / A telephone conversation with Marie Laurencin

For ten minutes she talked of nothing but her teeth; she had one pulled out three weeks ago and another yesterday; they were wisdom teeth, and she is shaken by it. She was complaining of her forty years, of her weakness, of the poor circulation which is going to oblige her to leave for Bagnoles. She hates hotels, and she is planning to go in September with a woman friend to the South of France, where she has a cottage. She added that she can't work anywhere but in her own home, and even there it's only thanks to her maid, who knows what she needs at every hour, as she needs so much care and so many different medications.

She asked me if I've been to the Cigale to see Picasso's ballet, of which she said she understood nothing, that it was too highbrow, that she can't make out why he turns solids into steel wire, that he takes himself too seriously because he is Spanish.

On Marcel Proust

I have been questioning Ollivier, the headwaiter of the Ritz, on the writer's life in this hotel which he frequented so much during the last years of his life. "Marcel Proust," he told me, "would come quite unpredictably, five times a week, or else disappear for a fortnight,

[1] Subsequently in the Barton Jacobs Collection, Baltimore.

which he'd spend in bed with his window shut, never opening it. You can't imagine how stuffy it was in his room. I often went to his house, generally toward midnight. I would stay on until three or four in the morning, almost unawares, such was his charm."

I asked Ollivier if Proust would question him about society, people in society, their scandals and so on, and he pleaded guilty: "He managed to pump you, and without noticing, you'd be amazed to find that you had confided things best kept to yourself."

"But tell me, Ollivier, did love or any woman play a part in his life?" "Oh, no, the body was worn out; only the brain was left; he was all brain. The miracle of his brain was what kept him alive at all and made his body go on, that damaged thing, his body which for some time past he had sustained with nothing but liters of coffee, liters a day, especially during the long periods when he didn't eat. But when he did eat, as he used to here, his appetite was astonishing; he'd have to have two kinds of meat, and he always had second helpings, washed down with the best wines. He ate around eleven or midnight, often in a little back room, when everyone had left; but I would show him upstairs when there was a salon empty; a servant would light him a searing fire and I'd often be terrified that the Ritz would catch fire because of him. He'd sit right up near the fireplace. His tips were extremely generous. On the other hand, he exacted the most absolute courtesy, in spite of the fact that he was able to come down to anyone's level and could put the humblest person at ease. He was extraordinarily sensitive; one evening, for example, he arrived at the very moment when an elevator operator was going off duty and the man did not altogether hide his ill-humor. This put Marcel Proust in a wild rage; but when I asked him if he wanted me to dismiss the man, he was firmly against it. He wouldn't even hear of his being suspended for two days, when I wanted to chastise him in this way."

I asked Ollivier if the writer used to come to the Ritz with friends. "Yes," he replied, "at the beginning, but his friends wearied of those long nights with him and came less and less, which he didn't seem to mind. He used to sit for many hours just thinking: he thought a great deal. Sometimes he corrected proofs, but never when he was eating, for then his attention was absorbed entirely by his food."

July 4 / The Prince of Wales

I've spent a few days in England. From a dealer I bought a beautiful Boucher oval of two cupids, *Night and Day*. When I left for Paris, the prince was on my train. At Victoria Station his guard consisted of only three policemen and there was not a spectator in sight; but in Paris, home of the Republicans, there were two military bands to receive him, the municipal guards presented arms, and the crowd was overwhelming. What a contrast!

At the Molier Circus

Next to me, a woman was saying to her friend: "Really, Countess, you weren't very pleasant to that distinguished diplomat." The Countess replied: "He's only the ambassador of a republic."

A Poussin

It was Nathan Wildenstein who bought the Poussin from the Duke of Westminster for more than £6,000, more than 500,000 francs at the present rate of exchange. It's a pleasant Boucher-like picture, which is why he liked it. But I don't like it, despite the pictorial qualities, for Poussin is a serious painter and the seriousness is missing here.

September 6 / Lunch at Alphonse Kann's

He has left Paris and is living in Saint-Germain, 7, rue des Bucherons. He has just bought a Cézanne for 400,000 francs from Georges Bernheim and Hessel; it's *Young Girl with a Doll,* a very fine work which he is leaving in his will to the National Gallery, together with another Cézanne, a still life. He told me that he is reserving Oriental objects for the Louvre. On a panel, along with eight Renoirs, he has hung Cézanne's *The Blue Plate,* from the Mirbeau Collection, to prove the superiority of the latter.

He has kept only a few pieces from his former eighteenth-century collection. He showed me a bidet, which rather shocked the ladies; but at that time such objects were to be found in drawing rooms and were called "in cases."

I talked to Kann about Marcel Proust and he told me: "I knew him very well as a child; we played together on the Champs-Elysées and he bored me; he was a hair-splitter and already, at that age, a frightful snob. Besides, when he depicted society people in his first books he did not know them yet and described them badly. Only later, when he was lionized by them, did he get them right. I couldn't stand him. He would come over very early in the morning and stay with me while I dressed, I couldn't get rid of him. One day I practically showed him the door, and I received this strange note: 'Monsieur, I have left my gloves at your house, would you kindly have them sent by your servant.' Later, around 1913, I met him again; he had told mutual friends that he would like to see me again, that our estrangement was due to a misunderstanding. I accepted, but couldn't bear him any more than before, although some of my friends, like Robert de Montesquiou, spoke very highly of him and said they adored him.

"I preferred de Montesquiou; he had the most brilliant mind; his conversation sparkled. I was unkind to him when he read me his verses; I simply left the room. He used to get angry but he always came back to me, telling himself: 'Kann doesn't know anything.' Marcel Proust also read me his pages when he was sixteen; I appreciated the intelligence in them. Perhaps if I hadn't known the man I'd appreciate his work."

While I listened to Kann, I asked myself if people of his kind don't bear a grudge against the writer for having laid them bare. Kann must feel put out at having served Marcel Proust as an anatomical specimen.

September 7 / With Crommelynck in Chartres

I took him along; he has spent a fortnight on the Belgian coast. I had talked so much to him about cathedrals that he rushed to Rouen, then to Amiens, where he had a long conversation with the keeper, who informed him that around 1895 Marcel Proust spent a week going over the church from top to bottom and went to all the places in the city and country nearby from which it could be seen, so as to study it from all angles. Returning there subsequently, Marcel Proust met the painter Liebermann, who was busy restoring the Palace of the Popes. That day at Amiens a tomb was opened, and a very well preserved body was found, as a vacuum had been created by the burning of hot coals in the tomb; but when the tomb was closed again in the presence of these two men, no precaution was taken and the body must since have turned to dust. The keeper had taken a bit of ribbon from the body, and all three took pieces, and Marcel Proust was as happy as a schoolboy with it.

The keeper told Crommelynck the story of the destruction of the Amiens stained-glass windows. These were taken down during the war and sent to Paris, first to the Trocadero, then to a restorer, who deposited them with one of his nephews. The nephew had a garage and put the windows there; the garage caught fire with the windows in it, and they were completely destroyed the following morning when the firemen, wielding their hatchets, came to make sure the fire wasn't smoldering under the stained glass.

With Fernand Crommelynck, who came to lunch

How brilliantly analytical he is! At our first meeting he only listened to my recollections of Marcel Proust; the second time Forain hadn't given anyone a chance to speak; today we were alone together and the writer showed himself to be a man of penetrating logic. He absolutely plumbs a subject; I can't see him finding a sparring partner of his own stature. He stayed on until four and talked exclusively of Marcel Proust. "Proust annihilated the whole of the nineteenth century," he said. "He tore it to shreds and nothing will remain of it, not even a poet, for he is the greatest of poets." Crommelynck started to quote entire sentences on the death of the grandmother and on Méséglise and Vermeer, and truly splendid they were. "Of Flaubert's works, *Madame Bovary* stands," he continued, "and perhaps *The Sentimental Education.* Compared to Proust, Balzac is a ludicrous romantic. As for Baudelaire, and Verlaine, he sweeps them away, he crushes them utterly. He wrote in prose, but now that verse is no longer being written, all poets write in prose. Do you know that Albertine is a man? Through her he described his love for a man. At least that's what people say. It's also said that all the homosexuals in Paris were at his funeral. The truth is in danger of being clouded by the efforts of this special world to claim him for itself. What a mystery it is! I can see the nausea he sometimes felt; profoundly too, not superficially; and isn't it all very like Charlus not being able to stop himself from speaking of his vice? Why did Proust write on this subject so incessantly? What did he want to say? What is the concluion? Of course we must await the conclusion of *Time Regained*. But what *is* the mystery? What did Proust want? Man wants to know himself, that's why he invented words; they enable him to converse with his neighbor, to know him, and in knowing him he thinks he will eventually know himself, for this will be impossible unless he can compare himself with others. Indeed a man alone on earth would not go on living, he would kill himself. Art was invented by man as a means of defense. What does it mean to speak of paradise? Do animals go there? That's the question to which I must have an answer, and it is one of the weak points in the spiritual aspect of Proust's work that he says nothing of animals.

"Socially, Proust was too rich; being wealthy, he didn't enter the abode of the people. Still, he might sometimes have mentioned a dumb creature, an innocent dumb creature. He took great delight in his own world, believing in it tremendously, and what pleased him was the sensation that so many of its members were superior. Proust studied everything around him with a stereoscopic precision; he wanted to know himself; I might say that he wrote minutely where the others who came before him wrote large; that's why to start with we've all had so much trouble reading him. It took me a year, and I had to start again three times. I had, I was certain, read some extract of his in *Le Matin* before the war; I had found it astounding but had forgotten his name, and that annoyed me; when I began *Swann's Way* I remembered. How deadly I found those first fifty pages with their mass of insignificant details; now I couldn't enjoy them more. Gradually you come to understand how greatly Proust struggled for knowledge of himself. How is it possible? The nature of the species throws men and women together; but Proust wished to submit to no law, he did not want to be the instrument, he loved himself so. Proust shows us how he loved himself when his old servant speaks to him, urging him to get up, calling him 'big lazybones' "
. . . (Crommelynck quoted the exact sentence.)

"And what does Man learn in this form of possession, what does he give? Little enough, and Proust is hardly interested; but he does want to know the exact proportions of the exchange. I've said that by questioning his fellows, man thinks to arrive at self-knowledge; but the law of procreation gets in the way of that, so that the same sex starts to go toward the same sex, and then there is equality, proportion, balance; that's what Proust wanted to arrive at; that was how he thought, that was how he acted.

"I have just read *The Captive*; his work has fallen off, it's less successful, there are too many repetitions, and he's started making fun of himself. La Berma he no longer remembers, and he calls her Sarah Bernhardt. And then he is mistaken in wanting to create historical figures that are not real, that never existed. Saint-Simon's works are alive still because his characters were, and Proust in one or two passages has expressed a desire to create a work which will survive. Such remarks are typical of a writer of prose, for poets are convinced that they will be the sole preoccupation of future generations. It is Voltaire we find telling a woman that she'll be immortal if he sings of her. Ah, Proust drives himself, drives himself terribly."

I told Crommelynck what Kann had said to me about Proust, that he did not know the world of high society when he first started writing, and I added that Proust died once he had finished his work, that he couldn't have died before but that once his novel was concluded, he no longer had enough strength to stay alive.

"That's quite true," said Crommelynck, "and I said the same thing to my brother a few days ago. What Kann says is also true. At the beginning he was watching the society world from the outside, but later he had plenty of elbow room and could move in it with ease. I am eager to read his correspondence, for he certainly saw my play *The Magnificent Cuckold*. He wrote twenty pages about it, twenty pages of commentary. I'm not saying that he was inspired by me in the way he presented his character, far from it, but I do say that these pages are a commentary on my play; if I had been asked for commentaries, I would have written those twenty pages, and even now I would cut them out and send them to a magazine under my own name. Yes, he must have spoken of it in his correspondence. Unfortunately I didn't know him personally. One day I nearly went to look him up to talk to him of Swann, but I didn't act on the impulse. 'Will he receive me?' I asked myself. The worst thing is that I did in fact know him; I am almost sure that I met him once and didn't pay any attention to him. I have a frightful memory for faces: I can be introduced to the same person three times in ten minutes and believe I've seen three different people. I must have a letter from him, but I don't open my letters, it takes up too much time; I mustn't let myself be absorbed by what is useless, and I yield easily to the temptation. That's why I work at night, from nine in the evening to six in the morning; nine hours, not only without noise, but without appointments, without the telephone, totally absorbed by my work, with coffee, cigarettes, and the window open. I could work just as well in the morning; I adore the morning for working, but a beautiful sun would send me running to the country. I would set off with Verlaine's stick, which I've had from Verhaeren's widow; it's only boxwood, a nobble, which somehow in its every aspect reminds me to an astonishing degree of him. I shall have it authenticated and sell it to an American. I'm not the man for relics, I don't understand all that."

I asked him if he writes novels. "Yes, I have one, but it isn't finished. It's hard work, I drag it out of myself; that's an idea, I'll put you into it. In fact, no, that's impossible. I'm quite incapable of judging others, everything comes out of me, I take it all from myself. Some critics have said that I'm a psychologist, but they've been wrong. And that's where Marcel Proust was mistaken. The critics assured him too assiduously that he was a psychologist and this made him lose his breadth of vision."

When I told Crommelynck that I had a letter from Proust in which he called the place where we used to sit together every evening in the hotel at Cabourg "the retreat of the damned," he said to me: "But that turns up in his book, the retreat of the damned, and I'm astonished that he hasn't put you in it." "To begin with," I replied, "I don't remember the passage, and I see myself nowhere in his work; he might more likely have put me in *Within a Budding Grove*, or where he speaks of Vermeer. In one of his letters to me he wrote: 'It's Vermeer who brought us together.'"

At this point young Crommelynck showed his brother Hofstede de Groot's book on Vermeer and explained to him my discovery that the man on the left, in *The Courtesan*, is the painter himself. None of the properties in the picture really stands properly, and the shape of the table can't be made out. Nor does the head of the procuress fit into the composition: it seems to grow out of the wall. The picture was painted in front of a mirror. There are still a number of other observations to be made which I shall go into more deeply.

September 16 / On Vermeer

In *The Courtesan* the painter's shoulder is too elongated because he is looking at himself in the mirror. The left arm is distorted; I should think he painted it without looking at his own arm, or he put it in later on. Again, the painter's head is in the far background, while his arm is in the foreground, because the mirror doubles distances. His face is pallid, again because of the glass, and Crommelynck tells me that a white canvas would have reflected white rays onto the painter's face.

September 17 / An Ingres and a Renoir at Hector Brame's

Hector Brame is an old dealer, an eccentric, who shows his pictures only to people whose faces he likes. He always has one or two beautiful pictures in his back room. He was telling me about a Belgian who was related to King Leopold and who had a very fine collection. He had slipped a fake picture into it, and always started by showing this fake to visitors; if they went into raptures over it, the collector would vanish, leaving the barbarian in the care of a secretary, who had instructions to get rid of him expeditiously.

The Ingres he showed me is perhaps the picture of this master's with which I should most like to live; it is *The Iliad,* a subject treated again in *The Triumph of Homer,* and this study is more complete than a large picture. Brame has just sold it for nearly 200,000 francs. The Renoir is the portrait of the architect Lecoeur, a small canvas about fifteen inches high called *The Man in White.* On a sort of blue placard, in the upper right-hand corner, the artist has written GALAND JAKO. He's the genuine bourgeois of the period.

Marvels at Duveen's

A small Dürer, a portrait of a man in armor; his beard ends in two long points sinuously coiled. Lord Spencer's Frans Hals:[2] the back of a chair, with a man seated, from the back, but his elbows seeming to burst out of the canvas; and a great black hat. A landscape on the right; it's

[2] Since sold to Wood of Toronto, Canada. (Note appended May 12, 1925.)

something rare in this painter, and is treated a bit like a Van Goyen. A marvelous Hoppner, the portrait of Lady Beauchamp; her hat has a ribbon of so lovely a blue that it casts upon her face an azure haze which fills her eyes with love. A fine Reynolds, a woman and child, of a Lady Spencer seated on the ground with her baby: an English version of Jean-Jacques Rousseau. A bronze, as insignificant as it is huge, by Luca della Robbia. It's a pity that this artist ever discovered this mawkish craft more akin to porcelain than to sculpture; he lost his sense of form in it, and then his grandeur. Great artists should stick to stone, marble, and all kinds of hard stone. His talent softened like his clay.

September 26 / With Crommelynck

We were chatting and looking at the Dürer book. I showed him how well the painter drew his own hands, and told him how I first noticed at the Louvre, when looking at the Rembrandts, that in his self-portrait the artist didn't know how to draw his hands, and that when I subsequently saw the Rembrandt book I noticed that this applied to nearly all his paintings.

"Last night I had dinner with Derain," said Crommelynck, "at a place on the rue des Fosses-Saint-Germain run by a kind of paint seller who does the cooking. You get a very good meal with bottled wine for ten francs. You're cheek by jowl with stokers and Americans, but the latter will pretty quickly spoil the place. Derain is a sharp fellow from Picardy, he's got wit, he's droll and he made us laugh. He was talking a great deal about the war, and knows a heap of anecdotes, of which he is invariably the hero. He told us that he looked after his own skin in the war; that was all he thought about. He'd be given instructions to 'go over,' and if the position showed signs of danger and if he knew it was a shell trap, he simply wouldn't go where he was told. He hates the modern-painting dealers, he says, because they didn't recognize him when he was young. These days he is surrounded by shady middlemen, parasites who live off him."

October 5 / At Strasbourg Cathedral

The master builder of the cathedral must have been depraved. He seems to have used the portal for a black mass. His women are beautiful.

but their bodies are lewd and shrouded in a veil of sadistic perversion. His evocations of the Virtues have breasts for the picking, their bellies are like fruit on the point of bursting, and their legs, which are more or less apart, writhe as though caught in the grip of a spasm.

October 10 / Fernand Crommelynck comes to lunch

My niece Muriel was there. As we were talking about Shakespeare, Crommelynck told us that he thought of *Othello* when he wrote his *Magnificent Cuckold*. He had some criticism to make of Shakespeare's play. "Someone else induces Othello to be jealous, but jealousy is not like that, it's a passion which grows of its own accord and without reason. This is so true that in order to make Othello more plausible Shakespeare made a mulatto of him, a weakling, who believes on the spot everything he is told." Crommelynck admires the "life-quality" in Shakespeare, his popular genius, and all those sayings he created which have become a part of the language.

October 13 / Fernand Crommelynck on the death of Anatole France

He said to me: "It strikes me as splendid, that long-drawn-out death which didn't give the lie to his life; magnificent, that ten-day agony with those smiling awakenings. 'I'm going to die.' Generally speaking, however much one may be prepared, one doesn't know if at the last moment some default, if only purely physical, may not spoil the whole work of a lifetime. I would wish my death to be prolonged like that one; I should wish to be able to converse with it. This good fortune was granted to Anatole France, and he knew how to preserve in it the dignity of his life. I really think it was splendid."

A gesture, 5, quai Malaquais

The Champion Ancient and Modern Library is closed, and on the door is a card: "Closed in respect for the memory of Anatole France."

Anatole France and the antique dealers

Throughout his life he spent a great deal of time in book and antique shops. I saw Leonardon, a dealer in Gothic articles who has his shop on the quai Voltaire, and I asked him if he knew him. "Very well," he replied, "and he even put me in *The Revolt of the Angels* under the name of Guinardon, because I had told him about the theft of a book from a library, a story which he transposed into his tale. You know Lambert on the rue Bonaparte, the priest turned antique dealer; Anatole France used to go to his place when he was preparing *The Revolt*, to get documentary material on the mentality of a defrocked priest."

A Watteau

Nathan Wildenstein asked me to see about a Watteau of Lord Iveagh's, *The Comedians*, or *The Italian Comedy*. He told me it could easily bring thirty thousand pounds. At the current exchange rate that amounts to 2,250,000 francs.

On Anatole France

I went to see this Lambert. In fact he knew Anatole France very well and is extremely proud of having served him as a model.

He has letters from him, two of which are particularly curious. They aren't dated, and I advised Lambert to put the year in in pencil. They were written in 1915 and 1916. In one of the letters he speaks of the war, of the people in high places who kept coming to whisper secrets in his ear, secrets which he had in fact read about in the papers. In the other letter these are more or less his own words: "France is proud of her army and its fortunes and the bourgeoisie does all it can to accumulate more and more debts. You know the story of Don Quixote and his friend Sancho. They bestride their wooden horses, their eyes blindfolded, and they rear up, while the bearded duennas cry to them: 'You are high up in the clouds.' You know how the story ends."

Lambert told me that his favorites among Anatole France's books are the volumes of *Contemporary History*. He admires the exactitude with which he depicts the clergy. "He seems to have second sight," he said. The priests, who cannot fail to recognize themselves, exclaim: "Ah, how nasty he is!" But Lambert disagrees. According to him, Anatole France was all kindness; no other man gave him so much encouragement in his business; the writer often bought objects from him which he didn't really need, with the sole aim of helping him to earn some money.

The Princess Murat

I met her at the Théâtre Caumartin, where a rather good play, *The Talking Monkey* by Alfred Savoir, is on. She asked me if I had seen the house which Marie Laurencin has bought in the forest of Sénart; she said she thought it was frightful but that Marie is so nearsighted she finds it exquisite, and that anyway with her taste perhaps she'll succeed in making it charming. The princess was talking so fast that I didn't manage to grasp whether Marie Laurencin had bought a picture by Delacroix or by Douanier Rousseau, or the countryside reminded her of the two artists, or she was going to do a landscape in the manner of one of these painters, or if she is going to copy two of their canvases. Anyhow, I did understand that it's for her maid's daughter that she has bought this house, and the princess, like a great lady who alone can pardon such a foible, added: "It's a delightful thing in Marie Laurencin's life, the story of her maid's daughter."

October 16 / A Manet at Hessel's: "The Beach at Boulogne"

It's a wide canvas and valued at 450,000 francs. Hessel told me that it takes Vuillard three years to finish a portrait.

October 18 / At Villa Saïd, where Anatole France died

I went there together with my son Ernest at 9:30 in the morning. It seems strange that this man had such fine taste in literature, yet the walls of the house are hung with the most ordinary drawings and pictures. His influence will long endure, for I saw filing past his coffin only youngsters of twenty.

Anatole France originals

I possess the manuscripts of *The Amethyst Ring, The Elm in the Walk, The Wicker Basket*, several chapters of *Monsieur Bergeret in Paris*, part of the manuscript of *Life of Joan of Arc*, parts of the manuscript of *Crainquebille*, with the printer's proofs. I have *The Wells of Saint Claire* in the Livre Contemporain edition, copy 17, with the name of Berthon and fifteen handwritten pages. I have the autobiographical notes for the preface of *Herodias*—forty-two pages. Also the "Vocation" chapter: sixteen pages, and copy number 1 of the first edition of *The Red Lily*.

The funeral of Anatole France

I didn't want to hear the speeches; one can read them in the papers. I mingled with the crowd and crossed Paris on foot from the rue Spontini to the quai Malaquais. We have some good ideas in France. His bier was raised on a platform in front of the house where he was born and near the quays which he described at such length. The loud-speaker made it possible for everything to be heard a thousand yards away and more. I was surprised at the respectfulness of this crowd and at its youth. Some people were hoping for a political manifestation. The free-thinking government has its free-thinking corpse, which had of late been close to being that of a Communist. But the hawkers are offering the insidious little red flowers in vain, the wild rose doesn't sell, whereas photographs of the writer are being bought. I came across Helleu, who told me that he had seen a red flag, followed by slovenly brawlers with highly intelligent faces. He continued: "One day I said to Anatole France, 'I adore Carpeaux, he was perhaps greater than Houdon; he had imagination, verve, and humor.' But Anatole France, raising his finger, replied: 'Houdon.'"

I left Helleu. The procession was supposed to turn at the Pont du Carrousel, then follow the right bank of the river, along the Louvre and the terrace of the Tuileries, which was already black with crowds. I went up the Champs-Elysées again around 2:30 and the crowd was enormous.

Such a delay in the funeral ceremony is quite unheard of, and I had an appointment at home with a Mrs. Joe Thomas, née Fargo, an American whom Kelly sent me with an enthusiastic letter in praise of her beauty and artistic sense; she paints and decorates. She wanted to meet Beltran Masses and write two articles for *Arts and Decoration* and *The International Studio*. She is indeed a very beautiful woman. I offered her tea and we went to call on the Spanish artist, whom we did not leave until 6:40. Thus I missed the funeral of Anatole France, and I was very annoyed about it. I hoped for the impossible: the speeches might have lasted indefinitely. I said all this to Mrs. Thomas and suggested: "Supposing we go to the Neuilly Cemetery?" She agreed. When we arrived there, the cemetery was closed; but cemeteries have bells and I gave the caretaker twenty francs while a dog barked, the dog which guards the buried dead. The man picked up a dim lantern. It was quite dark. In front of us we saw the lights of Neuilly with a vast halo accentuating the shadows and making the agglomeration of tombs look like an Oriental city, a criminal city, where there are no buildings save palaces. Mrs. Thomas shuddered. The procession had got here so late that the undertaker's men, insensitive as they are, left their tools on the ground, cluttering the entrance to the cemetery, and abandoned hundreds of garlands along the paths, heightening the Oriental illusion. The heavens seem to have bestowed a garland on every tomb. The tomb of the great man, who was idolized such a short time ago, has been hastily covered over with a tarpaulin, which our guide lifted up so that we could see the bier with the famous plate which was a point of contention, as certain people wanted to see the words "of the Académie Française" added to the inscription, though finally this was not done. The general impression here is one of flight and abandonment. Obviously they felt it was time for dinner—and so it looked as though Anatole France was going to spend the night out of doors.

The caretaker informed us that instructions had been given that the flagstones should not be sealed, as he'll be taken in two months' time from here to the Panthéon with Jaurès. Is that the law? Now he is resting side by side with his father and his mother, his mother on whom he called during his agony; he sleeps with the Thibaults. His mother had originally been buried in a provisional plot in this same cemetery, but on his father's death France bought this tomb in perpetuity. The caretaker didn't know where his first wife was buried. We stayed a while to meditate and then we left.

October 23 / On Anatole France

Seymour de Ricci, who is to write a book on the author's first editions and to whom I showed the *Crainquebille* manuscript, remarked that the work was originally entitled: *The Jérôme Crainquebille Affair.* He crossed out "Jérôme."

Ricci, who has a prodigious memory for everything he has read, doesn't remember a single word of the writer whose house he used to visit every Wednesday morning before the war. France liked to receive young people.

October 25 / On Anatole France

For 5,000 francs I bought a manuscript of fifty-nine sheets: two speeches which he delivered in Argentina and Brazil a little before the war.

This manuscript belonged to Eugène Richtenberger. It is astonishing that Anatole France was so little concerned about his manuscripts, but some words inscribed in this one show that he didn't care a rap for them. Here they are: "My dear Richten, I chide you and thank you for the care with which you keep these sheets which ought to be left to scatter to the winds."

This manuscript also shows that before sending a letter he would make a draft, full of scratched-out passages. This one is addressed to the Argentine minister in Paris.

On Gauguin

A lady told me that she'd heard Lanessan, governor of Tahiti when Gauguin was there, say that the painter had a contract with Vollard, who paid him five francs apiece for his canvases. I can scarcely believe it.

Marie Laurencin—Laboureur

I meet the engraver at the painter's. Laboureur's human figures are so slender that I imagined the artist would resemble them, whereas on the contrary he is small, stout, and jolly. He told me that at the age of ten or eleven he thought he would become an engraver, not knowing what this meant, except that it was something to do with copper, and that pleased him.

While he was working, Marie was painting a fantastic picture in which the women's arms and legs are so mixed up that they can't be disentangled. With a few brush strokes she painted in a shoulder, then a foot, and then some tulle, never spending more than five minutes on the same bit. She told us she is to illustrate a book by Raoul Duval, whose talent she greatly admires. "He's living in poverty," she told me, "and his wife came around two days ago to borrow 2,000 francs from me." Marie talked to us about her country house, which looks like a seventeenth-century stage set. The garden is a little like one of the public squares in Molière, where the various characters can pop out of the windows, which are close to the ground so that the actors won't break their legs.

December 23 / The newest Carel Fabritius discovered

It belonged to the wife of a minor employee in a provincial English bank, who sent it between two pieces of cardboard to Christie's with a letter asking its value and instructing them to sell it if it should bring more than ten pounds. She received an answer that it was a very good painting, and a minimum price of £1,000 should be set. The husband rushed up to London, thinking there was some mistake; in fact, Christie's had grossly erred in their estimation, as the canvas brought £6,000 and was purchased by the National Gallery. At that same time, a boy who had inherited his uncle's estate found in the bank vault a pile of Rembrandt etchings to which he attached a value of only a few hundred pounds, especially as each engraving had on it the purchase price, which in no case exceeded a few shillings. But this lot came to more than twenty thousand pounds; a single etching brought £3,000.

January 2, 1925

I set out for Florence to show Berenson a picture which I believe to be by Bellini and which he formerly attributed to Vivarini, then to Lotto.

Pisa

Nothing would be further from my mind than any thought of scorning the term "dead city," which is used so often. Quite the contrary. The cities of Italy know how to die, and that is their greatest virtue. Thus I hasten toward those towns thought to be vanquished by material changes, which have in fact bestowed on them an ability to preserve forever their spirituality. In refusing to expand, they become greater; by staying motionless, they become immovable. What a lesson in repose they give to man, who doesn't want to stop, or indeed to live! In death, those dead cities retain their youth and look to us exactly as they did when we ourselves were adolescents.

With its buildings of green-veined white marble, Pisa always reminds me of a bride dressed for her wedding. The façades of her houses are silken. The four landmarks of human existence stand side by side: the Baptistry, the Church, the Tower, the Cemetery. The cemetery is unique, a rectangular cloister infinitely elongated, surrounded by a plain, not very severe wall.

January 4 / At Berenson's

He will have it that the picture is a Lotto. It is in poor condition but was painted by a greater master. But Berenson hates Wildenstein, inveighs against him, and says: "That man goes about telling everyone that I'm a swindler, that I can easily be bribed; I've other things to do than sue him for slander."

In his book on Lotto, Berenson did mention this picture, which was attributed in the Stuttgart Gallery to Jacopo di Barbari, and he then believed it to be by Alvise Vivarini. If Berenson doesn't like Wildenstein, he cares still less for his own countrymen. "In Florence," he commented, "the Yankee becomes an art lover between a visit to a little girl and one to a little boy, a flourishing trade here. The middleman who deals in works of art follows close on the heels of the procuress; often they are one and the same. They invariably know how to find somewhere in the same town the twin brother of the picture admired in the museum, and the American flings himself into this new kind of debauchery at fantastic cost. But there at least he isn't risking the dread disease; only the picture is contaminated!"

The Florentine countryside

The museums were closed and I was walking in the Boboli Gardens surrounding the Pitti Palace. It is a strange garden, in fact it is merely a cascade of paths; but at the top, as compensation for the terrible climb, there is a hanging terrace from which the view, bounded by the neighboring hills, extends from the direction of San Miniato to the south of the Florentine countryside. The air is so mellow that apart from the indomitable black cypress, the foliage of all the trees takes on the color of the olive tree, a pliant color exuding a mist, a vegetal cloud; a lovingly seductive mood of Nature, who understands better in Italy than anywhere else that veilings are essential and must never be torn away to come closer to her; this is the Florentine miracle.

January 5 / At the home of Fra Angelico

These days the Convent of San Marco is a museum. Here is what the guide taught us.

If Christianity had hoped to create—and I hasten to deny this—a place from which all human warmth was excluded (if that were possible), it was the nineteenth century, alas, which was successful when it invented the museum. When shall we be rid of it? Such thoughts assailed me as I went round these despoiled holy places. I'd seen nothing, so I started my tour over again at the first cell. Fra Angelico—who yourself adorned perhaps twenty-five of these cells with paintings—I earnestly implore your forgiveness. I should very much like to have known what Anatole France, less celebrated, thought of you. He'd have declared that you led all your companions into hell. Somewhere in his works, in *Penguin Island,* he has old Douillard explain that the prostitute is closer to God than the woman who gives herself to Him, for the latter has joy and passion as her sole motive, while the former does it rather than commit suicide, which is forbidden by God, and she takes no pleasure in it, quite the contrary. Anatole France would have said of you, Fra Angelico, that you did not gain paradise because you brought it to your convent. You lived a life of joy, palette in hand, and your scenes of beauty led your brothers from the path of austerity. Worse, the neighboring orders envied you; you aroused jealousy among them, while in your own temple you destroyed the harmony of the cells.

Fra Angelico, I have been disrespectful, and I ask your pardon, I who might have dreamed of being poet to you! But I am exorcised by this sacred edifice, and its transformation into a museum.

What I would like to do is to establish in a reconstituted convent a holy week in your honor. From all points of the globe, once a year for seven days, all lovers of your work, chosen and selected, would come in pilgrimage. I don't know whether I might even permit a few, who had lit candles to you or performed acts of piety, to spend a night in one of your cells.

No, on second thought, it's the least deserving who would have to be accorded this signal favor: they would go home better men, for it is goodness which you, Fra Angelico, expressed above all. Never before or since has any artist dared to render this greatest, this only quality of man, for the other virtues, whatever their names, are but petulant, degenerate children.

I venerate you, Fra Angelico, who painted man's heart.[3]

[3] I have just discovered a marvelous Fra Angelico from Russia. It is only a fragment, an angel's head, probably cut out of a large picture, but it has a supreme beauty. (Note appended 1935. The Hartford museum bought it from me.)

January 6 / Across Florence

Unfortunately it was a holiday and the museums rising on every street corner were closed, but the churches were my consolation.

I entered the one named Santissima Annunziata. Though this applies even more to the churches of Rome, these Florentine churches often seem built in the image of their name, like this one, redolent of marble, feminine freshness, superlative decoration. The entrance consists of an atrium painted almost entirely by Andrea del Sarto, who was not a great painter but who had the merit of being the last, as decadence approached, not to cross into mawkish sentimentality. His adolescents have the slightly faded grace of blonds in warm countries, but his women on the other hand are robust and make advances to them. I find it hard to believe these young men can suffer their embraces.

In these great religious compositions there reigns an innocence totally denuded of faith; I see here that Andrea del Sarto, gentle pagan that he was, took a sweet pleasure in inspiring joy in the souls of the faithful, and so applied himself to deceiving them into living more happily.

Inside the church nothing has changed; the spirit of yesteryear reigns supreme. It was raining outside, and the day was somber, it was almost dark inside, and in a hollow in the wall an illuminated crib was streaming with light—the stable in Bethlehem, in relief and in color, modern, in rough-hewn wood. In this vision each god—and let us not destroy the idols—is tangible, the lovely tale . . . and the magic force of electricity. The effect is so striking that the good people of Florence pass unseeing before the frescoes of Andrea del Sarto and hasten to kneel down in front of these hacked bits of wood.

January 7 / Venturi

I've come to Rome to make the acquaintance of this celebrated scholar and art critic. Perhaps it is because he has studied everything in art that he does not understand sculpture like Bode or painting like Berenson; but he has stuck his nose in everywhere and his nose is large, and the scholar has done much unraveling of Italian art. He has done a great deal to bring art closer to the layman. He is extremely old. His head is triangular, a triangle drawn out by a white goatee surmounted by black teeth. He's a very nice man, and welcoming. When I told him about my idea, which I haven't given up, of bringing out *The Arts,* he was enthusiastic and talked to me of the treasures of the French museums. He has discovered a Lippi in Nice, two Pisanellos in Le Mans, a Velázquez in Tours, and many other wonders of which he declares our museums are full. "You have some sensational pieces there," he said, and continued: "You French have felt the lack of a Vasari, a fifteenth-century historian who would have recounted the lives of the painters and given their names. But by searching your archives there should be a way, at four hundred years' distance, to find a substitute for him and investigate your admirable fifteenth-century school." He told me that Scotland and Ireland are full of Italian treasures. He saw a Veneziano in Ireland which has no equal in Italy.

January 9 / Rome. Michelangelo's Moses

He looks like a very intelligent old man, but he has seen too many popes and is no longer a prophet. He strokes his beard instead of tearing it, and he is seated; he is a clever politician. Marble is the silk of minerals, but the Egyptians used granite, impervious granite. The sculptor's touchstone is hard stone. The naked leg is marvelous; the sculptor has bent the tibia into a beautiful curve. Michelangelo is the greatest of couturiers in sculpture; he is a couturier in marble.

January 14

I leave with my youngest son Jean, bound for New York.

NOTEBOOK 13

January 20–November 14, 1925

January 20 / Germaine Taillefer

A dull crossing. This young artist, this beautiful young girl, is the only interesting person on board. She belongs to a group of seven musicians who play modern music. Her artist's life brings her into the freest milieux, and she knows all their deviations. Just now she was up on the captain's bridge and she thought the spectacle was marvelous. "To put to music," I said to her. "No," said she, "nature and its forces cannot be put into music, which can only express sensations. Last year I went to the edge of the Sahara; friends wanted me to put the desert into music." "But Wagner," I suggested, "rendered 'fire.'" "I prefer real fire," she replied, "although I admire his fire, his water, his wind." She told us she will be spending three months in New York, where she will stay at the house of the American painter Dougherty; when I told her that he has talent (though I think it's pretty thin) she was as happy as a child, and said to everyone sitting around the tea table: "You see, you hear what M. Gimpel says; my friend Dougherty has talent. I'm always so glad when people speak well of my friends."

In a charity concert this evening she played works by Poulenc and

Stravinsky. She swears she isn't a pianist, that in New York she won't play; she will simply be present at concerts where her music is performed.

At John D. Rockefeller, Jr.'s

This morning Mrs. John D. Rockefeller showed me over her mansion; she has bought the worst kind of Gothic statues; and the La Rochefoucauld tapestries are placed in a tiny room, where there's not an inch of wall space; it's horrible. She's a nice woman, but quite absurd in her affectation of simplicity. She was talking of one or two objects which her husband bought her this winter: "He's been so nice to spend this money on me, but I have been good, I haven't asked him for a thing for several months." Rockefeller bought David's *Lavoisier* from Wildenstein for $160,000; it is hanging here but is destined to go to his Institute. She has a set of third-rate Chinese objects, apart from a single good wood carving. She takes pleasure in lighting incense in the Chinese room, and she enjoyed showing me how it burns and forcing me to put my nose over it. She wants to buy a sixteenth-century Italian portrait because the profile resembles one of her sons. She went into rhapsodies over Rockefeller Senior's horrible pictures by Sargent. She has a fine Lawrence, a woman with a peacock, but it's a bit like a poster. She has some remarkable black Chinese vases as well as a vast collection of the green variety, but all in disorder, showing a wicked bad taste.

March 6 / The tragedy of the motion picture

I had dinner with some people from California; they live in Los Angeles, and were telling me about the motion pictures and how the king of the Belgians and Marshal Foch couldn't drag themselves from the studios. People stay for hours watching the artists redo a scene. It's the city in the world where one sees the most beautiful women, for they flock to it from everywhere, France as well as the remotest parts of Russia, England, Egypt, India. These marvelous creatures arrive with dreams of happiness and conquest, but when they appear on the screen it turns out that their faces are not photogenic. The dream collapses, the tragedy begins. Fit for nothing else, they become maids of all work—inevitably, as they have no profession. They have used up their savings to pay for their fare, and after having believed they would conquer fortune, they are reduced to servitude.

March 13

John D. Rockefeller, Jr., came to see me today. I didn't know him and I found myself confronted with a marvelous creature. He delivers sermons in church on Sunday and has in fact something of the priest about him. This man, the greatest philanthropist the world has ever seen, does so much good on earth, cares so much about all our miseries, that I'm not surprised he seems to be somehow of divine origin. This constant occupation, the occupation of goodness, has surely fashioned his face in the likeness of his spirit; the face of a man who gives every day cannot resemble that of the man who takes every day; the face of a man who not only doesn't know how to refuse but doesn't want to, must be quite different from any other countenance ever seen. Such is his face, and it is a wonderful thing to see. He came to look at my pictures and art objects, about which he doesn't understand a great deal, but he makes an effort. He asked me prices because he has the impression that they indicate a certain degree of beauty. He believes that the religious objects come straight from the churches. I don't know why it interests him to learn whether religious objects come from dealers or from collections. He has Buddhas in his house, and yet he is astonished that one can live with religious objects. He, who is so religious, does not understand them. However, he adores my Fra Angelico.

March 15 / On Mark Twain

I dined in Detroit with Mrs. Julius Haas, who collects, and with taste. But the moving spirit, the pioneer of this city, is Ralph Booth, the president of the museum. He is the heart and soul of it, and his wife, who shares the same tastes, is an invaluable help to him.

The daughter of the American humorist Mark Twain was sitting next to me, and talked to me of her father's journal, which is just being published. I asked her some questions about it, and she replied: "A lot of people are expecting a scandalous narrative but they're mistaken, although some overintimate passages have had to be suppressed. To my mind, a journal must be absolutely precise, or at least on an even keel, quite the opposite of my father, who was of such a changeable disposition, sometimes so vindictive and full of anger, then suddenly forgetting his quarrels, even his hates, and throwing himself on the neck of the man he'd been abusing the day before; so that what he wrote one day, the next he no longer believed."

March 19 / Modern German painting

If France were to study it carefully, she would realize the dangers threatening her. I came away disturbed from the home of Dr. Valentiner, a German museum director with a collection of young artists from his country who, upon my word, are not without talent, such as Emil Nolde, Kokoschka, E. Munch, Nowsigier, Otto Mueller, Kirchner, Franz Marc, A. Macke, Schmidt-Rotluff, Rohlfs, Klee, and the sculptors R. Scheibe, G. Kolbe, and Lehmbruck.

I've often heard it said: "He who understands the ancients automatically understands modern art." There aren't two arts, ancient art and modert art, each far removed from the other. Thc artist of the past formed us in our beginnings, like his brothers the man of letters, the musician, the moralist, the philosopher. We are what we are because a Moses, a Christ, a Mohammed lived; we owe our brain to a Plato, a Sophocles, a Shakespeare, a Pascal, a Goethe, a Van Dyck, a Velázquez, a Rembrandt, a Watteau, a Wagner, so that we can readily understand everything that has been done up to the day of our birth, but it's the day after that that the difficulty begins. Does an artist manage only to imprint his sensibility on an epoch or does he portray the sensibility itself? Like Pasteur I believe only in great men and I think we owe everything to them. A Pasteur owes nothing to the masses; his discoveries direct them like the works of a Victor Hugo or a Wagner. When our parents were painted by Manet, they said: "We aren't like that." They would like to have been painted as their parents were. We say: "Look how well Manet has portrayed our parents and their period." So Manet was right. He wasn't ahead of his time. He was the absolute present; and he evolved because he was himself, the moving sensibility of his time.

Rembrandt is all Holland of the seventeenth century, reflective, powerful, rich. Manet was therefore in the right, as our parents were not, who didn't appreciate him, or rather who didn't understand their epoch. But a modern artist teaches only a few initiates; first and foremost he is preparing the next generation, and then above all the ones to come after, in whom his spirit will sing and who will understand him without explanation. I well know, on the other hand, that not everyone can readily comprehend a Gothic statue, as since then, so many sensibilities have come to superimpose themselves, but is the retrospective effort not always necessary? Since the artist of the past formed us, while the modern artist forms future generations and in his own epoch has, especially in painting, only an insignificant influence (for example, how many people knew Cézanne when he died?), he who understands ancient art does not necessarily understand the modern. Having been formed by the ancient, we all understand it, but the number of those who appreciate the modern is small.

As for the modern artist, he doesn't have to understand the whole past, since his art contains it in its entirety. If, in order to create, he had to go back like an expert to all the sources of art, he would be gravely encumbered with this baggage, which would weigh down his talent and even crush it into nothingness. To sum up: I am afraid, when I gaze on this modern German painting, which must as a matter of course represent the present-day sensibility of Germany. Furious, violent heads, drunk with blood, murderous, demonic, and not in the ancient manner but in the modern: replete with the scientific, with poison gases. The ancients invented and depicted the world of sorcerers, but the world of hate is a modern invention, the invention of Germay laid bare on these canvases. The demons in the Gothic pictures are child's play beside these human, or rather these inhuman, heads of a turbulent humanity, avid for devastation, which line the walls, baring their black teeth, teeth of steel, eyes bordered by live coals, blood-tinged nostrils. They'll revel in cutting into living flesh, the Germans of tomorrow!

April 16 / Reflection

An American sculptor said to me: "What surprises me in Paris is the way drivers use the names of vegetables as abuse to hurl at one another."

May 28 / Henry Ford

He must be the richest man in the world today, ahead of Rockefeller. He was the first to think of making an automobile for popular consumption. You can find a second-hand Ford in Detroit for $25. Nothing can deflect him from his idea. Schwab, a steel magnate, said to him one day: "Your automobile is too light, it can't hold the road." Ford replied: "If you don't buy one this heavy immediately, in two months it will be too late, as my new machines will weigh five pounds less." These days Ford turns out 7,900 cars a day in his factories, and 500 tractors for agriculture. Mr. and Mrs. Edgar Whitcombe, who are friends of mine, invited him to meet me this evening at the Book Cadillac Hotel, where I am staying. I was what they call here the guest of honor. The Georges and Ralph Booth and some twenty other people were present at dinner. The reception took place in my suite. I ordered the dinner, which was of the finest. There isn't a better chef in Paris than the one in this hotel. Ford is in his sixties and, like nearly all the great captains of industry, has retained the simplicity of his early days of struggle. He has nothing intellectual about him—quite the contrary— and yet he has the head of a poet, of an English writer. He takes gleeful madcap pleasure in announcing that square green peas are about to be manufactured. He said in court one day that history is bunk. This added to his fame. He said this evening that he prefers the photograph of a picture to the picture itself. However, the man wants to better himself and believes he can succeed by his efforts to revive old dances; he buys the rarest ancient instruments for his own orchestra. Is he trying to obtain forgiveness for his comment on history by buying up historic inns throughout the country, to save them from demolition? He's also organizing a museum of arts and crafts.

Ford is terribly thin, and so is his head, which looks like an anemic egg. He doesn't lack distinction. He has a great admiration for France, and especially for French engineers. "It's with French skill," he said, "that the Ford was constructed." He recounted how one day he and his engineers found themselves faced with an old French car which didn't look solid, but when they dismantled it they were astonished at its resistance as they tried vainly to smash the steel to learn its composition. Ford enjoys repeating remarks that are going around about the Ford, such as: "Why pass a Ford when there's always one in front on the road?" Apart from his facile banter, he comes out from time to time with a trenchant phrase that throws light on his genius. This evening someone said to him, I can't recall in what context, "You'll remember," and he replied: "My life has been one long remembering."

His wife is small, so very small, and most unassuming: she was the companion of the time when he was poor. She lacks distinction, but one senses in her the virtues of a wife and mother. She has, moreover, produced a son, Edsel, whose qualities are vaunted by everyone. America is becoming less used to seeing the sons of rich men show the endurance of their fathers. Until recent years this country has had such a struggle that it is now beginning to demand pleasures, so the children tend to be a letdown.

We are going to see Ford next Thursday; he's giving a ball for us.

May 29 / Nungesser, the ace

He brought down five hundred "Boches," he says. This morning he arrived in Detroit, where the mayor welcomed him.

June 3 / Nungesser

I invited eighteen people to a party in his honor; we had dinner in my reception rooms and afterwards we went to the cinema to see his film, which would shock France. He plays the role of Nungesser the Hero! At one point he lays flowers on the tomb of the Unknown Soldier.

June 4 / Nungesser and Ford

Today the aviator took me into his confidence. He was an engineer in arts and crafts, was already quite taken with aviation in 1909, was looking for an airplane, became a pilot, it must have been in 1912, and the funny thing is that at the beginning of the war he was in the cavalry. He told me he had lost three fortunes in aviation; that's why today he is starting out again on a left foot; if it must be through the cinema, it must, but he has to recover his finances, and then he will devote the money to aviation.

At eight in the evening we went to Ford's to see the old dances. Ford lives at Dearborn in a house that is considered magnificent here but which is really only a vast country house. All the walls are dark. He has a very pretty Corot, and a Jacques and a Maris which aren't worth a great deal; moreover, he admits to me that he understands nothing about all this, that he's not interested. I've mentioned that there is considerable talk in the city about his old dances and his old instruments. One of these is a most up-to-date Viennese xylophone; the only thing that is old are its strings. There are five rather poor musicians. Thus has a legend sprung up. Ford is not accepted in Detroit: the good families live on the other side of the city in an area called Grosse Pointe. Ford has said to Mrs. Ralph Booth: "Come with ten or twelve friends." She tried to bring some people from Grosse Pointe but had a hard time doing it.

I've never seen anything as comical, as laughable, as ridiculous, as this evening. If the man were not so oblivious to it all, I should say he was impudent. To begin with, the ball, if it can be called that, took place in an enormous garage, in an exhibition hall for thousands of cars, a building he calls his "business office." If he wants to invite the wife of his third engineer or the daughter of his second accountant, with a pack of commercial travelers, that's his business; if a Mrs. Booth goes there, that's her affair; but he should not ask her to bring her friends, people from the best society, into this squalid place. We left at midnight without having been given anything to eat. Nothing at all. Not a sandwich, not a piece of bread from the richest man in the world. You might think he would have orangeade distributed; no, it was water, and not even ice water, just ordinary water as in factories or big offices here, in enormous bottles of the siphon kind. And what did he give us to drink from, the super-wealthy Ford? Paper cups.

Ford's secretary telephoned us all to say we could wear white trousers or gray suits. Even that was too good for this ball. And what about the old dances, the revivals? Did we see men and women dancers in costume? We did not. Ford roped us in, chained us to it. We were the ballet, we the victims. He had us stand in a circle, there was no backing out, no chance of sitting down quietly and watching. He called to his assistant instructors, who separated us roughly from our friends with an order to "take" the sixth dancer, or some other, always the one designated. Sixty persons in a ring, all holding hands, and the instructor cried: "All together now, left foot forward!" Just as Ford turns out his cars in series, so in series he turns out dancers who must all pass beneath his Caudine Forks. Suddenly a voice shouted: "Five minutes' rest!" And then: "Everyone to their feet." You'd have to be either poor or abject to come here again. The thoughtlessness of this couple is without equal in the world. They watch how each guest does his steps. At one point when I got confused, Ford put his arm around me and counted 1, 2, 3, chanting tatata, tatata. A little later a woman picked me out to teach me some other step she is expert at, then she passed me back to an instructor.

Ah, you'd better not dare go out for a breath of air. They wouldn't look on you with greater displeasure if you committed rape before their eyes. It's difficult to get back into the hall without being seen. It's deadly, people were yawning at the end of an hour, the constraint is so wearing, and the lesson lasted four hours. We left at last and with what pleasure (the only pleasure of the evening). The richest man in the world and his wife! May they rest in peace and may they let others do the same! But on the pretext that I love singing, when they come to Paris I shall invite them to my house and after dinner I'll organize a chorus of my guests and make the richest man in the world sing scales and arpeggios; he won't see the joke but will open wide his mouth like a fool.

June 5 / Nungesser tells me

"During the war I refused to exploit my name; I was discharged number one, with thirty citations. Spade offered me a million to give my name to an airplane; I refused and went to the ministry, told them about it, and asked to join up again, and got fifteen decorations; but since the end of the war I've fallen on very hard times."

June 19 / Nungesser is nearly killed

The announcement of this accident has affected me profoundly. In the West, at Grand Rapids, in an aviation meet he took off and one of his wheels came away; other aviators went up at once with a single wheel to make him realize what had happened and get him to come down on the water; he understood but wanted to land on the airfield and, acrobat that he is, came down rolling at an angle on one wheel; in stopping, however, the plane overturned, and he suffered a broken arm— which didn't prevent him from going to the theater that evening.

June 27 / On the "Homeric"
The transatlantic liner left New York during the night, at 1 A.M.

July 4
I've reached Cherbourg after an uninteresting crossing.

July 5
Armand has told me that the Michel Lévy sale brought 7 million francs, when Wildenstein made a private offer of 9 million. Watteau's famous *Ensign* brought 450,000 francs. I have already spoken of it. When Michel Lévy started a public argument to prove that he and not the Kaiser owned the original, our government, afraid of irritating the German emperor, instructed the French Society of Art History to quash it.

July 6 / At 57
Wildenstein showed me a superb Roger Van der Weyden that he wants to sell for $250,000 to $300,000.[1]

July 28 / Vézelay
It is the pink church of Christendom.

August 4 / Maurice de Rothschild arrives at the hotel in Biarritz
He waylaid me, though I never even looked at him, and started talking to me about my affairs. When I told him I had considerably enlarged my clientele this year in New York, he said with interest:
"Oh, then, you must bring me your Americans, you must put them in touch. I have my Renaissance jewels, I have a Goya, a bullfight, I have lots of things they may like, primitives too. What do they want? I am ready to buy whatever can be sold to them. I have Persian armor, an Assyrian high-relief, the two pieces bought from Demotte. Tell me, who would buy that sort of thing?"

August 14 / Encounter with Helleu on the avenue du Bois
He is very embittered and I exasperated him by saying that Sargent is a bad painter, quite inferior to Bouguereau, Benjamin Constant,

[1] He sold it to John D. Rockefeller, Jr. (Note appended April 1927.)

and Meissonier, who are themselves second-rate. But, on the other hand, he is right that the last Renoir sale, which produced 12 million, was a scandal. He called the expert a brigand, said that he should be thrown in jail, that he's got the face of a convict. Helleu railed against all the modern-art dealers. He called Vollard a blackguard and said his apartment was frightful. According to him, the modern art shown by the Bernheims and the Rosenbergs is strictly for laughs! He went a few days ago to visit Claude Monet, who said to him: "The Bernheims brought along to me the biggest brute you ever saw: Vlaminck, a painter." Helleu added: "Modern painting is brutes' painting."

Journal of Marie Bashkirtseff

Every man who reads it is bound to imagine he would have loved this woman. Her secret notebooks have just been published. We learn that her journal was an abridged version and now the ardent young girl is revealed to us, but we shall understand her only when her journal is put together again in its entirety; for her notebooks, which speak only of her loves and her rebellions, give as false an idea of her as her first tame journal. Floury tells me that he knew her, or rather saw her several times in the bookshop where he was employed, that she was beautiful, that she was made for a throne and that, despite her eternal despair at not being understood, she was already beginning to be quite well known; and she was only twenty-three.

September 4 / A letter from Proust

I found it in my boxes of business papers; it isn't dated but it reached me September 24, 1920 or thereabouts. (I had once more lost track of Proust, but he had been awarded the *Légion d'honneur*, and I had had a little cross of diamonds and rubies made at Cartier's.)

Here is the letter:

> 44 *rue Hamelin*
> [*confidential address*]

Dear Friend,

I must seem ungrateful, and I'm exactly the reverse. Here is what happened. I had a temperature of 40 degrees, following a chill, when your letter reached me. Thus I could answer neither your letter nor any letter.

The day before yesterday (I am telling you all this very badly, but I have had another small relapse) the firm of Cartier asked for my new address, having a delivery to make to me. The thought that it might be a remembrance from you could not have been further from my mind, or I believe I should have rushed there myself. Nonetheless, since, hoping if not to find peace at least to finish my books, I haven't been giving my address since the fatal day when, my landlord having sold the house in which I lived to a bank, I packed up in terror of the noise (it took a year's work to convert the house into a bank), I sent my chambermaid's sister for the object, afraid that if I had it deposited at the Ritz, where I take my meals when I can eat at all (I generally lead the life of the mayor of Cork), it might be mislaid. Cartier declared after an hour and a half's search that there must have been a mistake, that there was nothing for me. So I sent again this morning (Friday) and at 9 this evening, when I had just got up, the delivery comes of the ravishing jewel which moves me more than I would know how to tell you. Immediately a mad whirl began in my head to think what I could send you as a token of friendship. Alas! on leaving the boulevard Haussmann (once again thanks to Guiches, whom you saw I believe at Cabourg and without whom I'd have found nothing) I decided that I couldn't take along what I had into the only "furnished" flat vacant in Paris (a strange phenomenon), and I sold whole collections of marvels for a song. I've some pictures still left in storage at antique dealers', but although they are not without merit they are too mediocre for me to dare to make you a gift of one. I recall de Montesquiou saying to Mme Jules Porgès, who wasn't exactly thrilled by it: "But these are Ferdinand Bols you're showing us as Rembrandts." Mine, I'm afraid, would be at best pupils of Ferdinand Bol. Dear friend, you can't imagine the hell my life has become, because of my health and, more, because of bad habits of hygiene. Thus it has become very trying for me to see anyone. But nonetheless I would so much like to see you again! Do you go to bed late? Can I, one day when I feel well (relatively), have you telephoned to ask you to come to dinner at 9 at the Ritz or go to see you at midnight? I would wish that in these lines—by me who reply to no one—you might sense my gratitude and my affection. I treasure the memory of your merriment, of the violet overcoat that made you laugh at Cabourg (what a happy time); I cannot wear it, because the moths, those experts on wool, have judged the outer part excellent, and have taken it over. But the ludicrous sateen still leads me sometimes to "Remembrance of things past." Where will I hide your ravishing cross? I cannot display it. I don't go to official receptions. I shall look at it sometimes in secret, in recollection of the sentiments whose most affectionate expression I implore you to find in these lines.

Marcel Proust

October 17 / At Maurice's

I was shown into the smoking room, where I waited for several minutes. Wildenstein has sold him quite a lot. I noticed a fine portrait by Aved, *Woman at Her Dressing Table,* the painter's best picture, but this artist is merely a good craftsman. He's a plodder, the kind of man who is industrious because he cannot rise to any heights. Below this picture there's a poor sketch in the manner of Romney, but not by him, the painting is heavy, thick, and muddy. To right and left, two beautiful sepias by Guardi. On the panel opposite the window, two Prud'hons, the portrait of Viardot and that of his wife and daughter. Prud'hon is truly great only when he gives rein to his sensibility; he is the painter of Bacchantes in their last two minutes before losing their chastity. Farther down there are two Guardis, Venetian fetes, which once belonged to Edouard Kann, two tiny Chardins, a monkey and a seated housewife; a circular Lawrence, two youthful heads. To right and left of the chimney, pictures of slight importance: a man, an oval by Greuze, a Chardin still life, a small Lépicié.

October 19 / Michel Lévy's "Ensign" by Watteau

It was pushed into the sale by the family and bought back for 400,000 francs. I've seen it just now. It is genuine and wonderful. I have already spoken of it, and I didn't believe in it. I've already described how before the war the French government had been so afraid of antagonizing the emperor of all the Germanies, who owned the other *Ensign,* that it had indirectly ordered the French Society of Art History to undermine its repute. This assignment was given to the aforesaid Alfassa. Michel Lévy's picture is a marvelous Watteau, and certainly the true *Ensign,* for its treatment is bold, matching its intention; whereas Wilhelm's picture is made for a drawing room. Perhaps I shall buy it one day, to keep for myself.

November 6 / A masterpiece by Prud'hon

I bought it for 40,000 francs from Edouard Jonas, who didn't realize what a marvel he possessed.

November 11 / Maurice de Rothschild telephones me

It is Armistice Day, but there is no daylight for the dim-witted. He wanted to know if Rockefeller, Jr., would be prepared to buy his crockery.

November 14 / Some prices in America

I was looking over some accounts this evening. I see that my father founded his American branch in 1902. He died there in 1907. His biggest sale of the 1902-3 season was to the Metropolitan Museum of New York, a marvelous Nattier and a Largillière for $70,000. Then he sold a marvelous Watteau to Edward Berwind, *The Comedians*, its figures perhaps one-fourth life size, together with a Boucher, for $50,000. Today the Watteau alone is worth more than $200,000. I took an option on two Falconets and a Clodion from P. A. B. Widener for $15,000. The sales in New York, even for that first year, amounted to $162,279. It was a good beginning. But the following season the total rose to $237,115. This included $100,000 and $76,780, respectively, for the famous Romney *Lady Hamilton with Her Dog under Her Arm* and the Lawrence *Lady Peel*, today in the Henry C. Frick Collection. Jules Bache bought the four Bouchardon marbles, *The Four Seasons*, bas-reliefs of the fountain of Grenelle, for $20,000. We made fresh progress in 1905, and reached a total of $571,000.

The firm was really launched, and with extraordinary rapidity in a difficult country hostile to a new arrival. My father had remarkable charm, and it's thanks to that that he overcame the initial difficulties. In the history of the introduction of old art into America, that year was rich in consequences, for we saw my father persuade J. B. Altman to buy old pictures for the first time, which started that famous collection that is unsurpassed in quality. It was from the day Altman bought such beautiful pictures that collectors like Widener and Frick became harder to please as to the quality of their purchases. Altman's example engendered that host of Jewish amateurs who were and still are among the greatest collectors of this country. For a long time Altman had collected the finest Chinese porcelain; he had also bought Barbizons, and pictures of the nineteenth-century Dutch school, such as Mauve, but he hadn't gone in for old painting. That year my father sold not at all badly to the Duveens. Henry Duveen sold Altman china, and my father, to avoid arousing Henry's hostility, fostered his interest in sales, and I even believe he gave him shares once or twice in the purchase of pictures. When the Duveens realized the money there was to be made in old paintings, they became interested; in 1907, as a new departure, and spreading themselves enormously, they bought the Kann Collection with us. No one has been as successful as they in importing masterpieces and enhancing the American artistic patrimony—none of which would have taken place without the arrival in the United States of my father, so modest and so simple, who achieved tremendous results, and met death in the country to which he had rendered this incalculable service; he died there very suddenly on January 7, 1907, of diphtheria. This is a statement of fact and not the imagination of a son who adored his father. He and the Duveens were the pioneers of great art in the American home, and they deserve a place beside the men who made roads, railways, cleared the forests, built churches and schools.

NOTEBOOK 14

November 15, 1925–
March 24, 1927

November 15 / Some American prices

I neglected yesterday to give the main sales of 1905. A very fine Romney, *Mrs. H. C. Cottow*, to David H. King for $25,000. And on January 23 a Rembrandt *Portrait of a Man* to Altman for $120,000.

One of the finest Greuzes, *Madame Mercier*, went to Sir William Van Horne in Montreal for $30,000. I see that J. P. Morgan gave $49,000 for a purchase made in Paris the previous season, but I don't know what it was. The Duveens bought a Vassé bust, a Falconet, a Mabuse, a Clouet, a Pigalle group for about $55,000. And then there was Altman, who bought the Comtesse de Pourtales's famous Hals for $32,000.

A fine Solario, the portrait of Cesare Borgia, went to Colonel Payne for $22,000. My father initiated a major client: John W. Simpson, a lawyer. He sold him *Child Blowing Soap Bubbles* by Chardin for $22,000, and a still life for $2,800.

The year 1906 brought in something like $700,000 in sales. My beloved father died on January 7, 1907, and on December 8 he had sold two pictures to Altman, a Hals and a Turner, probably for $200,000. (Altman returned the Turner in 1908.) On December 8 he made out a bill to

John W. Simpson for $141,000 and on December 29 for $82,250 for the two famous circular paintings by Fragonard, *Mademoiselle Guimard* and *Mademoiselle Colombe*.[1]

On the first invoice I see a small Boucher, *The Good Mother*, from the Montesquiou Collection for $9,320. A Lancret, *The Gallant's Awakening*, for $7,360, from Mme de Polès's Collection. A portrait by Hoppner shown at the Exhibition of One Hundred Masterpieces in Paris, *The Princess*, from the Anderner Collection in Edinburgh, for $48,340, and Gainsborough's *Dorothea, Lady Eden*, from the Goldsmith Collection in London, for $76,000.[2] In February my father had also sold him a *Cupid and Folly* by Fragonard for $18,420. And in March the two Paters which were exhibited at the Hundred Masterpieces, for $45,000. At the beginning of that year, Altman had bought Rembrandt's *Woman* from the Anderson Collection for $124,185. To Colonel Payne, through the intermediary of Stanford White, the architect subsequently killed by Thaw, my father sold one of the most beautiful Constables in the world, *Salisbury Cathedral*, for $20,000. W. K. Vanderbilt, Jr., bought a marvelous fifteenth-century French statue. And P. A. B. Widener, some small pictures. At the beginning of 1907 we bought with Duveen Brothers the famous Rudolph Kann Collection for 17 million francs. We sold it through that year and 1908, but the prices don't figure in these books which I have before me. The Altmans, Wideners, Huntingtons, Morgans bought to the tune of millions and millions of francs. It must have sold, all told, for more than 40,000,000. During those two years I find only two large and beautiful Bouchers which were sold to Berwind for $45,000, and for $30,000 a Gothic statue to Mrs. Blair, a *St. Catherine*, which is now in the New York museum in the J. P. Morgan Collection. Three-quarters of the Kann Collection was liquidated in two years, but the sale of small pictures and art objects was prolonged and difficult. During this time the brother, Maurice Kann, died, and we set about buying his collection too, which was smaller in number but superior in quality. This time we preferred to buy the fine canvases at higher prices and leave the rest, which would prove so difficult to liquidate. The Du-

[1] Collection of Baroness Nathaniel de Rothschild, Paris, and P. Walter, London.
[2] This picture was sold for 428,000,000 old francs at the Erickson Sale in November 1961. (Editor's note.)

veens made a proposition to me and my partner, that we hand the busi
ness over to them, allowing them to buy us out. They were such cumber
some and monopolistic associates that we accepted. The two Kann
brothers had made their fortune at the Cape. Rudolph had twelve Rem
brandts, four Hals, perhaps the most beautiful of Ruysdaels, and one of
the loveliest Hobbemas.

November 18 / Proust anniversary mass

There were scarcely seventy people there—mainly old men. In
other years one saw some elegant young women, but these have vanished.

Maurice de Rothschild

He asked me to come and see the Renaissance jewels, and the
Greek ones that he'd like to sell to Rockefeller, Jr. He told me how once
a marvelous antique without arms or head was shown to Joe, who cried:
"Arms and heads for Duveen Brothers."

November 19 / American prices (cont.)

The Rudolph Kann Collection contained six Van Dycks, five Rubens, four Cuyps and four Hobbemas, a Vermeer of Delft, Steens, Ter-
borchs. Of the Flemings: Dierick Bouts, Gérard David, Isenbrandt,
Quentin Metsys, three Memlings, three Roger Van der Weydens. Of
the Italian school: there was a Benozzo Gozzoli, an Andrea del Cas-
tagno, a Ghirlandajo, eight frescoes by Luini, some Guardis, some Tie-
polos. Of the Spanish school there was a Velázquez, a Greco, a Goya.
The great eighteenth-century masters were represented by Watteau,
Lancret, Greuze, Nattier, and Fragonard's *The Swing*. To return to my
business in New York, the year 1909 shows an increase of about $450,-
ooo. I sold two manuscripts to J. P. Morgan for more than £8,ooo. To
William Salomon a Lancret for $10,500, a Fragonard for $14,500, two
Paters for $15,ooo. To Blair, two Boucher tapestries for $15,ooo. To John
Simpson, a Fragonard for $14,ooo and a Watteau at $30,ooo. To Mrs.
Potter Palmer, a Veronese and a Falconet for $58,ooo. A Holbein to Alt-
man for $55,ooo, a Fra Angelico for $71,500, and a Sansovino for $70,-
ooo. The Otto Kahns bought a wonderful Gérard David from me for
$10,ooo.

The year 1910 was slightly less good. Altman bought a terra cotta by Clodion for $50,000 and a terra cotta by Pigalle for $55,000. Also a Velázquez, *The Pilgrims of Emmaus*. When I showed this picture to Altman and he asked me the price, I said: "I shall give it to you tomorrow, but note that there are three figures on this canvas, and a head by Velázquez is alone worth $100,000." I left and Altman said to his secretary: "I understand what Gimpel was getting at; he's going to ask me for $300,000 and I like this picture so much that I will give it to him." The following day I asked him for $150,000 and he accepted. After Altman's death his secretary reminded me of this incident. That year I sold a superb marble by Rossellino to Thomas F. Ryan for $37,500.

In 1911 I came up with only one sale to Altman: a bust by Germain Pilon for $55,000. A marvelous Goya, a very beautiful actress, to George Baker, together with a small Cuyp, for $36,000. A Goya, a bullfight, which is now in the Metropolitan Museum of New York, to Leonard Thomas for $24,000. To Schiff, a sixteenth-century jewel for $41,000. A small Fragonard and a small Chardin, *Fanchon the Hurdy-Gurdy Woman* and *The Blind Man*, for $23,000 to John W. Simpson. Quite a handsome take in small sales that year to Warburg, Huntington, Dreicer, Rogers, Bacon, Clarence Mackay, P. Lydig, etc. A Ruysdael for $24,000.

The year 1912 is very interesting; unfortunately my accounts stop here, in fact, before the end of the year. Sales must have risen to nearly $900,000. Altman paid me $220,000 for a Holbein which I had bought for £20,000 or £22,000 in England. It was, I believe, my last sale to Altman, who was to die in 1913. Mrs. Charles B. Alexander bought a Guardi nearly six feet long from me for $55,000. In March S. R. Bertron bought a Nattier for $54,000 and in the summer a Boucher portrait for $45,000, a Pater for $45,000, a Largillière for some $15,000, Fragonard's *The Good Mother*, $85,000, a Lancret, a Perronneau pastel, a La Tour, and two Greuze pastels. I sold a Velázquez *Portrait of the Queen* to Duveen Brothers for $75,000; it is now with Baron Maurice de Rothschild, to whom they sold it. I had bought it in Paris at an old German painter's who told me he had acquired it, perhaps forty or fifty years before, at a liquidation sale by the Berlin Museum. How much did I pay him for it? I believe some 50,000 francs, which was what he asked. It was not authenticated, and at that time there was only one man in the world who knew Velázquez: that was Beruete. Even after his death, no one has replaced him, and my canvas was worth just barely 10,000 francs if it was not by the master. I left for Madrid, and stopped off at the Ritz Hotel. I took a drawing room, set up my picture in front of the window, and Beruete came to see it. I recall the scene, the room was immense, and Beruete, who was so slow to move, so cautious and circumspect, cried from afar: "There's a Velázquez!" He hurried up to it in delight with a celerity that amazed even himself; he looked at it for a long time in silence, and then said to me: "This picture is so beautiful that in it I find all the qualities that generally are scattered among the different portraits of the Queen, and I am tempted to believe that this canvas was a study he used in finishing the great portraits—for which the Queen did not like to sit, or only rarely, as she didn't care for Velázquez."

"Give me an authentication," I asked Beruete. "I'm leaving in a few days for America."

"Well," said he, "write to me from America."

"No, that'll take too long. I want to show it at once to a client."

"Then write to me from Paris."

"Monsieur Beruete, here are pen and paper, write me the authentication."

"No, I'll write it for you, but I want to reflect, not to go so fast, but to do a real study of it; the picture is worth the trouble."

He went on refusing, but still I insisted and literally put the pen into his hand. I left with the authentication in my pocket.

I wished to sell the picture to Altman, who, like all Americans, bought only on authentication; I left Madrid next day, arrived in Paris on Friday, or I think rather it was Saturday. Opening the *Herald* on Sunday, I read that Beruete was dead.

To return to Bertron, he was a very distinguished man who had made his fortune very quickly, had bought a house on Fifth Avenue and wanted one very fine example of each eighteenth-century French master. That year I sold him a superb tapestry done from subjects by Watteau, for about fifty thousand dollars. Except for some furniture, a beautiful Regency wainscoting and two Hubert Roberts from the Roussel sale, he bought only from me. Shortly after, he lost a great deal of money, his own and others'. He sold his house to Whimpfeimer, with the furnishings, wainscoting, the Largillière and the Roberts. I subsequently resold Watteau's *The Castanet Player*, which I had sold to Bertron for some $45,000. I sold Dreicer a picture of the school of Schongauer for $22,000.

The following years saw some fine sales. If I continue to look over the books and papers as I am doing just now, perhaps I may be able to reconstitute them. The archives of the important dealers hold precious documents on the minor history of art. I sold James Speyer a Nattier and a suite of furniture for $69,000, and another Nattier to the C. Denfields for $20,000.

November 20 / With Maurice

We have drawn up an estimate of Renaissance jewels and objects, and arrived at $2 million for thirty-one pieces. The whole of a collection like his is worth perhaps 100 million prewar gold francs, perhaps more.

He had invited Bokanowski to lunch and said to me: "I have some instructions to give him for this afternoon's speech."

Laws to do with finance are being voted. The extremists want to fleece the rich. The wealthy are defending themselves. One works on both sides of the barricade.

November 21 / At Maurice's

I told him that the best way of selling to Rockefeller was to invite to his home Rockefeller's architect Bosworth, who was delighted to view the collection. Maurice received him amiably but after two minutes bolted like a rabbit, having learned that Rockefeller, who was expected here in two weeks, won't be stopping in Paris and will be back only in a year's time.

Former prices

The man who was perhaps most instrumental in building our fortune was Ernest Crosnier, whose entire collection my father made and whose sale took place in 1905. Not all the pictures were in his sale, as he made exchanges. His wife didn't like his collecting, so he left all his pictures with us, and my parents kept them in their bedroom. At that time our shop communicated with our apartment, two rooms of which were given over to business, and Crosnier came a good four times a week in the afternoon to contemplate his pictures, a joy which was denied him at home.

On copies of invoices, here is what I find: January 27, 1899, Watteau, *The Italian Concert*, 120,000 francs. March 14, 1900, sketch by Gainsborough of his celebrated picture *The Garden Party*, 8,000 francs. May 19, two signed pastels by La Tour, of the Count and the Countess of Coventry, from Mrs. Gilbert Coventry of Sherridge Lodge, 130,000 francs. May 31, a signed and dated portrait of a woman by Nattier representing *Madame Challes*, 40,000 francs. January 29, 1901, a picture of a woman portraying *Emily, Duchess of Leinster* (W. Wilkins and Fred. Clark Collection of Great Cumberland Place) by Romney, 50,000 francs. Two pictures by Pater, *Rustic Pleasures* and *The Bath*, which came from the Bernstein Collection and figured in the 1892 Exhibition of the Hundred Masterpieces in Paris, for 200,000 francs. These pictures he didn't keep, for my father sold them to John W. Simpson of New York. On that same day, March 22, 1901, for 191,000 francs, Crosnier bought *The Betrothed Village Girl* by Antoine Watteau, a picture from the H. F. Broadwood and Humphrey Ward collections in London, which had been shown at the Royal Academy's Burlington Exhibition of 1892 (mentioned in Goncourt's book on Watteau). Crosnier wasn't to keep this picture; we had it for a very long time. It is now in Cleveland in the collection of Mr. Severance's sister. On July 4, 1901, he bought a picture which he wasn't to keep either and which is today, I believe, in the Cognacq Collection: a Hoppner, *Miss Devisme*, from the A. Greene Collection, Surbiton, for 135,000 francs. Crosnier was a great speculator. And when he lost he didn't ask you to take back the canvases, but to resell them on his behalf. November 1: a decorative picture by Watteau entitled *Repose, or the Sleeping Lovers*, 140,000 francs.

January 18, 1902, a picture by Watteau entitled *Rustic Pleasures*, from the Stirberg Collection and formerly the property of Louis-Philippe, 190,000 francs. April 29, a portrait by Reynolds for 40,000 francs. May 29, 1902, a picture entitled *Nature*, portraying Emma Hart, later entitled *Lady Hamilton*, by Romney. This picture came from Mr. Fawkes; it had been in the Charles Wertheimer Collection in London and figured in 1886 in the Royal Exhibition of London as well as in the Romney Exhibition in the Grafton Gallery; 500,000 francs. My father resold this picture on Crosnier's behalf to Henry C. Frick of New York with the Knoedlers as intermediaries. March 26, 1903, La Tour's pastel of *Schmidt the Engraver* for 55,000 francs. This marvelous pastel was bought by Veil-Picard, who still has it. June 5, 1903, my father sold him a Gainsborough, *Portrait of John Campbell of Stonefield,* from the Lee Wright Collection for 180,000, and a signed and dated pastel by Perronneau, from the Boisville Collection at Abbeville. On that day my father took back Watteau's *Betrothed Village Girl.* June 12, La Tour self portrait, 75,000 francs. August 26, 1904, two Fragonard panels from the Duke de Fezensac's Collection, 650,000 francs, and the repurchase of Romney's *Lady Hamilton.* The two Fragonards, which are marvelous, are with Edouard Kann.

How did Crosnier begin? It's a very curious story. At 9, rue La Fayette there were three shops. At the corner a horrible antique shop, then ours, and then a dealer in modern furniture. One day Crosnier came into our shop, mistaking it for the one on the corner, and he was astonished to see so many beautiful things. That was in 1898. He started out in a small way. In another book I see that his first purchase was for 1,000 francs on November 8, a sketch by Carle Vanloo. Then a genre by Pater, *The Bull,* for 10,000 francs. In May 1899 he bought a sketch of *Lady Hamilton* by Romney for 39,000 francs. That same year, a pastel of a child by Russell, and Watteau's *The Theater.* Then two marvelous pictures, Fragonard's *Woman Reading,*[3] for 81,500 francs, and *The Woman Playing at Knucklebones,* for 33,000 francs, which I have sold since for more than 450,000 francs to Mrs. Barton Jacobs of Baltimore. In January 1900 he bought a fanciful Watteau, *The Italian Concert,* for 120,000 francs, but returned it shortly. My father afterwards sold this Watteau to John Berwind. One day he also bought the famous Lawrence *Lady Peel,* and must have returned it at once. I find no trace of it on the books. Only its resale for 300,000 francs to Knoedler for Frick, on the day he bought the Romney *Lady Hamilton* from us.

December 28 / My bindings

For a fortnight I've been in the grip of a new passion; I have been

[3] A canvas sold for 437,000,000 old francs at the Erickson sale in 1961. (Editor's note.)

spending all my evenings doing designs for book bindings. Some artist friends like them very much. I am doing some for my manuscripts and I shall display them. I'll be speaking of them again.

Recently I've again set about buying manuscripts, such as a part of Anatole France's *Monsieur Bergeret*, and *Là Bas* and *The Oblate* by Huysmans. *Ubu Roi* by Jarry. The notebooks of the Goncourts.

On Botticelli

I showed Armand, who had recommended that I buy it, the book on Botticelli by the Japanese Yukio Yashiro and he said to me: "It's a pity, though, that it contains inaccuracies."

Lord Lee's picture *The Trinity*, with Mary Magdalene and St. John the Baptist, is not by Botticelli, any more than the picture in the Louvre, *The Madonna and Child*. Berenson tells me that it's the copy of a lost original and I agree.

I said so to Armand. I added that I didn't believe in the authenticity of the *Madonna and Child* on a throne in the Chapel of the Vennella in Settignano. Nor does Armand believe in it. He informed me that the *Madonna with a Child and Six Saints* in the Florence Academy is a discovery of Berenson's. It's his opinion that the painter had some assistance with the Virgin and Child, that moreover Botticelli is one of the most difficult masters to know thoroughly; after Leonardo da Vinci he is Italy's greatest painter. He was ten times greater than Raphael but was too decorative to rise to the genius of Da Vinci. Berenson only recently acknowledged the *St. Sebastian* in the Berlin Museum, and only when he saw the enlargements of the photographs done for this book; Armand had the photographs taken for the Japanese. Armand showed me the portrait of the man—plate xxviii—this is the one he discovered three years ago, for a few thousand francs, at Trotti's in the Place Vendôme. It is not yet sold, and Armand himself said: "It's not a wonderful picture because it is the portrait of an aged man and Botticelli attained perfection only in painting youth." He is the painter of youth, the painter of spring, of the daisy. Florence understood only adolescence. His old men's faces with the wrinkles cut as with a knife are ridiculous. His landscapes are not of perspectives, but of flowers. Venice, on the other hand, understood autumn. Titian's men are painted at a ripe age.

Giorgione painted the melancholy of sunsets which the Venetians contemplate every evening on the Adriatic. It is said of these painters: "Color is all they contributed to art." But with color they brought repose, wisdom, quietude, tranquillity. They understood the strength of the man who has left his adolescence far behind him. Rembrandt is great in his old men. He paints the entire expanse of a lifetime.

January 9, 1926 / At Zarraga's, where I take young Tooth, the London dealer

Tooth wanted to meet French painters and organize exhibitions of their works in London. The painter showed us a superb nude, a sort of Venus with her arms raised, holding a bowl in her hands, and he informed us that it was commissioned by a husband who was very much in love with his wife's body and had him paint it. He changed the facial features so as not to cause a scandal.

April 3 / Some prices

Business in America has been good. I learn that this year Jules Bache bought a Fragonard, a woman pushing a cart, for $100,000; a large Hubert Robert for $65,000. The marvelous Rembrandt *Standard Bearer*, for $250,000; a full-length Van Dyck *Portrait of a Young Man* for $300,000, or a bit more; the Pater from the Carnarvon Collection for $160,000.

April 4 / The horse show

This is my new passion; I have one or two horses which my wife rides. She has taken part in three shows in a week and won three prizes. The less good horse, the one named Peter Pan, which I found in Ireland, is, I believe, going to become a crack.

April 6 / The horsewomen's prize

My wife won it today with Sherry Golden. It's the prize that we wanted to win. A big success.

Soutine

He's a star rising in the firmament of modern painting. Zborowsky, a dealer on the rue de Seine, introduced us. His canvases, which a year ago couldn't find a buyer, are sold these days in the ten-thousand bracket and are going up every day. He is small, sturdy, with a thick crop of hair whirling round his head. He has deep, round hooded eyes; they are of hard stone. Zborowsky told me he's a man in torment. He paints a great deal, but he will suddenly slash the canvas, tear at it, like one possessed.

In this gallery an exhibition is about to open of someone named Lasserre, an animal sculptor, a boy not yet twenty. In many sketches the Japanese influence, which he is, however, beginning to shed, is too strong. He has a great future before him. I bought eight sketches at 300 francs apiece. He is asking 18,000 francs for a marble cat.[4] But his felines are not cruel enough.

General strike in England

It's the greatest strike in history: perhaps two and a half million men are involved. It began at midnight on Monday. I left for London yesterday to attend the X sale, which took place today and at which I bought two ovals by Drouais, two children, at the current exchange rate for 2,100,000 francs. A Nattier, *The Duke de Penthièvre*, was sold for nearly the same price; I dropped out at 1,200,000 francs.

My friends in France thought me mad to go. "You won't get to London," they told me. "Think what dangers you're exposing yourself to!" I knew that their fear showed an ignorance of the English character, which really emerges only in time of action and trial; not in the confrontation of two politicians, but when their native land is endangered by the threat of revolution.

When one sees on the Dover docks those young people from Oxford, the tall, blond, blue-eyed, sophisticated descendants of Norsemen, smoking their pipes and carrying trunks on their backs, doing it simply and with spirit, unaffectedly, all of us would do well to envy this elite, who feel no hatred of, or disdain for, the people, but who take their place in a moment of disorder. Vigorous blood flows in the veins of the British, and centuries of greatness must surely still be in store for them.

[4] I subsequently had it bought for my brother-in-law Ernest Duveen.

May 15 / An old château. On Toulouse-Lautrec and Rodin

I went with Mori, the picture dealer, to the Château de Canon, near Mézidon, home of Count de Beaumont, to see two Drouais, two bad pictures for which he's asking £6,500, more than a million at the current exchange. We were taken for a walk in the park, which must certainly have been very beautiful but has now fallen into neglect. There used to be a theater in it. The Beaumonts have archives. A certain ancestress wrote to her husband in Paris telling him of the bathroom just completed in the park. "Oh! how I wish you were here; the bath has been installed and I don't know how it works, and I haven't been able to find anyone in the village who wants to try it." In a subsequent letter she speaks of one of their friends who finally had the courage to take a bath.

Mori told me about his acquaintance with the painter Toulouse-Lautrec, who lived in licensed brothels simply because he was so deformed and repulsive that only there did he find a refuge where women would not treat him harshly. He loved women and hated woman; when he painted them and drew a bitter crease at the corners of their lips, it was above all his own bitterness that he was expressing. He painted for Ohler, the manager of the Moulin Rouge music hall, a dance by La Goulue; it hung there for a long time. Arnold Seligmann owns it now and has refused 400,000 francs for it.

Toulouse-Lautrec used to draw in all the cafés, on scraps of paper which Mori carried off because they amused him, not at all because he considered them to be of artistic value. He told me that once, when one of his girl friends, who had spent the night with him, needed some squares of paper in the morning, he passed her a bundle of the artist's drawings. Mori, who knew Rodin very well, also talked to me about him and told me that he was extremely fond of women, and that even when he was senile he always had to have them round him to pet. He was particularly mad about a certain Javanese girl, whom his fingers never ceased caressing.

June 14 / Those worthy Americans

I repeated Forain's latest sayings to Mme Steiner, and she told me that one day she wanted to sell a Forain to an American. The subject was a woman undressing. The collector was horrified, crying: "Madame, how dare you offer me such a scene, how could I hang it in my house, a woman undressing in the afternoon?"

At Claude Monet's

I have bought two canvases from him for 200,000 francs. They are among Monet's masterpieces. They are not actually a pair, but both depict women in boats. What a book could be written on the subject of fine Sundays in nineteenth-century French painting! The impressionists are particularly great there, reaching the summit of their art when they paint our French Sundays, so typical of our people. There is candor in them and gaiety, color, a gracious ease, tenderness, and silences and clear intelligent faces; there are the couples who are faithful to each other, the first call to love, conscious desire but always tinged with romanticism, the eternal Lisette or Mimi Pinson, the little working girls, sunlit kisses, lunch on the grass, repose, work forgotten, unabashed relaxation.

I don't know which of my two pictures I prefer: they are large horizontals. In the first there are two women in pink; in the second, which is smaller, two women in blue. The women in pink are in a pink canoe passing fleet as a dart, close to shore, just under the low foliage that overhangs the water with a dark green shadow. In the shadow the two women are illuminated like torches by reflections glancing off other reflections. It is one of the most skillful effects ever achieved in the art of lighting. They pass so swiftly, these two women, and we are on the other bank. They pass like a dream, or like desire that cannot be satisfied. All of us, in adolescence, have been in the country on such a sunlit day, and without a companion in our arms; and always we saw her whom we lacked on the opposite bank, unattainable and lovely. And we imagined that we were her happiness; chaste Mussets singing the charms of Rolla —the river is so broad. The two pink pelicans in their pink boat speed on, graced with inordinately long pink oars; through the wake in the water trail our hearts, fast sinking into the depths, and melancholy enfolds us in its pernicious snares; the day is spoiled, nothing but an unavowed sob.

The other canvas is very different pictorially and in its emotion. The first is treated sketchily, especially the figures; the second is quite finished, for Monet seems to be seeking the ultimate limit of the science of a thousand reflections of light. The first is the more poetic in spirit because it's a little sad; the second is at once grave and more tranquil. A heavy boat of rustic wood with damp moss, thick and cool, caressing its flanks. The two women converse, dressed in their Sunday best, their rounded figures contained in corsets as was the fashion of our mothers. They are almost too elegant; there are fair, grave, serious, touching Frenchwomen.

Monet talked to me of his portrait by Renoir, sold the other day in the Decourcelle sale, but he said that it might possibly be that of Pissarro. "It's not," he added, "that we looked alike, but we were of exactly the same build. So much so that one day I went to the home of the tenor Faure, who was then exclusively our customer, and the servant said to me: 'It's useless to see Monsieur; he won't take anything from you, as he's just bought a canvas for a hundred francs from M. Monet, who's been here and gone.'"

Monet asked me for twenty-four hours to sign the canvases, but I was so afraid that he might change his mind and keep them that I made my escape with them hastily by automobile.

July 17 / With my wife, at Claude Monet's

My wife did not know him, and for a long time she was supposed to go to see him. He received her accompanied by his daughter-in-law, and they were both very pleasant. My wife fell in love with his *Water Lilies* and his *Poplars*; he sold me the two canvases for 150,000 francs; they are, comparatively, much more expensive than the boats, which some dealers have valued at 500,000 francs apiece, perhaps a million. Today he told me that the two women who served him as models were his daughter-in-law, who was there with us, and the daughter-in-law's sister, who has since died. The latter is at the back in the blue picture and is rowing in the pink picture. In Monet's studio there is still another canvas with these women in pink. It was the preliminary idea, done more sketchily, and the execution is not good. The pictures my wife has chosen are very beautiful. After these ten years during which we have come to Monet for many paintings, there is not really a great deal left, apart from two women, who are, I believe, his daughters-in-law, standing with parasols;[5] and a picture as beautiful as a Vermeer, a woman passing before a french window in a wintry landscape. My wife discovered the poplars in a pile of other paintings. He told us that these trees were at Limay, near Giverny, and that one day he saw them marked with red paint. "They're going to be auctioned off and felled," he told himself, "and it'll be the sawmill nearby that will buy them." He hurried round to the owner, to ask what price he was going to buy them for. "Go higher," he said to the timber merchant. "I'll pay the difference, but let me have the time to paint them."

Monet's daughter-in-law told me that the pictures of the boats date from about 1887 or 1888. Monet informed me that since my last visit he has destroyed perhaps sixty canvases, though his daughter-in-law says fewer. It is she who starts by making an incision in the canvas with a knife and detaching a piece of it, then they are burned in their entirety and Monet stays by the fire so that nothing may escape destruction. But although his daughter-in-law approves his gesture in principle, she has moments of reaction when she grows nervous and agitated; Monet notices and the work is postponed to the next day. Monet showed me some very beautiful flowers which he was going to destroy. He took advantage of my last purchase to take down all his canvases again, and we found him in his studio, where he was busy rearranging them. We talked of modern painting; he knows very little about it. Of what he has managed to see, he said: "I don't understand it, but I'm not saying that it's bad. For I remember those who didn't understand my works and who said 'It's bad.'" My wife asked him if he knew Manet and he replied: "Yes, he was a great friend, a great friend. I saw him two days before his death. He had phlebitis and it had been necessary to cut off his leg, but he hadn't been told. When I approached his bed, he said: 'Now watch out for my leg. They wanted to cut it off, but I said they mustn't and I've kept it. Watch out.' And he died without knowing that in fact it had been amputated. It was just when I was settling in at Giverny here. His brother sent me a telegram, I believe I received it the first Sunday I spent in this house."

As my wife and I were walking with his daughter-in-law, I said to

[5] Claude Monet's son gave them to the Louvre immediately after the death of his father.

her: "Then, Claude Monet can no longer paint because of his eyes, but does he take pleasure in walking in his garden?" "Why, no," she said, "his eyes are very good, or, rather, very good with glasses. He has spectacles for seeing close up as well as for distance, but it's energy he lacks. He no longer has the strength to paint, it drains him. He had a bout of tracheitis this winter which made him suffer frightfully for two months. It upset everything inside him, even his stomach, which used to be so strong. He wasn't eating any more; now he eats but no longer smokes, as right away it chokes him. He can no longer take alcohol. He has a lot of trouble seeing close up. Signing is worse for him than painting."

This woman's devotion to Monet is marvelous. She took me aside, anxious to know if I thought he looked better than a fortnight ago. She seemed to think he did; she must be right. She keeps track of him minute by minute. But on the other hand she doesn't seem to care very much about Monet's son.

He lives there, she said, at the other end of the house and doesn't work. She gave the impression of being fed up with him. He is very spoiled by his father. I had never seen him except here, at this luncheon. Without his daughter-in-law, Monet would live in a seclusion that would kill him; it is she who keeps him alive for us; posterity must not forget it.

July 22 / On Claude Monet

I showed my picture *The Water Lilies* to Mlle Cladel, who says: "The Greeks might have done that."

August 4 / I leave on vacation

I am always mortally bored in the month of August. I believe it is because I choose fashionable beaches, where I go only because the hotels are good and doctors near at hand. This year I'm going to Menaggio, a secluded corner of Lake Como. Pierre and Jean went on Saturday with the governess; today we leave with Ernest the eldest and the two dogs Saïda and Yva. We are stopping at Geneva.

August 5 / Ernest's birthday and memories of childhood

He is thirteen. The day before yesterday I took from my library a guide to Switzerland, I opened it and saw it dates from a long time ago. I saw the words "Anchet, August 12; Geneva, August 24, 1892." Anchet is a village in the Jura where I believe my maternal grandfather was born. At all events, he retired there. He lived in a small house, a peasant's house. At that time I spent some time there with my mother; I was ten years old. My grandfather's name was Vuitton. My mother often told me how with his elder brother Louis Vuitton he had come to Paris as a young man and both had made and sold trunks there. The Franco-Prussian War of 1870 ruined my grandfather, as many people didn't pay him, but he settled his debts. He hadn't the energy or the heart to start again. I never saw as much of him as during those vacations of 1892, this grandfather who never came to Paris. My mother went to see him often; he spent his days with a dog, and both hunted. It took me a long time to realize that I was the grandson of peasants. I spent longer seeking out affinities on my father's side because of the importance given in his family to things of the mind. My paternal grandfather was headmaster of a school in Mulhouse. I considered that this grandfather was the repository of all knowledge and learning, I even thought of him as slightly superhuman. I always trembled lest he question me, although I was a rather good student. He too perhaps trembled at the thought of examining me, which he never did, so that I was able to live with him in perfect harmony. I used to recite a lot of poetry to him, since I was very good at it, having spent much of my imagination on verse, and he was enchanted with this.

My father, more interested in art than in literature, very quickly became a great expert on pictures. Circumstance would have it that for a long time I directed my gaze only toward my father's family, but subsequently I've not overlooked the fact that it's impossible to expunge the influence of a long line of peasants, and when I think of my mother, though she was utterly Parisian, I can well discern the sturdy forces that constituted her spirit. Her moral influence on me was enormous. She explained good and evil to me so clearly, simply, and in few words; not very strong on religion and without any special knowledge of philosophy, she knew wonderfully well that all life turned around forces from below and from above, and that it sufficed that I should be well instructed for my life to unroll on a straight line. To my last day, I shall give thanks to her for it.

My father had joined us in Anchet, and we went on a circular tour in Switzerland; I was almost eleven years old. Today, with my eldest son, who was thirteen yesterday, I am once again in Geneva, on the lake, and on the boat taking us to Lausanne. Ernest is playing with two well-brought-up little American girls, one from St. Louis, the other from California. One day he will do this same circular trip with his son.

August 6 / Ernest saves Yva

She was drowning in a sort of little waterfall in Milan, not far from the station. The current was very strong, the bank high and steep; with my stick I tried to catch the dog by the collar, but at each attempt, and despite my own efforts and the animal's to hold out and move toward me, she was swept farther away. I have the impression that it was quite deep. Everything was happening very fast, the animal being carried farther and farther by the swift water; but there was a little bridge, and Ernest, with marvelous presence of mind, slipped down into the water, and the animal was saved. Some twenty yards farther down there was a grating, and if the animal had drifted there, she would have been swept over it to perish in the sewers.

September 3 / On Renoir

Dimier, Jr., told me that there are many of the master's canvases in Dieppe, where he spent his vacations and where he had many friends, to whom he expressed his thanks with presents of paintings. He would even give some of them as tips to servants. Dimier knew a valet who quite recently sold a small canvas for 8,000 francs.

September 25 / Departure for New York on the "Mauretania"

A business trip.

October 1 / A crossing of little interest

The only artist on the boat is Sert, the Spanish painter, whom I prefer not to recognize. He displeases me. He has the air of having been sculpted out of a cosmetic stick.

February 3, 1927 / The journal

I've never gone so long without writing. To begin with, I'm so busy! But there has scarcely been enough material these days for twenty pages. I spent eight weeks in Detroit. In the museum I organized a marvelous exhibition of eighteenth-century French art, worthy of a treatise. I delivered a lecture in front of the pictures. At the French Institute of New York I gave two lectures: the first on Renoir and Claude Monet, a summary of what they have said to me; the second on Marcel Proust. Since then Claude Monet has died peacefully, without any of the illnesses of old age. His old friend Clemenceau came to close his eyes and wept. Durand-Ruel told me the other day that Claude Monet has destroyed canvases all his life. He assured me that there are still some in boxes that I haven't seen. I doubt it. How many people are already dead who have passed through this journal, which dates back scarcely eight years! Monet's family say for the moment that they don't want to sell. His canvases immediately went up in value. Three cities in the United States are organizing exhibitions of the master—Boston, Chicago, and New York. I don't believe two canvases can be found as beautiful as the two which belong to me of women in boats.

Durand-Ruel told me he bought many impressionist pictures in the United States and resold some in Paris. Moreover, since the 1830 school no longer sells well here, many canvases return to France. Today the Stillman auction was held. A Rembrandt *Titus*, which he had bought very cheaply from me, has been sold for 1,350,000 gold francs; it was bought by my brother-in-law Sir Joseph Duveen (who was made a baron last January by the king of England). But if it hadn't been promoted by another dealer, a friend of Stillman's, it would have brought in only 675,000 francs. Last month Joe sold $4 million's worth to Henry Huntington of Los Angeles, who is founding a museum, and $2 million's worth last October. Joe Duveen has bought the Lawrence *Pinky* at auction in London for more than 1,600,000 gold francs. He had run up an order of 2,500,000 francs. It was my brother-in-law Ernest who sold 1,-250,000 francs' worth to Lord Michelham.

At the Stillman sale a picture which is not by Nattier has been sold for 75,000 gold francs (375,000 paper francs). Recently, in going through the book on Botticelli by the Japanese Yukio, I realized that the picture *Portrait of an Aging Man*, which belongs to the Duveens, is not by Botticelli; one of these days I'll explain why, but in Paris when I have the photo in front of me. It's a marvelous book from the point of view of its reproductions. It proves that the day of small photographs is past. All the little books written on artists will be superseded by big ones. You can only study from big reproductions.

In Detroit, the museum is making considerable efforts to expand. In two or three years a wealthy collector will be found on every street corner. Unfortunately Dr. Valentiner has such bad taste, and he is the chief adviser! Museums in the United States inherit considerable sums. This year Kansas City received 75 million gold francs. Cleveland too will be rich when its two or three great collectors are dead. Recently Mrs. Barton Jacobs of Baltimore called me in and said: "I'm going to give my collection, my money, and my house to the city of Baltimore. I'm getting on in years. Will you agree to be its official counselor by provision of my will?" "Yes," I told her, "provided you give me full powers and specify that everything bought be of similar quality and taste to the things in the Wallace Collection." Mrs. Barton Jacobs had been collecting for years when the dealer from whom she bought committed suicide in 1908. Whereupon she called me in and learned that in the French school she had nothing but fakes—filling two enormous galleries. She was paralyzed by this for several years and began buying again only in 1914, on July 28. The war broke out several days later and she wired me from Cherbourg that she was giving up the lot she had chosen in my galleries. A great admirer of France, she spent her money during the war exclusively in relieving our sufferings. She began thinking of her gallery again only in 1919. And since then we have been replacing the poor canvases with very fine pictures. She has since acquired an admirable Greuze, a La Tour, a Chardin, two Hubert Roberts, a Nattier, etc. It will one day be America's Wallace Collection.[6]

It is not known what Ford, Jr., will be able to leave to the Detroit museum. At present the American government is bringing an action against Ford's former partners to claim tax from them, and it is disclosed that 500 gold francs lent to Ford when he started out have brought in 5,000,000. He has become the world's richest man in twenty years, and he emerges greatly enhanced from this suit. A man named Couzens, who

---

[6] Unfortunately her shares collapsed in 1929 and she did no more buying. As she no longer had the money to make a museum of her house, she bequeathed the incomplete, and not entirely purged, collection to the museum. (Note appended 1939.)

has since become a senator, had lent him 4,500 francs; today he has an income of 50,000 francs a day. Ford's business is going less well, however; the factory is producing fifteen hundred fewer cars a day. As he grows old, the big manufacturer persists stubbornly in not changing the horrible shape of his cars. If he sold his cars at cost, he would still make 150 million francs a year on spare parts. Because of this enormous automobile industry, money from the entire world pours into Detroit, and these people are becoming so rich that they don't know how to spend their money. A rich young girl's coming-out party may cost 120,000 francs. Many people who have only modest means spend it all in the hope of marrying their daughters well, and take three years to settle their accounts. There are some tragic instances of this. In this journal I have not dwelt on customs, and sometimes when I see such enormous changes come about in a few years, I regret not having noted them down; I am stunned by the speed with which so many things die out. I don't know, for example, what future generations will think of today's fashions, these women whose skirts end above the knee when they sit down and who have long since given up wearing undergarments. Last summer at Le Touquet a society photographer showed us snapshots he had taken of women seated or practicing sports, revealing all their most delectable secrets. Alcoholism in the United States, and particularly among the upper classes, is beyond anything one could imagine. At the Stillman sale this evening, among this wealthy and artistic crowd, the fumes of alcohol were suffocating. I was at a funeral today and in the car taking us to the cemetery one of the men took out pocket flasks of whiskey and offered them around. Prohibition brings in so much money to hundreds of thousands of men that this army of crime has become the most powerful defender of the law; they would be ruined if it were repealed. In Detroit I'm told about a leading bootlegger who buys pictures, and expensive ones. But for added assurance he lives on the other side of the lake, in Canada. The American who violates this law daily becomes inured to breaking others. Twenty years of this regime will lead the United States to disaster. Women are dying in great numbers, especially among the wealthy. I have lost two clients like this, Mrs. Dupont and Mrs. W. Coe. The other day a senator was able to say to his colleagues in public: "Only three among you respect the law. Instead of having drinkers arrested, you jump for joy at the sight of a cocktail."

In Detroit a ball to which all the well-off people are invited is given every evening in the month of December. They come away at four or five in the morning and don't arrive at their offices before noon. They leave them before five, so as to be able to sleep a little before dining and continuing their dance. The rich American no longer even organizes his life to work a little; he lives exclusively for pleasure. The gold seems to gush out of the ground like oil. Not long ago an amateur theater was built, costing more than $100,000, for five or six performances a year. Detroit is famous in the United States for its amateur groups.

The last word in science. You can telephone London by Hertzian waves. Our children won't find anything wonderful in it, our grandchildren least of all. But when the news was announced to us a month ago, a thrill of admiration shook the world. The other day Joe Duveen telephoned his office in Grafton Street, spoke to his brother and three other people, and heard them as clearly as if they were all in the same room. Twenty minutes cost him more than 2,000 francs. It was all about the purchase of a Holbein, a small portrait of a woman, which was in Poland.

Now let us speak of New York itself. The noise there is becoming frightful. Construction is on the increase daily and the riveting is deafening. Traffic is horrible. Some of the tall buildings are extremely interesting. Because of the narrowness of the streets and the lack of light, they have to be built in the shape of pyramids! And under pressure of necessity, a number of architects have achieved quite picturesque results. The tower has become very fashionable. To live on the fortieth floor is the last word in smartness. So people are literally living in the clouds. From below we often can't distinguish the tops of these towers. Only multimillionaires can afford these apartments, those anxious to keep healthy and those who aren't poets. They often cost more than one million (paper) francs, and the rooms are scarcely larger than small cabins. A tower of 110 or 120 stories is going to be built, which won't I believe be far from 1,200 feet high. As it will considerably surpass the Eiffel Tower, I hope that latter will be pulled down. I begin to think that New York will become the oldest city in the world, as such constructions must stand for all eternity. In Europe it is said that the life of a house doesn't on the average exceed 120 years. The New World will become the Old World. It's inevitable.

February 4 / Charlie Chaplin and Mlle Taillefer

I met him this evening at Mrs. Clara Thomas's. The motion picture was born yesterday, say twenty-five years back, and he's the only artist it has produced, but what a genius! He has an inner life like a fine work of art. I sometimes amuse myself by doing imitations, caricaturing the cinema. It is impossible to imitate Charlie Chaplin, for his face is all but immobile. I watched him this evening, and he keeps his eyes nearly closed, the lids always lowered, so that at times he has the look of a blind man. The most popular artist the world has seen seems very shy. He is simple and silent. I met Mlle Taillefer, who has just married an American, a caricaturist; she told me that Charlot is one of their great friends, that the other evening at dinner he described to them a film he is making, and he showed marvelous intelligence in his explanations. Just now Chaplin is having the most frightful troubles. He married a woman who was after his money and who, in divorcing him, is claiming an enormous sum. She is raking up such scandal that in some small towns Chaplin's films have been banned. It always was a puritanical country. The newspapers are on his side and his situation has improved in the last fortnight. But if he went to California, he could be arrested. I was introduced to him, but I didn't have a chance to speak to him. So I observed him, and sought in vain for the reasons for his immense success, for in his private life he ceases to be an actor. He is an Englishman, an English Jew apparently, though he isn't the type. He is quite small and very distinguished, built on a kind of miniature scale.

February 5 / Mlle Taillefer and Charlie Chaplin

My wife and I went to have tea with her. A film by Barton was shown in the studio, presenting Charlie Chaplin with Sacha Guitry and his wife Yvonne Printemps, in which she reveals herself to be a gifted motion-picture artist. She does a rather piquant caricature of it all. Germaine Taillefer told us that Sacha Guitry, normally so grandiloquent, turned very simple and was even a little overwhelmed in the presence of Charlie Chaplin. In this film Charlie Chaplin caricatures Charlie Chaplin, rolling his eyes at a hundred miles an hour. Then he does some tricks with two cigarettes, making the smoke come out of his ears. Sacha Guitry repeats the same acts but as if he were performing a rite: he is very boring, while the less imposing Charlie Chaplin is completely natural and seems to juggle with the smoke as if it were alive, parodying himself without a trace of self-consciousness. The father of the two Boutet de Monvel brothers was also present at tea, and behaved like a motherly cardinal.[7] Among the French contingent we were talking of Charlie Chaplin's divorce and agreed that if things go badly for him here, he'll have to be made a ward of the French government ("It would be sad," says Lepape, "if he were turned into an official personage") and installed on the Riviera, given land and studios, thereby retrieving from America a part of its supremacy in the art of the cinema.

February 9 / Charles B. Alexander was buried today

His wife leads all society here. With him, a moment in American life comes to an end. While he was sinking, the pickaxes of the demolition people were tearing down the Vanderbilt mansion next to his; forty stories are to rise on the site of a very dignified residence. Industrialism imposes its hallmark on the architecture and shows the whole country's independence of Europe. The New York of yesterday, an English city with eight or ten steps in front of each house, will soon be no more than dust. Dust, too, its patriarchal customs. Vertigo has replaced the beauty of space and spaces. Yesterday fortunes were made by offering people a chance to subsist, by building them towns and giving them quite simply a bit of comfort; today, by means of instruments of pleasure: the auto, the phonograph, the cinema, the photo. The new magnates are often no more than procurers, and they look their part. They are as far from Europe as what they build. The pioneers borrowed money from us; their sons lend it to us. But there were friendships too that distilled from us a little of the essence of distinction and some refinements; the apoplectic newcomers demand girls from us, our daughters.

February 10 / The John Quinn sale

He was an American lawyer who for a decade collected young painters. He is dead, and the best pictures have been bought privately by dealers. The public auction lasted three days, from morning till evening. This evening I bought three large pictures for very little money, on behalf of the Detroit museum. For $1,900, an immense canvas by the English painter Augustus John, who is not without talent, but who has too

---

[7] I have since learned that it was the elder brother, the dramatist.

many French derivations, without the joie de vivre. I prefer John's drawings to his paintings. This painting is a kind of fresco called *The Mummers* 1912 (English bohemians), measuring nine feet in length. Another, not without charm, by an American artist, Arthur B. Davies. I'm very taken with Prendergast (1859-1924), and bought his *Promenade*, six feet in length, for $1,400. It's a sort of *pointilliste*, or rather *carréiste* work, its daubs being considerably larger than Signac's; with its more beautiful colors it's like a Monticelli if he'd taken lessons from Seurat. For myself, I have bought a boat by Derain, a water color called *The Red Boat* and signed "For André Derain, Alice Derain." The light boat is borne aloft on a hard, leaden but dreamy sea.

February 11 / With Ralph Booth at the New York dealers

First we went to John Levy's with its unforgettable army of salesmen who supply all the picture dealers in the United States with hundred-dollar chromos. From time to time he sells a canvas for $100,000. We saw a fine Millet, $40,000. Then we went on to Scott's. He has some beautiful Van Gogh flowers. They're reproduced in Duret's book. He said they cost 6,000 dollars. Wildenstein, opposite, is asking $60,000, the equivalent of 1,500,000 francs, for a large still life with a blue carpet by Cézanne. But since no Cézanne can bring 400,000 francs in France, it's a handsome profit. Cézanne is sold according to the size of the canvas. The Bernheim brothers, who have set up this year in New York and who are at Jacques Seligmann's, are asking 750,000 francs for a picture half the size. They talk of $20,000 for a Matisse—500,000 paper francs. It's more than 400,000 francs' profit.

February 19 / The Detroit museum

This afternoon Ralph Booth showed me the new building that will be inaugurated in October. It's a palace. Without Ralph, this city would possibly have had to wait fifty years for a museum. He found the $5 million required, obtained from the local authorities, but he has been working on it for twenty years. What perseverance!

February 21 / Dinner with Snowden Fahnestock. A charming evening

I met his aunt, Mrs. Griswold, Lecomte du Nouy, and an Engishman. Du Nouy told me that an American woman who has spent part of her youth in France is likely to be disorientated in America, where she'll always feel unwell. Such is the case with his wife. Because of her, he is going to give up the Rockefeller Institute, return to France, and work at the Pasteur. Snowden, in spite of Prohibition, served us very fine wines, and the young scientist enjoyed them greatly. He also claimed that the American woman who appreciates a good wine is psychologically more sensitive than the one who loves a cocktail, but also more sickly. He insisted that the gulf dividing America from Europe will never be closed because of the centuries that cannot be recovered.

Two days ago the censorship suppressed Bourdet's fine play *The Captive*, a chronicle of Gomorrah, of a man who can't keep his wife, drawn and called as she is toward another, as by a siren. It had been on for several months. I gather that it was closed because over here plays are not allowed which couldn't be seen by a little girl. However, Bourdet handled the subject with marvelous tact, without shocking the public. Like Proust, he draws no conclusions. He exposes the fact, and if he doesn't defend it he doesn't offer any protest either. Du Nouy said he was amazed—it was beyond his comprehension as a Frenchman—that a group of women teachers are protesting against the *withdrawal* of the piece, on the grounds that every young girl should see it.

February 23 / Some visits

Today I saw Mrs. G. Stevens, director and trustee of the Toledo Museum, a museum which has received about $20 million. She has the air of a character out of a story by the English writer Barge—very intelligent, at once dreamy and extremely precise, soft and authoritative, smiling and grave. A trustee, Mr. Gosline, also came to see me; he is melancholic and intellectual. Life in these provincial American small towns brings sensitive people together, but the years go by and one day the group breaks up. This is what has happened in Toledo, and those remaining find themselves relegated to a kind of cemetery, as it has become impossible for them to have any dealings with the younger generation, who want nothing to do with them. Here the older man is looked upon by the young as a kind of plague carrier.

February 25 / Dabo, an American painter whose parents were French
comes to see me

He used to know Whistler and Anatole France intimately. He admired my Gothic exhibition, as he adores that sort of thing, and said to me: "What enabled the cult of the Virgin to grow with such intensity in the thirteenth century is that God and His Son had become very distant grandees, while the Virgin was a woman of humble origin and so most appealing to the poor. She herself had been so poor that she had had to take shelter in a stable for the birth of her son. On one side there were the nobles and the rich, and on the other the serfs, without any intermediate class. And that's how it was with the divinity, God and Christ were inaccessible. The Virgin came just at this moment, offering her consolation, and all the cathedrals are dedicated to her. Notre-Dame de Paris, Notre-Dame d'Amiens, Notre-Dame de Chartres, Notre-Dame de Reims. And the villages vied with the cities."

February 27 / Reflections

Among the world's masterpieces there is not a single sketch. The masterpiece is not only a finished work, but a highly finished one. The artist must never forget this.

February 28 / At the J. P. Morgan Library

He was the last American grandee.

With Dabo, who lunches with me

I showed him my Fra Angelico. "Degas," he said, "would have written of such a work: 'She's to go to bed with.'" Dabo continued: "Here it's the price that's valued. Someone like Clarence Mackay says: 'It's mentioned in Venturi, reproduced in de Ricci, it's the most expensive painting in the world.' He cannot see how drawings or any other comparable piece can be put in a museum. He showed us some books. He's the typical connoisseur. This American aristocrat was the son of a woman who did laundry for miners. She was the widow of some carter by whom she had a daughter, subsequently Princess Colonna, who became a considerable protectress of artists in Rome. Mackay Senior was a miner. Today the son owns the transatlantic cables. It's impossible to talk to these people. To begin with, they don't welcome you. You don't realize it, because you're a stranger and that's why they entertain you, but they don't want you. Look at the society columns; you'll never see the name of an intellectual. The Queen of Rumania eventually got fed up with meeting so many bankers and journalists and said at the McCormicks' house in Chicago: 'But I still haven't seen a scholar or an artist here, where are they?'

"When an artist in the United States has talent, he can go hang, like Whistler. That's all his own country cared about him—I knew him well, he was my friend. All of us used to go to Princess Mathilde's, and in lounge suits. Here a salon for discussion is out of the question. From the East Coast to the Pacific. Whistler knew that the portrait of his mother was his best canvas; he sent it to the Metropolitan, then directed by a Greek American. 'He isn't a painter,' this man replied. 'Pack that up fast, and off it goes back to Paris.' It wasn't colorful. The American is a savage, he loves color. Whence his taste for the primitives, whom I myself adore, but for other reasons. In disgust, Whistler created a mask for himself, and in spite of the books of Roger Marx and Arsène Alexandre he is not known, giant though he was. His jokes, his bon mots, and his sarcasm all hid the furious worker. If he had said, 'I'm working,' he would have been laughed at: 'Ah! Ah! He's working.' I was his pupil. He influenced me. Being his pupil meant sweeping his studio, going out for vermilion and paying for the tube without being reimbursed. America let him be turned out three times by the British bailiffs, and to be turned out over there really means the street, you're not allowed so much as a change of shirt. Luckily, Freer of Detroit, who had made a great fortune out of the first steel railway coaches, happened to be around. He left a sum at his banker's in London for the painter to draw on. Each summer Freer chose from the works in his studio. The whole collection is in Washington and it's marvelous. Whistler was pure-minded as a young girl, and if you could have known his sense of elevation when he worked; as great as Fra Angelico's, who would pray before painting. He was influenced by Mallarmé, who, like him, had been influenced by Poe. There is such repose in his works, by which I don't mean immobility. A work that doesn't budge isn't art. I haven't succeeded as a painter. If I didn't have a certain gift for lecturing, I'd be dead of starvation. My painting wouldn't have kept me two out of twelve months.

"I've had some success in Germany, also in Japan. Chinese art also inspired me. I've had lunch at Potsdam with the emperor, who also painted, huge pictures with warships and vermilion spurted out of a tube. That's how he made the fire spit from his cannons. The best German painter, Liebermann, made fun of him, and Wilhelm II hated him, saying: 'He's a Jew, not a painter.' He closed the doors of one salon to him. Liebermann founded another himself and the young intellectuals followed him there. The empress, a sweet German bourgeoise, asked me what I thought of her husband's painting. What was I to tell her? That he had talent. I did. She was happy.

"Well, among the unappreciated painters was Puvis de Chavannes. He had a small income; otherwise he too would have had it. Then a Russian princess married him. It was a perfect marriage. Do you know where he found certain gestures? Just as Sargent did, in synagogues. A splendid gesture is that of placing or holding the Torah on the head, an ancestral and grandiose gesture. I often go into poor synagogues —what rhythm, what settled, established, solid grandeur! Movements perpetuated with a music much more extraordinary than that of the Christian church. With the Christians it strikes up and then fades away, while in the Jewish temple it envelops you and bathes you from head to foot in its harmony. These gestures, this music are worthy of archaeological study! Archaeology, what a marvelous, powerful instrument it is! We shouldn't know anything about Egypt had we not reconstituted her whole past through the hairpin of one of her harlots!"

Lepape dines with us at Pierre's, with the Ridgway Maeys, the Snowden Fahnestocks, Mrs. Charlotte Satterlee, the Count de Maillé

Lepape, the draftsman, arrived extremely late, and that was the evening's great source of amusement, as he is a very entertaining man and takes the offensive himself. He got the time wrong by an hour. He told us he had once arrived very late like this at a severely bourgeois household, at the moment when the host, in an icy chill, was cutting the piping-hot leg of mutton. Lepape's first words were: "I love overcooked leg."

He talked enthusiastically about Charlie Chaplin. He was at the Charlie Chaplin–Sacha Guitry performance. "The latter," he said, "has and can manifest enormous talent, but he's a performer, while the former has genius." Guitry was pretty well diminished next to Chaplin. Chaplin seemed astonished that he is considered such a genius in France. He does everything well, plays the piano marvelously, has an exquisite voice, draws perfectly. He treats life as a kind of vaudeville. At eleven o'clock the restaurant lights went out and Snowden swept us along to his house, just nearby. I don't know what made him talk of the Hôtel de Crillon, but it seems that he discovered a room there high up, just under the roof, with a delightful view onto the Épatant Club. One day Polignac, an old nobleman, very much a Frenchman of the old school, who had lived in the house before it was converted into a luxury hotel for travelers, came to see him and exclaimed in wonder and horror: "But you've been put in a servant's room!" This same Polignac told him another story: An American woman came to see his château, and in front of the first portrait he showed her she asked him the price. "But it isn't for sale," he said, "it's an ancestor." She tried to acquire the second, the third, and so on, until Polignac showed her one about whom he said: "Now that one was guillotined." The woman was moved, truly touched by the drama, and said: "Ah, I too had a grandfather who was hanged."

March 8 / Arthur Lee

He was furious when I said to him on the telephone that the artist simply must belong to his own time and to his own country, and he rushed over to argue the point with me. He thinks he's a Greek and that in two thousand years' time if his works were to be unearthed they would be taken for ones executed four centuries before Christ. How mistaken he is! "The artist of genius," I said to him, "is the one who expresses the soul of his country, and he creates a masterpiece when he catches and isolates the very minute." As in Botticelli's *Spring* and Rembrandt's *Nightwatch*. The *Spring* could not have been done sixty miles from Florence. To survive for all time is to express all the beauty contained in a certain place and in a fixed second of eternity.

March 17 / Industry

Henry Cravoisier in Paris had asked me to find him some American patents. The latest great American invention was the automatic electric refrigerator with the ice in a compartment of its own, and the heating apparatus fired by petroleum. The oil replaces coal. I've brought back these two patents.[8]

March 19 / "Aquitania"

My wife and I embarked yesterday evening, with Pierre, Yva, and a new little sheepdog who hasn't yet got a name and is very frightened of us all. On board we met Mrs. Charles B. Alexander, who thanked me very much for my letter of condolence, which she sent on to her daughter Mrs. S. Whitehouse in Paris. Mrs. Hamilton Rice, who has the most delightfully decorated house in New York, was also there. Her first husband was George Widener, who went down with the *Titanic*. I've also met Sorine, a Russian artist who paints women as beautiful as motion-picture heroines, and brings in enormous prices. He is dark, lugubrious, and as deadly as his pictures. I got away from him quickly.

March 24

Tomorrow we disembark.

[8] Cravoisier didn't bother with them. They were the refrigerator, then unknown, and heating by fuel oil, also unknown.

NOTEBOOK 15

March 26, 1927–
January 20, 1928

March 26 / Helleu

He died two days ago, I believe. He should not be altogether disparaged. We always ask too much of these fashionable draftsmen. The perspective of time lends them a certain charm, as with Gavarni and Constantin Guys. Helleu showed us the woman of 1900, who knew how to recline because she wasn't yet familiar with the automobile. She wasn't the languishing type, because she was already beginning to make her mark. I would say that she ventured to show her ankles, if not her thighs, but only on her chaise longue. She was a coquette, not yet a hussy. It was the period of the froufrou, the rustle; Lepape styled the jersey. As the popular singers of Paris used to say: "It's the froufrou of woman that troubles the soul of man." Those were the days of the slow waltz, and of cadence as well, of heavy curls gently drawing down the head of a woman onto the shoulder of her conqueror. Bonfils and Barbier show us the jazz band, Negro dances, clinging bodies, bobbed hair as feather-light as the head. Helleu's faces were more aristocratic; the modern ones are all a bit too much American republic. When I think of the abyss dividing 1900 from 1925 or 1927, I see how unfair it would be if Helleu disappeared altogether. He belongs in a museum of fashion and manners.

March 28 / Willette

He is a draftsman of a superior order. His studio was sold the other day. The prices brought by his drawings were too low, but it wasn't at all the same with his paintings, which will one day be much sought after. He is to painting what Charpentier is to music. He paints the French spirit and above all the spirit of Parisian adolescence; he's the Paris gamin of the pencil.

April 7 / Horseshow. The spring prize

My wife has won it on Sherry Golden.

April 10 / The New York museum has bought two pictures for high prices

They are not by the masters to whom they're attributed: Antonello da Messina and Titian.

April 20 / Two fake Watteaus at the Louvre

For a fortnight there has been a great outcry over two Watteaus bought by the museum for 1,500,000 francs and considered very fine. They are of Watteau's period and done by a man named Pierre Quillard, who died at about thirty, after spending several years in Portugal. A Watteau in Edinburgh is by him, so is the Uffizi one, and I have seen others. What a disgrace for our museum! A man not altogether lacking in talent, whom one could rank with a Pater, but with somewhat less personality; one day he will bring a good price. Two years ago the Louvre bought for 375,000 francs a portrait of a man which the curators mistakenly attributed to Watteau. It had been going around all the dealers for twenty years and had been for sale six months before for 25,000 francs, a sort of portrait of an actor. But a week after the purchase the Louvre learned that the picture had been remounted and that, twenty years before, several people had read "My portrait" on the back and had seen a signature which no one remembers, but it was by an artist of the second half of the eighteenth century.

April 21 / On Claude Monet

Georges Bernheim has gone to Giverny. "Monet," he told me, "left a lot of money and everything else to his son, but gave his daughter-in-law a great deal directly. She's the one who will stay on in the house. The son has bought an estate in the neighborhood. The two get on very well these days. She is starting to paint again, and is doing very well; I have bought some canvases from her. The son told me confidentially that he'll sell a canvas from time to time when he needs money."

April 22 / A singular tale

I have been to Dodge's, the American antique dealer. A Greek followed me in, and when he left, Mrs. Fahnestock told me: "That man's begun collecting; he is married but never buys anything for his home without consulting his mistress. The first day he comes alone, the second day with his mistress, and the third with his wife, who signs the check."

May 3 / Forain at his window

Fortunately I was walking along the opposite sidewalk, because I saw him spit into the street from his second floor.

May 15 / At the Brussels Museum

We went to see it before catching the train. The room of primitive Flemings is more beautiful than our old Salle Carré; the new Salle Carré is abominable. The northern sky gives precision to line. The great Flemings are greater than the great Italians, and they owe it to their light.

May 19 / The Daumiers of the X sale

They have been auctioned off today, and drawings have brought 400,000 and 500,0000 francs, or from $16,000 to $20,000. A stir which on the whole is unjustified, as at such a sale no distinction is made between the mediocre and the very fine, between the caricature and the image of life. It is precisely when Daumier abandons the caricature that he ascends to such heights. For instance, a painting of Don Quixote and Sancho came to some 1,500,000 francs—$60,000—which was a mistake;

even when one looks at it as a painting and nothing else, it's a bit wooden. When Daumier paints misery, the world of the poor and their woes, he is sublime, but the artist of the *Charivari* is somewhat less worthy of respect, as his art depends exclusively on the trick of deformation.

A particular incident marked this sale. The most beautiful picture was of a laundress climbing the stone staircase of a steep river bank; the auctioneer announced that the Louvre was entering the lists. At 600,000 francs someone hidden from view behind Lair-Dubreuil was pushing; whistling broke out, the bids went up by 50,000 francs, and the mysterious collector (it was the family) dropped out, but the canvas already stood at 701,000 francs. The Louvre was right to buy it, but instead of following in the wake of others, why has it never taken the lead? Fifty years ago the Louvre could have bought a hundred works by Daumier for 50,000 francs. One day it will similarly buy Derains, Picassos, Segonzacs, etc. The state is as deplorable a Maecenas as it is a merchant and industrialist.

Nungesser

If a diary can be *shown* to be of any use, I would like the case of Nungesser to be an example and an encouragement. Nungesser, who wasn't afraid of dying, was afraid that in spite of his exploits he would die without being sure that the honesty of his bravery was known.

I greatly admired him on the evening of that ridiculous Ford ball when the richest man in the world, a positive lunatic, mad on old dances, forced all his guests to play the monkey, under the direction of two dance instructors, with himself and his wife joining in. I was one of the buffoons, together with some of the richest inhabitants of Detroit. But before going to Ford's, Nungesser had said to me: "I don't give a damn about Ford." "He's exaggerating," I said to myself. Not at all; he really did not give a damn for him. He alone refused to play the fool. Ford, his wife, and the two instructors surrounded him like a wild beast; he had taken a young woman in his arms and was teaching her the tango, the most modern of dances. The four fanatics couldn't separate them; he neither listened nor heard. They looked like clowns running after a race horse.

Lindbergh the aviator

He has taken off alone from New York for Paris. Let's hope he succeeds.

May 21 / Lindbergh arrived at Le Bourget around 10:30 yesterday evening

Thirty-four hours of flight. What a date in the history of aviation! His progress was signaled from Cherbourg on—200,000 people were waiting for him. Indescribable enthusiasm, rising to such a pitch that eight people were injured and had to be taken to the hospital. The crowd ripped the canvas off his aircraft for souvenirs.[1] He is twenty-five. It's his first visit to France. He had only a few sandwiches, and no wireless. He said he was bored to death. Shut up in the airplane, he had visibility only through a periscope; he knows practically nothing of navigation, had only a small, insignificant compass. It passes understanding how he was able to find his way. He also had a ridiculous map of the coast of France. And yet he managed to make it right to Paris. He always gets where he wants to, thanks to what one might call his flair. It's what I had said in speaking of Nungesser. There are birdmen, men who have a sense of the air, Icaruses. He is another, and a formidable one. The crowd at the Opéra was once again as dense as on Armistice night. A fine gesture, with France in mourning for Nungesser. The Americans mustn't forget him.

May 22 / Lindbergh

Early yesterday morning, Nungesser's mother left her card at the embassy, where Lindbergh is staying. He went to call on her in the afternoon. "You alone," she said to him, "can bring back my son."

For the first time ever, the government has ordered the American flag to be flown at the Louvre and the Foreign Office.

May 24 / Lindbergh at Le Bourget, where 200,000 people awaited him

Climbing out of his airplane, he said simply: "I'm Charles Lindbergh."

[1] This report was inaccurate.

Henry Ford

He has contributed $1,000 to the American subscription for the Nungesser and Coli families.

June 1 / On Lindbergh

I have seen Mrs. Charles B. Alexander, mother of Mrs. S. Whitehouse, wife of the first secretary at the American Embassy. She saw quite a lot of the flier during his brief stay here. He left on Saturday for Brussels and from there on Sunday for London. I think he is due to return tomorrow, to embark on Saturday on a warship. All Europe wanted to see him, but the United States was afraid of diplomatic complications if he went to one place and not another, and he was asked to return home immediately. He said to Mrs. Alexander: "The trip has taught me three French expressions: *formidable, épatant, pas possible!*" He told her that the night hours, which we think so fearful, were the most beautiful, for he had four hours of moonlight during which he flew above the clouds, with the birds following him—a magic sight. She added that he never uses the singular, he says "we," meaning the airplane and himself. "We found our course." "We made a good landing." "We were acclaimed."

June 3 / English snobbery

Armand, back from London, was telling me about English snobbery, which always amuses him. "To be really smart in London, there are three things one must have: a box at Covent Garden, a Rolls Royce, and a son or young brother killed in action; oh, not in the Great War, too many died there, above all too many on both sides of the social barricade: no, the son or brother must have been killed in a colony, where only the elite go; for the common soldier doesn't count in England, he's a thief, a hooligan, a drunkard. The height of elegance is to have been killed somewhere around the Mediterranean basin, but that doesn't happen much now. Egypt no longer offers a good family this opportunity; India's still fine, very fine indeed; Australia would be rather pathetic."

June 9 / At Forain's

I told Forain that, reading the life of Arthur Rimbaud the other day, I saw that he had known the poet. "Why, yes, I knew him well," he replied, "so well that I stayed two months with him on rue Campagne-Première, in a frightful hovel, which suited and pleased him—he had such dirty habits. There was only one bed, he lay on the springs and I on a mattress on the floor. We had one water jug the size of a glass, yet it was almost too big for him. I myself used to wash in the courtyard, just as if I were in the army, naked to the waist. Our way of life bothered the concierge, and one day while I was streaming with water he came out to engage me in conversation and asked what I did. I replied that I drew. 'Ah,' he said, 'I thought you were a locksmith.' Living with Rimbaud was impossible because he drank absinthe, and in huge amounts. Verlaine used to call for him, and they both despised me because I wouldn't go with them. That was the extent of their vice. There has been talk of homosexual relations. Ah, no, I saw nothing of that; no, I don't believe that at all. Wretched, that alcohol! Rimbaud stank of genius, he really did; he was wonderfully clever. He wrote a few verses, a few essays, and stopped, exhausted forever; he never wrote another line. I had some manuscripts of his and some of Verlaine's, and I am sorry that I haven't kept them. When I went into the army, I entrusted Rimbaud's to a sort of actor-writer, who didn't return them to me, and I found them again at Barthou's."

I don't know how I came to speak of Proust to Forain; he didn't care for him four years ago but now regards him as a genius. "It's fantastic, the likeness; everything he writes is true to life." I wonder whether future generations will be able to realize this, they may perhaps think that he distorted the scene, but they'll be wrong. The Guermantes are perfect examples of that kind of people, always talking too loudly. As for M. de Charlus, who was in fact Montesquiou, I knew him well. He had considerable and indeed exquisite wit. He organized a fete near Croissy, near Chatou, and in the morning a notice appeared in *Le Figaro* announcing that it was canceled on account of bad weather. Six of us, including the Besnards, didn't read it; neither had Montesquiou himself. A sorry jest: Montesquiou was waiting for the guests with a bouquet in one hand and verses by Verlaine in the other; he wore a violet-purple dress coat. The fountain basins were heaped with rose petals. The moon rose, the stars lit up and were extinguished, the moon disappeared, we six stayed the whole night. So next day the poet went to *Le Figaro* and upbraided the woman who handled the social column; she was an Italian. Now, for *Le Figaro*'s social column she had assumed the title of princess. "I received a note," she said to Montesquiou. "I'll read it to you." And she began: "Madame la Princesse . . ." Montesquiou interrupted: "And so you believed the rest."

June 12 / *Forain, his wife, Mme and Mlle Trarieux, Bosworth, and Armand lunch with us*

Forain recalled the time and place at which my two Monet pictures, the women in the boats, were done, and that it was Montgeron.

Over lunch we talked about Latin, and Forain quoted Maistre's statement that he knew of nothing complex which could easily be learned. Then our artist murmured that so much has to be learned only to be forgotten.

The conversation turned often to animals. Forain said he couldn't understand how a group of ten men who always go to the Épatant Club could talk only of races every evening. But he did somehow appreciate the attitude of a certain lord who went to see a famous horse, Great Monarch, and found himself facing its rump. "So!" said he, "I take off my hat to Great Monarch's rump!" Armand described his experience two years ago when he was having coffee at the home of a grand Polish princess and saw a horse enter the drawing room. "He comes every day," the princess told him, "for his sugar, and his blood is as royal as mine." "Well, it's a diversion in the country," said Forain. He knew a horse fancier who invited the painter Lewis Brown to lunch and asked him to come and take coffee in the stable.

At the table I heard Forain, who doesn't agree with Mme Trarieux as to politics, say to her: "A nation must always retain a feeling of danger."

We talked very little today about art. My wife mentioned Claude Monet to Forain, who hasn't grasped a thing about the impressionists; in everything he says about them he's quite wrong. The very modern painters likewise exasperate him. My wife, speaking of her visit with me yesterday to the Salon des Tuileries, asked him if he'd been to it, and he replied: "Certainly not; it's catching."

September 23 / On Claude Monet

I went to see the Durand-Ruels. At one point the conversation touched on Monet, and I learned that at the age of sixteen, to earn a living, he did caricatures in Le Havre under the name of Oscar. These have in fact been brought in to them recently, but are of no interest; they didn't buy them. I also learned that the artist drew a great deal in his youth, but destroyed all his drawings. Some of them have had a miraculous escape, as he had sent them to be reproduced in journals, and for this reason they were all signed. They showed me two: a study for one of the two women with the parasol which Monet's son has just given to the Louvre, the other depicting the top of a cliff. The wind and the movement of the woman with the parasol are caught in it; it is marvelously rendered, although his drawing has the insubstantiality of his painting, save that the outlines are forcefully set off. It is also very graceful.

Grandfather Durand-Ruel one day bought for perhaps a hundred francs a canvas signed "Monet," an Algerian scene with camels, very much like Fromentin as to composition and execution. Some time afterward he showed it to Monet, who said: "It's not by me; I've never done any camels." This couldn't be; at the time Durand-Ruel bought it, fake Monet's weren't being done, the painter had no value. Grandfather Durand-Ruel was somewhat surprised at this statement, but when he was about to go, Monet said to him: "I should like to keep that canvas; I'll give you another in exchange." Durand-Ruel realized that Monet must have painted it in Algiers at the time of his military service, that needing money he had done a kind of fake Fromentin, but he had failed to sell it and had signed it later on.

Around 1889 he had decided, so to speak, to give up landscapes. He had discussed the matter with Renoir and his other friends, who had strongly advised him to study the human figure. He had come to Paris to look for a model and found and engaged a very good-looking young girl, who agreed to come and live at Giverny; but when he returned home his wife said to him: "If a model comes in here, I walk out of the house." That's why we're missing a Monet who paints portraits and the human figure. He did of course do some: for instance, Durand-Ruel showed me a portrait of a man, painted at Bordighera, which may be lacking in solidity and construction but not in life, not at all. The blood flows in the face somewhat in the manner of Hals, but it is a more dilute, swifter blood, sunny like the Midi and like the painter's landscapes. Durand-Ruel added: "Painters are always injured—their talent suffers—when they marry social women: they don evening clothes, go out too much, work less; the fashionable world doesn't allow them to do beautiful things, only pretty ones, and they work against their instinct. A society woman won't let her husband paint their maid, and the maid would often be the best of models."

We talked of the exhibition of works from Monet's studio, soon to take place at the Jeu de Paume. I said that nothing can hurt the artist but that the exhibition will be rather regrettable; on my last visit I had great difficulty in finding two good pictures. We all went back to the studio and I had to choose canvases from some series of water lilies and poplars, nothing out of the ordinary. I told Durand-Ruel how between my two visits a fortnight apart he had burned so many canvases. And he informed me that prior to doing a series the artist would do a good seventy studies of each before finding a definitive form, and all these sketches he destroyed.

October 4 / My birthday

I am forty-six.

Gold

This evening I showed my children a twenty-franc gold piece, they'd never seen one; the eldest is fourteen. They looked curiously at this coin, which was current before the war; for my part, I have to make an effort to remember using it.

October 5 / Rosalie leaves us

She has been our cook since our marriage fifteen years ago, after having served my grandfather for a long time; she was not so very old, but she underwent some serious operations. How I lament the departure of this faithful servant who looked after three generations of us; when she was very ill, while I was in Egypt, she had only one fear: of dying without seeing me again! Rosalie.

November 25 / Wilhelm II does a little dealing

He has offered Joe one of the Potsdam Watteaus, a theater scene, and the Lancret *Camargo*.

January 10, 1928 / A new Vermeer

In London I've bought a picture from Scotland. It was in the W. A. Coats Collection, which also contained Vermeer's *Christ in the House of Mary and Martha*, recently bequeathed to Scotland. But my picture was coated with a varnish which had darkened it, and none of the Vermeer experts had perceived that it was an original. But then it is an early one and doesn't possess all the master's qualities. I am going to write a study of this picture.

January 13 / An American collector

This summer Kleinberger showed Jules Bache a superb head of a man with a somewhat sullen air, by Memling, and the American exclaimed: "Oh, no, I don't want a man who looks as though he got up on the wrong side of the bed that morning; give me pretty women. Even if I do spend an evening with a woman who isn't pretty, she maybe knows how to sing."

Kleinberger's nephew, who was assisting at the sale, then said to the American, indicating the Memling: "Perhaps he could be taught to sing."

January 20 / On Marie Laurencin

Armand talks of nothing else, and in a most interesting manner. He's the one who ought to write a book about her. He will be her poet. What strikes Armand most is the miracle of seeing her retreat entirely into the world she's created, and as the sublime fantasy clarifies and enlarges itself, become ever more its prisoner, and in truth an egoistic prisoner in spite of her great heart—an egoism born of sensibility. She is adored in her village of Champrosay, where she has her little country house, and where she performs acts of kindness for everybody, for mothers, for children; but even so, if she is so concerned, it is because the sight of misery troubles her dreams—that's why she goes on trying to alleviate it. She has many friends and is devoted to them because she doesn't listen to them or indulge in confidences with them; but since she muses aloud, they know her intimate thoughts and even her observations about them; she isn't sharp-tongued, but she considers it base not to condemn base actions. For instance, at the moment she's quarreling more and more sharply with Mme Groult, a friend of twenty years, the best next to Suzanne, her maid, whose sister was with her several years ago. It's not Suzanne she loves, it's "the maid," this essential being who knows how to carry out orders and so makes it possible for her to paint and thus subsist, for she says she paints for a living, she doesn't love painting, if she were rich she'd never touch a brush. When she says things like that, she is sincere, as she always is at the moment of speaking. But she loves her pictures to bring high prices. She sent Armand to ask the prices of her drawings and water colors at the dealers'. She doesn't understand anyone being a dealer; it seems to her the last resort. She excuses them with the phrase "They're necessary." She understands only poets and painters, or rather she doesn't comprehend that anything else exists, and if she grasps the poet's art, she doesn't understand the painter's. She will execute a very good painting, saying: "I don't understand it." She loves princes and takes up their defense. She lunched with the King and Queen of the Belgians, but was disillusioned with them on learning that Belgium is so small. Neither did she have any real grasp of the war; the war wasn't in her dream. But, ah, if the war had taken place later, after they had grown up, the children she has painted, and if the people in her dream had had their hearts and heads shattered, then the war would perhaps have killed her, she whose health is so delicate, who doesn't seem called to a long life, whose eyes are already so weary, large eyes which she turns on the world like a magnifying glass and which by enlarging details eliminate them, preserving only the mass.

Yesterday when she telephoned Armand and asked him what he thought of the daughters of Louis XIV, he replied: "They don't interest me, they were too badly brought up." "Oh, don't say that, I'm painting them at this very moment. Saint-Simon speaks of them and I'm reading his memoirs, so I've had the idea of doing them."

"They are new figments of her dream," continued Armand. "No, I'm wrong when I say they're new; they're just like the little girls in *Les Malheurs de Sophie* and all the little creatures of the Bibliothèque Rose, who are the source of her view of life. Speaking of pink, Louise Hervieu has been awarded the *Légion d'honneur,* to which Marie's comment was: 'I don't want the *Légion d'honneur;* oh, yes, I'd love it if it were pink, but red is vulgar.' "

"She always speaks a lot about her mother," Armand tells us, "and like all emancipated women is very proud of the fact that her mother was extremely strict, her ambition being that her daughter should speak good French. One day little Marie ran to her mother, saying: *'Je m'ai brûlée'* ('I'm burned'). 'No,' said the mother, *'je me suis "brûlée"'* ('I've burned myself'). She was so badly burned that she didn't sleep all night, but the mother was more concerned with the damage to the French language than with that to the child."

NOTEBOOK 16

January 22–September 10, 1928

January 22 / On Marie Laurencin

Marie Laurencin is criticized for always doing the same face, even in commissioned portraits. "Each person I paint is different," she protests. "The public is mistaken. It is said that I do the same eyes, but the eyes don't count; it's the look."

"It is thus," adds Armand, "that the daughters of Louis XIV, daughters of different mothers, will have for Marie Laurencin the same eyes but not the same look in their eyes." Lately she did a water color, a Scotsman, very accurately rendered. Armand asked her if she thought all the Scots were like this one. She replied that she'd only seen one, from which she'd drawn this one, and that was on a bottle of whisky.

February 11 / A Vermeer

I've discovered another Vermeer, a portrait of a woman like the one in Budapest; it's a rather curious item, as the woman, who is relatively young, is wearing a collar that was not seen in Vermeer's time except on the necks of old women. But it is signed in the lace with that mysterious signature that I have found on almost all the "unsigned" Vermeers. I shall speak of it again.

February 17 / Carvallo on Velázquez

He is a naturalized Frenchman, a Spaniard by birth. He has married a rich American woman and owns the Château de Villandry in Touraine. He is taken up with pictures and speculates, his specialty being the Spanish school. And this morning I was astounded to hear him talk so marvelously of art. He gave me a magnificent lesson on Velázquez. He demonstrated Velázquez's ability to plant a man on his two feet, and also the perfection of his drawing. He says that the portrait of the little girl in the Louvre is not by Velázquez and that the only original of the master that we possess is the portrait of a man marked *Unknown* and given by Princess Mathilde, a head seen again in *The Forge of Vulcan.*

February 18 / With Carvallo at the Louvre

Yesterday he invited me to go around the museum with him; he led me up to the most beautiful Greek and Egyptian objects, which are not those that everyone looks at but which I myself show to friends. He then showed me how to appreciate the art of Ribera and Zurbarán, painters I have never really thought of, to whom I have scarcely allowed any merit, but who have a marvelous science of painting. Fashion will bring them back again, since fashion has so much to do with our knowledge of art. I am astonished by Carvallo, I've never met a man with whom I'm so much in agreement. He was speaking to me of his gallery of Spanish pictures at Villandry, and asked me to come down for a night. I accepted with pleasure.

May 20 / On Marie Laurencin

Armand was telling me that she is put out at not having the *Légion d'honneur,* and that her annoyance inspires her to make some very droll remarks, such as: "It would give the women who have it too much pleasure."

June 28 / At Derain's on the rue Bonaparte

Two antique dealers who have known him for a long time and have sold him Gothic objects took me along to see him. They were telling me that if he had a lot of money he would buy wonderfully well, as his taste in antiques is perfect. He has, they assured me, a very fine collection of Negro art. (If this art can be fine. I don't find it so.)

He lives in an old house whose front flight of steps is clean, well kept, and has an aura of a crinolined grandmother about it. The interior is unpretentious and most untidy. He must have painted many masterpieces here; he has lived here for a long time and is leaving it in a few days to go to the Parc de Montsouris, where he has built a house. First comes a low entrance hall several yards square, where some forty boxes of drawings are piled. Derain brought out two for us, studies of female nudes. He showed us into his vast studio, where Negro sculptures were scattered about, as well as astronomical instruments, and antique musical instruments, picked up no doubt at the close of some rustic concert. There is, in addition, a very large canvas of such a rustic concert, and he told us that he had been working on it for ten years. Its surface is hard and I wondered how he could paint on it. He replied to my question that, on the contrary, he paints best on worked-over and dried paint. Derain is, like all painters, preoccupied with the decomposition of colors and he no longer paints with any but earth colors, which alone, he insists, don't alter. I don't agree; we have too many canvases by old masters which have stayed as they were when first painted. I said to him that the man who perhaps best knew the technique of colors and to whom modern art is closest is Rubens, that he is a very great master, though fallen into neglect these days, that he knew how to prepare his canvases, his foundations, his undercoatings. And when Derain heard me say this, he was overjoyed; he is mad about Rubens, places him at the top, calls him one of the greatest geniuses that painting has seen.

I had an idea of Derain's face from his self-portraits, but a false idea, as I found them invariably lacking in distinction. He has painted himself as an indifferent bohemian, still under Flaubert's influence, dressed sloppily and not too well shaven, whereas he looks to me very much the established man, yes, large and vigorous, fleshy but in well-fitting clothes, a blue suit. Besides, these days artists take pains over their appearance. Derain has the air of a gentleman of some learning who has studied a little of everything and therefore knows the limits of knowledge and maintains a wise man's reserve. He is all moderation, and that's what struck me most during this rather brief hour. He didn't speak a great deal, listened attentively to the observations of the antique dealers, and was interested; he was taking our measure without showing it. Anything one says to him seems to reach him slowly, as if through a process of sorting. One senses in discussion with him—all the more so since he doesn't give the impression of thinking swiftly, but nothing said to him is lost— that if one wanted to pile up arguments to convince him overwhelmingly, they'd get there, as the theory of relativity tells us, with some necessary delays, and perhaps make a different point, but they'd have the benefit of a coordination and balance they didn't have to start with; so that these arguments, transmuted and linked together in his brain, no longer confused but all arranged in their exact order of value, would give him the total picture as if mathematically and proved out by nines.

I made a quick tour of the studio; there are hardly any pictures: a small landscape, some rather scattered trees, a kind of spaced-out forest landscape; but I've never seen trees so precise in their design, and herein lies the difficulty. A small portrait of a woman which is pretty, done very lightly, unfinished; then a nude, no more advanced, rather large, a woman standing, full-face, her arms reaching down to her knees; it's delightfully subtle, she isn't too innocent, she has an easy naturalness about her.

Derain explained to us that if he has so few pictures it's because he has painted only one all winter; he has only sketched. He brought in three full boxes: always the same woman, in the most difficult positions, foreshortenings such as are seen only in the privacy of the bedroom. Why all these sketches of the model, five or six months of work, three or four a day, four to five hundred studies, why? "To find a certain position," Derain told us, "and I haven't found it." He showed us the one he considered best and he is right: it's the woman of the upright portrait, done like this because it's simple, lifelike, just like everyday—adorable.

Derain seems to be under the influence of Dunoyer de Segonzac, the first, I believe, to have tried these extravagant studies of nudes in unexpected poses, nearly all of them reclining; but while in Segonzac the women nearly always seem to be experiencing a bestial, if sometimes grandiose, vertigo of lust, this is not the case with Derain; to begin with, it's pure design and not a delving into emotion, it's a line, and it's this line he has failed to find, and probably because he has gone too far, he hasn't remained the simple Derain who is close to ordinary observations. The question too arises, when one sees these drawings and thinks of Segonzac's paintings, whether these men and their school are not influenced by that new invention, the cinema, which puts out a multitude, a succession of lines.

All the artists have been studying the cinema, which has brought them precision in the observation of movement. But won't they go beyond this cinema and paint what it cannot give us, such as these delectable, twining nudes, impossible before the objective lens, where they become coarse? A piquant detail having to do with fashion: Derain deplores bobbed hair. He says, "It's all very well in the street, at the theater, in a drawing room, since the couturiers have created an aesthetic of bobbed hair; but the female nude, whose beauty is no longer either shielded or protected by these veilings now cut off, doesn't emerge to advantage from this last fall (that of the hair). Her hips seem too bulky, and her shoulders too narrow; when I find a model who still has her hair, I give her five francs more." After this, Derain talked only about the need to sketch, the piano exercises, the endless study, the eternal set task; the line is the road, a rigorous track, elongating and losing its shape if it isn't precise and ever more precise. One can sense what agony this drawing must have subjected the artist to this winter, worse than his poverty when his canvases weren't worth even fifty francs, as he couldn't sell them, and his mother begged him to take up something else. His parents wouldn't support him, hoping to get him to change his profession—the old story—until the day Vollard bought the entire contents of his studio from him; there were thirty to forty canvases in it; and suddenly his mother began to have confidence, with this first amount, even though it was less than a thousand francs.

July 2 / Mintchine

He is an unknown Russian painter whose canvases sell for a few hundred francs, but he will have the talent of a Renoir. It seems that he is very young, around twenty-four. For three weeks I've been buying everything of his I could find, about eight pictures in all. Only in this past year has he freed himself of various influences: Cézanne, Utrillo, Marie Laurencin. His color is fluid, and that's where the great masters can be recognized. To be a Velázquez, a Rembrandt, a Manet, you have to get free of your medium. When these men paint fluidly, they are at the peak of their talent. Mintchine already has that art in his palette, with the beauty of colors that Renoir was master of at thirty-five. I shall speak of him again.

September 9 / The Jewish artists

Zborowsky, the Polish art dealer, a person of great sensibility and himself a Christian, told me that the two greatest artists of the generation after Derain, Matisse, and Picasso are two Jews, Modigliani and Soutine. There is also Kisling,[1] he added. He thinks that there is a renaissance of spirit in the people of Israel, an evolution from the critical to the creative temper. He considers that it isn't the mission of the Jewish people to create art, that their role in the world must be dynamic, to prevent debilitation.

September 10 / Briand

I arrived in Geneva this morning. We want to enroll our son Pierre in school—he's too thin—and we have turned up nothing satisfactory, except Le Rosey, which he'll be entering in a year. I caught sight of Briand, who is to deliver an important speech tomorrow at the League of Nations, and I wanted to take a picture of him with the motion-picture camera I bought a fortnight ago, but the minister disappeared into the Hôtel de la Paix, where he was going to confer with the Germans.

[1] Very bad. (Note appended 1939.)

NOTEBOOK 17

September 21, 1928–July 16, 1929

September 21 / Deydier

I don't know if I've spoken of him. It was he who showed me a
Mintchine for the first time. Today he brought me six, and I am going to
buy five of them from him for 10,000 francs. This Mintchine will attain
a beauty like Renoir's. He hasn't yet extricated himself from certain influences, not even from Cézanne's as yet. Not as solid, not as well drawn,
but fluid colors, delectable as creams. Deydier loves nature; as we crossed
the Tuileries he gazed at the colors edging the treetops; he's a sensitive
creature. He loves this vista of the Louvre, but said: "In spite of everything, you know, all these trees, all these flowerbeds, all the flowers, it
isn't as beautiful as a simple field in its perennial vigor." Deydier is right,
of course, for a garden is never anything more than nature subdued. We
crossed the Seine; he was right again when he criticized those steel
bridges, saying that only stone went well with water.

September 23 / Mots

Deydier was passing my door as I was about to set off by auto for
Mortefontaine Golf Course, and I took him along. He would leave a
woman for a chance to go to the country.

He knew Anatole France in the last years of his life. Speaking of Verlaine, France said to him: "He certainly wasn't hard of hearing!"

Deydier told me how one day in Tréguier Renan, already very old, bowed quite low to the Christ borne in a procession. One of his friends said in amazement: "What, you salute the Christ?" Renan replied: "We salute but we don't talk to each other."

September 25 / On Derain

I went in to Heim's, an antique dealer who is a friend of Derain's. He showed me the portrait of Derain's wife which the painter did after the war when she was engaged to him; Derain has worked over it; he has added or finished the hand, put in a collar; the dealer has made himself some money.

Heim showed me a nearly life-size horse, very stylized, done by Derain in the manner of his first period. Heim has just bought it in Denmark or Germany. Derain has worked over this one, too, giving it powerful hoofs. The paint is very thick. It is his way of going back over paint hardened by the years; he hopes that this way the retouchings won't flake off.

It is rather rare to find a painter going back over his canvases. People will be surprised, at a later date, to find the works different from what the first photographs, for example, presented. They may well believe that certain works were repeated and others lost, and forgers will be able to take advantage of this to improve some works.

October 24 / The United States

My wife and I left today on the transatlantic liner *Paris:* the modern-art decoration is old hat, as I complained when the ship was launched; they had made the mistake of approaching antique-art decorators for designs. Only the Lalique salon justifies its existence, as does the smoker.

We have left our eldest son Ernest in Paris with his aunt Emilie Vuitton and an English teacher. The two other boys, Pierre and Jean, are in England, in a small country school. Jean is at the top of his class.

November 30 / In the United States

I've been here four weeks and I've written nothing. It's very wrong of me. I've been extremely busy and had a great many invitations.

The American collector is prey to the hugest swindle the world has ever seen: the certified swindle. Thirty years ago the American bought so many fake pictures that eventually he wanted authentications; expressly for him, experts were created and promoted; the dealer let the responsibility rest with all these irresponsible creatures, and the client no longer had anyone to whom he could appeal for justice. For instance, I went to see Bache, who pays enormous prices but has a Bellini, a Botticelli, a Vermeer of Delft, three old pictures which aren't by the masters. At Ernest Rosenfeld's, a profile in marble by a sculptor like Rossellino, but it is fake. The Detroit museum also has a fake marble bust bought by the deplorable expert Valentiner. All this is done in Italy. Americans have bought within a short period $10 million's worth of pictures whose certifications are indefensible.

The movement in favor of modern art is intense, and not only for impressionists but also for living artists, like Matisse, who is the most expensive. Derain, Modigliani, and Utrillo are very much sought after. There is a positive furor for modern decorative art, but only in the past six months; it's the result of the Paris Exhibition.

December 3 / Austin, director of the museum of Hartford (Connecticut), comes to see me

He is about twenty-four and has been at this museum only a year. The town was asleep, his youth and intelligence have conquered all hearts, and he has made the money flow in torrentially. He has obtained about $600,000 for a museum which had nothing. How has he brought about this miracle? By giving a ball in the museum. Everyone enjoyed it and after that they all swore by him. Who can say what future may be in store for this institution, thanks to this Don Juan, friend of the great masters?

He has come to acquire my Fra Angelico and an enchanting Avignon primitive, *Christ on the Knees of the Virgin*.

Holmes, the director of the Boston Museum, comes to see me around six this evening

You have to admire the activity of these museums. I've been showing my objects only for a fortnight, and I have already had Detroit,

Toledo, Fogg, Hartford. This Holmes, whom I hadn't met before, paused in front of my best things.

December 25 / Elinor Glyn

Her book *Three Weeks* launched her. She has done better since. She makes a lot of money with her novels and some scenarios. Her sister Lady Duff Gordon, also shocked England twenty-five years ago, but by setting up as a couturière.

I met Glyn at dinner with Mrs. R. T. Wilson, who always has amusing company. She has a dulcet way of speaking and expresses herself magnificently in French. Montaigne, she said, was her first teacher. She also said she kept Sterne's *Sentimental Journey* by her bedside. She adores the eighteenth century and really knows it. This woman isn't superficial. She has a strange face with hair in the Venetian style, sharply divided by a madonnalike parting; but she has modernized this coiffure with a kiss-curl coming down on her cheek. Her eyes are disturbing, but not troubled. They are outlined as if ringed with a dark brazen color like Egyptian eyes that had gazed upon the lagoon. She told me how when she lived with the Luynes at Dampierre she rummaged with the duke through old papers of theirs. Their ancestress, the duchess at the time of the Revolution, practiced mounting to the scaffold on some steps made out of packing cases, but she escaped it.

December 27 / The Grand Duke Alexander

I left yesterday evening for Cincinnati, where I arrived this morning. I've come to see M. E. W. Edwards and this evening I dine at his brother's. The Grand Duke is the guest of honor.

December 29 / Pre-Columbian art

I arrived in Toledo around six yesterday, and I plan to leave on January 2 to go fox hunting for several days in North Carolina at Percy Rockefeller's, with Mr. and Mrs. Joe Thomas. My friend Billy Gosline was waiting for me at the station and I'm staying with him. He's an excellent letter writer and his wife is full of wit. Mrs. George Stevens, widow of the former director, has organized this exhibition. This art of the inhabitants of America before the arrival of Columbus and the Americans is most curious. It is to be found near the Gulf of Mexico, but also much farther north, in the very state of Ohio, where Toledo is. The Indians seem never to have produced such beautiful things. We may assume that other men lived here in the fifteenth century. A vanished race? It is a mystery. The Aztecs lived on the Gulf of Mexico. But here—so high up! The so-called mounds have been discovered in Ohio, vast quadrilaterals built a little like pyramids, but not coming to a point. I believe they are made of earth, and the exterior must be shored up with stones. I don't know if they served as tombs. From these mounds objects have been collected, the most remarkable pieces being animals sculpted in hard stone; these are tiny, only two-thirds of an inch to a little over an inch high: a wonderfully lifelike bear, massive and sturdy, planted on its hind legs, looking comical and formidable; skillfully made pipes, whereas those by the Indians are infantile. Frequently animals serve as ornament. These sculptures evoke Egypt more than anything else. I knew a little about the Mexican findings, but was ignorant of the art of the Mound builders, and the United States has not yet given it due attention. The whole of this collection comes primarily from museums of natural history, where these objects in their showcases are relegated to the status of curiosities rather than works of art. It's the first time they've been put on exhibition in this country.

January 1, 1925 / *Yva, our little Aberdeen terrier, is dead*

My wife just telephoned me here in Toledo a few minutes ago. It is ten in the morning. I wept. Yva was very ill when I left. She was being looked after in the dressing room; in the last two or three days her little muzzle had already shriveled. When I left her, she gave me such a sad look that I was certain I should not see her again. She was about ten, the same age as my third son. She gave us much joy. She had great intelligence, a friendly understanding of life, she loved only us and she adored the children. I wept.

February 3 / *Poiret the couturier*

We went with Mrs. Ridgway Maey to take tea with Mrs. Elisha Walker, whose husband is American. She is of an old French family from Martinique. They have the marvelous Beauvais furniture from the William Salomon sale.

Poiret arrived with the Perrins of Lyon; he never fails to cause a sensation. He has trimmed his mustache and beard and has the air of an old unemployed actor. The women here wear dresses that reach just to the calf when they stand and go a good deal higher when they are seated. He assured us that Frenchwomen don't wear such short dresses, and that the Americans won't hear of having them lengthened. "In 1912," he said, "I brought over a film showing short skirts, and it was banned by the censor as obscene. Last year in Chicago I gave a lecture against the short skirt. There were three thousand women there. The first row of the balcony was fronted by open ironwork, and I felt like telling the women to come and take my place and see what they would see!" Perrin asked him if he was able to continue with his lecture, and he replied: "Yes, because I was reading and had my eyes lowered!" He claims to have been the apostle of the short dress, but stated that he never thought it would rise so high. I amended: "And so close." He says the public is intolerable, even the ordinary people, they want only one design, in a few years they'll be asking the women to wear a uniform, already their clothes are just about that; women will end up wearing sacks.

February 8

With Clara Thomas, her husband, and the Count and Countess de Forceville, we have gone to North Carolina for a foxhunt at Overhill, as guests of Percy Rockefeller.

February 9

Rain: there's our first day. North Carolina—sand, pines, woods hacked to pieces, gray thickets. Not beautiful. We are staying at the clubhouse situated on the Rockefeller estate, fifty-odd yards from his own house. He already has fourteen persons staying with him. The club is a way of giving you independence. Percy invited my wife and myself to dinner. They are numerous in this country, rich people who live miserable, enclosed, restricted lives, who don't know how to eat or drink.

February 11 / Proust and Reynaldo Hahn

The Countess de Forceville is the musician's niece. We followed the hunt by automobile, but only in a manner of speaking; we raced around after it for two hours while it never budged; for five hours it was beating the woods for a fox that it didn't find, and my wife came back out of humor. She had a poor horse, which dragged, and she complained about it to Joe Thomas, who is a kind of spoiled, childish dandy.

The countess told me that Reynaldo Hahn is a gourmet and that wherever he is invited, he runs to the kitchen. At Robert de Rothschild's he didn't dare go see the chef. Robert had for a long time been promising him a certain recipe for sauce which he never received; so that evening Reynaldo Hahn asked the butler to go get it from the chef. The recipe came up in an envelope addressed to Reynaldo Hahn, but Lord Robert opened it, read it aloud, and at the end he found this revelation: "Add a clove of garlic, but above all don't tell Monsieur le Baron."

The countess, who must be about twenty-eight, knew Proust. She saw a lot of him during the war and has a voluminous correspondence from him which she doesn't want to make public. She reminded me of Esther in Proust's work. She didn't tell me anything of interest about the writer, except for this: Proust was much attached to her parents, and one day, in the early years of the automobile, he went to her mother to ask if a woman going off on a two- or three-day auto trip would take one veil or two with her. He often worked at their house in Saint-Germain.

February 12 / Departure

There was another hunt today. For two hours it could almost be followed on foot. I got it on my movie camera. My wife had a good mount, and there were some gallops, but they don't jump here.

Having previously known only the Northern United States, I was astounded by the poverty in the South. The Negroes live in miserable wooden huts. Vehicles lie about with single wheels, agricultural implements are in a deplorable state. The Negro earns some ten dollars a week and often has half a dozen children. I have to pay a typist forty dollars a week in New York. As everything used by the Negro comes from the Northern factories, living is as expensive for him as it is everywhere else in the United States. There is another side to mass production.

February 28 / At Mrs. E. S. Fabbri's

An interesting dinner party of more than thirty people: Professor

Osborne, head of the Museum of Natural History, who talked a lot to my wife. Colonel House, President Wilson's confidant, who had been writing his memoirs of the war and his association with that friend from whom he parted mysteriously one day. Colonel House was the gray eminence; his arrival was never announced, or his departure; and it was never made known whom he had seen; but everything said about his power was true. I am told this evening that his memoirs have cost him his power, as he has been considerably censured for having spoken so soon. His books diminish Wilson and show him up as indecisive. The impression given is that House often abused the President's confidence, to get him to make decisions. House is urbane and doesn't strike one as a fighter. The Republicans, as well as the Democrats, will have none of him. No political party loves men who expose the leaders.

After dinner I found myself with him and Mrs. Pindleton; we talked of art and he was surprised by my theory of weight, which I haven't yet noted here. He was almost sorry to be convinced by my arguments that weight, vulgar weight, has such a connection with art. He would attribute it all to the spirit. I concede that the spirit never loses its rights in art. I was pleased to hear this man of action, a realist, defend the intangible rights of the spirit in art. I explained to him that my theory was more a practical means, a sort of rule of three for those whose spirit is not so sensitive, so spontaneously able to recognize beauty.

Historical Museum

A collector of Italian pictures took me there, and I discovered in it a pretty Hubert Robert and some other very good eighteenth-century French pictures.

At Mrs. Austin's

We discussed modern portraits; she told me that a painter who wants to be successful here must slim down the hips and fatten the pearls.

I said to her that Whistler painted neither as a Frenchman nor like the English, that he is therefore American, that his masterpiece, the portrait of his mother, which is in the Louvre, is essentially American. "Whistler is Whistler," she replied, "but he isn't American. How can an artist be American when there isn't any environment here? When he painted the portrait of Lord Riversdale, now in the National Gallery, he painted a work as English as the portrait of his mother is American. Naturally his mother recalls America to him; he couldn't escape the memories and the atmosphere they evoked, but he avoided it in all his other canvases. Our countrymen cannot create unless they go abroad. It's sad."

March 4 / The fake certificate

The scandal of the fake marbles, which I mentioned at the beginning of this notebook, broke this winter. The Italians have sold Americans two million dollars' worth of marbles done by Dossena. A laughable sum, compared with the amounts obtained by means of certificates given daily by German experts to German dealers. Just as there were paper marks, so there are paper canvases, an easy way of bringing dollars into Germany. I went this morning to the Van Diemen Gallery, which has an exhibition of sixteen Venetians. Three pictures are good, apart from the Guardis and perhaps the Longhi.

Last Sunday's *Times* devoted an entire page to reproducing this scandalous exhibition, which gives only a faint idea of what is brought in.

Bode, the director of the Berlin Museum, died two or three days ago. The king is dead, long live the king! The Mayers, the Gronaus will replace him. The German title of Doktor impresses the Americans.

The museums are even more intent than the collectors on defending their fakes or their mistaken attributions.

March 5 / President Hoover in the White House

He entered it yesterday. Mrs. Austin attended the ceremony. "A new President of the United States," she said, "is sometimes the history of a people, and his election can indeed bring about a change in world history. I caught some colorful notes in the ceremony, but felt no character in it because Hoover is a weak man."

March 11 / Henry Barton Jacobs Collection in Baltimore

It's the work of Mrs. Jacobs, who doesn't even let her husband give an opinion. They've removed nearly all the bad pictures that had been bought; and the first gallery, consisting mainly of eighteenth-century French pictures, begins to have great distinction. Mrs. Barton Jacobs had asked me to take on the administration of her collection after her death, but now she has almost made up her mind to give it to the city museum when the building is completed.

Duncan Phillips

I often reproach myself with not having noted down descriptions of American collectors, but I declare I have nothing to say about them, as they have so little personality. They show you all their pictures like rich children showing off their toys. A great personage was Mrs. Havemeyer, who died fairly recently, and left her collection to the New York museum, where it fills some deplorable gaps.

Another considerable figure that has come forward in the past four or five years is Duncan Phillips, who is forty-four. One of the first things he did was to purchase *The Rowers* by Renoir from the Durand-Ruels, then he threw himself eagerly into the modern movement. Duncan Phillips is an intellectual and expresses himself on art in too literary a way; he's a bit of a socialist, but he is a person of infinite sensibility. He has reddish hair and a lively face equally red, with a rather protuberant mouth that seems to gobble up life. Like a picture dealer, he has veritable reserves in rooms filled with nests of drawers. Collectors of modern art try these days to collect all the styles of a master, as the Chester Dales of New York do. Duncan Phillips has bought some old pieces but a great deal of nineteenth-century items, especially early nineteenth. He has some fine Daumiers, a master that has just been rediscovered. He opens his house to the public two or three times a week. This man will leave his mark on the history of the development of a taste for modern French art in America. He speaks of France with the same fervor as we speak of ancient Greece.

March 16 / The deplorable Hoover

Mrs. Austin was right. His inauguration address was stupid. At a time when the world is faced with such vast problems, he has chosen the paltry theme of Prohibition enforcement.

March 23 / Return to France

My wife and I left yesterday evening at midnight on the *Aquitania*.

April 10 / A surgical operation

My wife is going to undergo an operation for appendicitis. We have consulted Landowski and Gosset and have seen an X ray: it must be done. My wife is ready and talks about it as of a pleasure party. But she insists on riding tomorrow at the horse show in the mixed prizes, after which the surgeon can do what he likes with her.

April 11 / Mixed prizes

She won third prize on Sherry Golden, with Lieutenant de Niort on Lindbergh, whom my wife bought in America this winter and named thus because he is brave and flies over obstacles.

April 12 / Nursing home on rue Bizet

My dear Florrie was taken in at five o'clock. A tragic place. But the invalid burst out laughing and made fun of my long face.

April 13 / Operation

It was much more serious than a simple appendicitis, and when my wife was told this, she replied: "These surgeons always want to make complications."

April 14 / Marie Laurencin

Armand was talking to us of her at great length. He met her when Lady Cunard commissioned her to do her portrait, which she painted with a horse in it, but a fantastic kind of dream horse, the only sort she'll do, and naturally very far from anything seen in England in the way of horses. The lady, who was not satisfied, sent the portrait back from London to Marie Laurencin, and customs imposed a 12 per cent luxury tax on it. She refused to go to their offices, Armand took care of the formalities, and she didn't have to pay anything. The matter, though settled with the customs, was not settled with Marie Laurencin. Her honor as an artist was offended, and she made Lady Cunard get down from her horse and get on a camel; she told the story and showed the picture to everyone. Lady Cunard heard of it and came in all haste to Paris. Lady Cunard, who for years had been trying to scale the last rungs of the English social ladder, Lady Cunard on a camel! What a fall! Absolute horror of seeing the canvas exhibited or reproduced in the *Burlington* or the *Tatler*. She had Armand sit down and think of something and commissioned a whole ballroom from Marie Laurencin. The artist has long since ripped up the canvas.

Marie Laurencin is much taken up with Armand and he says she won't be pleased when he marries.

April 28 / Marie Laurencin

Armand came to dinner. Yesterday a water color by Marie, which she had sold some time ago for 500 francs, brought 14,000 francs at public auction, whereas Armand would have paid her around 7,000 for it. She claimed that such a price gave her no pleasure. This was sincere, but nevertheless she found everything charming today. She even sketched on, and very well too, the four panels of a folding screen which she had had for two years and never touched. It is in black lacquer, with a white inset, on which she's to paint, on each panel. For two months she had scarcely picked up a brush because of all the trouble she had had with her apartment.

Marie Laurencin is quite well off these days. She must have nearly a million in canvases. She has very good shares, and her two homes, which are worth some 800,000 francs. The Friends of Modern Art, which bought one of Matisse's canvases from him for one franc, came to call on her, but she replied that she wasn't interested in museums, although her mother had loved them.

May 7 / Mintchine

Since becoming acquainted with this painter's work, I have bought about thirty-five of his canvases. Some are quite uneven, but that in itself is some proof of talent. I recently met the Manteaus, husband and wife, the dealers who have a gentlemen's agreement with him. Mintchine arrived from Russia about four years ago, and his poverty was appalling. Married, and with one child, he barely managed to scrape together a hundred sous a day to live on; he wouldn't eat, and, dying of hunger, he would say to his wife: "Eat. Mintchine isn't hungry." Now that he's attained a measure of comfort and his health has deteriorated, he continues to deprive himself for his wife, repeating: "Mintchine doesn't need anything."

Marie Laurencin

Marie Laurencin's former husband has an exhibition on the avenue Rapp at a bookseller and publisher's whose wife was ill this summer; the wife needed country air and Marie lent them her house for two months. They wanted to thank Marie by organizing this exhibition, but she didn't understand. Armand went to buy a canvas, for 700 francs, and one or two other friends of Marie's have also acquired paintings, to please her; but she didn't realize what it was all about. The husband still less. But he is satisfied. Marie also. He has a mistress, a German woman who got a divorce for his sake and who has some money. She adores Paris. She is pretty, and Marie, who is quite pleased, says: "My husband has taste." She sends flowers to the girl friend. Yesterday a lamp fell on Marie's dog, a Tonkinese, and he had to be killed. Marie was absolutely shattered by it. She was working on a portrait of the niece of Governor Fuller of Boston; the young girl had a big dog in her arms which the painter had put there. Today, under the stress of emotion, she removed this dog and replaced it with her Tonkinese.

April 30 / On Soutine

Dimier, Jr., knows him well. He met him at Zborowsky's, with whom the artist has now fallen out; it was this dealer who discovered him and enabled him to make a living. Dimier looks on Soutine as a savage, a rustic savage. At one time they used to go out walking a great deal together. One day, passing a butcher shop, Soutine bought an entire ox for 4,000 francs, a still life for 4,000 francs. The butcher, accustomed to supplying his meat piecemeal, had never seen anything like this. Soutine had the animal delivered to his studio and painted it twice, on Dimier's canvases, and then let it rot, to the great scandal of the neighbors, who were bothered by suspicious odors. Soutine himself kept well away from his studio. It smelled of death, of carrion. Soutine was nowhere to be found. In the end the City of Paris Health Service had to be called in to remove the putrefying mass.

Soutine is at present in a château in Burgundy. When he is invited to a fairly elegant household, his joy is almost delirious.

May 31 / Georges Aubry

Someone else writing a journal which should be of interest. He knew all the painters and literary figures of his generation when they were impoverished. He bought Utrillos for five francs (twenty-five of today's francs), he sold them for nine, and even then would throw in some molding costing him one franc fifty. He made most on Picasso, as he sold for fifteen francs the canvas for which he had paid him eight.

He asked me if he should publish his journal; he was afraid of scandal but said it would be thrilling all the same. I advised him to continue writing, although in my view the great period of his journal is over, as Aubry has become a bourgeois, living in the country and scarcely seeing his friends any more. He is, however, still on very friendly terms with Picasso. One day he went to an exhibition with him where a Dunoyer de Segonzac was being shown, and the artist knocked his stick on the four corners of the canvas, saying: "It makes the same sound everywhere, it's provincial band music."

We also talked of literature. Aubry said to me that Montherlant is the author of the day, which is also my view. The writer has been going through a terrible crisis for two years. He has burned everything in his apartment—his books, manuscripts, art objects, pictures, and, I believe Aubry said, even his furniture.

June 1 / Mauny dines with us

"It's no longer possible," he said, "to organize exhibitions in Paris; there are too many galleries; people haven't time to see one in ten. Then the dealers only want to show what you've done in the past year. The rest isn't worth anything to them, as it's no longer in fashion." He has been to Doucet's and seen his new modern setting, done entirely by Legrain the bookbinder. He insists that he is indeed a great decorator, that he stands for the hopes and tastes of the younger generation. Mauny is crazy about him. He is equally impressed by the Doucet Collection. No one knew how to select the way he did. He is bequeathing a Douanier Rousseau to the Louvre. The Louvre has turned down his Picasso, which must be the most beautiful in the world. At the Louvre, at the Luxembourg, no one in the official world wants to understand Picasso. He is a marked man. A new group, a society, has been formed to get the moderns into the Louvre and not repeat the errors of yesteryear, but the first purchases have been deplorable, except for the Matisse which the artist donated himself. Mauny swears only by Picasso, one of the greatest masters, he says, that the world has seen. The Spaniard may do three pictures in a day. Mauny must be exaggerating. At all events, his work is prodigious, and goes on by night with electric reflectors. Mauny spent two hours in Nice with Matisse, whom he ranks very high. Matisse, whose canvases appear to be only rapid sketches, works on them for days without any let-up. Just now he is absorbed in sculpture. Mauny has seen him mold clay and swears that he is the greatest modern sculptor. He gets up very early and models until eleven; then practices sports, then lunches; and in the afternoon he paints. He surrounds himself with antique and modern fabrics, will put a Coptic fragment beside one of his canvases and derive inspiration from its color harmonies. His love of color is consuming. He draws and paints from a model. His eternal odalisque of these recent years is a Basque woman.

June 2 / Armand and Marie Laurencin

The other day Armand was at Princess Murat's, who said to him: "You who are close to Marie, try to find out who her Argentine is. It won't last. That's how it is with Marie. He has a Rolls, which appeals to her. It's an amusing story, that's all." Armand told us that at the time he didn't find the story amusing and he demanded explanations of Marie, who replied: "But the Argentine is you. Last year when I was taking the waters in Normandy, you came for me and we went by taxi to Argentan, from there to Evreux by train, from there to Trouville by taxi, from Trouville to Le Havre in a boat, from Le Havre to Dieppe in a taxi as far as Dr. Gosset's, at whose door you left me. Asked how I had come, I lost my head a bit, I felt I'd look a fool if I described our silly means of transport, and I invented the Argentine with the Rolls Royce. I was looked on as a greater artist. It was good for my painting."

June 12 / Mintchine

This painter is a genius. I have fifty-four of his canvases, many very uneven. But when they bring me high prices, I shall exchange two or three mediocre canvases for one good one. Some are marvelous. They must have cost me around 70,000 francs. Mme Manteau, who sells them, was talking to me of the artist's conscience and the intensity of his emotions. When he starts painting, he is more absorbed in the subject than in the painting. In Toulon last summer he did vagabonds, which I like rather less, as they resemble Cézanne's figures, but he prefers them. As he studied his models, he thought only of them and their life. He told himself that it was beautiful to be a vagabond, to sleep in a thousand places, to have the open road to oneself, to belong to no one and have nobody as one's slave. He painted, and on his canvas he no longer saw his vagabonds. If he paints a flower, he thinks of nothing but the flower and is lost in a reverie, a reverie with a flower.

When he saw Soutine's ox at a dealer's, he turned pale, remained in front of it for ten minutes without saying a word, then left, arrived at the Manteaus' after a quarter of an hour and said to them: "Soutine has robbed me." "He has robbed you? How has he robbed you?" "He has robbed me of something I shall never again be able to do." For three days in Montparnasse he was so haggard that his friends thought him demented. It was admiration.

Forain

I met him on his doorstep and talked to him of the impressionists. He knew very little of them and admitted that at the time he didn't understand them. He said this: "It is because I started as a sculptor that I love solidity, foundation, whites and blacks, and I don't understand subtleties of color. I've never even tried them."

I told him that Monet didn't always recognize his canvases, and he talked to me of Hoschedé, the fellow whose wife Monet married. "He was a generous man," he said. "All the artists, good and bad, used to go to him in the country on Sunday, and he bought from them all. It was very gay. In the summer we even used to go and stay near his estate. One day it was given out that he had disappeared; he was well liked, we were worried, and then too he owed us money: two hundred francs to

Sisley, sixty to me. In those days you didn't live badly on such sums. He returned, but he was ruined; his wife had some money, which remained to them after the bankruptcy. So Monet married her and she supported the whole family, her husband included. It was in the following ten years that Monet, safe from want, was able to devote himself to the most interesting and useful research into the art of color."

Forain used to meet Renoir mostly in a Montparnasse grocery, and he describes him as a man who, when he was thinking, always pushed up his left nostril with the index finger of his left hand. This is his sole recollection of the painter. It's little enough.

June 21 / In England

I have just returned after having spent a week there. I've bought two marvelous Hubert Roberts and a delicious little Pater. England is showing real taste for modern art. Bignou of Paris has some marvelous impressionist pictures on exhibit at the Lefebvre Gallery.

Mintchine in person

I met him in the Alice Manteau Gallery; he was with his wife and their baby girl, whom they wanted to show to the dealer. He has painted her often and she is very much like her portraits; she has a little disk of a face. He is terribly Slavic, with the winding, Asiatic lines of his eyes. His nose protrudes, the nose of a tamed eagle. He must stand five foot three, he is thin, dressed in gray and very neat. His upper lip caps the other like a penthouse roof. I imagined him so wretched that I was astonished to find myself confronted with this man who is not at all lacking in gaiety. He was playing like a boy with the child! His wife, tiny and thin, looks like some Turkish girl born under the Wailing Wall in Jerusalem and has a perpetually astonished air. Just now the first Mintchine exhibition is being held in the gallery. I showed him the pictures I have bought like flowers in a florist's shop window: a pink house, a green house, *The Cathedral of Paris*. He speaks French very badly, chewing his words to the point of indigestion. He tells me he worked on that cathedral for a fortnight without stopping, that it gave him unimaginable trouble, that *The Cathedral of Paris* is a ship, that any cathedral is a bridge, a bridge leading to heaven. He added that he is very religious. There is a bridge,

ar to the right, in his picture, leading toward the cathedral, and there is
nother on the left, this one ascending to the sky.

At this point I took Mintchine off in my auto, stopped in front of
he cathedral itself, and said: "No one has ever rendered the Gothic
athedral because no one has rendered its weight, no one has understood
he immensity of its weight. Look how weighty it is, look at the way it
its, look at its base; it is as heavy above as below, except for the towers,
s they are of a later period. So long as you, Mintchine, do not render
his weight, you will fail, like Claude Monet, like Utrillo." Mintchine
ointed out how tiny, how Lilliputian, the people are against the portal.
had never noticed this, and was startled at the discovery. He asked me
f he ought to paint them, as no one would ever believe that they were so
ittle. I could not reply. We returned to Alice Manteau's, he placed him-
elf before his picture *The Cathedral* and at once hit on the least well
ainted part; he hadn't known how to shore up the stones; and he was
ully aware of this. He is leaving for the Auvergne, as he has been hear-
ng about the red soil. He asked me if the churches in Italy were as
eautiful as our cathedrals. I told him that they weren't, because they
vere less solid. He wanted to know if he was making progress and I
eplied that his progress was quite marked even within six months and
hat his flowers were best. They were of less interest to him, he said,
ecause they were easier, too easy, and did not entail any deep study.

une 27 / On Mintchine

Mme Manteau told me that the criticisms I offered the painter
ave made a strong impression on him. "Before," he said, "I didn't
nderstand stone, not the union of stone and earth, nor their solidity;
ow I shall try to capture stone." He is leaving on a two-month trip.

uly 1 / Fénéon

I was taken by Zarraga to visit him with Malvina Hoffman. He is
ll repose. But what a fighter! Painters strive to build something, but
hey don't lead the battle; they love art too well and money too little. It
s the Fénéons who fight for them. He discovered Seurat, Cézanne,
Gauguin, Picasso. He has an incalculable number of studies by the late
Seurat, proclaimed in 1929 the greatest painter of the year. When I

mentioned Seurat to him, he said he knew him very little, the man worked so much that his friends didn't disturb him. Zarraga will shortly be telling me that Fénéon was an intimate friend of the artist. Looking at these sketches of Seurat's, massive as they are, one wonders how he could have invented pointillism. Fénéon lives in a tiny apartment in Montmartre. His wife asserts that all these pictures bore her. She reminds me of a clergyman's daughter who, tired of sermons, turns chorus girl. Fénéon's politics were red; at one time he was said to be an anarchist. He was a radical in art, and that's why he has on his walls works to the tune of several million, which have made a petit bourgeois of him.

July 16 / Legrain is dead

It is a catastrophe for French art. He was forty. He had started as a bookbinder, then had taken up decoration. It is said that the room he designed for Doucet is a sheer masterpiece. After that effort it was felt that he would lead French art toward new goals. I knew him. Some time before the war he did a design for me for a little book by Maurice Barrès, as an inset. His work was then quite average. I have two beautiful bindings by him: part of the Anatole France manuscript, *Monsieur Bergeret in Paris,* and part of the manuscript of *Voyage to the Orient* by Lamartine. It was Daurat, the modernistic goldsmith, who gave me the news: he was shattered by it.

Mintchine

Mme Alice Manteau showed me a letter dated from Toulon, where the couple have gone with their little girl Irène. The Auvergne didn't inspire the artist and he has made for Toulon, where he painted last year.

NOTEBOOK 18

July 23, 1929–January 15, 1930

July 23

I am leaving this evening for Florence to spend two or three days with Leon Schinasi, an American collector who bought the Fra Filippo Lippi of the Carl Hamilton Collection at public auction the other day in New York for about $120,000.

July 24 / Pisa

The train passes in a semicircle around its three monuments, and from the window I tried without success to analyze my emotions. What a vanguard to Florence is Pisa—compact, scaled down, and alert! Pisa doesn't display banners, nor does she sound trumpets. Pisa is the jewel of the ancients, rich as they were.

July 25 / Florence

I am staying at the Excelsior Hotel. My window overlooks the Arno and frames the *Chiesa* in its entirety.

I can see the whole church from my window, I hold Florence in a frame, a frame which I cannot displace, which keeps me from stirring, as a pace to right or left would carry off my dream, substituting reality. This is Florence: this frame in which dream and reality are secured with remarkable permanence in studied angles, in a cruel immutability. In Florence everything must be seen from a certain point. Even the countryside outside it. Florence imposes itself on its beholder; it commands. Those who do not understand her do not wish to obey. Let them buy postcards.

July 25 / Donatello

Youthful St. John the Baptist, Donatello has made an old man of you. Although you have not, like your namesake, met a Salome, the artist has devoured you with the same essence; and impassioned young women, looking at you at the Bargello, must feel the same desire as men who, before the image of Mary Magdalene, are touched with regret, erotic regret; they love her only before her conversion, when they might have possessed her; they envy the vulgar lovers of this mistress singled out by Christ, she who exists only through Him. The youthful St. John the Baptist is indeed the best morsel at the feast, he too denies himself, and that's why Donatello has made an old man of him; but with a young, hale, slender body with the ligaments flowering from the bone, and all his bones like armor. This body, incomplete from within, would need only an embrace to blossom out; but that embrace will never come to this young madman who's too much in love with the spirit of wisdom. His intellect bursts forth, and it is wretchedness; his translucent flesh is burnt by the furnace in his skull, that plate of red-hot iron. He is too intelligent and bears on his face too many griefs to come, but he does not deserve them, this young shepherd, as every animal in his flock would crush him like young grass. He does not ask for pity, as he is suffering for his beasts. His pace is decided.

July 25 / "Spring"

Every time I spend two or three days in Florence, I can speak of nothing but this sublime painting! This time I have looked only at the flowers strewn on the ground, and their perfume has impressed itself on my mind. This picture is the spell the Renaissance has cast on the world, to be served for all eternity with bended knee and hands clasped on high.

Jealous, violent goddess who gives herself to all passers-by. Their tremor returns unto her, impassioned sorceress. I hate the Renaissance for holding me under its sway. Why lose oneself in the inaccessible!

July 29 / Vacation

We left by car with the three children, in a new Cadillac. We spent the night at Dijon.

August 18 / On Lake Como

The cypresses along the shore of this lake are masts grounded in the soil, masts with no further need of their boats; their lost hulls have been drawn away to extinction by the drifting hearts of the millions of lovers who have come to take refuge under the iron hand of hope. She brought into being this countryside as lacking in relief as is the desire it expresses.

August 21 / On Dunoyer de Segonzac and Marie Laurencin

I have had to come back on business. I am staying at the Hôtel Trianon in Versailles and Armand came to have dinner with me. This morning he had a visit from Dunoyer, who is going to the United States, invited by the Carnegie Institute to sit on their jury. He is pleased to have the opportunity of studying the country, but he isn't going there to sell. "He's a man of the soil," Armand said to me, "like his friends Marchand and Lotiron, who although they're also members of the Paris school, constitute as solid a group as a French village. And they don't understand the subtleties of a Picasso, a Matisse, a Braque, a Marie Laurencin; they're not a clan in the full sense, but they have ancestral ways of thinking, of expressing themselves, and they are profoundly opposed to those other artists, there is no love lost there; they don't understand one another."

A conversation with de Segonzac is always interesting. He says that it's a frightful thing for an artist to have a dealer; it's horrible to have someone pushing you to produce at any cost. He stays with Marseille because he is a small dealer who wouldn't dare try to impose a formula on him, not even the size of a canvas. Dunoyer does fifty drawings, then a painting—fifty drawings in two months; then it doesn't take very long to do the picture, as he lives on the drawings. But he says tha[t] the painters who paint to order for the big dealers ("to order"—that'[s] got a taint of the brothel about it) do one drawing and fifty canvases.

August 30 / Wagram Collection

This marvelous collection has just been bought by the Knoedlers. The prince, of whom I spoke in 1918, was killed in the war. When h[e] acquired these pictures from Bernheim Brothers, at high prices for th[e] time (but I must say they are masterpieces), he came to believe that th[e] dealers had swindled him; he brought charges against them, and for [a] while it looked as if they would land in prison. What! To go to jail fo[r] having sold 30 Courbets, 50 Renoirs, 47 Van Goghs, 28 Cézannes, 4[0] Monets, 26 Sisleys, 20 Pissarros, 10 Puvis de Chavannes, 11 Degas, 1[2] Manets! I take these figures from the memoirs of his sister, Mme d[e] Gramont. The Bernheims were acquitted and began yelling that th[e] government owed them reparation, i.e, the *Légion d'honneur*. The gov[-] ernment probably did owe it to them, as it gave it to them. The prince'[s] sister inherited the collection and has sold it, for perhaps twenty-five times more than it cost.

September 10 / Marie Laurencin

She always talks like this about her husband: "I'll bequeath him my canvases on condition that he sell them; he loves drink and he'l[l] think of me when he's drinking. He had forgotten me after three months of marriage. Men aren't faithful to me. People talk of how I threw Apollinaire out, yes, I shut my door on him and have been at- tacked for it. He adored me, he loved only me; it's true that he suffered frightfully, but what people didn't understand is that I was twenty-five and he was sleeping with all the women, and at twenty-five you don't stand for that, even from a poet! Ah, today I'd see life differently. For instance, I'd marry well, I'd have to have a man who makes money; I couldn't live with someone I was supporting. I'd also want an older man to care for me; and he'd have to leave me alone on days when I felt a need of repose."

September 12 / I buy a Soutine from Zborowsky for 32,000 francs

It's the portrait of a poetess, a Polish woman. It is marvelous, a masterpiece. This evening I placed it beside some portraits by Mintchine; they pale into nonexistence; their shadows are too dark, the flesh lacks blood, the bone structure is neither deep nor on the surface, as in great works. I know quite well that Mintchine hasn't yet studied the portrait. When I place a large and beautiful still life by the latter beside the Soutine portrait, certain parts start to blend, especially the backgrounds. My poetess is adorable.

September 18

In Geneva with my wife, en route for Rolle, where we are taking our second son, Pierre, who is entering the Rosey School.

September 19

Mintchine is still in Toulon and has sent several canvases: one of them depicts a man with a bottle seated among large rocks. I've bought it. This picture will be shown in the Salon d'Automne. I also took a canvas depicting only rocks with beautiful red colorations. I don't care for a view of the port of Toulon, barred by an enormous steamer ugly as a German toy. And he has painted some curious canvases with vines looming rather gigantic in the foreground; on one of these a town perched like an eagle's nest can be glimpsed very far off. I prefer a little vine stalk, very convincingly knotted, a labor of love. He has produced less this summer, but has lingered over his work. Mme Manteau tells me that Mintchine has greatly profited by my counsels in his study of stone; indeed, his rock has a remarkable feeling of weight. The artist will remain in Toulon until October.

October 7 / Isadora Duncan

Aubry made me read her memoirs. They're prodigious and in miniature they're like the memoirs of Casanova. What a frenetic scene: Isadora, a virgin, meets Rodin, who pants around her like a faun, feverish and possessed, pressing every square inch of her flesh. Then later, the eternal regret of this woman at not having given the colossus that flesh to crush, her flesh which had since known the ardent embraces of so many.

Aubry relates that the sculptor's sensuality was so keen that in the course of a conversation his hands would caress and crush every breast and phallus within reach.

October 16 / On Soutine

My brother-in-law Ernest, who was crazy about my picture, had the luck to find a sketch for it for which he paid 22,000 francs, but it wasn't signed; he delegated Armand and the dealer who had sold it to him to ask the artist to affix his signature and bring it to Duveen Brothers in the Place Vendôme, which he did. But in repainting it, he literally destroyed it because he no longer liked it. He said so to Armand, who replied: "You're a lunatic." When Armand told me this story on the phone, I replied: "It's you who are the lunatic to have sent Soutine the canvas, when everyone knows how many canvases he destroys—like so many masters: Degas used to do it. Monet would ask me for twenty-four hours to sign a canvas, and I'd take it off at once for fear that next day he wouldn't hand it over to me." Soutine talks of replacing the work, but Ernest adored that charming head and is afraid of receiving one of the monstrously ugly ones the artist takes delight in painting. Armand has spoken to Soutine about my picture, he wants to see it again and will be here tomorrow morning.

October 17 / Soutine here

A clumsy man. A singsong voice rising from deep to shrill. The flattened face of a muzhik; his nose comes out in a rectangular cube and his nostrils move like wings; large sensual lips that speak as fish breathe out of water, with the same rapid tragic beating. He seems always to be looking into the air, the way large dogs do.

I have hung his picture very high, for fear that he might damage it; and there he was telling me that it was pilfered from him and enlarged, and that the hands are fake. The hands are in fact very poor. He told me that there are people out to harm him, that Pierre, on the rue de Seine, has bought a fake Soutine for 80,000 francs, that a rumor is going around that since he can be imitated he can't be painting too well now. Who are the forgers? They must be found. Who is this recanvaser who finishes his pictures?

He talked on in this way, rather unconvincingly; he didn't seem very anxious to find the guilty parties—he could lodge a complaint if he wanted to. He asked my permission to take the canvas and I replied: "You are too dangerous." He assured me that it was with the intention of improving Ernest's picture that he ruined it, he didn't mean to destroy it.

When the artist was calmer, I took down my picture; but I asked my secretary, Miss Philipps, to be present, with orders not to leave the canvas if I were to be called into another room. He swore that the hands were fake, and they must be, for he criticized the glaring defects marvelously. I authorized him to remove them, but he would have to do that in my presence. When I went to get the turpentine, I was told that Dimier was in the small drawing room; I went to him, explained the situation, and asked his opinion. He could not reply, of course, not having seen the picture, but he told me something unheard-of, that very often it is his best canvases that Soutine lacerates, so that the dealers may recanvas them, as after the recanvasings they are more beautiful than he could make them.

On my picture I had indeed noticed mysterious strokes which I could explain only as the work of a knife, but when Soutine repeated that the canvas had been added to, I contradicted him, assuring him that I knew all about it, as it is a common practice with old pictures, and that he was mistaken; whereupon he agreed that it hadn't been enlarged.

When the conversation touched on the unevenness in quality of canvases by the great painters, he declared that only two Rembrandts moved him in the great Dutch exhibition in London this year, that what is called unevenness is only a relation between the works of the master, and that it's this alone which must be considered. I find his explanation remarkably powerful; it opens up a new horizon to criticism.

He took off his thick dirty coat and started to remove the fake hands, revealing in its entirety the blue of the bodice, which is like that of the background. He recalls having left a finger at the base of the canvas, there where he claimed to see an enlargement; a trace of it does exist. His cleaning has diminished the blue slightly, but he promised me to return with brushes and color.

Soutine told me that the woman was a Pole, a professional model. The canvas is unsigned.

Dimier told me that formerly he often used to ask Zborowsky to sign his canvases. Claude Monet's canvases were often signed by his daughter-in-law.

October 25 / On Soutine

Zborowsky came to see me. My canvas was indeed one of eight pilfered from Soutine by one of his friends. The painter had slashed them too, as he considered them poor, and he has since bought them all back from Paris dealers, which cost him about 40,000 francs. He would like to work over mine, but he shan't have it, and besides he now finds it quite satisfactory. He has never been as impressed by any house as by mine, which he calls "a palace." He didn't know what to say. Zborowsky had the picture at third hand. Soutine was so frightened by that band of crooks, his so-called friends, that he's fallen back into the arms of Zborowsky; the latter told me that the painter destroyed Ernest Duveen's canvas quite intentionally.

The Pellerin Collection

This man who owned so many Cézannes is dead. Three of them, which are said to be very fine, he has left to the Louvre. Is the family going to sell? I've let it be known that I am a prospective purchaser of the collection.

On Marie Laurencin

I hadn't seen Armand for a long time. Marie is furious with Rosenberg: he paid her 7,000 francs for a canvas that he sold to Professor Gosset for 50,000 francs.

Today she painted a water color, a woman in the guise of a fury, with black hair streaming up; and when Armand asked her what it represented, she replied: "A woman who isn't afraid of Rosenberg."

She has begun to get free of him, and sells to various dealers who come to see her. Rosenberg, livid, has spoken to her like a warring general: "You are selling to my enemies."

October 28 / The market for modern paintings

The dealers would have made up a combine of 60 million to buy the Pellerin Collection, which should be worth 80 million. There should be about 120 pictures.

Bardac saw the playwright Bernstein last night in a dance hall where he spends every evening. "For 25 million," the writer said, "I'd sell my collection."

It is perhaps worth 5 or 6 million. Alphonse Kann also wants to sell his moderns.

Othon Friesz

I met him at Georges Bernheim's. He must be fifty-one. He loves antique furniture in modern settings.

He is a born painter and yet has done little beyond the good average; his oil too much resembles the fresco and lacks transparency, fluidity. But what an agreeable face he has! It is full of laughter, despite heavy eyelids and jagged-edged teeth, khaki-colored and pressed like seeds one against another. The head of a modern Fragonard, whose waving locks seem to prolong the jiggle of his laughter. He is strong, bursting with health. He arrived the day before from the south and was still wearing a lightweight suit.

October 29 / On Soutine

An artist by the name of Cheval, laureate of the Casa Vélasquez and a friend of Soutine's, was telling me how the latter went to a butcher to buy a calf's head to paint it, but he wanted to choose and explained to the butcher: "You do understand, I want a calf's head of distinction."

October 31 / Jacques Doucet is dead

This couturier was the great gentleman of our time, the Medici of our circumscribed age. More than fifteen years ago he was the first to see that our country was going to revolutionize the world with a new art form and he slammed the door on the eighteenth century, which, it is true, we had brought back into taste, but whose mission was over and done with. He sold his Fragonards and his Houdons, to buy Manets and Cézannes. His greatness goes beyond that, to his having, at sixty, fought on behalf of the artistic youth which was to lead France towards new honors.

November 1 / Marvelous water colors by Marie Laurencin in Armand's apartment

For the first time I can understand the infatuation for these little studies, a bit rapid, a bit facile, a shade fragile. He has two beautiful, even splendid drawings of La Fresnaye. A woman with a hat, resembling a Dürer. He has a fine picture by Marie which she calls *The Angels* and prefers above all others.

Marie is furious with Rosenberg, who informed her three days ago that because of the American crash he couldn't give her an increase. "He gives me raises like a maid," says she, "a hundred francs at a time. I told him: 'I need money, here's a Chanel coat that cost me 7,000 francs!' 'Don't order any more,' he replied. 'It isn't the moment.'" Marie telephoned Guillaume, who said to her, "You ought to have ordered yourself ten coats." At which she informed him: "I'll have two canvases for you next week." Armand assures me that what Rosenberg gives her just covers her current expenses. She has securities but doesn't understand anything about stocks and shares. She has Suez shares bought at 10,000 which rose to 25,000 but have recently dropped to 20,000. Armand told her so and she replied: "Those are fabrications of the newspapers."

November 2 / Jacques Doucet funeral

There were very few people at the church on the avenue de Neuilly. I marveled at it to Mme Jonas, who replied: "He was very old and scarcely any longer of use to anybody."

November 3 / At Théâtre de la Madeleine

Very bad play by Guitry, as always. But it's the first time I've seen valuable pictures hung on the set, four or five Renoirs and some Utrillos, at least a million franc's worth of canvases lent by Bernheim Brothers. How such advertisement cheapens art!

November 6 / On Soutine

Dimier tells me how, during a stay in Marseilles, the artist didn't wish to put up at a hotel but at a brothel, and Zborowsky offered him the finest in the city for twenty francs. But Soutine disappeared. Panic; the city was combed and he was discovered in a five-franc brothel, because he had felt quite ill at ease in the first.

Dimier added that Soutine and Toulouse-Lautrec have many points of resemblance, like this love of brothels. The latter would sometimes immure himself in one for a fortnight. His health was very delicate and it often happened that he fell ill there; it was the countess, his mother, who would go to fetch him.

Today, with Dimier and Kraemer, I have laid the foundation of an association to sell modern pictures.

November 7 / Picabia

I went into the Briant-Robert Gallery, where an exhibition of the painter is being held. He was there and the dealer introduced him to me. I was astounded to see that a revolutionary could be so plump, and I didn't conceal it from him but expressed myself in the following terms: "I've never seen such a rational sort of man in front of painting that seems so irrational." He replied that painting existed to express ideas, and that the same applied to color, that he didn't consider it a substance to be struggled with, it was a matter of knowing how to grind it, how to juxtapose. He has always considered that technical considerations are easy, that they do not even exist, that his works were as easy to do at sixteen or eighteen as they are today.

I left him. He was with friends; and I carried away a lasting image of this man, small, solid, plump even, the type of the Basque ball player, of a peasant from a village near a fashionable beach; with a rough, tanned skin; eyes round as clocks, whitening hair; a very established sort of man who turns out canvases in which an eye is displayed on a buttock, or a dolphin is entering a woman's mouth, or six pictures are superimposed on the same canvas, like a film registering six shots.

For twenty-five years he has not settled down. He uses a fine dark putty line, he has fluidity; it is unfortunate that he isn't disciplined. How could he be when his parents are Catalans and he was born in Paris! Horrible accident! His painting feels the effects of it.

November 9 / Mintchine

He had been to lunch nearby at Deydier's, with his wife and little girl, who came to see me with him. He stayed from two to four and wanted me to talk all the time; he wouldn't even let Deydier interrupt. I gave him my point of view on what I call beauty in the art of painting, and he said to me on leaving: "You are the person who will have had the greatest influence on my art." I was flattered by this. He reminded me of our walk before the Cathedral of Paris and said that he had been thinking all summer of our conversation. I said I have noticed, he really has given precise weight to some of his rocks. He is terribly anxious and asks himself how this blessing could have come to him, to have the makings of a great painter and perhaps be called to a high destiny! He is assailed by doubts about his own talent. He is immensely troubled by his ignorance of painting technique, and he doesn't know where to learn it. I assured him that it was a lost art, that Rubens was probably the last painter after the primitives who had known it, and supremely. We decided to go to the Louvre together. He didn't like my *Polish Woman* by Soutine, but he did not say why. I placed two of his canvases, *Field of Tomatoes* and the *Fortifications of Toulon*, near my lovely Derain, a beautiful sunlit pathway in the Midi, and showed him that he hadn't yet acquired fluidity, that his shadows still lacked transparency, that badly painted parts alternated with better ones; one feels that he hasn't yet got full possession of his abilities, like a tennis player or a golfer who must concentrate on the position of his feet, legs, knees, forearm, elbow, and each individual finger—all at the same time—and who always forgets something anyway.

He accepted all my criticisms, almost with joy in his heart. He greatly admired my Monets and especially *The Pink Boat*. Although he admires the ancients, he finds ancient painting sad. He told me that his constant preoccupation, when he paints, is much more to give life than to represent an object. To paint a tree is to paint a corner of nature, to put it on the canvas is to isolate it and give it an immense place, whereas in the vastness of nature it is such a little thing; the tree takes on value through what it receives from its environment, by direct or indirect reflections, near or far off; from a color projected by the shadow of a distant hill or by a wide green or yellow field near at hand.

These aren't the exact words used by Mintchine, who has a certain difficulty in explaining and expressing himself, but this is what he was thinking.

He saw a *Saint* in my house, a red polychrome, Pisan, and he would love to paint it. I gave him a piece of eighteenth-century red vel-

et with which he was very pleased. Deydier asserted that art was nature
embellished by the artist, and Mintchine replied: "Perhaps not."

The Saint-Hubert

My wife hunted today with the James de Rothschild party. She
tells me: "I don't understand this blessing of the pack." I replied: "But
the dogs do!"

November 12 / On Soutine

Kraemer has told me that one of his friends, who owns a Soutine,
is bringing a suit against the artist because he claims that the picture is
not by him. The truth is, he just doesn't like it.

Henner used to authenticate fake Henners because he didn't
want to admit that he could be imitated.

November 13 / At Robert de Rothschild's

I have viewed with pleasure the two full-length Rembrandts that
Marcel Proust so longed to know, but without the presence of the horrible heads of the baron's father and mother. What would he have said of
Robert's head? The *Standard Bearer* of Rembrandt, if I may say so, is a
fine Hals.

November 14

Georges-Henri Rivière is brilliantly reorangizing the ethnographic
museum of the Trocadéro, neglected for thirty years. He took me
through it.

He told me that André Masson, whom I don't know, is a great
painter and that the sculptor Giacometti is great too.

November 16 / Weight and beauty

A mining engineer, Goetz Philippi, of English origin, came to see
me to ask me for an opinion on two bad pictures; I questioned him
about the weight of metals, with a view to the documentation of my
theory: the relation between weight and beauty, which are perhaps one
and the same thing, like taste. An apple falls from the tree at the instant
it attains its maximum weight, and that's also the instant when it should

be eaten. Of two apples from the same tree, of the same weight, with the same exposure to the sun, the smaller will be the better, as its density will be greater. If we measure the density of the wood of several apple trees, we discover that the densest gives the best fruit. I'll go further and say that where the earth is denser it will produce better apples. If I had melons on my property, I would weigh them before pulling them up and would eat them when they decreased in weight.

The engineer was a most interesting man. While he was speaking to me of the infinite beauty of nature, I showed him a remarkable German work, photographs of plants enlarged fifteen times, revealing the fantastic beauty of design of nature. He told me he could make as beautiful a book with enlargements of minerals. He had been all through Africa and spent the best years of his life with savages, because they were better than whites, he said—they had so few needs. He added: "They don't find us as remarkable as we suppose, and when they are superior to us, they know it. I was searching for a vein of gold that I had lost, and a savage found it for me, showing me a plant that was thrusting up just where it ran."

Mintchine

I've seen his three latest canvases at Alice Manteau's. A sort of concierge in a large blue apron, cutting apples. The painter still lacks solidity; certain parts, like the nose, are too sketchy. A life-size head is very hard to treat sketchily and demands a skill which Mintchine doesn't yet possess. Fragonard needed years of accumulated work to be able to do his beautiful heads in the Louvre. The sketch is more acceptable when it is small, and it is easier.

I much prefer the baby standing in its cradle, with flowers in a vase, a little trumpet with a bit of red thread. It is in a small touch like that that Mintchine reveals greatness.

I liked an extended view of Paris less, with a white house at a distance and a brick wall to the right with a flight of stairs. Two or three human figures beneath a heavy, rather leaden sky.

November 20 / I go in to Lucas Moreno's, the dealer on the rue de Provence

"We are the prey of German experts," he told me. "We've created them and they devour us. Mayer, the director at Munich, has arrived with Frau Heinemann and is no longer willing to recommend the wares of other dealers. The incorruptible Friedländer now has a mistress, and for her he acknowledges all the pictures he had previously condemned: Van Eycks, Gérard Davids, Memlings."

Mintchine

In the Manteaus' back room there is a collection of average Mintchines, really not a bad collection. I bought two good canvases for 5,500 francs: a child holding an apple, seated behind a table covered with a cloth on which two books rest, one open and the other shut and of a beautiful red. There is a fruit bowl full of gleaming apples. I also bought the child in the cradle, which I mentioned the other day; it is marvelous.

The painter Terechkovitch has started to pursue Mintchine with his hatred. He went to a collector's house to advise him not to buy from him, but our painter said: "We'll see where Mintchine is in five years."

The Manteaus mentioned that two Cézannes of his first period had been discovered by a young man in his father's attic, painted on bedspreads. When Cézanne's son was told about them, he remembered perfectly that his father had painted on bed covers. They are going to show them to me.

On my advice, these dealers have just signed a five-year contract with Mintchine, who also gives paintings to Deydier surreptitiously because he is an intimate friend, his little girl's godfather, and was the first to discover him, to buy from him, and give him the wherewithal to eat.

November 21 / Weight and beauty

An artist paints a woman in a silk dress beside a table covered with a common cotton cloth, and he takes as much trouble in painting the cotton as the silk. On his canvas the cotton will become as beautiful to behold as the finest silk. But why, when the difference between these two materials is so enormous in fact?

In America this year I gave a lecture at Mrs. Pendleton's and in a girls' high school: "How to Recognize Beauty in Art." I showed them a flat steel ruler and said to them: "If I ask all of you, here and now, to draw it for me, you'll all be able to do it. But which of you will present me with the most beautiful drawing? It will be she who gives me the impression of steel in her line, and that impression can't be given me if the weight of the steel is not put into the line. As in life, weight and matter are inseparable, so in art, weight and beauty are indivisible. The material, even the most ordinary, becomes beauty. It is beauty, it is truth, and there aren't two grades of truth. The cotton truth is the same as the silk truth. The nearer the artist approaches to the matter-weight verity, the more nearly he touches beauty. Chardin is all perfection, and if he paints a loaf of bread weighing eighteen ounces, it weighs eighteen ounces. A painter one degree inferior to Chardin will give me sixteen ounces, and so on. It is impossible for the artist to give me the exact weight if he doesn't paint the exact matter. While nature gives us matter and weight, art must give us the impression of matter and its weight."

November 27 / Dunoyer de Segonzac

Vincent, a painter who deals in old art, is a great admirer of the artist, and very sincere, and he said to me that since Dunoyer's arrival in the South of France, he has made no progress; the last exhibition at Devambez's disappointed his friends, it was porcelain. I replied to Vincent: "It's because Dunoyer wants to move on from the earth tradition to the air tradition." I explained the Zarraga theory to him, and he said that was it exactly, and that it opened up new horizons for him.

November 28 / De La Fresnaye

Countess d'Armancourt, lunching at our house, told me that this painter was a cousin of her sister's husband and that the artist's father, an ardent traditionalist, was enraged by the complete modernity of his son's art, and destroyed all the boxes of drawings at the Château de La Fresnaye.

December 10 / On a Cézanne

"Six months ago," Georges Bernheim told me, "I went to see Monet's daughter-in-law, who showed me a tiny picture by Cézanne, a canvas with apples; she told me that this work cost her two hundred francs (a thousand of today's francs). I asked her to name a price. She refused. I insisted. She then mentioned an enormous sum: 500,000 francs. I accepted like an idiot, because I wanted it. If I had bargained,

the woman wouldn't have said to me the other week: 'Ah, you did me
down!' "

December 13 / Modigliani

Yesterday Hessel bought a fake Modigliani for 55,000 francs, and
having swallowed it, he is obliged to shut his trap, as he is the expert at
the Hôtel Drouot. He is furious. It was Zborowsky who showed him his
mistake.

Ah! The experts!

"The Berlin dealers," Armand told me, "engaged the prettiest
typists in town to send to B., who was senile, to ask for certificates of
authentication." Armand saw the indisputable expert write scandalous
testimonials and was amazed to hear him say: "But I couldn't refuse, she
had such pretty legs." Armand saw him use sibylline language at times,
such as: "I've never seen such a Jan Steen."

The same comedy continues these days with his successor, Friedländer, who is madly in love with a dealer's wife. If she slept with him,
it would be quickly finished, so she keeps her garters fastened. On
the basis of such certificates, American collections are formed!

The writer A. Flament has invited four women to lunch tomorrow, four queens: the queen of painting, Marie Laurencin; the queen of
letters, Colette; the queen of the theater, Valentine Tessier; the queen
of fashion, Chanel. Four women who never lunch out; but Colette said:
"I'll come for Marie Laurencin." Marie Laurencin said: "I'll come for
Colette." Tessier and Chanel each said: "I'll come for the three of
them."

December 17 / Mintchine

He came in to the Manteaus' with a very fine eagle on a red
background and said to me: "When I painted it, I was thinking of you
the whole time: take the feather and give it its weight."

Just now Mintchine is working every morning on a nude done
from a model. "It's difficult, that," he said. He goes on painting, afterwards, till dark. Tomorrow I'm taking him to the Louvre, we've arranged
to meet at two o'clock; he asked me what I would be showing him and I

said: "Ancient Greek art; the *Peaches* and *Loaf of Bread* by Chardin *The Condottiere* by Antonello da Messina; Raphael's *Castiglione*, as ar example of a studied background; the Botticelli *Portrait of a Young Man*, believed to be Filippo Lippi." He wanted to know what I think of his latest picture, *The Child at the Puppet Show in Front of a Balcony* "It's the first time," I told him, "that you've given the impression of having studied a background." And he replied: "I studied the other backgrounds a lot, but I didn't succeed with them."

December 18 / Mintchine at the Louvre

I took him up to the ancient Greek statues, first showing him the Hera and then the most beautiful of the motion studies of athletes. I explained to him that our eye sees only masses (that may be why the discovery of anything infinitesimal is so slow) and details not at all, that the detail which we see is only an illusion, for if I look at the stuff of my coat the way an inspector would, I receive quite another impression of detail. The artist is concerned only with those masses which his eyes take in; the supreme art is the exact balance between the masses seen and the detail perceived. Too much detail causes the feeling of mass to be lost; too great a stress on mass eliminates the detail. The Hera, which is perhaps the most beautiful work of art in the Louvre, lets no detail be seen; its surface is prodigiously worked over, though we see this only by literally putting our noses up against it, and that's how the Greek artist was able to preserve the mass. In the athlete in motion, I showed him that every inch of flesh has its pigmentation; the buttocks have their weight, the skin of the belly is stretched and breathing, the arms fall with a weight accelerating down to the fist. Even the scrotum has its weight and its interior vitality. Looking at the Hera, he said: "It starts out like a column, it's matter transformed into life." He asked me if this was Greek art, if this was what it meant. Despite the legend of Galatea, I told him that Grecian art was something vaster, and I took him before the head of Athena, which to my eyes is above all the head of a warrior chief, an empire builder. I described to him the battle of Salamis, at which the Greeks dared to engage the colossal Persians, whom at a later date the Roman Empire itself dared not attack. Themistocles, commander of the Greek fleet, sent a spy to the enemy to tell them that the

Greek ships could escape through a channel the Persians didn't know about, which was true, and that the Persians ought to block it, which they did. When the enemy maneuver had been executed, Themistocles told his troops and sailors: "We are trapped like rats. We have no choice but to conquer or die." All this can be seen in this head of Athena: the sacrifice for their country, the abnegation, the courage under duress, the order within the city—all of it making up a vast part of the Greek sensibility. I showed Mintchine the Greek athlete and said: "It was with the athlete that Themistocles was able to conquer at Salamis, the athlete, in whom the chieftain could always find an instrument to carry out his decisions. And their mothers were built with the solidity of Hera, to give birth to these sturdy warriors and produce beings whose minds held the depths of the spirit."

I furthermore explained to Mintchine the union of the Greeks with nature; with the air, the vital element! I gave him a brief account of that religion of nature which Christianity has not encompassed, a religion which gave the Greek artist the power to make the air whirl tumultuously around each of his personages. Then we came to stand before the *Winged Victory of Samothrace*, which he knew already and adored. I pointed out to him the soft nap of the feathers, a nap of marble, then the bony structure of the wings and their interior armature. I insisted on the fact that the *Winged Victory* was nearly as immobile as the Hera, for grandeur resides in quasi-immobility; it is the whirling of the head wind that forces her into this attitude of flying-buttresslike resistance.

I took him up to Chardin's *Peaches*; he didn't like the colors, I don't know why; I suspect that he prefers his own red. I wanted him to look at Lépicié's *Child Drawing* beside it, a mediocre work because everything in it is too light. What a difference between that chair and the baby's chair in *The Blessing!* I had already explained to him that a masterpiece is a work which shows us the highest values of a race on the day the work is created. "France," I said to him, "comprised at that time 15 million men, 14 million of them like those whom Chardin painted; you, Mintchine, see these simple French interiors every day, and in them find the qualities of *The Blessing*, and that's why we are in front of a masterpiece. Fragonard, who showed only one side of France, doesn't attain the greatness of Chardin with his 14 million models. Now look at

Chardin's *La Pourvoyeuse*, and the loaf of bread she is holding, which is only an inch or so square and which none the less weighs several kilos; any baker would give you the exact weight of that loaf; and I promise you, the less great the artist, the less exactly he renders weight. Look at Chardin's candle standing amid the musical instruments; it's the best-painted part of this canvas since its substance and weight are exactly rendered." It was Mintchine who took me up to a Poussin; he rhapsodized over an Adam and Eve in the terrestrial Paradise, especially the woman, and he murmured that it was a fragment comparable to Da Vinci. We passed by French primitives and I stopped only in front of two panels, the Avignon Pietà, to make him note the mass represented in the donor, and the apparent suppression of detail, as in the swaddled baby with its milk-fed hands. He wanted to go to the Rembrandts, and was transfixed in front of the St. Matthew, remarking: "Rembrandt painted with white and then glazed over it. He couldn't possibly have done otherwise, he wouldn't have achieved his subtlety of tones. Look at the brush strokes all in one direction, one direction only, and so vigorous, then the glazed colors running in every direction. See the angel behind St. Matthew. There's an angel for you; he's ugly, but he is a man, he is intelligent; that's what an angel should be: intelligence and virility!"

Then we retraced our steps and paused before the Vermeer and one or two small Rembrandts. We returned by the large gallery, stopping before Rubens' *The Artist's Wife*, and here he could see how the artist prepared his backgrounds. Mintchine adores Tintoretto, and in a somewhat reddened woman with a child, he found the robust qualities of the Hera, that matron who gave her race its solidity.

We lingered before *La Gioconda*. Mintchine was full of contradictions and said: "It isn't the picture I was expecting. When you've waited for something for years and years, you want something more tremendous. And then I don't understand the picture. What is it? It's the photograph of an angel." When I pointed out the Mino da Fiesole in the Gustave Dreyfus Collection, he described the personage in one stroke: "What a politician!" He was pleased that I liked Tintoretto's *Paradise* and said: "Take away the personages, and the clouds remain, prodigious clouds, an immensity of clouds, a very paradise of clouds." I asked him whether he often went to the Louvre. Once a week. Did he feel he learned anything there? He said he did. I took him up to Raphael's *Castiglione* and declared that the background was one of the most beautiful in the world. "Yes, and it is insubstantial," he added. "It isn't a wall, it isn't stone, wood, or paper, it's nothing known to us and it's extraordinary. As for the man, he is so obviously an intellectual and has such finesse, such Jewish diplomacy." I had Mintchine pause before the Antonello da Messina and he said: "Above those qualities that you extol, substance and weight, there is light. I prefer Renoir and Cézanne to your Antonello da Messina; they would have put in the light which is lacking here." He had already said to me in the large gallery: "Dark backgrounds aren't for us any more; we shouldn't look for them; our rooms are bright. There was a time when people were placed near a window; in our time the dark background is a heresy." "Light has a weight of its own," I replied, "and is also a sensibility. The sensibility for light was perhaps as keen then in Venice as it is today with us, but what gives it more breadth in our time is that it is within everyone's reach." We came to stand in front of the portrait of Botticelli's young man, and Mintchine was both moved and astounded at the harmony of this troubled countenance. "This picture," I said to him, "is more beautiful than *The Condottiere*, because this young man more than the other represents the greatness of his country. It is the image of the Renaissance Italian, disturbed, melancholy in his joys and in his aristocracy, whereas *The Condottiere* represents force, surprise, cruelty." He said by way of conclusion: "I have still more to learn from Renoir, from Monet, from Cézanne. I've thought a lot about Cézanne." "I agree with you," I replied. "The painting of Rembrandt, of Poussin, was contained in Cézanne, but that of Cézanne is not yet in you, you are too close to it; it will be in our children by the miracle of ancestral memory."

December 21 / Arrival in London, with my wife, Ernest, and Pierre, from
    Switzerland
  Jean was waiting for us at his Aunt Eva's in Whitechurch.

December 23 / International Sportsmen Club
  For the first time I visited the club of which I am a founder. One

of these days we'll be seeing one in Paris. A swimming pool, an ice rink, a gymnasium, a tennis court; it's really very fine.

December 24 / The British Museum and the Kensington Museum

We went through them with Ernest, Pierre, and Jean. Ernest pointed out to me Persian objects, and immediately understood them, though they are a completely new art to him.

December 25 / Reflection

"In a tunnel," said my wife to her sister, "aren't you always afraid of being kissed?" "I'm not that optimistic," Eva replied.

December 27 / Fake Perronneau at the National Gallery

Since 1921 the National Gallery has been showing a fake picture which dazzles all visitors; everyone buys the postcard of it. It is the Perronneau called *Girl with Kitten*, given by Joseph Duveen in 1921. If museums didn't defend their fakes even more fiercely than private owners, it might be surprising that this pastel has been so long on the walls of a famous museum! But it is astonishing inasmuch as a few years later the gallery bought a superb Perronneau, the *Portrait of Madame Legrue*, an acquisition which would have been pointless if *Girl with Kitten* had possessed the qualities of the master. The comparison is all the easier since the two pastels are on the same panel.

Perronneau's great quality is that he draws his faces with a crayon point, a point that marks the trace of its passage everywhere in parallel lines as on the Legrue portrait, a method of working which is entirely missing in *Girl with Kitten*, which is treated only with the stump. Perronneau always highlights his faces with white, more accentuated on the nose and lips, whites which are in the portrait but not in the other picture.

Like all great artists, Perronneau marks the bone structure in a very pronounced way, it is marvelous in *Madame Legrue*; one can divine everywhere the skull beneath the skin, for the great artist knows as well as Houdon how to do it. No skull in *Girl with Kitten*, but a bone supporting her round, puffy chest, which is the most horrible part of the work. The poor little girl is like a deformed, unwanted child; her left shoulder is shrunken; Perronneau would have formed her delightfully. The hand is terrible, it isn't flesh but some transparent substance impossible to define; the index finger is trying to bend but looks like nothing so much as a hooked nail. As for the other fingers, which are bent, they are quite shapeless. The wrist, which is an exquisite thing in a child, seems padded like the arm of a stuffed doll. One of the cruelest details is the total absence of arm between shoulder and forearm under the stuff that the forger has made transparent. In the background, to the right, one can see a little flat brown spot, vaguely triangular; it appears that this is a chair on which the child is to be seated. Knowing Perronneau's decorative talents, one can fully appreciate the absurdity of this bit of cardboard.

The poor little girl has no nose; see how vibrant it is on the other pastel. Let us continue. Perronneau places his eyebrows with definiteness and gives them a magical life, as in *Madame Legrue*; but in *Girl with Kitten* they are drawn with the regularity of a compass, as are the eyes and lids, all uniformly rounded. In *Madame Legrue*, we have the living, sinuous quality and even the moisture at the rim of the eyelids. Moving back from the wall and looking at the two portraits together, we wonder at the consummate skill with which Perronneau lets the light fall on his people; it gives them strength while bathing them in an atmosphere of marvelous creaminess. *Girl with Kitten* is dusty, dust taking away the character, but something the forger always goes for, to give credence to the antiquity of the work. The clothes, with Perronneau, are drawn with the same care as the faces, with splendidly established planes; the silk cracks at its corners, as in *Madame Legrue*. It is difficult to find, even in a third-rate painter, material as badly drawn as in *Girl with Kitten*. The ribbon round the neck has no shape, none at all; the lights have the look of bits of white macaroni stuck on the blue. We must look at the ribbon on Madame Legrue's bodice with its beautiful lights, its beautiful transparencies, and also look at her fur, which is full of life. The bottom of the dress in the *Girl* is just a scribble. Note as well the right arm glimpsed between the cat and the bodice: it is a comical, nameless thing; it doesn't enter the sleeve.

Some of these points are not clearly visible in photographs. However, a rather common phenomenon, the lens shows us, on the one hand, qualities and, on the other, defects much more patently than we

see them when we are standing before the work itself—like the marvel
ously wrought hair in *Madame Legrue*; it waves and is alive, the ai
passes through it and stirs it, giving it a luminous, pleasing, fetching
intensity; while the hair in *Girl* has a dull aspect, no air circulates round
it, it is in heavy common tufts. What the photograph also shows u
better is the marvelous work in the background of *Madame Legrue*, a
background every inch of which is studied, whereas the other resemble
the dusty backcloth of a photographer.

We must also note the forged signature on *Girl*, shriveled, poor
hesitant; while Perronneau's signature is beautiful and decisive, like the
handwriting of a nobleman.

December 31 / Exhibition of Italian art

I went to the private viewing, accompanied by my niece Muriel
we skipped lunch and stayed for five hours. It is so vast that it would be
ridiculous to speak of it today.

January 1, 1930 / An unknown Pater in the National Gallery

In room XVIII, No. 4079—called here "School of Watteau." It is
a Pater, from his early days, the time when he was working with Watteau
I am acquainted with several of these, such as the one belonging to S. R
Bertron in New York.

January 5 / A new Houdon

A new Houdon has been discovered by M. Souffrice, a very able
middleman. He has shown it to me and there is no doubt. He has
learned that it is the *Portrait of Alembert*. He showed it to Giacometti
who doesn't know a great deal but recognized it.

January 8 / Marie Laurencin

Armand came for dinner. The luncheon of the four queens fell
through, as Colette was unable to come. Marie spent Christmas at Dr
Gosset's. Armand has just been to see her, and she was busy spreading
out furniture covers—pink ones at that.

January 9 / Mintchine

Yesterday I bought a nude by Mintchine for 3,500 francs; it is prodigious, a very vigorous woman, head lowered, drawing down the whole body, breasts pendant but full; there is a prodigious foreshortening of the head, and thick bushy hair thrusting up like a forest, and it's splendid.

Mintchine said: "To do a head or hands isn't all that much, with the rest of the body covered by clothing. Material is easy. But in a nude every square inch of flesh has to be studied."

January 11 / Mintchine in person at the Manteaus'

"I am glad, M. Gimpel, that you have the nude of my wife; I did it thinking of the athlete in motion, the Greek athlete you showed me at the Louvre. It isn't smooth, that marble, it's composed as if in thicknesses superimposed just like paint; it's fantastic. I tried that with my canvas, which is no smoother and whose surface, whose substance resembles stone. Now I am working on flowers. I used to think it easy, but the flower is lighted from the other side, always by transparency, and that's what is difficult."

January 15

I left this evening for America on the *Paris*, and without my wife, for I plan to stay only six weeks.

NOTEBOOK 19

January 16–December 20, 1930

January 16 / On the "Paris," two decks of which were recently burned

The company took advantage of this to make a new ship out of the old one. In the twenty-five years that I have been making this crossing, all the initiative in matters of comfort has been taken by the transatlantic liner. It has brought us the dining room with small tables, the first elevator, the newspaper by radio, the orchestra, the puppet show, the cinema, and above all modern art. It's the first time that a promenade deck has been well lit; one can read anywhere on it. There's another novelty: a stock-exchange hall; it's sad. The speculators turn their backs on the sea; they deserve it.

January 17 / On Italian art

I thought back to the London exhibition. I told myself that, allowed time to cool, my ideas on such a vast subject would clarify themselves. The great victor is Piero della Francesca, and the great vanquished are the Luinis, the Francias, the Boltraffios, the Ambrogio di Predis, the Lorenzo di Credis, the Pinturicchios, the Bronzinos. It is the French nineteenth century that has killed these painters, our portrait-

sts: Ingres, Corot, Manet, Renoir, Degas, Van Gogh, Delacroix, and
ven *The Fisherman* by Puvis de Chavannes. The exhibition is in chron-
logical order, the decadence accelerating swiftly from room to room, as
n the Trocadéro Museum the architecture and sculpture after the thir-
eenth century. It's tragic to behold.

Luini sometimes rises above this. And I feel moved to say: poor
otto, poor Cariani! These men don't hold up, beside a mask by La
Four, a painter who still awaits his great place in the sun. Because of the
aps, it is not a considered exhibition of Italian art. No Cimabue; the
Giotto is postcard size. Botticelli and Raphael have brought something
ew to pictorial art. We find here Botticelli's *The Birth of Venus*, and
is eternal insipid *Madonna and Child*, meant to milk your tears of love
or her. We have *La Derelitta*, which tears us apart; it's terrible to en-
lure, and I grit my teeth.

But the sad Botticelli of the National Gallery is missing. If ever I
vere harrowed by some frightful grief, I would go up to those panels, I
vould look at those people he painted and, seeing how much Botticelli
uffered, how much more he suffered than anyone whosoever because he
vas more sensitive, I would know that my grief could not equal his;
measuring my suffering against the excess of his, I would regain courage
n this terrible life. But Venus is born . . .

anuary 22 / The United States

I don't know if I am tired or lazy; it is very difficult for me to write
ere. What have I done this past week? Mauny was waiting for me at
he docks, he was very nice. He has had an exhibition at Jacques Selig-
nann's and has sold a considerable amount; it ended on Saturday. He
as had a thousand-dollar commission, a portrait of an aviator commis-
ioned by an admirer of the young man. He told me about the famous
eptember panic, comparable to the one caused by the Scottish financier
aw in Paris. Fortunes of a $100 million vanished in an hour in the
vhirlwind, shares falling from 4 to 1. The whole country had been spec-
lating, from the multimillionaire to the Negro. The women were more
renzied than the men, and often brought ruin on their households.
Many wives of former millionaires are earning their living by hard work
hese days. What is admirable is that they don't talk about it any more;

they wisecrack. Everyone's starting again. This attitude is a form of wealth as great as the other.[1]

On the day of the panic it was impossible to get a thousand dollars' cash on twenty thousand dollars' worth of jewels. A hundred thousand cars were for sale: but three months after the crash there are as many cars in the streets as before. The restaurants are full, the theaters too; it's astounding. The government has lowered taxes and the Ford Company has raised the salary of its workers. The antique dealers are starting to do business again; Wildenstein has sold the Fould Collection for $800,000, except for the pictures, to the Philadelphia Museum. It cost him $400,000. The Jacques Seligmanns have been selling for the past month. My clients seem disposed to buy. I suggested the Pellerin Collection to Mrs. John D. Rockefeller, who is very interested. The Pellerins are asking 120 million francs for it. I spent Monday evening with Mrs. Rockefeller. She has a superb pearl necklace, neither too long nor too large; there is none better. On her walls she has seven or eight primitives of the first rank, such as two French portraits, a man and a woman, heads of the kind of bourgeois who are invigorated by the country. She has a Holbein and a rather tired Piero della Francesca. You ascend her staircase between tapestries on the walls that are as beautiful as stained glass windows. She is interested in modern art and with several friends has founded a museum of modern art; the first exhibition consisted of Cézanne, Gauguin, Seurat; a splendid collection. The second was deplorable, with American painters. The third is very successful and is on at the moment. Picasso is predominant. The finest belongs to the Buffalo Museum: two standing women, who have the dignity of figures by Piero della Francesca. Derains, Matisses, Dunoyer de Segonzacs. Matisse will be coming on from Pittsburgh; his canvases are to be shown in the museum. Mauny claims that American painters are fiercely jealous of French artists. What will they be saying soon, in the face of the steep increase in prices which is on the way? It's hard to get $20,000 even for the most beautiful Picasso. Mrs. Rockefeller wants me to help her buy young masters; the Toledo Museum as well, and I don't know if I can work for both. There are few great living painters.

[1] As the crisis has lasted a number of years, this attitude has changed very much. (Note appended 1935.)

The train is at this moment carrying me toward Toledo. I stayed for two days in Philadelphia, where I went with Stettenheim, a New York collector. We saw the Widener Collection again, spoiled by too many English pictures. The Romney is deplorable, the Gainsborough deplorable, the Hoppner deplorable. The only two who knew how to paint were Raeburn and Reynolds. I'm not speaking of the nineteenth century, for Turner was a genius, and Constable too, now and then. Widener's Italian pictures, except for one or two, like his fantastic Bellini, are rather unfortunate. His two Vermeers are splendid, especially *The Tonkinese*. At the museum I again saw *Woman with a Lute*, which has always been attributed to Vermeer but which is quite a poor copy, probably eighteenth century. How could it ever be taken for an original?

I met Mr. Kimball, the director of the museum, who in four years has obtained millions of dollars for his museum.

January 25 / I am appointed adviser to the Toledo Museum for the purchase of living masters

The museum has bought a beautiful canvas by Goya, a bullfight. It is genuine, while the one in the Metropolitan Museum is by Lucas. The first is transparent and fluid: that's Goya's style; the other is daubed with an inkpot background. The museum has also bought a Clouet.

February 16 / In Boston, which I visited last Friday with Leon Schinasi and his wife

He is a person of feeling, and so is his wife. We lunched on Saturday at the Paul Sachses', and on Sunday with the Forbeses. Sachs and Forbes are directors of the Fogg Museum, an adjunct of Harvard University. They have just bought a Botticelli from Agnew for nothing, a mere $30,000, a Christ pronouncing a blessing; the Detroit Museum believed it had the original. Schinasi has just given me fifteen iridescent glasses for Toledo.

Bache and Erickson collections

If Bache lives another ten years, he will have a finer collection than Widener's, which would be easy to match, as fifteen splendid Rembrandts and five or six supreme Van Dycks, which are the backbone of

Widener's collection, could be found for Bache too. I don't believe in Bache's large Bellini, any more than in his Botticelli; his Dürer of Venice is poor. His Fra Filippo Lippi is doubtful; his Vermeer, a portrait, is by no one special. But the rest are superb: Bellinis, Holbeins, Memlings, Gérard Davids, Titians, Rembrandts, a Bouts, a Petrus Christus, a Roger Van der Weyden, Signorelli, Cosimo Tura. He has Fragonard's *Billet Doux*. But two days before, at Erickson's, I saw *The Woman Reading* by Fragonard, from the old Crosnier Collection, bought at his sale by Professor Tuffier, a canvas which I consider more beautiful than the first and which, being less well known, doesn't perhaps receive its due. Erickson, now there is a collector with some fine paintings—for example, *Aristotle Contemplating the Bust of Homer*,[2] from the Rudolph Kann Collection, profound if theatrical. Rembrandt was great enough to paint a man and show us the philosopher in him without having to introduce the bust of Homer. His mistake was above all in having placed the thinker's hand on the head of the Greek. A painter must never indulge in the theatrical if he wants to reach the heights. Erickson has a small head by Rembrandt, without bust, which is nearly as beautiful, and as philosophical in spirit as the *Homer*. The collector has bought a Crivelli from Joe Duveen for $350,000. That is madness, for Crivelli, after the manner of Perrault, who turns men into pumpkins, transforms the earth and its beings into lacework. His palace may well be a marvelous thing, but it's only decorative art. I owned the *Homer* in 1907, and I rediscover here an old picture of mine, Gainsborough's *Lady Eden*, which I had sold to John W. Simpson. There is a fine Titian, *Man with Falcon*, a Holbein of the familiar sort, and a vulgar Hals, of a fishmonger.

March 7 / On the "Ile-de-France"

A fine transatlantic crossing, but the paintings in the dining room are frightful. The general effect of the modern-art décor is very good.

March 19 / Marie Laurencin

Armand came to dinner, bringing a host of fresh anecdotes. "I

[2] This canvas was sold for 1,127,000,000 old francs in November 1961 at the Parke-Bernet Gallery in New York. (Editor's note.)

prefer cooking to painting," Marie told him, "for the results of the former do at least disappear." She doesn't like having her own paintings in the room where she is working, as they prevent her from renewing herself.

A paper, *Vu*, I believe, has just published photographs of Colette Willy, of Mme de Noailles, and of Marie, with the caption: "The three most famous women in France." The painter's comment was: "I was pleased, Armand, to see that those two women are older than I." F. Buisson, president of the Chamber, a tactless creature, thought to please her by flinging at her across the table: "Madame, your pictures are going up." On the other hand, an aviator told her that her paintings resembled what he sees from an airplane, and that pleased her greatly.

March 20 / Kisling

Here we have a painter who looks like his paintings, the color of a nice glass of hot chocolate. I got the impression that if he undressed he would have the body of his stocky models with broad creased folds of flesh. He has the round black eyes of his women, as sad as tormented birds. His conversation is that of a bouncer; he was telling me of his old drinking bouts in Montparnasse, when the police would pick him up and take him to the station house. There was even one night when he was arguing with his wife on the doorstep and a police officer hit him over the head from behind. Turning around, our painter laid him out with a terrible punch that broke the officer's jaw. He was hauled off to the station house in handcuffs, roughed up, put in the black maria, and kept in prison for three days. Six thousand francs settled the matter.

April 9 / Valentine Prax

She is beautiful. Her face is drawn with the precision bad painters bring to their portraits of pretty women. A mathematical regularity, an absolute balance between the two sides of the face. Her lips are like the fine wings on the feet of the god Mercury. Melancholy gray-blue eyes—gunmetal gray. She told me that she is thirty, and she hardly looks it. She is rather sturdy; a fine girl from the Mediterranean hills. Her manner reveals a hidden distress, but she is as gentle as the call of a child, and keeps her nerves in check with a will that has had is buffetings. She lives in Paris and no longer works. She suffers. At this juncture, life is hell for her in this house full of workmen, and dust coming in through every crack. She had about thirty canvases turned face to the wall and started by showing me flowers, which she treats very well; they're among her best things. She is married to a sculptor, Zadkine, and her figures are influenced by a nostalgia for snowy plains—does she know it? She speaks with fear, she has no voice. I had to chat with her for an hour to get a breath of animation out of her.

April 25 / At Baron Gourgaud's

Rather lordly, although he has married an American. He has some magnificent moderns, a beautiful *Harlequin* by Picasso and a life-size Douanier Rousseau as beautiful, he says, as Holbein's *Princess of Milan*.

Rouart and Degas

He came to see the portrait I have of his sister by Degas. She was eighteen at the time, he told me. I was astonished, I would have thought her to be forty. Degas was to do a big canvas of the Rouart family like the one of his own family in the Louvre and this portrait was a study for it. The work was never completed, as Mme Rouart died. Rouart still has the chair and the Egyptian statue, Old Empire, which one sees in the picture, and he informed me that a canvas to the right in this portrait is by Corot and that his brother owns it. He also told me that he posed for the portrait of a poet or a painter with his family, on the Place de la Concorde.

May 12 / Toledo Museum

My first purchases: a Picasso gouache, *The Blind Man*, which is fabulous: it is the last Christ (110,000 francs). A Bonnard. I find fault with him: although he came after the impressionists, he brought nothing new. However, mine is brilliant (114,000 francs). My friend Stettenheim of New York has given me the money for a turkey by Soutine— I've not seen a more beautiful one (40,000 francs)—and for a La Fresnaye, the portrait of the poet Mire (50,000 francs).

Picasso scandal

His mother has sold four hundred of his drawings for fifteen hundred pesetas to a Spaniard and an American, who have in turn sold them to Mme Zak, the painter's widow. A blue Picasso is among them and she passed it on to Georges Bernheim, who asked me 200,000 francs for it the other day. Picasso lodged a complaint and appeared at all the dealers, surrounded by police; Sûreté detectives, in fact, in plain clothes. The dealers, who have helped build his reputation and fortune, are furious.

June 23 / With the cubists

An interesting evening. The Baroness de Rebay was giving a farewell dinner. She had had an exhibition at Bernheim Brothers, which had some success. About twenty people were invited. I was seated next to Léger, the cubist, who is so much admired—he can hardly know why. These days it isn't always the artists who push themselves; they are thrust forward by an intangible, intellectual group. In Léger we have the good straightforward sort of man, in his fifties, very bourgeois, probably still given on occasion to singing a little song over dessert. His conviviality and masculine briskness must be responsible for his success as a painter. He doesn't even use pretty colors. He told me nothing of interest; to be sure, he had on his right a rather attractive woman, the wife of a German embassy attaché, to whom he was paying a good deal of attention. After dinner she tried giving something of herself to everyone, she was so eager to please, and that's unpleasant. I had Mme Cappiello on my left, the wife of the poster artist. She told me that she paints too. Grand and beautiful, she is a sensual but distinguished-looking Jewess, a sort of Latinized queen of Zion. Cappiello is Florentine and with the head of a small eagle which wasn't ever an eaglet. He hasn't found the means to renew his talent, but in his day he really did have a feeling for posters. He was just telling Le Corbusier that he preceded the cubists and heralded them. He claimed that he liked them very much. It is so unpopular these days not to adore them! Fénéon the critic was also present. I had a chat with Othon Friesz, who started by telling me the story of his life and why he paints boats—because he is a sailor's son, and so he loves the sea. The Frieszes were corsairs; grown rich on an English prize, they became shipowners, then their fortunes declined from generation to generation; his father was a captain of long standing, but reviled the sea when steam replaced the sail, and he set Othon against the profession.

Friesz is only a second-rate painter; I might even say, as in tennis, third-place, which is still honorable. His facileness made it seem that he had talent. Twenty years ago he painted as well as today. So many painters have talent at twenty-five or thirty, everything seems possible for them, but they don't advance one step—for example, Vlaminck. The critics can so easily be mistaken, and it's impossible to see ahead.

Dr. Reber from Lausanne was present this evening. He has, I believe, eighty Picassos; he is a modest, almost a timid, person. Le Corbusier the architect made an American woman jump by saying to her that New York ought to be blown up, that maybe the Americans do build big but it's of no account since they have no philosophy of building. She didn't understand. She was startled when he said that he has drawn up plans for a Great Paris with buildings two hundred stories high, but spaced out, interspersed with parks. She said it's a fine thing to be an architect, and he replied: "Being an architect is nothing; you have to be a poet. There has been much discussion about the qualities, the merits that an architect must possess. What he needs is to be a poet. It is sad that in our time you have to be more of an engineer than an architect, whereas in fact it is essential to be more of a poet than an engineer, more of a poet than an architect. Poet, poet, always to be a poet." And then Le Corbusier told me of his struggles, of the old guard who will have none of him, a redoubtable band who defeated him over the League of Nations, for which he wasn't able to obtain the Palace; he came in second, the competition was a joke; Briand didn't want him and had already made his choice. From the League of Nations the architect went on to speak of the next war, and he asserted that the only city that will be able to defend itself will be one with tall buildings, well-spaced, armored at the top, so that the people can take shelter in them, high up, away from gases. The Russians wanted an underground city. A mistake and an impossibility. Le Corbusier, who is perhaps not far from forty-five, has the air of a schoolboy in his first suit, hands in pockets, balancing himself. He deals in teasing paradoxes, and when he has struck, when he has carried your thoughts beyond the clouds or over the horizon, he pulls you sharply back. He is like lightning, which, having launched its spear, returns to its point of departure. He throws out a paradox and follows it up with a precise interpretation like this: "But Louis XIV was a revolutionary; he rejected everything and in many instances demolished everything he had inherited from his predecessors. When he created Versailles, it wasn't only new; it was modern, unlike anything ever before seen." Is Le Corbusier the greatest architect in the world? You wouldn't believe it from looking at his flat, nay, concave stomach. I spoke to him of Mrs. Rockefeller, and said I'd give him a note for her, as he is going to New York this year for the first time. "It was Rockefeller," he replied, "who ruined my project for the League of Nations; I had plans the cost of which beat all competitors, and he threw an enormous sum of money into the balance." Then, like Friesz, the architect embarked on the story of his life, which was all too soon interrupted by some intruder: "The Rockefellers, I don't know if they interest me; I'm a sort of adventurer, I catch life from day to day, and I've tried all the professions. I was in industry, commerce; I've tried everything, I started out from here, from nothing—zero point—and the way I stretch out my arm I thrust my line. I left school at twelve, so you can imagine. I've not gone through any school of architecture. In France you don't need a diploma to build." At this point the intruder showed up.

June 27 / Mintchine comes to see me

He was shaven and neat; I remarked on this and he told me that it was especially for me, that he'd come to say goodbye to me. I showed him his canvas that I had just bought from Manteau for the Toledo Museum. Three thousand francs. I then advised him to study the transparency of shadows, which is a failure of his. I brought out some ten Claude Monets; he saw my point and assured me that after each of our conversations he makes enormous progress. He is leaving for the Dordogne.

July 5 / Marie Laurencin

Armand had dinner here. "I could write a book on Marie," he said once again, "made up of sixty sayings a year. And they'd matter. She said to me yesterday: 'It's curious, when I begin a picture my women are girls to start with, but then they all become princesses.'" Apropos of a real princess, when Marie was redecorating her house, Armand gave her the address of his upholsterer; she in turn recommended him to Princess Marie Murat, who had just bought an apartment; the princess wished to see Marie's curtains in her absence, and asked the upholsterer, who had the key to Marie's apartment, to take her to it; but he replied: "I have to telephone M. Lowengard to ask his permission." This story has been all around Paris. "You're compromising Marie," I told Armand, "and what does she say about it?" "She says it flatters her because I'm younger than she." She was born in 1883, but all the books say 1885. When anyone asks her age, it's always Armand who answers the letters, signing them: "Armand Lowengard for Marie Laurencin." She says: "Armand, I'm a natural child, and the age of a natural child is always a mystery; it's neither real nor a dream; it's not fixed by a date." "It's uncertain," Armand added, "but what is certain is that she takes two years off her age."

July 8 / Gleizes

I had tea at his home. He came the other morning to see my thirteenth-century heads from the Cathedral of Thérouanne. He spoke for a whole hour in front of them, and I understood nothing. The cubists are too intelligent, too complicated, too far removed from nature. There is nothing wild about them; they do laboratory work, they scrutinize only the infinitesimal. Today Gleizes explained to me his theories on the Gothic, illustrating them with drawings. He is preparing a book and read me some very apt, very clear passages. But it's with his cubist way of thinking that he interprets the Gothics, who themselves were no hairsplitters. The keystone of Gleizes's thought is the return to craftsmanship. I questioned him on surrealism. He doesn't admit of fantasy in painting, of making the sky the color of love. He looks for an absolute truth; the rest is for the poets. His truth is represented here, in his apartment, by a pile of small canvases. Some present a rotary movement; it's the work of a painter-cum-engineer. It makes me sad to think of these lost artistic lives, lost to themselves, even if others profit by them: decorative artists primarily, for cubism is decorative art, though the cubists didn't suspect this at the outset; but what are we to call an art which represents nothing of what we see in nature? A confusion of planes, lines, colors automatically becomes ornamentation. Just as the Arabs, whose art is always decorative, employ nothing of what they see in nature. Once cubism passes from a canvas to textiles, paper, or bindings, everyone understands it; women gladly wear dresses with cubist designs but are loath to have a cubist picture in their home. The great merit of this group consists in having brought us back to volume, which is always a factor at the start of a great period, and it was perhaps necessary to harp for twenty-five years on the same string; we shall probably owe all to the Gleizes, the Delaunays, the Légers, in their sincerity.

The sincerity of Gleizes is beautiful to behold; it is ebullient, like his face, his eyes, his cheekbones. When he grows animated, it all swells, shifts, bursts, rebounds, and multiplies.

July 25 / Modern frames

I have decided to put all the pictures I buy for Toledo in modern frames. Two women are in charge. Rose Adler, whose acquaintance I have just made, an interesting person of whom I shall speak again, and Mme Nathanson, keen and intelligent. As yet the movement is in an embryonic phase. It began only a few months ago. I have, I think, ten canvases. One of these women is doing two frames for me, the other is doing three. Impossible to find anything for the Bonnard. I shall frame the four other canvases with one or two of the only moldings of his in existence. I consider that Legrain made overcomplicated frames; I have been to see his son three times and haven't gotten anything; this boy won't get anywhere.

August 2 / Lake Como

We arrived at Menaggio to spend the month of August here. We came by automobile, having stayed overnight in Dijon and Montreux.

August 23 / Coming into Florence

I have missed my appointment with my beauty. I told the chauffeur: "Hurry!" He drove at eighty. "Faster, she won't wait a second for me." He hit ninety. "Faster." "I can't," he said. "But," I retorted, "the machine can do a hundred and twenty." "It's dangerous." "What's that to me?" "The road," he said, "twists and drops, the dust is fright-

ful." "Turn with the road, charge into the dust." "But I'll kill ten people." "Kill them, I have an appointment with my beauty, she won't wait
a second for me." I could see her before me, all in mauve, enveloped in
it, clothed in a million mauves. How stupid man is to have created so
few words for so many colors. I was coming from Menaggio. From the
hill I saw her, it was no more than a glimpse; it was 7:15, the fatal minute. I was still a quarter of an hour away, I hadn't made the rendezvous,
she withdrew and I saw her withdraw, never once losing her from sight,
sadder still. The air a few moments before had been so clear, I had been
living at the heart of a world of crystal; in an instant the night swathed
her in darkness and when I embraced her I held nothing but mourning
crepe. O Florence!

August 24 / Hugo Van der Goes at the Uffizi

This man of the North, I bear a grudge against his genius; he is a
criminal to have come as far as this. I shall never assert that his *Adora-
tion of the Shepherds* is the *most* beautiful picture in Florence; I shall
write that it is *perhaps* the most beautiful; this is the sole satisfaction
he'll get from me. Don't consider me unjust. Though what do I care? I
believe in injustice. Let them perish, those impartial judges who would
award him the palm, for they would destroy Florence; let them die horribly under their own saw. Besides, it is not the most beautiful; it cannot
sparkle in all its beauty in this clear light of Tuscany; those northern
colors need the mists of their own country. Here the veils are lifted; the
personages stand clear, for want of unity, and become silhouettes, sublime perhaps, but only silhouettes. Down to the planes, which lack relativity. And then, the picture is too chaste; fie on such solemnity. It's not
thus that shepherds adore the infant God in Florence. The Italian bambino is precocious and has no need at all of a portentous face to show
that there is man in him. When he holds his mother's chin he knows
only too well that it is a woman's; he is almost Eros. He is differentiated
from the Greek god only by his submissiveness; he listens to his mother
but knows how to take her, he has the art of the caress, this conquering
God child.

August 26 / Francesco Vianni

Our stay in Florence has been spoiled. Since Sunday Ernest has had a fever, brought on by sinusitis. We left at once, thinking that two days by the sea would do him good, and went to Viareggio, a kind of ignoble beach-fair, but I was astounded to discover here a magnificent monument to the dead, by Francesco Vianni.

September 23 / The Prince of Wales[3] went this afternoon to Duveen Brothers and Armand received him

The Prince has just been appointed curator of the National Gallery, and he told Armand very modestly that he was flattered by this honor, that he must learn about art, for he won't be able to be of much use to the institution otherwise. "But that isn't the case," replied Armand. "It'll be enough if you take an interest, you'll be a great influence, getting people to acquire taste and a desire to come to the museum, which is always rather empty. And then, if a large purchase is called for, you will find the money; England loves her National Gallery."

Armand says he's a real prince charming. He made some apt comments. He considers the frames in the Duveen establishment too ornate —that is because they're made for Americans. He has a sense of proportion and standards. He asks questions, how frames or plinths are made, for example, what recanvasing or transposition consists of. "He is thirty-six," Armand added, "but acts too young for a king of England. He is well dressed but not snobbishly, not nattily; loose clothes as for sports, no stick, no gloves, a soft hat, a smart casualness. He speaks French well."

September 29 / The portrait of Vermeer of Delft

It's now ten years, I believe, since I recognized in the gay *Cavalier with a Glass of Wine*, in the Dresden Museum, the portrait of Vermeer of Delft, and today, here in Brussels, at the Congress of the History of Art, I spoke in public of it. Here, in a quick résumé, is what I said:

The painter seen at the back in the Czernin picture is certainly Vermeer himself. I stationed myself between three glasses and saw that it was the only position he could take to paint himself. It is the same man, in the same costume and with the same beret, as in *The Courtesan*.

This latter is in the position of the painter doing his portrait and so looking to the left at it.

[3] The Duke of Windsor.

The planes are not precise, the right sleeve is in the foreground while the head is on the third or fourth plane back.

His shoulder, as when we look at ourselves in the glass, is twice as long as it should be.

His face glitters, becoming blurred.

He is holding his lute in his right hand and his glass in the left; it ought to be the other way around, but this again is an effect of the mirror.

The artist can't draw his glass, which in reality he wasn't holding; he doesn't know how to draw it, its ellipse is all tremulous, the base quite clumsy.

The neck of the lute isn't long enough, it's no longer than the hand holding the glass. Moreover, it's not in its proper plane. If the lute were not a creation of fantasy, it would push up from under the rug that hides it.

The hand holding the glass is gigantic compared with the other, and in fact isn't even holding this flat glass that's stuck on to it.

The left forearm is too high; its distance from the chin, which ought to be one and a half times the extent of the head, isn't even that.

The right hand isn't holding the instrument, which, instead of being clasped between the forefingers, is affixed to the palm. Or rather it's the hand that was affixed afterward. If the neck were sensibly held by the fingers, it would have to go to the right instead of to the left. It must also be noted that the painter's hand in the Czernin picture, which Vermeer did not do from life, is very poor.

The right forearm, which again he did not do from life, is a cripple's—perhaps too short by half. Moreover, there's no junction of arm and forearm; there isn't any elbow.

The diminutive table in front of the courtesan goes neither with the furniture of the period nor with Vermeer's. How to explain the tapestry in the foreground? How is it held? How does it go back? It's on air. What imbalance! Everything is clear when we see that Vermeer's head is much too large compared, for example, with the courtesan's. The fact is that Vermeer did not paint himself at the same time as he painted the group he posed. When afterward he placed himself before the glass, he had lost all sense of proportion. We have seen the mistakes he made in

he simplest problems, he couldn't draw an object when he didn't have
t before him. Vermeer was standing. If he had drawn himself as far as
his feet, he would have gone right off the canvas, whereas the other people are well within its confines. Vermeer was short: we see this in the
Czernin picture. Here he would have been perhaps six feet tall. To cover
his mistake, he resorted to subterfuge: he threw a tapestry over a bar,
here, in the foreground, thus glossing over his errors.

It can even be seen that when he posed he didn't have his beret
on his head; it isn't velvet. It is so rapidly stroked in that it is hacked, its
shape is inexact, the sky beneath appears through wide patches.

October 6 / Mintchine

I was so busy last month that I didn't have time to go to the
Manteaus' to see his work, including the two canvases meant for the
Autumn Salon; possibly the best of them all depicts a man pushing a
wheelbarrow full of pears. A market in the Midi; a large boat—his boats
are on the immoderate side. A canvas all in red, masts like spears. He
says that's how he imagines Venice. He has certainly made progress with
the transparency of shadows. To give play to his sky, he now adds little
red touches. There wasn't a real work of art there; I am worried. It's true
that when a master is evolving, it takes time to grow accustomed to his
new manner. I shall pore again over this latest consignment. Mintchine
was there and awaited my verdict in silence.

November 3 / The portraits of Maria Lani, at Georges Bernheim's

They are less interesting than might have been supposed. Here we
have a woman painted by fifty artists, and it's rather pitiful; few painters
stand up to the challenge. Derain has done very well. Bonnard average,
but a masterly average. The best canvases, by Matisse, Soutine, Vuillard,
have already been sold in America.

November 27 / Jean

Jean, aged twelve, was crying. His brothers were making fun of
him because he didn't know who wrote *Vanity Fair*. I said to him: "If
Thackeray had known when he wrote the book that in a hundred years'
time a little boy of twelve would weep because he couldn't name its
author, the novelist would have felt the greatest joy of his lifetime. It's

your finest tear, Jean." For whom will little boys a hundred years hence be weeping?

December 4 / Mintchine

The Manteaus can no longer manage him and I am going to take him over from them next January, giving them compensation. The painter won't deliver me pictures every month. "It's terrible," he was saying, "this obsession, these canvases that must be handed over on the thirtieth or the thirty-first, unfinished, often all wrong, about which there hasn't been time to form an opinion: which need to be reconsid ered and lived with. Ah, M. Gimpel, I'm pleased to be working with you, because I know it will be more difficult than with Manteau. You see, I couldn't work with Deydier, he's sensitive but he wearies me 'That's pretty, that's ugly,' he'll say to me. That isn't criticism. You say to me: 'Here you lack transparency, here weight, there relief.' That's criticism; you put your finger on the spot. But Deydier's 'That's pretty' or 'That's ugly' means nothing. A lot of canvases it's better not to sell they're studies, thoughts, annotations, they're rough drafts. A writer is allowed his drafts, but not a painter; it's madness. One day one may start a canvas well and finish it badly; one wants a layout. A picture is a thousand things, a thousand things which the collector doesn't think about, but it's not for him to think over a picture, it isn't made for words but for the eyes. In Russia one day a group of artists were arguing in front of a rather incomprehensible picture by a painter who was close to genius, and while they were raving, a peasant said: 'It's beautiful.' 'But what do you know?' the artists demanded. 'This blue, this blue,' he told them, 'look how beautiful it is.' He was right, he had understood."

December 6 / Mintchine

I met him at Manteau's, where I talked about Chirico's latest, very poor, canvases that I have just seen at the Vignon Gallery, and I pointed out to him how many painters go down fast. Derain is drunk every evening.

December 14 / Zadkine and Valentine Prax

Zadkine is her husband, he's a naturalized French citizen, a Russian by birth, who fought in the war. He seems a boy next to her, but a formidable boy. He has brows like lianas in a virgin forest; his hair too is tight-woven and lusterless, giving him somewhat of a rough appearance; his upper jaw comes down like a roof; keen eyes are creased by movement. He loves the gigantic, as people of small stature do; his art doesn't impress me. This man invents nothing; he does Negroid art, fake Gothic, cubism, Modigliani. When I talked to him about the rather good statue in the Pimienta Salon, he said: "I'm satisfied: it's first-rate."

He can't be easy to live with; there is a photograph that shows him knitting his brows furiously. I even said to him: "You look wicked in that." And to soften the phrase, I added: "Not easy, being a master." I feel that Valentine Prax must have a lot to suffer from him. But how tenderly and proudly he speaks of her art. Then, when she went out to make tea, he eagerly asked my opinion, delighted to hear me speak well of her. As to her art, I'm afraid it's only pretty decoration. She's not working close enough to nature, she does everything from imagination.

A fake Houdon

A fake Houdon, a marble, was sold yesterday in New York at the Countess de la Béraudière sale for 2 million francs. It actually belongs to Piazza's widow. It is of Mme de Sabran.

December 19 / Fake moderns

Georges Bernheim told me that his syndicate is holding conferences at this very moment to determine whether pictures are genuine or not, and opinions are sometimes quite divided.

A Sisley catalogued in Sisley's sister's sale has just been submitted to them. It would seem to have a sure guarantee; but far from it, since Sisley's sister finished all the canvases left by her brother in the studio. "How to explain that?" demanded Bernheim.

He told me that six hundred canvases were left in the Rosa Bonheur studio and that over a period of two years Georges Petit had them finished, and no one protested.

December 20 / A Vuillard

I have been shown a very fine Vuillard: a woman telephoning.

NOTEBOOK 20

January 12, 1931–March 10, 1934

January 12 / Ethnography

I went to lunch at Georges-Henri Rivière's. He had invited two of his friends, Marcel Griaule and Michel Leiris, of the Trocadéro Museum of Ethnography, who are going off with four other experts to study all the races in our African colonies. It is the first mission of this kind that France has sent. We are fifty years behind the great nations. Griaule is the head of the expedition, Leiris will keep a journal of their progress. These people all have some professional distortion. Griaule considers it time for the white race to crossbreed with the Negro, on the grounds that mulattos are on the whole much more intelligent than whites. Rivière declares that the Frenchman is characterized by his ugliness, which he attributes to unwholesome, overspicy fare with too much butter and too many sauces. The American diet is more wholesome. Griaule agrees and affirms that the great quantity of phosphate that the American absorbs gives him his solid framework.

March 2 / On Vermeer

I have come to Berlin to see Friedländer, the director of the museum. He agrees with me: the Jules Bache picture, *The Head of a Young Man*, is not by the master. He also shares my opinion that the Mellon *Laughing Young Girl* is not by Vermeer.

Mme Cassirer has shown me the photograph of a newly discovered Vermeer, it seems superb to me, a woman with a hat, looking to the left. Friedländer says it's splendid, despite some wear and tear.

This afternoon I met an expert who knows Vermeer well: Plinch, who also says, of course, that the Bache Vermeer isn't genuine. At one time he thought the Mellon *Laughing Young Girl* was authentic; he now gave me to understand that he no longer believes in it. But Plinch, now employed by a dealer, must keep a certain reserve.

The Strogonoff Collection

The Soviets are selling it. It is a minor Wallace Collection. A sequence of six Hubert Roberts—the most beautiful canvases by that painter ever seen. Two Houdons, including the marble Diderot. Furnishings, as rich as the Rothschild ones; some unfortunately of Russian manufacture. It is said that the Soviets have fixed such high prices that virtually nothing will be sold.

April 7 / On Degas

Lerolle showed me his father's collection; he was a painter and a friend of the impressionists. He has a superb Puvis de Chavannes depicting a sort of hermit in the desert, and he has some fine Degas canvases given by the artist. He told me that at a certain period Degas was very keen on photography; that he took some photos in this very drawing room in which we were standing, and in the evening too, with oil lamps. He composed his photos exactly like his pictures; he didn't place you in some extravagant manner but in foreshortened studies not always comprehensible at first glance; often half the person would be outside the plate, as in some of his canvases.

April 9 / Toulouse-Lautrec Exhibition at the Museum of Decorative Arts

It will never be possible to do it again, the painter's works are too dispersed, and such fine ones are in America!

The greatness of Toulouse-Lautrec is his humanity. It is in humanity that the great masters excel. It isn't enough for a work to be a masterpiece of color or technique, like *The Painter's Studio* by Vermeer. No, other merits being equal, it is the canvas with the greatest humanity which will always be superior. That's why I much prefer *Embarkation for Cythera* to *The Painter's Studio*. That too is why Chardin is greater than Vermeer, who painted only images, whereas Chardin rendered in definitive form the warmth of the French home.

The work of Toulouse-Lautrec is a thing of the heart. It should be entitled: *The Greatness and Misery of the Courtesan.*

April 25 / Mintchine, the genius, is dead

I received the following telegram from his wife, dated 4:25 P.M.: "Mintchine died suddenly. Alone, without money. Coming at once. Madame Mintchine."

I was thunderstruck. He couldn't have been more than thirty. It is terrible to learn that a genius has died in the prime of life. I weep for the future. I weep above all for the works he did not create; the unknown now vanished. I weep for what the world is losing, for the joy he would have spread, the joy he brought forth from grief. During his nearly four months in the Midi he wrote to me three times. There are one or two magnificent passages, one especially, on grief. And it must not be forgotten that he was a Russian; he spoke French very badly but could write it with beauty. He would have become a Renoir, perhaps even greater! I weep for him. He had told the Manteaus and Deydier of his privations in Russia, and even in France; it must have been tragic to hear him. Two years ago, I believe, he had had a kidney removed. I went to see Deydier's cousin, as Deydier is away, and she told me that the painter must have been suffering from tuberculosis. Where will he be laid to rest? Perhaps at Toulon, which he so loved. A few years more and the world would have been kneeling at his tomb; today it is almost a common grave. Poor corpse! Deydier, the Manteaus, and I are the only ones who realize the disaster. All three of them had given him hope and confidence in his genius. He had fire and would speedily have acquired repose. He was of the stuff of Rubens, Fragonard, Delacroix. It was in fire that he too would have created his most beautiful works.

I believe that in his last months he really looked on me as a tutelary spirit. He had found material repose, and peace was essential to him. He knew that my counsels were wise, that they didn't fasten on details but were general comments. He was irritated when others told him, for example, that he ought to have placed a trumpet to the right and not to the left; to make progress he didn't need anyone. What he was anxious to know could quite simply have been taught him in school, if such a school had existed; a school in the ancient manner, a school on discipline, tradition, tools, technique—he would have liked to learn all this, so as not to waste time finding it out—a school on preparation, foundation, blendings, chemical reactions.

Of all that I could tell him nothing.

Not "poor Mintchine" but "poor world," which has lost him! I was alone when I heard the news and fell asleep in this darkness, this hell. Of what consequence is it to note down facts, when beings like Mintchine are facts in themselves, creators of facts? He envied Soutine for having been in France fifteen years longer than he. Paris and France were an inspiration to him, the spring of his talent, the first source. He wanted to become naturalized; he didn't know how ill he was.

June 10 / Hayter

An English engraver to whose house Malvina Hoffman took me. His paintings are detestable, cold as fresh plaster, but as an engraver the man has talent.

June 14 / Matisse Exhibition at Georges Petit's

I went with my wife and her sister Eva to get an overall view. It is many years since an exhibition of this painter has been presented, and we needed to refresh our memory. My impression is that he is an artist of great talent, but he isn't a genius, he isn't a Manet, a Degas, a Cézanne, a Delacroix, a Renoir. I don't even know if he is a Monet: yes, if he had developed his canvases to the full. What bothers me in this vast exhibition is not finding a masterpiece; thirty-five years of painting, and not one masterpiece; no finished picture, and a masterpiece can't be found in unfinished work. Incompleteness keeps Matisse from enveloping his works in quantities of air, and masterpieces are bathed in it.[1]

[1] Since then, Matisse's art has grown considerably in stature. (Note appended 1939.)

July 12 / Forain is dead

I returned at 7:15 from the Tir aux Pigeons with Pierre, who bought the *Intransigeant* and read the sad news. I got back at midnight yesterday with the children, saw lights in all the windows of his house, and said then that Forain must be dying. He had breathed his last at 11:27. He was seventy-nine.

I rang the bell of the house and Jean-Loup received me affectionately.

July 15 / The French spirit

Forain's interment took place this morning with many flowers at Saint-Honoré-d'Eylau, but it was too much like a big funeral; that is, there was neither flame nor sadness. There were few people at the house of the deceased; the coffin was in the middle of the hall, which had been left in its customary disorder. On a table opposite, his last picture, unfinished: *The Pilgrims of Emmaus*, a grouping of five or six people.

This evening's *Le Temps* says: "When Pascal died it was said: this night intelligence has dwindled in the world." That's how I feel now that Forain is dead. Who will replace him? I don't know. For the moment, no one. All the people of spirit in France are dead. It must never be forgotten that the war killed 1,500,000 French. This butchery is responsible for our having neither a painter nor a sculptor, nor a musician nor a dramatist. It is sad to live in such a time!

I have been much tempted, with Forain's death, to stop writing this journal. I have the impression that they are all dead, those who have passed through these pages: Renoir, Monet, Marcel Proust, Caro-Delvaille, Nungesser, Mary Cassatt, and how many others! A star was rising: Mintchine, whose first hopes I was to shelter, and the first wind has carried him off. Ah, something of my past has indeed died with Forain.

November 13

Remark of Degas's at the first cubist exhibition: "It's harder to do than painting."

October 14, 1933 / My journal

It is two years since I abandoned it. Forain's death affected me most cruelly!

October 17 / At Rose Adler's

She was giving a tea party. Among those present was the sculptor Lipchitz, who didn't say a word! Am I certain of his talent? For me, he's too much inspired by primitive paintings. Is he playing at simplicity? I may be mistaken.

Rose Adler is secretary to the Doucet Library and is organizing a concert of modern music with Milhaud and Sauguet. My wife will be selling tickets.

October 17

My son Pierre today begins his studies, to learn about pictures and sculpture.

October 22 / Marie Laurencin

My nephew Armand, that cavalier of platonic love, said to me: "What troubles, and how am I to get out of them, with my women friends! Yesterday a little lunatic said to one of my closest friends, who hadn't told the first that she knew me: 'A friendship like that between Armand Lowengard and Marie Laurencin is the most beautiful thing in the world, almost beyond humanity. Men want us and we come to believe that it's love. But it's nothing, when you see the platonic friendship of that man for Marie.'

"So the friend who heard this said to me an hour later: 'I only come second.' And so forth and so on.

"Women don't understand. And it's not over yet, as the little lunatic is meeting Marie this evening, and she'll repeat her conversation. Marie doesn't like these friendships.

"It's a matter of indifference to her if I sleep with ten women, but she can't accept my having a platonic friendship with another woman; it's very unpleasant to her.

"Incidentally, I hear that you recommended Marie Laurencin's course in drawing and painting to some of your friends, and that they've found it expensive. But Marie makes nothing from it. She's done it to help that poor great Laboureur to earn a living. She would never have known how to give a painting lesson. When I asked her one day for an explanation of the course, she said: 'I've shown my dog to my pupils, a breed they'd never seen, that's instructing them.' Or she says: 'Today I bought a tart, a large tart, and ate it with my pupils; it was beautiful, that tart; that did them good.' "

Only Anatole France could have described Marie's courses and explained how with her grace, her ideas, her conversation on topics sometimes worlds away from art, she can teach these young girls a thousand times more than an Ingres would have done. No formulas, no metaphysics, no theory—just the unforeseen brought forth from its wrappings.

November 14 / The Doucet Library, at the Sainte-Geneviève Library

A committee meeting. Fortunately it has friends, this library; otherwise it would already be extinct, not buried by the old university spirit but by the university's old minds.

I had to donate a brass plate to get them to find a door for it.

November 26 / Marie Laurencin dines at our house with Armand and his sister Annette

On a piece of furniture here she noticed a little painted box she gave Pierre in 1922, when she did his portrait. She signed it on the spot and dated it 1921. It's a sort of stage set that she did from the window of her nursing home, one day when she thought she was going to die. "It's not the exact view," she said. "There wasn't any house right in front of me, but I love houses and staircases, staircases profoundly, but houses even more. How curious it is, I always see houses in my dreams."

Marie was perfectly happy to talk "dresses and hats" with my wife and niece. She adores Rose Descat's hats. Doesn't care for Poiret, but appreciates his sister's wit.

She spoke of Rosenberg, saying: "He hasn't got a hold over me as he has over Picasso and Braque. For instance, Ida Rubinstein commissioned me the other day to do a work with Picasso and Braque, and Picasso said to me, confidingly: 'What will Rosenberg say? Rosenberg's in America.' Picasso fills me with pity, he is like a child.

"Rosenberg came to see me before he left. He said: 'It's hard to cut down.'

'To cut what down?'

'Why, to cut down. For instance, you can't order any more Chanel dresses.'

'But, Rosenberg, you're not with it, my friend. I have only to sign an article or two on fashion, and I'm dressed from head to foot, for nothing . . . but not you. I own an apartment, but if I didn't have it I'd be somewhere else and just as happy. I've a bit of ground in the country because I like green, but the earth is everyone's. I've never had a car, but always a maid, and I still have one. You're not with it, Rosenberg.' "

December 20 / On the "Champlain" en route to New York with my nephew Armand

He's on intimate terms with the prince regent of Yugoslavia and was talking about him to me this evening.

"The prince loves art, he has an excellent curator in Belgrade who buys moderns. He buys from me in a lordly way without bargaining, and I respond to so much graciousness by letting him have things for nothing. He invited me to Belgrade, saying: 'You'll stay with my wife and me in our house.' He was telling me about the current European situation: 'France has only one ally in Europe, and that's us. Poland will go to right or left, she'll put herself up for sale. Italy will demand Tunisia as pledge of her neutrality. If Germany were victorious, she would take Algeria and Morocco, which properly exploited would become a new Egypt. My country has a million magnificently trained soldiers who would crush Italy. Mussolini has turned every man into a military type but not into a soldier.' "

Marie Laurencin

I hear Armand talking about her from morning till evening; she is in fact an inexhaustible subject. "She adores the artificial," he told me. "Her people are in fact fabrications—dolls, phantoms, beings that cannot possibly be brought to life. She loves clockwork birds enclosed in cages; she even loves artificial flowers. She can't abide flowers with a scent; that's why, at the beginning, I sent her a half dozen small green plants. She can see a forest in them, scenes and a thousand other things which we can't even imagine. Besides, when she paints flowers she paints only one flower and makes a bouquet of it by repeating it twenty times.

"She doesn't much care for visits, but loves correspondence; she would have people far away from her, so they could write to her. She answers to keep them at a distance and also retain her hold on them. Her style is delightful, alert. I have destroyed nearly all her letters because I haven't a drawer that I can lock and I prefer to destroy them rather than think that one of these letters, however trivial, might be read by my maid.

"A. Flament published a book this year, *Mariana*, consisting of her letters, with a very good preface. He suppressed some names and a few passages. It was a great success.

"Marie often eats in her kitchen, which cost her a fortune, as she's put silver in it everywhere. She eats in every room, but invites people to restaurants only, on the pretext that she has a horror of the smells that permeate the apartment. A slight change of routine takes place in the summer, when she leaves on Saturdays for Champrosay. I generally go down on Sunday morning, sometimes on Saturday evening. I return alone on Sunday and she on Monday morning. Her former husband and I are the only ones she puts up there. People come in only to tea. She wishes to preserve intact her right to solitude there, which allows her to continue to live in her dream; hers is a fierce egoism. I might tell her about a railway accident with forty dead, and she would say: 'Ah!' Not that this keeps her from being charitable and generous; she is godmother to one of Nicole's little girls, for example, and in fact spends as much money on one as on the other, treats them both to winter sports, entertains them in summer. Yet she knows a big buyer of pictures in Switzerland and I've asked her ten times to introduce me; but no, she doesn't think she will. In reality she only loved her mother, and she detested her father. She sometimes speaks of her youth and pretends that she had a very comfortable bringing-up, but I own a portrait of her mother, which she did at twenty, and I can assure you the woman has a most unpretentious air about her. When I said: 'Here is your mother's portrait,' she didn't answer, 'Yes, that's my mother.' She passed by. One day, however, I asked her to sign it, and she dated it: 1902. She remembered well enough!

"Men she hasn't loved. She has had some lovers; I have met them. One is a sports writer of considerable talent who writes for *Intran* and who has since married an actress. He is a rather handsome fellow. It amused Marie to enter, or rather look upon, the world of sport.

"Apollinaire loved Marie unto death. The poet's friends haven't forgiven her for having left him. She never speaks of him.

"No, she hasn't loved men. There is in her something of man and of woman which prevents her, despite her femininity, from giving way to an expression of love, it existed once in her, tentatively, but it was aborted; she tried it at one time but has since relegated it to the remote past.

"She has been on intimate terms with Berthelot, who was not her lover, contrary to what is reported. With her, friendships last, not loves. People don't pay court to her to get her into bed. That's what she has, a court. For the rest, Marie would dampen any man's ardor."

December 22 / On Marie

"She is beginning," said Armand, "to earn a good living again, has commissions for water colors and decorations, is doing articles and portraits for collectors. She has sold two canvases to the director of the Porte-Sainte-Martin. Alas, she is painting less well. She paints better when she is troubled.

"Her dreaminess prevents her from looking at nature; that's why I send her flowers, to force her to remember nature. She loves to pass from one canvas to another, has a horror of tarrying over the one at hand. But I force her. She no longer paints as much; she has her etchings, her drawings. She reckons that she still has ten years of painting, twenty pictures a year, or two hundred canvases."

December 25 / More on Marie

"She is more intellectual than other painters," Armand was saying. "Writers adore her. She dined the other day at Giraudoux's with some pretty good authors. They love to hear her opinions. She must receive a book a day.

"Joyce, the Irish writer, comes to her house; he's a very good-natured person. When his book was banned in England in 1912, he wrote directly to the king, to protest, and the king had him informed that he couldn't reply. He is nearly blind, reads with a magnifying glass, and as Marie's eyes are weak it frightens her to see Joyce and she can't receive him alone. She has to have someone with her to soothe her."

February 15

My book, *Notre-Dame de la Belle Verrière*, has just appeared in the bookshops, with some horrible misprints. My publisher tells me that Giraudoux liked it very much.

February 20 / Marie Laurencin

She told me on the telephone that she will come to dinner one evening, that she adores our children, they are her children; the youngest, she says, has a fine head. She appreciates the harmony in our family. She repeated that she adored my wife, her voice, her gestures. I told her that friends had often said to me that my wife was like one of Marie Laurencin's paintings—this, long before I knew Marie. Marie's answer: "A spiritual Marie Laurencin."

February 21 / Mme Bourdelle comes to see me

She would like me to help her sell some bronzes in connection with the final arrangements for the Bourdelle Museum.

She told me that Rodin never touched a marble.

On Rodin

I telephoned Mlle Cladel and passed Mme Bourdelle's remark on to her. She replied: "He didn't do all that much to them, but he would take them and apply the mark of his genius. He had his pupils take the work as far as they could. You should have heard Despiau, who used to say how splendid and how atrocious it was to work under him. His genius would bend the instrument the figure carver held in his hand; he would bend the man's will and lift it to the heights of his own mind. Then he would seal the work with his caress, and this is where it passed into the realm of the inaccessible."

"But this must be told, written, printed," I said to Mlle Cladel, "before it is too late, as Bourdelle has begun to assert that it was he who did all the Rodins."

"Bourdelle worked only on certain stones, he didn't touch the marbles," said Mlle Cladel. "At the beginning he adored Rodin, then little by little he said to himself: 'Why not me?'"

February 24 / Montherlant

When I read him, I say to myself: "What pride!" I think of the plastic arts, of music, which have the great superiority over literature that they don't show the artist's pride.

March 4 / Coutaud Exhibition

At the gallery of the senator's wife, Mme Cuttoli, Rose Adler said to me that she didn't understand it, but that Mme Cuttoli had done a great deal for the art of tapestry by asking Picasso and Lurçat for designs. She asked Rose Adler for frames and has had them reproduced by small jobbers.

March 10 / On Degas, Forain

Tea at Marie-Louise Bataille's, the sister of the deputy. It was she who organized the Goncourt Exhibition. I met a Rouart, I believe the elder of the brothers. The other brother came to rue Spontini one day to see the portrait of his sister by Degas that I possess.

How difficult it is to write even the history of art! The other brother had told me that my picture was an extensive study for a large picture of the Rouart family, but it was never executed because their mother died in the meantime. Today this brother told me that he didn't think this was so, that their mother died some years later, that he had never heard of any plans for a large picture except the portraits of their father and mother.

It's difficult indeed to write history. Rouart assures me he never heard Degas make any remarks about Forain, and yet he is supposed to have said: "Forain soars on my wings." Rouart insists that Degas said it, but about Besnard, and that the exact phrase was "on our wings." He wouldn't have said "my." He was referring to the school. Degas also said of Besnard: "He's a potboiler who started a fire." Certainly, he didn't care for potboiling. At the races one day Degas was standing next to Detaille, who asked him for his binoculars, and when he gave them to him,

Detaille said: "You'd think they were a Meissonier." Rouart didn't know Degas's joke: "Forain paints with his hands in my pockets." I said to Rouart that the remark had the sound of Degas, and he assured me it was his, but aimed at another painter; that it was Degas's way to use these capsule judgments to criticize the work of bad painters only.

The following remark ascribed to Degas was apparently made by Manet when he saw a cavalry charge by Detaille: "It's all steel, except the armor." Manet's bon mots, equally mordant, are less well known.

Rouart's father was at Louis-le-Grand with Degas; they had lost track of each other, but then came the Franco-Prussian War. Degas had enlisted in the infantry but was transferred to the artillery because of rather bad eye and was posted to the battery commanded by the elder Rouart. After that they were never apart.

This year marks the Degas centenary and the Beaux-Arts is going to have an exhibition. Rouart is in charge of it and insisted on full power of choice. I called his attention to a still life, as beautiful as a Vermeer, owned by the antique dealer Louis Guiraud. Rouart was astonished, and he didn't recall a single still life painted by Degas.

NOTEBOOK 21

March 13, 1934–
December 9, 1938

March 13 / With Braque

How often has Marie Laurencin said to me: "He's a noble animal, like some lyrical Saint Bernard." It's the way we must suppose the first Florentines were, architects, sculptors, painters, who, in making a life for themselves, built a city to immortalize their greatness.

He lives near the Parc Montsouris, at 6, rue du Douanier; it's a blind alley with artists' houses rising one above the other. His is larger than the others, but has no character. It's a little like a brick factory building. The maid showed me up to the second floor; I was early. It was Rose Adler who invited me. She was bringing Mme Solvay from Brussels, who was coming with Jeanne Bucher. Jeanne Bucher sells the more advanced painting, which, alas, isn't doing well in this crisis. She's an Alsatian. She told me right off that she didn't understand why there had never been a big Braque exhibition in Paris. It was held in Basle, where Jeanne Bucher heard even the most unsophisticated people say: "You must see it; it's really interesting."

The painter's studio is a large, high room with plaster walls. There were a few works on the walls. I noticed two trompe-l'oeils something like brass wires, black and white, running over the canvases, delineating silhouettes. I don't care for that kind of thing, but another canvas was beautiful and not especially cubist; it was small and Rose Adler defined it with: "It's jade." It was in fact the color of jade, only the pipe was white; there was a very vague apple in it, like something in a Chinese pictorial paradise.

Braque sells a good deal. Some fifty small pictures were scattered on the floor, all about eight inches wide, most of them cubist, with some charming touches; one or two of boats stranded on the beach. One or two rather broad canvases were right on the easels.

The studio was very neat, but the linoleum-covered square on which he paints was very dirty. His three-level easel was covered with a thick deposit of paint. Behind, there was an enormous canvas screen.

He took us up to what Rose Adler and I took to be an original picture, which in fact was a color engraving, printed on five plates: prodigiously done. Jeanne Bucher wanted to buy the reproduction rights for 10,000 francs, run off seventy-five proofs and sell them for 375 francs apiece, or about 38,000 francs the lot. Rose Adler asked me if I wanted to put 5,000 francs into the venture, but the crisis is so prolonged and money so scarce that I want to keep what I have for my business.

Next to this vast studio there was another large room with almost empty walls. As I had come early, I had about ten minutes alone with the artist, and I had talked with him of Marie Laurencin, he is very fond of her and will be seeing her the day after tomorrow. "I knew her in Montmartre," he told me, "with her pigtail down her back." I recalled the Montmartre of those days, the Montmartre I'd known—the bohemian life at old Adèle's or in Baron de Vaux's fortified tower. He had been there too, and if he doesn't altogether regret the passing of these days, he does lament the loss of what that hill was once, it's now modernized, the gardens destroyed, and no corner of the city has been able to replace what has gone. Then he spoke with awe of the eternal and the transient in art, of the works in the fashion of the day which disappear overnight, and the others, which live on; and he mused on the whys and wherefores of this.

"I myself at this moment," said Braque, "am illustrating a Greek text. And why not! Isn't today's art allowed to give its vision of past ages?"

When some moments later I saw the painter's designs, I understood how he could illustrate this work. His design was a sort of amplification of Greek letters, his lines, at first glance, appearing as incomprehensible as the reading of that language to someone who hasn't studied it; a mingling of strokes and unending curves, in which silhouettes of people and things are barely there. It has the spirit of Gothic illuminated lettering, with its intricate tracery, but transposed into a Grecian mold by a modern artist who knows cubism and surrealism; I felt that this interpretation, allowing full play to the imagination, was nearer the texts than an illustration, in the eighteenth-century manner, of episodes of Roman history or mythology.

But even Braque's interpretation doesn't resolve the question of illustrating books. In my view, only a modern text can be illustrated by a modern artist.

"It's Vollard," said Braque, "who has commissioned these drawings from me, and it's a pleasure to work with him, as money doesn't count for him. He has never done a book for profit. He'll redo a text, no matter what it is, for a missing letter, his editions often cost him a fortune."

Rose Adler confirmed that she had seen him destroy whole pages because of some small criticism she made, which at first she hadn't dared formulate. The smaller the question, the greater Rose finds Vollard. Before we left, Braque showed us one or two paintings in his dining room, with some antique rustic furnishings. The walls were hung with Negro objects and fabrics.

On leaving this great painter—though the visit had been most satisfying—I couldn't help regretting the time he had wasted in reiterating an interpretation which, it must be admitted, is rather facile. He bruised his great wings in the attempt, and so could not bring it to a conclusion.

France has lost in Braque a painter of genius, a Chardin. Yet he isn't so far from it.[1]

March 16 / Marie

My wife gave a tea party today at which Marie was expected; but

[1] His works in these last two years have become as beautiful as Chardins. (Note appended 1939.)

she was so tired, she is working so much, that she had to forego it. She i
preparing three canvases for Helena Rubinstein, the purveyor of beauty
products, who will have reproductions done for her salons. Marie ha
work until the month of July.

March 19 / At Jeanne Bucher's

She has given up her shop and has three small floors, but it stil
costs her 3,000 francs a month to live and she is finding it hard to earn
them at the moment. She showed me pictures by Ernst, the German
painter, the greatest draftsman painting; but his work is exquisite, some
what in the manner of Odilon Redon. Is he a surrealist? What does the
appellation matter? Since line and color are ways of thinking, the exact
reproduction of what is around us is not the only means of creating art
Jeanne Bucher told me that Masson, whom she sees every day, is a good
natured person. I noticed some canvases by an Italian, Brioni, a young
man with a promising future; and Jeanne Bucher, herself so advanced, is
afraid that he might get lost in surrealism.

At the home of the beautiful Alva Gimbel we had lunch with
Zuloaga, the Spanish painter, and d'Espezel, the editor of *Beaux-arts*.
Rose Adler, who was sitting next to me, told me that the book by Nijin-
ska, the dancer's wife, was an absolute must. She tells how he was be-
witched by Diaghilev; that on the day after their wedding night he admitted to her that he was the man's lover, and that Diaghilev continued
with his work of destruction; no matter what the distance, he worked on
the mind of the sublime dancer, who is today in an asylum; it must,
however, be admitted that a brother of Nijinsky's had already ended up
in an asylum.

Rose Adler informed us that when Nijinsky's foot was operated
on, it was discovered for a fact that his bones were shaped like those of
birds. She dined the other evening with Max Jacob, who strikingly resembles Chiappe, the former prefect of police, which leads him into a
number of misadventures.

A woman admirer of Chiappe's said to him: "Now that you are
no longer at the prefecture, I don't know how to get in touch with you,
give me your address." Max Jacob handed her his card. "She read it, and
I wasn't invited up," he added.

March 25 / Marie Laurencin

She leaves on Wednesday for Champrosay, and so can't come to dinner this week. She has read my book; I don't believe she understood it. She was talking to me of Giraudoux, who lives on rue du Pré-aux-Clercs in an old house; his son sleeps in a tower. She loves his style, as well as Green's, which is, however, less soaring. "Too set, too enclosed," she says. She asked me where I wrote and I replied: "Everywhere; at home in the evening, or in the street or the métro, but best away from home." "How well I understand that," she said. "That's why I need to go to the country, not to work there but for the movement; I find my best subjects for pictures on a train, and when I return to Paris I work better. But what an age! Poverty for writers. Jouhandeau has earned 1,400 francs this year. It's just as ghastly for a painter to devote himself to a canvas and then be faced with the impossibility of selling it. It seems that Picasso sells; I don't believe Braque does. I found him much aged the other evening, and he is a greater painter than Picasso; I mean, he does grander work; and he takes pains over his paint, which is of a marvelous consistency. I have a small Braque; it consoles you, a Braque does. If I turned neurasthenic, I'd buy Braques; I mean, if I had money, and this came on me. Braque is repose."

Marie asked me to tell Rose Adler that she loved Braque's work and she added: "I don't know Rose Adler, but I like her name, it suits her, and I believe in the influence of names!"

April 15 / Marie Laurencin

I went to see her with my wife and her sister Eva. Marie adores both these women, who resemble her unreal, fairy-tale world. Marie is going to give me colors for several walls for the old mansion I have just rented, at 37, rue de l'Université. Such modern colors on the old walls, what a revolution! I shall delight in people's exclamations.

I recently invited Marie to lunch, with Rose Adler, who wanted to meet her, and the two got on very well. They admire many of the same things, both place Braque at the summit of their paradise. They like Lacretelle and Jouhandeau. They recognize the talent of Christian Bérard. They don't agree about the writer Malraux. Marie finds his rendering of agony too facile. Rose claims that his art goes much beyond that.

April 19 / Nathan Wildenstein

My former partner died yesterday in his eighty-third year.

May 21 / 37, rue de l'Université

I moved in yesterday. A small town house between a court and a garden with immense gardens all around. An oasis!

May 23 / Marie Laurencin comes to dinner

She adores order, but loves the first disorder of a move.

She is extremely sorry not to be able to help us arrange the furniture. My wife talked to her of Gertrude Stein's memoirs, in which the writer describes the early artistic days of Picasso, Matisse, Derain, Laurencin. For all its enormous success, I find this book deplorable. For instance, when the author writes about Marie, it's in connection with an evening party at which Marie got a bit high on champagne. The reader is left with the impression that Marie is a drunkard. So I was not surprised this evening to hear Marie say that she never found Gertrude intelligent, that she was never snobbed (sic) by her. "Our youth," she added, "is perhaps the only thing of our innermost selves which we possess, and no one has the right to take it on himself to tear it from us. Gertrude Stein doesn't realize her own bad taste, her lack of tact; thus she can publish a photograph of Picasso and his first mistress when he is now married and has a child."

May 25 / Derain

I have seen twenty of his paintings and I said to a friend: "He's no longer a painter to buy but to sell."

September 4 / A royal marriage

A week ago the engagement of Prince George, fourth son of the king of England, to Princess Marina of Greece, was announced. Armand came to dinner with us this evening and told me: "I made that marriage. I had learned, through somebody's indiscretion, that the prince had said:

'There are only two girls in the world who appeal to me.'" Armand didn't recall the name of the first. The second was Marina. "I hastened to make it known to Prince Paul, who got busy creating opportunities for the young people to meet."

"Then you know the princess well," I said to Armand. In his colorful way, he declared: "Yes, I know her! She is exquisite. I've often said to myself: 'It's too bad she's a princess.' There is only one young girl in the world who can compare to her, and that's my cousin, your niece Muriel. They have the same grace and sweetness, the same joy of life, desire for happiness, tenderness toward the weak. Marina had been cast by fortune into the camp of the weak, of those receiving assistance. The war had put her family on the side of the fallen princes, and poverty was at the door. Marina bore up under it by laughing it off.

"She thought she'd never marry. She is twenty-seven and she told me regretfully: 'I'm destined to be an old maid.' There are three sisters. Prince Paul of Yugoslavia, who married one of them, was very unhappy to see Marina unmarried. He settled the other one last year with a Bavarian baron, a lord of beer.

"Every time I left for England, Marina would say to me: 'You're lucky. I love England so, and I can go there only once a year.'

"This little princess, who so modestly and quietly took her corner seat in the train bearing her to Calais, is going to find the royal yacht waiting for her in the harbor to ferry her to Dover. There may not be a cannonade, but there'll be better: flowers will be thrown at her feet, for 'the man in the street' has made her his own."

November 8 / Rose Adler

She brought me a very pretty binding of *Notre-Dame de la Belle Verrière* which she designed for an American, M. A. Higgins. She placed the H in the center of the plate in a way suggestive of a cathedral. It's certainly the first binding my book has had. But today one of her clients, whose mother-in-law has the same initial, commissioned the same binding from her.

December 12 / For New York

I left on board the *Lafayette*.

October 18, 1935 / On Picasso

Ten months have passed during which I've written nothing, but I'm going to open a gallery in New York with my friend Sidès, who is leaving the day after tomorrow; we'll be selling Greek art as well as surrealists in it, and I'm going to be more embroiled in the modern movement.

She is astonishing, this Mme Cuttoli who has succeeded in obtaining tapestry patterns from artists like Picasso and Braque. "It's difficult with Braque," she was saying. "He's sharp. He says: 'I'll do two designs and we'll see if they sell.' Picasso is easier, but he kept me waiting two years and gave me his first design only when he needed the help of my husband, who is a senator, to obtain a favor he had asked for.

"But how amusing he is with the tapestry, after it's been woven. He stands in front of it, gazing at it as if it were something totally strange to him, as if he couldn't imagine where, from what son or daughter of Eve, it could have sprung. He comes in with his wife and says to her in his Spanish accent: 'Look how pretty it is, how pretty, just look!'"

Mme Cuttoli will be giving me the American representation for her needlepoint tapestries by Léger, R. Dufy, Lurçat, and Coutaud, and her rugs signed by the greatest artists.

October 29 / On Matisse

Coutaud met him this year and found him most amiable. "It's astonishing," he said, "he works on a picture for six months, and with what anxiety, what minutiae! Before applying a color, he colors papers and fixes them on the canvas to see the tone relations!"

October 30 / Sidès

He left today for America to open my establishment there.

November 3 / Epstein the sculptor

I am in London. A Dutch dealer who is established here, Mr. Asher, suggested taking me to see the artist, whose works continue to create a furor. We went to his house with my son Pierre, who is spending a year in London. The artist lives at 7, Brendon Street, W.1, in a pretty neighborhood near the park. His house could be very attractive if it were looked after.

Epstein, a Polish Jew born in America, could equally well be an electrician's assistant or a men's hose salesman, with his rather fat, pale face. He is in his sixties. It's his birthday tomorrow, and his wife and daughter have given him a Negro mask.

Also present was a French dealer, likewise called Asher, who sells sculptures on the rue de Seine. When we left, he told me that Epstein had the finest collection of Negro sculpture in the world. This interest explains his art, not because of the heads of Negroes or Negresses that he has sculptured, but because there surges from his art a kind of hurly-burly which might have issued from some virgin forest.

The sculptor's daughter didn't take her eyes off my son Pierre. I was talking to the mother, a type seen only on the stage, who looks like a gigantic reddish mushroom. Strangest of all was her hair, which falls round her head like an umbrella. She must be American. She asked me if I had seen the bust of Bernard Shaw which had been such a success. Epstein informed us that it was commissioned by an American woman. While Shaw posed, he wanted to know what Epstein felt as he was modeling. The writer didn't like the work, but said nothing at the time. He complained about it only recently, in an introduction he wrote for an exhibition of another sculptor who had done his bust. He appreciated being represented as "a gentleman." Epstein added: "I neither looked for nor found the gentleman in him, for I saw only the diabolical being."

To conclude, Epstein complained again that the Amsterdam museum had bought nothing from him, nor had it sent him anything to do.

November 23 / A tapestry by Picasso

The first ever done. I saw it at Mme Cuttoli's, who executed it. This work approaches the purest tradition. She told me that she had had unprecedented difficulties, as Picasso used several sheets of paper stuck together, wrapping paper, for his pattern, which he painted on the back to give a transparency; and she has succeeded in actually transposing this effect to the woven fabric. The result is magnificent.

November 30 / At Marcel Garnier's

As the ancients affixed shells to walls to create a new kind of decoration, so this artist uses pebbles, taken mostly from river beds, to compose pictures, pictures in relief. He sometimes adds brick or slate and shows a genuine talent in his assemblage. It isn't a process, for he i a real artist; I realize that from the very good drawings and very sensitiv gouaches that he has shown me.

January 1936 / Rose Adler, Lurçat

I had lunch with Rose Adler at Colombin's. She had brought m her drawings in a very new style. Six months ago she had shown me he first efforts, stumbling attempts, and today her works are accomplished They're fantasies in black, in dark gray; they are what the spirit pro claims but what is never seen. She has already done a lithograph, and sh sent me a proof for Christmas.

The day before yesterday I was at Rose Adler's, with the firs laureate of the Friends of the Doucet Library: René Daumal. Our soci ety proposes to carry on Jacques Doucet's work and encourage th young.

With Rose we went on to Lurçat's, who is living on the rue de l Tombe-Issoire, in the Villa Seurat. His very modern house was built b his brother, who is a very advanced architect and also a Communist. Th two brothers are apostles of the new faith, but this house has plenty o comforts and a religious feeling too. Lurçat owns a beautiful, shy Af ghan hound, with that Arabic muzzle they have.

January 19 / Marie Laurencin

I telephoned her; she hasn't been well this winter. She has had a throat infection for weeks. I told her I'd seen the fine Braque Exhibition at Rosenberg's and she replied: "He's a greater painter than Picasso, he' expressed more; less experiment, more French, less toreador.

"Since his divorce," she added, "Picasso has taken on ways that you might excuse only in a woman. He doesn't paint any more, writes verses, and shouts: 'I'm a poet.' Will you believe it, he no longer paints because his wife is demanding millions from him for his canvases. He' like Marius on the ruins of Carthage."

February / At Othon Friesz's, 73, rue Notre-Dame-des-Champs

He's a lesser painter than Derain by far, and has gone down even more quickly. He is about fifty-five. His face is rather disarranged with age. His pointed nose takes wing and his cheeks, which were mottled, have gone hollow. His forehead, which lacks height, is nonetheless intelligent. Pepper-and-salt hair crowns it. He has energy and his voice is decisive. We talked of the position of artists, and he said: "With Derain, Lhote, Segonzac, we shall probably occupy whole walls at the new Trocadéro. It's time they thought of us who have not only been through such hard times but have renewed the art of painting. With Matisse and the others, we have retrieved the natural laws of painting, which had been forgotten. How will Derain react? He may very well say: 'Let the officials go hang; they discover us fifty years too late; let them keep their walls.'

"Actually there are few officials on the committee. We have always fought against them. The young have been striving and searching, while the old guard drew from the most insipid sources; they've been too long at the top! For instance, at the 1900 Exhibition, the ghastliest painters were asked to do ceilings, but there was nothing for Renoir. He could have decorated the Petit Palais, he would have covered it with masterpieces that the whole world would today come to admire, and would have left France a treasure. Happily a reaction has set in, and it will be pitiless toward the barbarians!

"Our friends Bonnard and Vuillard are rather destitute. [I don't agree.] Is it their age perhaps? It's fitting that we, the kings of the 1900's, should have the lion's share. Let them also give work to those of thirty or thirty-five."

June 24 / With Braque

I visited him with Einstein, the writer on art. The artist was working on a tapestry design for Mme Cuttoli and I told him the piece was much superior to his first effort, more like a tapestry. He explained to me that the first tapestry wasn't done from a pattern but from a picture of his which Mme Cuttoli had taken; that this time he was working with the medium and the craftsman's requirements in mind.

1938 / On Guillaume Apollinaire

The years pass, yet I never cease to be astonished at the dead who clutter this journal, which I might call "My Tomb."

Jacques Doucet appeared in the first pages. I also spoke of him on the day of his funeral. His last work was the creation of a library of letters. He had seen that the Institute didn't have the great poets, Baudelaire, Verlaine, Rimbaud, Mallarmé. The situation is even more tragic. He realized that the Institute didn't want them and was snubbing these poor dead! So he decided to buy their manuscripts and samples of their work and play the huge trick on the Institute of bequeathing it this collection.

Subsequently he added Valéry, Gide, Suarès, Apollinaire, and their illustrators, Picasso, Dunoyer de Segonzac: it is a veritable monument that he has left to his country.

The Institute accepted all the more graciously as these old men didn't understand. They gave the books a very fine place on the ground floor of Sainte-Geneviève, a site that threatened to become a mausoleum. Rose Adler alerted some friends. The work of Jacques Doucet was going to die out. It must be carried on: she rallied women in particular around her, and they have accomplished the miracle of augmenting this treasure in a marvelous fashion, and I may say with no funds behind them. Today at the library Max Jacob talked on Guillaume Apollinaire.

October 15 / At Soutine's

I called on him at noon with Pierre and Jean. Two ground-floor rooms, including one overlooking the Villa Seurat, the other overlooking a court or a small untidy garden, in the same disorder that reigns in his house. I believe his canvases are on the first floor.

M. and Mme Castaing were there, they made their money through discovering him, but their loyalty, it must be conceded, has always sustained the artist. He is profoundly grateful to them. He told me so himself. He calls them "the faithful collectors."

As the conversation touched on fake Soutines, I told him that the canvas in the Tate Gallery which bears his signature was a fake. I described it to him, but he no longer remembers the subject. He wants me to look into it. He isn't much concerned about fakes, sometimes he buys them back. But he considers it rather serious that a canvas of his should be in a museum as important as the Tate. He would like me to obtain a photograph and would go to London if necessary, though he hates the fog. He was there once in bad weather, had sinus trouble, and has retained bad memories of it.

He searched out one or two canvases for me, a peasant woman
before a gate, with a bodice of a magnificent pink; the whole is perhaps
not too carefully done, the color isn't clean throughout. The girl has a
most tragic look. He told me he worked out of doors and that it was very
difficult. He pointed out that the arms weren't finished.

After this he brought me a much smaller canvas, a woman in
nearly full profile with a bodice of a splendid blue. She too had a most
unhappy air. Next, two small, insignificant canvases, whitecaps viewed
as in diving, and a man seated astraddle a tree trunk, holding a child.

Naturally the Castaings will take his best canvases. Soutine understands nothing of modern art; he considers a Picasso pretty much a
swindle; cubism means nothing, it's cerebral, can give no joy. Yes, Picasso knows how to draw, but Ingres drew better. The best painter is
Matisse, and even so he dwells too much on relations, it's too much
literature. Utrillo had certain qualities, but it's a mediocre sort of art.
The true painter is Courbet, he's so direct, for instance *The Model in
the Painter's Studio*; some of his other work is somewhat less well finished. Corot too is a painter, he conveys the same sensation of the im-
mediacy of things. Ah, the giant is Rembrandt. He's a god, he's god. I
said to him: "No, there is no one god; there are all the gods of Olym-
pus." He disagrees. For him Rembrandt is the idol, excelling all painters. Velázquez is nothing beside him. *The Betrothed Jewish Maiden* is
probably the most beautiful canvas in existence, with its penetrating
study of the clothing, and the hands, which are so beautiful!

I asked to go to the Louvre with him, and he said: "Let's go see
the sculpture. I have loved sculpture for two or three years. I did not
appreciate it before, but it's growing on me, giving me great joy; I go to
look at Greek art and I am moved.

"A painter who doesn't move me is Cézanne. It's over, I've
passed that stage; I believed in him. I don't think that a great deal of
him will survive in fifty years' time, he's too studied, fastidious, difficult,
too cerebral."

December 9 / *With Rose Adler*

Five or six of us are preparing an exhibition of amateur painters,
at the Sainte-Geneviève Library.

Valéry draws very well. I have brought along quite a few drawings by Verlaine, the library is very poor in these. There is a prewar portrait of Apollinaire by Chirico, but done in a surrealist fashion even then. The painter has put a kind of hole in one corner of the temple, the place where a bullet hit the poet during the war; he died of the wound.

NOTEBOOK 22

May 25–September 3, 1939

May 25, 1939 / Marie Laurencin

I asked her if she was influenced by her painter friends when she started; she said she wasn't and added: "The greatest influence in my life has been Goya's. Many of my works on these walls are influenced by him. I lived with him a great deal during my five years of exile in Spain. I knew him before going there. Ah, I suffered deeply in Spain and painted only four canvases there. Suffering is like being possessed by a malady; how is one to paint when one is ill?" She told me that she has always been influenced by her environment, even by a hat, more by a hat than by a Braque; in this connection she told me that she had recently read Braque's reflections, found the work poor, and was therefore led to doubt his talent. "But speak to me," she said, "of Michelangelo's sonnets and of Leonardo's treatise on painting; those are reserved, yet beautiful."

I remarked on how strange it is to learn that great artists always knew one another in their youth, at the beginning of their careers, and she replied: "I dropped my bag once in Zurich, and a man picked it up. It was Rainer Maria Rilke."

May 27 / An astronaut

M. Melot is an interesting man. Before the war he planned to be a violinist; but he was wounded in the fingers and became an engineer. He studied rocketry with the idea of giving airplanes greater speed, and that's how he came to know and associate with the scholars who are studying means of reaching the stars; with my son Jean I have attended several of their meetings, which are most interesting. This morning we were talking about it with him; he explained that the thing was going too fast, or rather too far, with people thinking of reaching the moon or Mars right away. It would be more reasonable to try for Mars, as life there must resemble our own because of the atmosphere.

"For the moment," he said, "we must be content with working toward the high-powered aircraft that will enable us to leave the earth and make short trips of a few hundred miles into space, returning to earth; we can foresee many difficulties and counter them, but it is impossible to know how man will be affected when he is no longer subjected to gravity. As it is, we don't do too well upside down. We understand a vacuum and can create one, but no amount of calculation brings us to a true knowledge of the effects of an absence of gravity, we have to experiment to find a way to move in such an environment. Twenty years from now we'll have to start these little excursions which you, M. Gimpel, call to the suburbs."

June 1 / Paul Sérusier

He isn't lacking in talent, this painter who died eleven years ago, and whom Mme Zak is exhibiting. He might be called a tarnished mirror of Gauguin. He dwelt in the shadow of the great painter and translated it into a dimness. Gauguin set down an arabesque of melancholy, and Sérusier has given it flat tints, each of his canvases becomes in our eyes like a rather depressing stretch of wall.

June 16 / On Apollinaire

Sidès has organized at Charpentier's an exhibition of nonexpressionist masters, like Gleizes and Delaunay.

Delaunay, who was there, called me Gompel, so I called him Defaunay. He hasn't got a sense of humor, he gave me a puzzled stare.

He has found among his papers manuscript notes of Apollinaire's, notes on art and also notes for a lecture given by the poet in Berlin. The exhibition committee has had all of it printed and I am keeping a copy for the Doucet Library.

Delaunay was an intimate friend of Apollinaire's, who was imprisoned in connection with the theft of *La Gioconda*. He was suspected because his secretary had stolen Phoenician statuettes from the Louvre. When Apollinaire was released, Delaunay offered to let him live with him in his studio, and he stayed there for a month and composed his famous poem "The Window."

Billy mistakenly wrote in an article that Apollinaire composed it in a café with a merry party of friends.

Apollinaire outlined the beginnings of cubism and in a very different way from Max Jacob. He attached great importance to Derain's influence. He described, to begin with, Derain's meeting with Maurice de Vlaminck in 1902, when Vlaminck was painting at la Grenouillère and a young painter stopped to look at his canvas: it was Derain. The two were never out of touch after this. Vlaminck owned some Negro sculpture, perhaps because he found in them analogies with Gauguin's figures, which he valued highly. André Derain loved those carved images of Guinea and the Congo and began meditating about them.

In 1905 Apollinaire met Picasso, at whose house Salmon, Harry Baur, Max Jacob, Guillaume Jeanneau, Alfred Jarry, Maurice Raynal would gather.

That year Derain met Matisse, and the birth of the fauves came of that meeting.

In 1906 Derain joined Picasso; their association resulted almost immediately in the birth of cubism, and Georges Braque came to mediate between his two friends. In 1908 Braque showed a cubist picture at the Independents Salon, which led Matisse to utter the burlesque word cubism that made its way so rapidly through the world. Others joined the young school, and after 1910 it included Jean Metzinger, who was cubism's first theoretician, Albert Gleizes, Marie Laurencin, Le Fauconnier, Robert Delaunay, and Fernand Léger.

It was then that André Derain, dismayed at the result of his spec
ulations, broke away from cubism, while others joined it, such as Picabia
and Marcel Duchamp and somewhat later Juan Gris and Roger de La
Fresnaye.

June 20 / In Montparnasse

I met Rose Adler at a very advanced publisher's, who knows more
about typography than anyone whatever. Valentine Hugo was showing
his engravings and etchings there; Hayter said they were too photo
graphic, which is true. It's a clever jumble of familiar things.

Afterwards we went to Jeanne Bucher's, where we met Marcoussis
and Miró.

We found a wooden statue there, a female nude, by a young
Hungarian of twenty-eight, who is truly promising. The head is both too
Negroid and too archaic and the body too much of a "dance of death,"
but it is beautiful from all sides—a considerable merit, a three-cornered
proof. The body nonetheless lacks repose; but it expresses a great sorrow
rather than a great spasm, though you can see in it either of these two
extremes, depending on your inclinations.

June 28 / At Rose Adler's

At tea with Marie Laurencin: Gleizes, Serge Ferat, Chagall,
Templier the goldsmith.

We heard how, to protect himself from intruders, Picasso has
had a very high iron grille built right on his stairs.

Templier complained of the tendency of goldsmiths to return to
flower designs in the 1850 genre, when the trend was so clearly toward a
definitive modern style.

June 29 / At Louis Carré's

In Porto, where I met Pissarro's son, Rose Adler, Le Corbusier,
Léger, Laurens.

This great sculptor has a ravaged face, resembling some cross be
tween Quasimodo and Adonis. I saw him in poverty a few years ago;
fortunately commissions have come in to him, and today he is very pleas

antly settled; but his suit is black under this June sunlight, he seems to bear mourning inside him for all his dark summers.

Léger is back from America, where he has done frescoes for Nelson Rockefeller, and he said: "We cubists are beginning to win through."

As Léger is my age, I could say to him: "Your youth is past, your adolescence too, you've entered on ripe years, we're at the gates of old age, and that's when you are beginning to be appreciated! But success has never come so late to a school! The public has never been so slow, and it's very sad!"

Pissarro came toward us. I own a picture of his father's, portraying an adorable baby wearing a straw hat with a pink bow, playing in a garden. That baby is this old man now three-quarters bald, with eyes like glaucous balls, a low, twisted forehead, a small, dumpy, puffy, thick-set body.

My story of calling Delaunay "Defaunay" has gone the rounds among the cubists and they were waiting for Delaunay, to greet him with a cry of "Defaunay!" I didn't have time to wait, as I had to go to another reception at the Countess de Ginestet's.

Le Corbusier arrived as I was leaving. It is he who built the house of glass in which Louis Carré lives, on rue Nungesser-et-Coli. He has designed a magnificent curve to the passage.

July 13 / Marie on the telephone

She cannot stand the surrealists or the Cuttoli group and considers monstrous the tapestries by Picasso, Rouault, and Braque which are at present being shown at the Petit Palais.

I assured her that Lurçat possesses to a high degree a sense of the wall, but she refused to concur.

At Hayter's on the rue Campagne-Première

Rose Adler would love the Guggenheim Foundation to buy canvases by Hayter. He paints in imitation of Masson, but badly. On the other hand, he has considerable talent as an engraver, and great sureness with his graving tool. He has quite a few pupils; his school has its followers.

I shall be speaking about him to the Baroness de Rebay, who is coming to have dinner at my house. The taste of this apostle of cubism is for the fantastic; for instance, she bought hundreds of Bauers because of their sexual charm. She has taken one or two poor Picassos only and one or two Braques, so as to exalt her favorite. She is the Catherine II of this school. However, as a moving spirit she's not without a genuine spark.

At Albert Gleizes's new studio, 22, rue de Ranelagh, near the former Pimienta House

The artist is still making progress. He spoke to me of his youth. His father was an industrial designer and managed a powerful group. Born before 1870, he had been grounded in the solid foundations of artisans' sons at the end of the eighteenth century. Albert worked with him but wanted to paint and also moved in theatrical circles; he was an occasional student at the Conservatory. In 1910 he came into cubism, as did Apollinaire the writer. These days Gleizes is coming back to the figure, still bound up with the cube, but in a simplified form; his art has come through its testing, and its silhouettes are massive.

The Baroness de Rebay

What an evening! I'm supposed to be putting in a word for all of them, for Gleizes, for Sidès, who is exhibiting nonobjectives and wants to receive aid from the Guggenheim Foundation. I'm to speak on behalf of Hayter, who wants enough money to go to America.

July 18 / Visit to the nonobjectives

I met the Gleizes, Delaunay, the critic Rambosson, a gaggle of painters. Mme Bucher came by, and I found her superior by far, in her village simplicity, to all these theoreticians, philosophers, and overintelligent artists. "When I look at painting," she said, "it's as if I were eating young flesh. When I lean close to the paint, I feel the same sensation as if I were rolling in fresh grass."

Antoine Pevsner, 5, rue Jean-Sicard

He had given me his card. He exhibited a magnificent bronze the other day at Sidès'. I went all around it, craned, stooped; it was still beautiful. It's impossible to describe; like a bit of tree burst by a shell. But how carefully worked it is! Straight veinings rushing, running with sap, undulating like plants in the sea. Pevsner is too complimentary, it's disagreeable, but he is a foreigner. I promised to go see him in September. He's a simple sort of man, of a markedly Asiatic type, a rather thin Mongol.

At Hayter's, taking Rambosson, who had never met him

The Baroness de Rebay made some remarkable criticisms of his paintings. She put her finger on the weakness with an almost cruel precision. She was like some dedicated surgeon. Moreover, she was nearly as clever in her criticism of the engravings; but with the engraving tool Hayter has considerable talent. She noticed when a line was too long or too short by even a fraction. She took Hayter to task for letting his lines go off the scene and into infinity too often.

In my opinion Hayter has a worse defect: sometimes things seem to come from outside and finish up on the edge of the canvas.

The baroness bought an engraving from him for $15. She cannot brook the least recognizable human form in modern art.

July 22 / Vollard is dead

He died yesterday in Versailles as the result of a fall, at the time when we were in the Doucet Library. Marie Dormoy had acted as his secretary and had copied out his journal, his memoirs. I scarcely knew Vollard; he was a sort of alert old bear. He was the first to recognize the talent of Cézanne, Gauguin, Douanier Rousseau, and by collecting their canvases he made a fortune. Publishing was his hobby and he was remarkably good at it. At Gleizes' I was told that he was beastly to artists, that only Picasso was paid in full, at 20,000 francs a copperplate, or a total of 600,000 francs. But Rouault had terrible scenes with him over *Ubu Roi* and they were on very bad terms.

August 10 / Giraudoux

I have just read *Choix des élues*. Giraudoux hasn't the power to

rouse the reader's indignation, and makes him neither laugh nor cry,
there is nothing to fear from him, as there is in Stendhal, Proust, the
ironic France, Céline, etc.

August 24 / Geneva

The conflagration is not far from bursting upon us. We have
been here for forty-eight hours to see the Prado Exhibition. We shall be
staying a week. Death hangs over our heads, and if it must take us, this
last vision of Velázquez, Greco, Goya, Roger Van der Weyden, will
have made a fine curtain.

September 3 / Paris

We're at war.

INDEX